A PLANNER'S ENCOUNTER WITH COMPLEXITY

New Directions in Planning Theory

Series Editors

Professor Gert de Roo, Department of Planning and Environment
University of Groningen, The Netherlands
Professor Jean Hillier, Global Urban Research Unit (GURU),
School of Architecture, Planning and Landscape, Newcastle University, UK
Dr Joris Van Wezemael, Geography Unit, Department of Geosciences,
University of Fribourg, Switzerland

Ashgate's series, New Directions in Planning Theory, develops and disseminates theories and conceptual understandings of spatial and physical planning which address such challenges as uncertainty, diversity and incommensurability.

Planning theories range across a wide spectrum, from questions of explanation and understanding, to normative or predictive questions of how planners should act and what future places should look like.

These theories include procedural theories of planning. While these have traditionally been dominated by ideas about rationality, in addition to this, the series opens up to other perspectives and also welcomes theoretical contributions on substantive aspects of planning.

Other theories to be included in the series may be concerned with questions of epistemology or ontology; with issues of knowledge, power, politics, subjectivation; with social and/or environmental justice; with issues of morals and ethics.

Planning theories have been, and continue to be, influenced by other intellectual fields, which often imbue planning theories with awareness of and sensitivity to the multiple dimensions of planning practices. The series editors particularly encourage inter- and trans-disciplinary ideas and conceptualisations.

A Planner's Encounter with Complexity

Edited by

GERT DE ROO
University of Groningen, The Netherlands

ELISABETE A. SILVA
University of Cambridge, UK

ASHGATE

Published by
Ashgate Publishing Limited
Wey Court East
Union Road
Farnham
Surrey, GU9 7PT
England

Ashgate Publishing Company
Suite 420
101 Cherry Street
Burlington
VT 05401-4405
USA

www.ashgate.com

British Library Cataloguing in Publication Data
A planner's encounter with complexity. -- (New directions in planning theory)
1. City planning--Environmental aspects. 2. City planning--Philosophy.
I. Series II. Roo, Gert de. III. Silva, Elisabete A.
307.1'2'01-dc22

Library of Congress Cataloging-in-Publication Data
Roo, Gert de.
A planner's encounter with complexity / by Gert de Roo and Elisabete A. Silva.
p. cm. -- (New directions in planning theory)
Includes index.
ISBN 978-1-4094-0265-7 (hardback) -- ISBN 978-1-4094-0266-4 (ebook)
1. City planning. 2. Public spaces--Planning. I. Silva, Elisabete A. II. Title.

HT165.5.R66 2010
307.1'216--dc22

2010009588

ISBN 9781409402657 (hbk)
ISBN 9781409402664 (ebk)

Printed and bound in Great Britain by
MPG Books Group, UK

Contents

List of Figures

List of Tables

Notes on Contributors

Erel Avineri is a Reader in Travel Behaviour at the Centre for Transport and Society, University of the West of England, Bristol, UK. Applying behavioural economics and cognitive psychology, Dr Avineri is exploring what influences our travel behaviour, how to predict it, and how to design demand management measures to change travel behaviour.

Michael Batty is Bartlett Professor of Planning and Director of the Centre for Advanced Spatial Analysis (CASA) at University College London (UCL). His research is primarily on the development of computer models of cities and regions, with a recent focus on large data systems, and visualisation using virtual reality methods and GIS technologies. He has written many articles and books, the most recent of which is *Complexity and Cities* (MIT Press, 2005). He is editor of the journal *Environment and Planning B*, a Fellow of the British Academy and was awarded the CBE in the Queen's Birthday Honours in 2004.

Luca Bertolini is Professor of Urban and Regional Planning in the Department of Geography, Planning and International Development Studies at the Faculty of Social and Behavioural Sciences of the University of Amsterdam. His research and teaching focus is on the integration of transport and land use planning, on methods for supporting the option-generation phase of the planning process, on concepts for coping with uncertainty in planning, and on ways of enhancing theory-practice interaction.

Adele Celino is a Civil Engineer. She took her PhD in Policies for the Sustainable Regional Development at the Università degli Studi di Bari. Her research has been carried out at the Politechnico di Bari and has mainly centred on study and application of methodologies and tools to manage the process of knowledge representation in complex organisational environments. Her current research focuses on the role of transient constructs in organisational learning environments and in particular on the role of open content systems developed for decision making in environmental planning.

Kiron Chatterjee joined the Centre for Transport and Society, University of the West of England, Bristol, UK, as a Senior Lecturer in September 2003. Before that he was a Research Fellow at the Transportation Research Group, University of Southampton. Chatterjee started his research career at the University of Southampton in 1990 with a PhD study of accidents in road networks. After this he spent several years undertaking research on new traffic management technologies (driver information systems, motorway access control), in particular examining their impact on traveller behaviour and how this could be used to forecast network-wide impacts.

Elisabete Cidre is a Postgraduate Teaching Assistant at the Bartlett School of Planning and a Teaching Fellow at the Bartlett School of Architecture. Her main areas of research interest are urban design and heritage conservation, planning politics and institutional change.

Grazia Concilio is a Civil Engineer. She took her PhD in 'Evaluation Methods for the Integrated Conservation of Environmental Resources' at the Università Federico II di Napoli, and is currently Assistant Professor at the Politechnico di Milan. Her research has been mainly focused on the implementation of methodologies and techniques of knowledge representation for decision making in spatial planning. She is recently working on methods and ICT systems to support the production and the acquisition of action-oriented knowledge.

Joe Doak is a Senior Lecturer in Urban Planning and Development at the University of Reading. He has undertaken major research into the formulation and implementation of regional, strategic and local planning policies and was a senior planning officer at county and district levels of UK local government. His research interests span sustainability, local economic development and the property development process. Other academic interests include theoretical perspectives on the planning and development process, housing markets and planning practice and urban regeneration.

Marcel van Gils is Strategy Consultant with Strategy Works/Academy. For this company he does consultancy projects and gives lectures for international companies and public organisations in the fields of strategy and leadership. He is also working on a PhD about decision making processes around major spatial projects in the port of Rotterdam. A book edited by him and two of his fellow researchers (Menno Huys and Bart de Jong) on *Dutch Mainports Under Pressure: Looking for Development Force* (Spectrum Publishing) was published in 2009.

Jens-Peter Grunau is the General Secretary of the European Network of Construction Companies for Research and Development (ENCORD), a network of 22 major and active members from the European construction industry. He worked as a lecturer and researcher in the area of planning theory and complexity. He received his PhD in 2008 at the Institute for the Foundations of Planning, Faculty for Architecture and Urban Planning, University of Stuttgart, Germany, on the issue of 'Solving Complex Problems: Theoretical Foundations and their use in Education and Practice'. Grunau is also a licensed architect in Germany.

Janneke E. Hagens works as an Adviser at NovioConsult, Nijmegen, the Netherlands. This consultancy specialises in landscape policy and environmental planning. She graduated at Wageningen University in Land Use Planning (2002). After her graduation, she worked for the provincial authorities of Noord-Holland, departments of strategic planning and public administration (2002-2004), and as a Researcher at the Land Use Planning Group of Wageningen University (2004-2008). At Wageningen University, she has been working on a doctoral thesis, about the use of landscape concepts in Dutch regional planning.

Menno Huys works as a PhD Researcher at the Delft University for Technology, Faculty Technology, Policy and Management. His research projects are about understanding and dealing with inert policy and planning fixations in the field of environmental and transportation planning. In 2009 the book *Dutch Mainports Under Pressure: Looking for Development Force* (Spectrum Publishers) was published, edited by Huys and two of his colleagues.

Nikos Karadimitriou is a Lecturer in Planning and Property Development at the Bartlett School of Planning, UCL. His latest work is drawing on ideas from complexity and network theory to explore how space and place are socially constructed in the case of 'Sustainable Brownfield Regeneration'. His work is also exploring the implications of systems theory and cybernetics for spatial planning and the planning profession.

Kristina L. Nilsson is Professor in Architecture at Luleå University of Technology in Sweden with a grounding as an architect and planner. Her research interests are planning practice, planning and complexity, sustainability in overarching planning, sustainable urban development, and planners' roles.

Gert de Roo is Professor in Spatial Planning at the Faculty of Spatial Sciences, University of Groningen, and Head of the Department of Planning and Environment. He is responsible for various fields of research, all of which are related to decision making concerning interventions within the physical environment. Most of his research and his publications are focusing on decentralisation processes, in particular those concerning physical and environmental planning. Another part of his research focuses on the development of decision making models that support choices concerning interventions within the physical environment. De Roo participates in various national and international associations and organisations, all of them having in common the physical environment, quality of life, sustainability and urban development.

Walter L. Schönwandt is Professor in Planning and since 1993 Director of the Institute for the Foundations of Planning (IGP) at Stuttgart University. He studied architecture, urban planning and psychology at the Universities of Stuttgart and Heidelberg. From 1979 to 1984 he was at the Institute of Regional Science at

Karlsruhe University. After that he worked for nine years as a manager in the planning department of the 'Umlandverband' (a regional planning organisation) in Frankfurt/Main (UVF). His interests include traffic planning, landscape planning, housing, economy and infrastructure, statistics, cartography and the Information and Planning System (IPS).

Elisabete A. Silva is a University Lecturer in Planning in the Department of Land Economy, University of Cambridge. Silva has a research track record of approximately 15 years, both at the public and private sector. Her research interests are centred on the application of new technologies to spatial planning in particular city and metropolitan dynamic modelling through time. She is interested in land use, transportation and metropolitan planning, regional planning, integrated planning (urban/transportation/environmental planning), geographic information systems, planning support system and AI models.

Yos Sunitiyoso is currently a Research Fellow at the Transportation Research Group, University of Southampton, UK. He received his PhD from the University of the West of England (UWE), Bristol, in 2007 with his thesis in investigating the role of social interaction, learning and influence in the dynamics of travellers' mode choice behaviour by applying empirical studies and multi-agent simulations.

Joanne Tippett is a Lecturer in Spatial Planning in the School of Environment and Development, University of Manchester, UK. Her work has developed in response to the need to animate the process of planning for sustainability, and to maximise the value of participation in planning. She is a Director of the UK Systems Society and an Associate Theme Leader of the Sustainable Consumption Institute. She is the founder of a social enterprise, Ketso (www.ketso.com), and invented a kit for creative group work.

Chris Webster is Professor of Urban Planning and Development at Cardiff University. He first used the paradigm of transaction costs economics in the early 1980s to explain patterns of access to institutional credit for development projects in North East Thailand. Since then his research has focused on understanding the nature of urban order under the constraints of market and government institutions. In his modelling, empirical and theoretical work he sees transaction costs as a friction that helps explain social patterns and economic and spatial outcomes. He was recently awarded a higher doctorate for his essays on spontaneous urban order.

Joris E. Van Wezemael is an Associate Professor at the Geography Unit of the University of Freiburg, Switzerland. Prior to this he was a Lecturer at the Economic Geography Division, University of Zurich, Visiting Scholar at the Global Urban Research Unit at Newcastle University, and Director of the Centre of Research on Architecture, Society and the Built Environment at ETH Zurich. His teaching and research interests are focused on economic and political geography and on planning. His main research interest lies in the analysis of spatial decision making and social complexity. Research projects comprise policy analysis and studies on decision making in economic contexts. In theoretical respects he developed an action-theory based approach for spatial decision making analysis. More recently complexity thinking and its potential to move beyond anthropocentric and essentialist traditions of spatial decision making analysis constitutes a major focus of interest.

Preface

Complexity and spatial planning never have had much in common. This is somewhat strange, as spatial planning has accepted situations to be quite often complicated and 'complex'. However, the theoretical debate in planning still focuses very strongly on the communicative direction in planning. With this book we aim to challenge that situation.

The evolution of 'complexity' as a conceptual understanding of reality has hardly had any serious attention in spatial planning. Within spatial planning, only a few modellers, working on cellular automata, agent-based modelling and non-linear simulations, had a hunch about the exciting debates on complexity thinking being conducted within other disciplines of science. To take part in this cross-cutting debate, planners need to understand that complexity is not a notion expressing basic feelings about an encountered situation. On the contrary, it goes far beyond that. Complexity stands for a 'reset' of our positivist mind frame, to be able to view the world differently, to make the switch from 'normal' science to a 'post-normal' science...which presents an understanding of reality that could very well be more promising than the reality proposed by 'normal' science.

Delving into the subject of complexity, we will discover a cross-cutting academic debate, including a wide variety of theoretical arguments, regarding a reality that is totally unknown to planners. It is an emerging, adaptive and co-evolving reality; a reality with an intrinsic drive that supports change, development and – if you like – progress. It is a reality that is, by and large, self-organising, asking the planner to be not just the ultimate creator or the interactive mediator but to become a manager of change as well who attempts to avoid the negative and embraces the positive effects of change. The reality presented to us by complexity thinking and the concept of 'complex systems' might be more valid than the linear world with which we are so familiar from a technical-rational perspective. And it might be more promising than the representation of a networking society, happily collaborating all the way...

While planners appreciate debating about various rationalities regarding physical interventions within our physical environment, the issue of change, development and progress through time seems to be regarded as implicit, non-existent or of secondary importance. Complexity brings the issue of change, development and progress into focus, albeit with a twist. Change, development and progress are considered to be non-linear. This might be off-putting, and may require an alternative mindset to deal with it in planning. Nevertheless, with this book we hope to break down some of the barriers, inviting all to give the issue a chance, since we strongly believe that the reality offered to us by complexity thinking is very, very promising indeed…

Perhaps, at some time in the future, the emergence of the issue of 'complexity' within the discipline of spatial planning will be considered an example in itself, showing how the debate in planning slowly opened up again to influences and ideas from outside – and adapted accordingly, gradually and increasingly embracing the essence of the issue of complexity, non-linearity and self-organisation. Reflecting upon our own experiences so far, we can say that it has not been easy. We have had some notable experiences. For example, at the end of the 1990s we submitted an abstract on 'Complexity and Planning' for the annual ACSP conference. This produced the comment that Karen Christensen's 1985 contribution had already said everything about complexity…

Being very much aware of the risk of failure, in 2005 we proposed a Working Group on Complexity and Planning within the Association of European Schools of Planning (AESOP). In Vienna, at the XIX AESOP Annual Conference, the Working Group on Complexity and Planning had its first meeting. The group comprised 15 people, some of them very much at the forefront of the planning theory debate. Most likely, their presence was crucial to seeing the issue not as a curiosity or a freak show, but as a challenge in support of planning theory and practice. It was suggested to meet frequently, as there is much to be discussed and to be shared. So that is what we did. Since then, the working group has met in different settings at various locations: Reading in 2005 following the Vienna meeting, Cardiff, Mexico City and Cambridge in 2006, Stuttgart and Naples in 2007, Milan, Chicago and Thessaloniki in 2008, Liverpool in 2009 and hopefully many more to come. This book has its origin in these meetings.

At the AESOP Annual Conference in Liverpool in July 2009, another major step was taken: without the Working Group having to push for it, the conference programme contained an entire track (Track 17) on 'Complexity and Planning'. The following conference in Helsinki, in 2010, will continue this track on complexity and planning. Within the AESOP arena we were able seriously to address the issue of complexity, bringing together those who were interested, to place it on the theoretical agenda and make others aware of this new perspective. AESOP therefore deserves our sincere thanks.

We also thank the AESOP Board for supporting the publication of this book. We would like to express our sincere gratitude to all those participating in the various debates on complexity and planning, who have therefore been tremendous sources of inspiration. Thanks go also to Tamara Kaspers for upgrading some of the figures, to Corien Kuiper for critically assessing inconsistencies within and between the various chapters, and to Rens Baltus for putting together the index. Last but not least, very warm thanks go to our publisher Valerie Rose and her colleagues at Ashgate Publishing for having faith in the whole project, right from the beginning.

With this book we are trying to reach out to planners and their theoretical debate, presenting the issue of complexity in various ways, having invited those planners who have touched upon the issue of complexity to contribute a chapter. Hence this book is indeed *A Planner's Encounter with Complexity*.

Gert de Roo
Groningen

Elisabete A. Silva
Cambridge

Chapter 1
Planning and Complexity: An Introduction

Gert de Roo[1]

Planners have multiple perceptions of the notion of 'complexity' and how it should be considered within the planning environment. Complexity is a term that is used and misused in various ways: 'It is too complex to manage' and 'the complexity is rather disastrous', are statements with which most of us have been confronted. Put like this, the message is an effective yet destructive way of addressing undesirable situations, expressing frustration and a disguise perhaps for a lack of interest in taking appropriate action.

The planning community has by and large ignored a much wider debate in academia concerning complexity in relation to notions of co-evolving and self-organising realities and complex systems which are adaptive and emergent. Between these two opposing understandings and interpretations of complexity is a world awaiting discovery, in which complexity has a positive role to play in planning.

This introductory chapter attempts to address various interpretations of complexity within planning, producing a range of considerations, some of which will be addressed more substantially in later chapters. These chapters will clarify the reasoning, restrictions, consequences and, above all, opportunities available to us as planners if we are willing to remain open to the various debates concerning complexity and planning. Therefore this book is indeed *A Planner's Encounter with Complexity*.

1.1 The fuzzy understanding of complexity

Complexity and planning – how incompatible they seem. Some consider that complexity refers to a qualification of a state of affairs. While planning refers to a rational process which guides actions from an existing situation towards an envisaged future situation. In relation to planning, others hold an opposing view, finding little reference within the theoretical debate on planning that incorporates

1 Gert de Roo is Professor in Spatial Planning. He is Head of the Department of Planning and Environment, the Faculty of Spatial Sciences at the University of Groningen, the Netherlands. He heads the thematic group on Planning and Complexity of the Association of European Schools of Planning.

the temporal aspects of the planning process (De Roo, Chapter 2). There are also alternative views on complexity.

One arises from the interdisciplinary academic debate concerning theories of complexity and so-called 'complexity thinking'. Here complexity is considered as being very much time-oriented and representing processes 'out of balance', with realities emerging at the interface of order and chaos (Waldrop, 1993). As such, complexity represents dynamic realities and non-linear behaviour. These realities and this behaviour have not yet found common ground within the planning community.

Several concepts lying at the heart of planning are decidedly fuzzy in nature, where fuzziness refers to multivalence, or 'vagueness' as Bertrand Russell called it (Kosko, 1993). It contradicts conceptions of a 'true or false' nature (Lootsma, 1997, p. 5), pointing instead to the shades of grey that can be found between such black and white oppositions. Fuzzy notions are multivalent in nature, with the principle conception of this being that this can be 'most easily grasped if one has in mind that [...] one does not directly meet sets with a crisp "borderline"...' (Bandemer and Gottwald, 1995). The test is an easy one: ask any group of students to define 'complexity', or even better to define 'sustainability' as students have grown up with an emerging sustainability discourse. The definitions they arrive at will undoubtedly include opposing perceptions. In planning there are various notions and concepts that are fuzzy by nature, such as sustainability and liveability, urban and rural, and the 'communicative' nature of contemporary planning. Many people have defined these conceptual notions, interpreting them in a host of different ways. Clearly, this diversity of interpretation is also the case for 'complexity'.

In the case of most planners, complexity is little more than an adverb which has not been given much thought. Nevertheless within the planning community there is a growing understanding of the importance of the conceptual side of complexity. Complexity and how it might work as a concept within planning is, however, not yet well understood and has been given a variety of meanings. Thus, for many planners, 'complexity' is indeed a fuzzy concept. However, unlike 'sustainability', for example, it has particular theoretical implications. While the fuzziness of 'sustainability' affects actions and behaviour *in* planning, 'complexity' influences our understanding *of* planning. As such, it is necessary to search for the philosophical and theoretical principles of complexity. In doing so, we also need to unravel the different discourses, attitudes and prejudices associated with the notion of complexity within the planning debate.

This is precisely what we have set out to do in this book. Without attempting to be exhaustive (an impossible undertaking in any case), we have endeavoured to be open-minded in considering the multiple interpretations of complexity, both within and outside the field of planning. We have done so by allowing different authors to consciously engage with the concept of complexity and thus have their say. They share with us their interpretation of the concept and explain how they have grappled with it.

In *A Planner's Encounter with Complexity* we also seek to alert planners to a notable theoretical development concerning the term 'complexity'. Linked to the notion of complex systems, this development parallels that of systems theory in the 1950s and 1960s. However, it has implications for our understanding of reality that extend far beyond the significance that systems theory had for academic thinking and practice. Many academic disciplines take the theoretical side of complexity extremely seriously. Despite this, planners have long overlooked the theoretical implications of complexity and the affects of associated complex systems. However, the broad academic discussion of this subject – and this is the position adopted in this book – can no longer be ignored.

1.2 Planners' first struggles with complexity

Many planners view complexity as a qualification of and confrontation with reality, involving a complex situation, a complex constellation of interests or a complex process. They see complex interrelationships, a coherence that is difficult to predict and a potentially unmanageable situation that might prove too much for those involved (requiring them to be on the alert, aware of a range of possible eventualities). Most of all, the idea of complexity raises the threat of a barrier, an obstacle to a satisfactory resolution. Viewed in this light, complexity has a distinctly negative connotation, with many planning practitioners signalling to their peers that they feel their backs to the wall as things become 'far too complex'. From a practical and theoretical perspective this attitude is rather unsatisfactory.

There is more to complexity, however. And some of us have taken the challenge to reflect upon it. Particularly interesting is the conceptualisation of complexity which takes place in various ways within the work and ideas of planners. Some might consider the enormous variety of these conceptualisations to be unsatisfactory. However, the variety of considerations constitutes a first step in structuring a disciplinary debate on complexity and planning. This debate is unavoidable and sooner or later it will have to be addressed in the field of planning, given the rapid developments in the discussion of the issue of complexity within other disciplines. Therefore, we take as a starting point the question of how complexity as a concept is currently interpreted *within* planning, ending in Section 1.6 with planners' understanding of the concept of 'complex systems', an emerging understanding from *outside* planning, and how this might influence the planning discipline.

Some consider complexity to be synonymous with complicatedness, while others point out the fundamental differences between the two. Nilsson, in Chapter 4, takes the position that complicated matters should be regarded as complex in cases where the circumstances involve unbalanced power relationships. She demonstrates her argument with the example of the wholesale relocation of the mining town of Kiruna in Northern Sweden. Here, unbalanced power relationships not only created a suboptimum arena for decision making, but also created uncertainties about possible transformations within and between coalitions.

Some argue that it is our contextual environment – society in all its forms – that is becoming more and more complex, and that we must adjust our planning actions and behaviour accordingly. Others believe that reality is always complex, but that this is something we have thus far ignored or tried to avoid in our thoughts and actions. According to Berting (1996, p. 24), 'Social reality is always extremely complex and we can observe, somewhat ironically, that complexity in itself is not the problem, but acting on the basis of simplifications of the social reality'.

The idea of complexity as a barrier to further development is evident within the theoretical debate on planning. This concerns, first and foremost, the development of the debate itself. Although planners in the late 1950s embraced 'rational choice' as the essence of what planning should be about, confrontation with a stubborn (or 'complex') reality put this assumption severely to the test. This resulted in the first 'theoretical' crisis in planning, where the conditions under which 'rational choice' could operate effectively were shown to be limited (that is, 'bounded and incremental') because reality was simply too complex for the method proposed. In the late 1980s, theoreticians again pointed to a crisis facing the planning theory debate (Alexander, 1984; Poulton, 1991). Solutions arising from discussions about bounded rationality, muddling through and incrementalism had also failed to offer sufficient solace. Planners were ready to accept a paradigm shift: the communicative turn to planning.

Not surprisingly, some point to the developments in planning theory considering these to be a response to the growing complexity *within* planning. Within the theoretical debate there has been a move away from the rational choice model and its charming simplicity, to bounded rationality and scenario planning, and from there towards the communicative side of planning. Some say this is a process of developing an awareness of the limitations of certainty. In other words, the successive crises in planning have basically been about coping with growing complexity, accepting uncertainty and finding alternative ways of dealing with these issues.

In the late 1980s, the neo-Marxist school within sociology confronted planning theory, revealing it to have too narrow a perspective on reality. The ideas of great philosophers such as Derrida, Foucault and Habermas were also discovered, each of whom pointed out the limitations of an object-oriented approach. Habermas claimed 'that, far from giving up on reason as an informing principle for contemporary societies, we should shift perspective from an individualised, subject-object conception of reason, to reasoning formed within inter-subjective communication' (Habermas, 1987). In other words, along with an orientation to the object and the associated facts, intersubjective interactions and their resulting ideas should be equally important for our conception of reality and in planning practice.

Even more importantly, planning constellations are now increasingly made up of a multitude of actors with different interests and concerns. Often these 'complex' situations have proven to be much more relevant for planning practice than a factual analysis of physical reality, hence a shift in focus within planning theory and practice from technical rationality to communicative rationality. However, this shift is not without consequences: 'Rationality seen from a communicative-intersubjective perspective is no longer a matter of definitions, proposals, plans, and scenarios as the starting points, but rather as the outcome of decision making processes. Naturally, the role of the planner will also shift accordingly, and focus will shift from object-oriented goals to optimising interaction and participation' (De Roo, 2003, p. 114).

With the acceptance of a communicative rationality, all alternatives to the rational-choice model are in retrospect burdened with a political reality founded on power. Without question, planning thus becomes politicised, due to the idea that actors are more than objective factors, and as such are engaged in a game that is evident in planning practice. The sociological rules explaining practice with regard to intersubjective interaction are then captured within a rationality that we label 'communicative'.

At the point to which the evolution of mainstream planning theory has brought us today, it is not surprising to find some who consider constellations of networks, communicative, collaborative and participative behaviour to be issues which are typical of so-called 'complex decision making' (Teisman, 1992; De Bruin and Ten Heuvelhof, 1991). Some argue there is still much to be done within this communicative reality. This could mean, for example, incorporating communicative and participative theories in line with Habermasian and Foucauldian understandings, addressing more than before issues such as values, ethics and gender, and progressing further into the fields of communicative action, story telling, discourse analysis and so on.

1.3 Planning, fixed-state relations and complexity

It would be far from correct to say that planning theory and practice, as well as its concepts, views and instruments, have entered their final stage. At present, in the early 21st century, there is once again talk of a crisis within planning. Contrary to the faith of some in the communicative and collaborative side of planning, the number of those who doubt this approach is still small but rapidly increasing. If indeed another crisis might be around the corner, it is interesting to consider the paths which are being proposed to avoid or overcome this particular crisis. Although some of these proposals are strongly embedded within contemporary planning theory (see for example Allmendinger and Tewdwr-Jones, 2002), the role of 'complexity' is hard to ignore.

Some have proposed complexity as the one denominator which gives meaning to various positions across the range from technical rationality to communicative rationality. In other words, depending on their position on the spectrum between both rationales, issues can be seen as either non-complex (simple, straightforward), complex, or highly complex (chaotic). According to the argument presented in Chapter 2 (De Roo), complexity seen from this particular point of view should be understood as a relative constitution, superimposed upon a 'fixed-state reality'.

Clearly, this positioning and its subsequent characterisation in terms of various 'degrees of complexity' will have consequences for the handling of the issue from a planning perspective (Christensen, 1985; De Roo, 2001/2003). On this basis, Chapter 2 draws two conclusions: first, complexity can indeed function as a criterion for decision making within contemporary planning, and second, contemporary planning is atemporal, with a focus on planning issues in a 'fixed-state reality'. Within this frozen setting, the mode of 'complexity' is therefore also atemporal. De Roo argues in this chapter that this is in no way a negative judgement, as this understanding can be a logical stepping stone in planning for temporal, evolutionary and non-linear realities.

Others point to 'the fuzzy middle' between the two main discourses of technical rationality (assuming certainties and an ontological focus on maximising objectives) and communicative rationality (involving intrinsic uncertainties, which above all should lead to agreements through interaction, resulting to some degree in frameworks for practice, in ontological terms a process optimisation), where most 'real life' planning problems are to be found (De Roo and Porter, 2007, see also Chapter 2). The idea is that between the ideal worlds of technical and communicative rationality there is a reality in which not only object orientation or intersubjective interaction is meaningful, but where both need to be examined at the same time (see Figure 2.3). Is it perhaps here that we can identify processes of complexity emerging from a 'fuzzy middle', where 'order' (technical rationality) and 'chaos' (communicative rationality) meet? Or is this totally beside the point?

In addition to successive orientations towards the object and the intersubjective, so common within contemporary planning theory, Schönwandt points to the importance of a third orientation which focuses on the human being, the subject. Building on the work of the biologist Jacob von Uexküll, he considers that his 'approach [...] explicitly addresses not only the limitations placed on our perceptual abilities, but also the restrictions of our cognitive capacities and the limits of our ability to act' (2008, p. 25). According to Schönwandt this way of thinking also allows us to avoid chaos, confusion, inefficiency and misinterpretations, although these matters are not seen as constraints (bounded rationality) on planning practice. On the contrary, by showing the biological and psychological side of the subject, we also reveal the adaptive human being (see also Portugali, 2000). In Chapter 3, Grunau and Schönwandt will draw our attention to cognitive characteristics and the adaptive ability of the individual – the subject – as well as the implications and potential of these characteristics and capacities for planning practice.

This exploration of relationships and interactions between complexity and planning within the range of contemporary planning thought and its conditions and possibilities reveals to us – to some extent – the position that planning theory has taken. Planning theory, for example, by and large operates within an atemporal framework. This is somewhat curious, considering the motives that drive planners to plan. Planners are supposed to support society's development through interventions in the physical environment. We can appreciate the idea that, in doing so, there is a need for a suitable rationale to guide our actions and behaviour. However, should it not also include a focus on the future and therefore on time? How can it be that we have ignored time? This is precisely the question that De Roo addresses in Chapter 2.

In response to this question, we will take a step further, beyond the horizon of contemporary planning, to discover what there is to say about the issue of time, including the consequences this might have for planning as a discipline. This path will take us deeper into the world of complexity, to interpretations of complexity which include time, evolution, transition and change.

1.4 Evolutionary processes and complex systems

There are some who are very much aware of and unhappy with the restraints of a planning debate with a strong focus on rationality and a 'fixed state reality'. Some have turned to discussions taking place within other disciplines, such as psychology (Portugali, 2000), biology (Marshall, 2008), economics (Bertolini, see Chapter 5) and systems theory (Verma, 1998). In doing so, their aim is to address flows, transformations and evolutionary processes, taking the position that within a planner's reality these processes are not to be ignored. Building on the work of Darwin's *Origin of Species* (1859), evolutionary processes were introduced by biologists and ecologists in the 1960s and have since been adopted by various disciplines to explain progress and development towards higher levels of organisation on the basis of selection (Buss, 2004; Hagen and Hammerstein, 2006; Nelson and Winter, 1982). Furthermore, from this point of view, environmental conditions, historical developments and competition are considered to be determining factors for selection and path-dependency, and are therefore conditions for choice and change.

In Chapter 5, Bertolini proposes an evolutionary interpretation of spatial planning, inspired as he is by evolutionary economics (Buss, 2004). Bertoloni suggests a notion of 'evolutionary planning' which should be concerned with maintaining and increasing the diversity of planning routines and strategies, making planning systems both resilient and able to adapt to change.

Darwin enriched us with the concept of evolutionary processes, and evolutionary economics is in this sense derived from the discipline of biology, clearly referring to biology in its struggle to find alternative understandings of economic processes. However, what if evolution, in the biological sense, was merely one expression (genetic evolution) of a universal mechanism which drives the processes of development and progress within the physical, biological, ecological and social realms and their interaction? Systems theory might help us here, proposing an abstract framework which cuts across and forms associations between the various disciplines in science.

Systems theory is meta-theory strongly embedded within the discipline of planning. It is not strange therefore that some have used systems theory to respond to the desire to incorporate (non-genetic) evolutionary processes and the issue of time in planning (Verma, 1998, see also Chapter 2). The various system classes readily correspond to mechanisms in planning: closed systems are represented by blueprints, feedback systems are represented by scenarios, and network systems are well understood within communicative planning. There is, however, a fourth system class which as yet has no reference within planning. This class of systems contains the so-called complex systems (Wolfram, 1984; Waldrop, 1993) which show 'evolutionary' behaviour.

These complex systems and their 'evolutionary' behaviour are the main focus of the interdisciplinary debate concerning the meta-theories regarding chaos (Gleick, 1987) and complexity (Waldrop, 1993). This debate has numerous origins, such as systems science, cybernetics, fractal geometry (Mandelbrot, 1977), fuzzy logic (Zadeh, 1965), agent-based modelling (Von Neumann, 1966), cellular automata (Wolfram, 1984), meteorology (Lorenz, 1963), physics (Prigogine and Nicolis, 1977, Prigogine and Stengers, 1984) and biology (Kauffman, 1993/1995).

Mathematical suggestions, such as Fuzzy Sets, point to a reality where various shades of grey (multi-valence, see Kosko, 1993) exist, a reality opposite to a clear and certain, black and white world. Mandelbrot's fractal geometry depicts a mathematical, non-Euclidian and irregular world that repeats itself on the various levels of existence ('self-similarity'), with each level representing processes moving from order to chaos, from which a new order emerges at a higher level, and so on. These mathematical exercises proved invaluable as arguments and delivering algorithms to modellers, who were in the process of discovering that there was far more to systems than nodes and interactions within a stable and consistent environment. Due to newly found algorithms and rapidly emerging computer sciences, simulations with agent-based modelling and cellular automata techniques have been able to clearly reveal that some systems, under the right conditions, show surprisingly 'endogenous evolutionary' behaviour. This behaviour becomes apparent in situations that are unstable, dynamic and 'out of a state of equilibrium'.

Although these systems might tend towards equilibrium, they rarely reach it, and, if they do, this will generally be only for very short periods. Far removed from equilibrium, these systems adapt quite well to their changing environment. At the same time, these systems are robust functioning and structured entities. They are flexible in relation to their environment and resilient at the same time. While adapting to the external, encroaching environment, the system also evolves through self-organising processes (endogenous evolution). These processes can best be understood by iterative and self-enforcing mechanisms well known in ecology and demography (where the impact on one generation has consequences for the next) and meteorology (the butterfly effect).

In physics, these types of process have also been made visible. Prigogine takes thermodynamics as an example to pinpoint irreversible and unstable processes far from equilibrium. Such processes illuminate the importance of time, sensitivity to initial conditions and the path these processes take from the past towards the future. This means there is some sort of time-space related causality which is called path-dependency. It also means that the unstable and irreversible processes are a recognition of indeterminism and, as Prigogine (1997) states, 'the end of certainty'. The reality we are facing is progressing, and not because it is determined by universal laws. There is a time-space factor as well, which can be very specific, very local, context-dependent and real, having a major impact on situations which are far from equilibrium or out of balance.

These discoveries provoke a dramatic conclusion: instability is necessary for development. Not surprisingly, some speak of 'new science' when referring to complexity thinking (Wolfram, 2002; Turner in Eve, Horsfall and Lee, 1997). We should not turn our backs on dynamics, turbulence, non-linearity and the like. Situations that are 'out of equilibrium' are likely to be far more common than stable situations and are a necessity for development and progress. Systems in a state of equilibrium are systems in which time, development and progress play no role. This deterministic, balanced, Newtonian world makes no allowance for change. This is rather unrealistic, considering all the changes we are confronted with in daily life in a dynamic world where it seems that there is only one constant: change itself. The idea of systems being able to evolve over time in a non-linear, emergent and adaptive way adds to our understanding of change, development and progress. We call these systems 'complex systems'.

1.5 Social complexity

Complexity thinking and the social sciences are not opposites, although the discussion regarding complexity is perhaps even now seen by most social scientists as somewhat exotic. If relevant at all, it is considered best kept within the realm of object-oriented studies such as physics and biology. Nevertheless, in the field of economics (considered here as a social science) there has long been an interest in complexity thinking, and there have also been social science studies that have contributed to complexity thinking.

In his study of social systems, Luhmann (1990) concludes that these systems are, by and large, systems of communication and that they maintain their identity and existence through processes of constant reproduction, confirmation and self-creation. This process of self-creation is called 'autopoiesis', an acknowledged technique within social complexity studies. Autopoiesis underlines the necessity of highlighting the essentials of the system – distilling them from an over-complex environment – and thereby have these repeatedly confirmed.

Byrne (1998), Eve, Horsfall and Lee (1997) and several others have undertaken pioneering work that has led to complexity thinking being introduced into the social sciences. Byrne took Mouzelis' book, *Sociological Theory: What Went Wrong?* (1995), to be arguing that it is time to reflect critically upon contemporary thinking in sociological theory. The book argues that sociological theory is caught between modernism and postmodernism but is seeking an escape from this impossible dichotomy. Byrne's response is 'to assert, and perhaps even demonstrate, that thinking in terms of society as constituted as a dissipative and evolutionary system, thinking about it in terms of the conceptual structure of chaos/complexity, is a good way of resolving these questions' (1998, p. 46).

In this introductory chapter on 'Planning and Complexity', we have also identified crises in contemporary planning theory. We have used complexity in various ways, as an abstraction within contemporary planning theory and as a means to deviate from this theoretical debate without losing touch with it. Nevertheless, if we are willing to appreciate the evolutionary, adaptive and emergent approach within planning, there are consequences, with rationality once again under discussion (Van den Bergh and Fetchenhauer, 2001; Prigogine, 1997; Nelson and Winter, 1982; Byrne, 1998). The third crisis in planning theory, mentioned as an emerging possibility in Section 1.3, will then become reality and might be the beginning of a serious paradigm shift.

At this point we are slightly concerned about how to state our position: should we conclude that planning theory could benefit from complexity thinking, incorporating some of the aspects that it proposes? Or should we take complexity theory as a whole as the starting point for our consideration of how planning theory should reinvent itself? If so, a whole new set of concepts will have to enter the debate on planning theory.

1.6 Planning and complexity thinking

Some have taken this challenge seriously, including those present in *A Planner's Encounter with Complexity*. Some are true frontrunners, Batty in Chapter 6 and Webster in Chapter 7, for example, who are both very much involved in the complexity debate and contribute introductory and accessible chapters exploring the issue of complexity and planning. Batty presents the city as a complex system, and shows the city's evolving path through time. Building on this, he shows how this evolutionary process can be seen as an example of the 'self-similarity of spatial structure'. In doing so, Batty makes a distinction between the evolution of cities and the processes used in their planning and design. This distinction raises the question of how to consider city management in the light of complexity. In the words of Chris Alexander, cities being well-ordered systems 'are generated structures, not fabricated structures' (2002, p. 80).

In Chapter 7, Webster also takes the evolution of cities as an example of complex systems found within the realm of planning. Planners have developed various constructs regarding their involvement in the growth of cities, the way in which cities function and how control is being pursued. This may very well be in contrast to the various autonomous processes that take place, and through which the city organises itself. Webster wonders what theories of social order are consistent with the understanding of a city as a complex self-organising system. His particular focus is on transaction costs and property rights, building on Hayek's view of the price system as an emergent social phenomenon.

Themes

Webster is one of the few theorists seriously trying to bridge complexity and planning. The topic he uses to explore mechanisms of complexity is property rights. However, there are other themes being explored with regard to complexity and planning. For example, Huys and Van Gils in Chapter 8 focus on the patterns of interaction and mutual dependency of actors within planning processes, seen in the light of complex adaptive systems and co-evolution. They argue that this perspective allows a realist view on the matter, enhancing planning with tools to manage uncertain and evolving planning processes.

In Chapter 9, Hagens focuses less on managing evolving planning processes, showing more interest in conceptualising these processes in terms of complexity. She takes the standpoint that complexity thinking will introduce different kinds of spatial concepts that are better equipped to understand our complex spatial environment, and help us learn how to influence and organise these environments.

Celino and Concilio explicitly emphasise the temporal dimension in Chapter 10, as does De Roo in Chapter 2. The arguments in each chapter differ, however. While De Roo stresses the lack of time awareness in planning theory, Celino and Concilio see a temporal dimension emerging, particular within collaborative planning. They propose an evolutionary approach to planning, not so much as an alternative to other existing forms, as suggested by Bertolini in Chapter 5, but as a means of enhancing collaborative planning. The temporal dimension takes shape within 'scenarios', these being seen as 'temporal structures' generated by collaborative processes which make use of knowledge actors' awareness of historically, locally and socially constructed contexts. In turn, these actors make use of the scenarios to reinforce, adjust and change their awareness of time and space.

Modelling

Batty, already introduced above, is renowned as a modeller and as one of the first to incorporate complexity thinking into his work, as shown in Chapter 6. Within the planning community, modellers were the first to understand the power and the importance of complexity as a concept for the discipline of planning as a whole (Batty, 2005; Batty and Longley, 1994; Benenson and Torrens, 2004; Allen, 1997). The use of GIS, cellular automata and agent-based modelling resulted in a perspective that differed from the theorist's point of view. While planning theorists have a strong focus on the here and now (Chapter 2), the modeller's perspective focuses much more on processes of change. Computer simulations which made use of the various techniques mentioned proved to be their key to success. Through back-tracking and forward-casting, making use of movements, actions and the choices of individuals (agents), groups (actors) and contexts (factors), and identifying path dependencies and emerging patterns, an awareness of the non-linear processes involved in spatial development has arisen.

Silva, in Chapter 11, shows the strength of cellular automata techniques in simulating the various ways in which the city of Lisbon has dealt with the process of urban growth and urban sprawl. These techniques are not just algorithms digesting quantitative data. There is also room for qualitative interpretation, which makes these techniques of interest in the support of management decisions regarding future scenarios.

In Chapter 12, Sunitiyoso, Avineri and Chatterjee use the multi-agent simulation technique to investigate the behaviour of persons using the transport system. They see this behaviour as a complex process that cannot easily be reduced to rational choices per se, but is a product of self-organisation and complex interaction processes between individual agents participating in the transport system. Their study explores and demonstrates the potential of utilising a multi-agent simulation model to understand, influence and predict the changes in the behaviour of transport users in response to the introduction of new traffic-planning measures.

In Chapter 13, Avineri adds to this, considering a traffic network as a complex system. He finds that a traffic network has the characteristics expected of a complex system, such as self-similarity and symmetry across various scales. However, the consequence of this complexity is a hierarchy within the road network. For Avineri, these complexity properties provide evidence that capacity improvements in the road network do not necessarily result in improved traffic flow. Such measures could just as well result in increased traffic congestion.

Digging deep

Many evolving processes in planning appear if one is willing to look for them. However, while examples obviously support the argument, and this support is what this book attempts to achieve, the question is whether these examples provide 'true' evidence of the underlying mechanisms suggested by complexity thinking. Are we not still another step away from an evidence-based understanding that will shed light upon time-space causalities and non-linear processes? Furthermore, will we be able to underpin this with mathematical algorithms? Although answers to these questions might seem helpful to the debate, one might wonder how real this next step is. Nicolis (1995) points to the impossibility of reaching a complete quantitative understanding of complex systems. Barrow also has his reservations: 'Mathematics is [...] seen by many as an analogy. But it is implicitly assumed to be the analogy which never breaks down' (1992, p. 21). The best example is fractal theory, which presents structures as repetitive and similar across various levels of development and, as such, is an interesting analogy for the evolution of the city. While we might recognise familiarities between fractals and city evolution, they are not the same.

Can we find a bridge between metaphors and analogies on the one hand and quantitative analysis on the other? Or will pragmatism prevail? According to pragmatism it is not always important to understand how something works, rather, we should enjoy the fact that it does work. According to Lakoff and Johnson (1999), concepts and conceptual thinking are largely metaphorical, and humans construct meanings through metaphors (1980). As such we cannot do without metaphors as they are fundamental to our understanding, to the perceptions we have and to the actions we take while interacting with our everyday environment.

And perhaps we should acknowledge that the concept of complexity is not just a phenomenon to be positioned within a realist and objectivist world. Co-evolution, for example, is not just about evolving objects or matter. It also has a great deal to do with changes in perception, understanding and giving meaning to objects and the material world. It touches the worlds of relativists as well as idealists, in which both conceptualise realities that are dependent on the subject, time and place. The issue cannot be resolved in this book, but it is addressed in various respects.

In Chapter 14, Tippett explores the nature of scientific paradigms and metaphorical understanding in the context of ecological design, in an effort to develop new and more effective ways of incorporating participatory processes into planning. For Tippett, metaphors are not merely useful mental constructs. She appreciates Morgan's statement that 'Metaphor encourages us to think and act in new ways. It extends horizons of insight and creates new possibilities' (1997, p. 351). Thus, she considers that metaphors can provide a powerful generative framework for rethinking the way in which humans interact with the environment. Furthermore, an understanding of complexity may play an essential role in planning for sustainable human settlements, in particular in looking at the nature of change and resilience. This understanding can then be developed into ecological design principles which can be applied to the design of settlements.

In Chapter 15, Karadimitriou, Doak and Cidre discuss what they call the 'space-time configurations' of brownfields. Basically they explore networks of actors, the material world with and within which these actors interact, and the evolving socio-spatial relationships resulting from this network and the interactions. They argue that these evolving socio-spatial relationships give meaning to the places and structures we call brownfields. This process of giving meaning influences brownfield policy discourse, which is also influenced by much wider debates on sustainable development and neo-liberal market mechanisms. Discourses at the local and the global levels meet, with elements 'adapting' to the best fit in time and space, being responsible – at least to some extent – for the constant change in our conceptualisation of brownfields and the actions we take as a consequence.

In Chapter 16, Van Wezemael is inspired by the philosophy of Deleuze (1969) and by DeLanda's assemblage theory of social complexity (2006). Van Wezemael argues that DeLanda's assemblage theory supports a better understanding of planners' 'reality'. Deleuze and DeLanda consider our 'reality' to be not so much a present state, a 'here and now', as a perceived constellation of events. Crucial to these events are their past, the way they are actually perceived and their potential with respect to the future. Events are all we perceive, metaphors also being events, and it is argued that we must also let go of the notion that metaphors are the building blocks of concepts and systems, making them understandable. Metaphors are not about reality, as events they are part of 'reality'.

An assemblage perspective on reality attempts to grasp not just the actual state or final products of a system or concept, but also the origins of a system or concept and the way the system or concept emerges from this initial state towards the actual (what most of us perceive as the 'real' or as the 'product') and beyond. The generative processes which drive these emerging or evolving systems are essential in assemblage theory. This reasoning is strongly influenced by complexity and chaos theory; however, it is presented to us with quite a twist and in its own set of terms, notions and concepts. Deleuze talks about the 'complexity of divergence', which Rajchman explains as involving 'a peculiar sort of complexity where it is not a matter of finding the unity of a manifold but, on the contrary, of seeing unity as a holding-together of a prior virtual dispersion. This sort of complexity does not consist in the One that is said in many ways, but rather in the fact that each thing may always diverge into others' (2001, p. 35). Deleuze's philosophy does not recognise a single unified entity or causally determined event, but considers reality emerging continuously from 'multiplicities' in which we abstract or categorise situations or 'happenings'. Deleuze speaks of 'the manner in which thought "orients" itself within' (Rajchman, 2001, p. 35) conceptual space.

Although Deleuze and his ideas are still rather unfamiliar to planners, his language is already very much in use within the planning arena. Deleuze's book *Le Pli* (1988 [The Fold]) presents the idea of multiplicity, which relates strongly to ideas of complexity. The multiplicity of conceptual space is domain of elements out of which new kinds of situations or 'happenings' can be perceived, very much depending on the subject, the locality and the time. The multiplicity of situations or happenings makes us analyse what we perceive (multi-actor) as entities or systems at the various levels – micro, meso and macro (multi-level) – as well as the various stages of their emergence and the very many ways these entities or systems adapt continuously to their environment. This kind of analysis is undertaken within planning and decision making, for example to support transition management. Transition management is not totally new to planners. As such, complexity in planning is perhaps understood slightly better than planners are aware of.

In Chapter 17, using somewhat different language, Silva elaborates on how events might emerge from these multiplicities, while exploring phase-transitions and bifurcations. In complexity thinking, phase-transitions are often understood as changes taking place between phases of stability, and as such are evidence of evolutionary processes. Bifurcations are considered to be fundamental changes in a system's behaviour due to a small change in one of its variables or elements. According to Silva, these changes occur in multi-dimensional environments containing different variables evolving over time, with different waves of intensity (comparable to Deleuze's multiplicity). With regard to the behaviour of systems, she identifies moments in time in which multiple variables interact to produce substantial change in a system, with a phase-transition as an outcome. These outcomes represent discontinuous processes in the evolution of a system.

1.7 A window of opportunity…

Planning is about dealing with our environment. In the *Planner's Encounter with Complexity* we present an environment that is subject to processes of continuous change, being either progressive or destructive, evolving non-linearly and alternating between stable and dynamic periods. If the issue, situation or system that is subject to change is adaptive, self-organising, robust and flexible in relation to this change, a process of evolution and co-evolution can be expected.

This understanding of an evolving environment is not mainstream to every planner. However, in this *Planner's Encounter with Complexity* we argue that environments confronted with discontinuous, non-linear evolving processes might be more real than the idea that an environment is simply a planners' creation. Above all, we argue that recognising the 'complexity' of our environment offers a huge and exciting window of opportunity, opening up a range of thought, including entirely new perspectives on our world, our environment, planning theory and practice, and the *raison d'être* of the planners that we are.

References

Alexander, C. (2002) *The Nature of Order, Books 1-4*, Center of Environmental Structure, Berkeley.

Alexander, E.R. (1984) 'After rationalism, what? A review of responses to paradigm breakdown', *Journal of the American Planning Association*, pp. 62-69.

Allen, P.M. (1997) *Cities and Regions as Self-Organizing Systems: Models of Complexity*, Gordon and Breach Science Publishers, Amsterdam.

Bandemer, H., and Gottwald, S. (1995) *Fuzzy Sets, Fuzzy Logic, Fuzzy Methods with Applications*, John Wiley & Sons, Chichester.

Batty, M. (2005) *Cities and Complexity: Understanding Cities with Cellular Automata, Agent-Based Models, and Fractals*, The MIT Press, Cambridge.

Batty, M., and Longly, P.A. (1994) *Fractal Cities: A Geometry of Form and Function*, Academic Press, San Diego.

Benenson, I. and Torrens, P.M. (2004) *Geosimulation: Automata-Based Modelling of Urban Phenomena*, John Wiley & Sons, Chichester.

Berting, J. (1996) 'Over rationality en complexiteit' [About rationality and complexity], in P. Nijkamp, W. Begeer and J. Berting (eds.), *Denken over complexe besluitvorming: een panorama* [*Thoughts about complex decision making: an overview*], SDU Uitgevers, The Hague, pp. 17-29.

Bruijn, J.A., de and Heuvelhof, E.F. ten (1991) *Sturingsinstrumenten voor de overheid: Over complexe netwerken en een tweede generatie sturingsinstrumenten* [*Control instruments for administrative authorities: About complex networks and a second generation of control instruments*], Stenfert Kroese Uitgevers, Leiden.

Buss, D. (2004) *Evolutionary Psychology: The New Science of the Mind*, Pearson Education Inc., Boston.

Byrne, D. (1998) *Complexity Theory and the Social Sciences: An Introduction*, Routledge, London.

Christensen, K.S. (1985) 'Coping with uncertainty in planning', *Journal of the American Planning Association*, Winter, pp. 63-73.

Darwin, C. (1895) *The Origin of Species*, Penguin Group, New York/London (reprint 2003).

DeLanda, M. (2006) *A New Philosophy of Society: Assemblage Theory and Social Complexity*, Continuum, London/New York.

Deleuze, G. (1969) *Logique du sens*, Éditions de Minuit, Paris.

Deleuze, G. (1988) *Le Pli: Leibniz et le Baroque, Collection 'Critique'*, Éditions de Minuit, Paris.

De Roo, G. (2001) 'Complexity as a criterion for decision making; a theoretical perspective for complex (urban) conflicts', paper presented at the 1st World Planning School Congress at the College of Architecture and Urban Planning, Tongji University, July 2001, Shanghai, China.

De Roo, G. (2003) *Environmental Planning in the Netherlands: Too Good to be True: From Command-and-Control Planning to Shared Governance*, Ashgate, Aldershot.

De Roo, G. and Porter, G. (2007) *Fuzzy Planning: The Role of Actors in a Fuzzy Governance Environment*, Ashgate, Aldershot.

Eve, R.A., Horsfall, S. and Lee, M.E. (eds.) (1997) *Chaos, Complexity and Sociology: Myths, Models and Theories*, Sage, Thousand Oaks.

Gleick, J. (1987) *Chaos: Making a New Science*, Cardinal, London.

Habermas, J. (1987) *The Philosophical Discourse of Modernity*, Polity Press, Cambridge.

Hagen, E. and Hammerstein, P. (2006) 'Game theory and human evolution: A critique of some recent interpretations of experimental games', *Theoretical Population Biology*, vol. 69, p. 339.

Kauffman, S. (1993) *The Origins of Order: Self-Organization and Selection in Evolution*, Oxford University Press, New York.

Kauffman, S. (1995) *At Home in the Universe: The Search for Laws of Complexity*, Oxford University Press, New York.

Kosko, B. (1993) *Fuzzy Thinking, the New Science of Fuzzy Logic*, Hyperion, New York.

Lakoff, G. and Johnson, M. (1980) *Metaphors We Live By*, University of Chicago Press, Chicago.

Lakoff, G. and Johnson, M. (1999) *Philosophy in the Flesh, The Embodied Mind and its Challenge to Western Thought*, Basic Books, New York.

Lootsma, F.A. (1997) 'Fuzzy logic for planning and decision making', *Applied Optimization Series* no. 8, Kluwer Academic Publishers, Dordrecht.

Lorenz, E.N. (1963) 'Deterministic non-periodic flow', *Journal of the Atmospheric Sciences*, vol. 20, pp. 130-141.

Luhmann, N. (1990) *Essays on Self-Reference*, Columbia University Press, New York.

Mandelbrot, B. (1977) *Fractals: Form, Chance and Dimension*, W.H. Freeman and Co, New York.

Marshall, S. (2008) *Cities, Design and Evolution*, Routledge, London.

Morgan, G. (1997) *Images of Organization*, Sage Publications, Thousand Oaks.

Mouzelis, N. (1995) *Sociological Theory: What Went Wrong?*, Routledge, London.

Nelson, R.R. and Winter, S.G. (1982) *An Evolutionary Theory of Economic Change*, Harvard University Press, Cambridge.

Nicolis, G. (1995) *Introduction to Nonlinear Science*, Cambridge University Press, Cambridge.

Piaget, J. (1974) *Biologie und Erkenntnis. Über die Beziehungen zwischen organischen Regulationen und kognitiven Prozessen* [*Biology and Recognition. About the Interactions Between Organic Regulations and Cognitive Structures*], Fischer, Frankfurt.

Piaget, J. (1976) *De Äquilibration der kognitiven Strukturen* [*The Equilibration Between Cognitive Structures*], Klett, Stuttgart.

Portugali, J. (2000) *Self-Organization and the City*, Springer-Verlag, Berlin.

Poulton, M.C. (1991) 'The case for a positive theory of planning. Part 1: What is wrong with planning theory?', *Environment and Planning B: Planning and Design*, vol. 18(2), pp. 225-232.

Prigogine, I. and Nicolis, G. (1977) *Self-Organization in Non-Equilibrium Systems*, Wiley, London.

Prigogine, I. and Stengers, I. (1984) *Order Out of Chaos: Man's New Dialogue with Nature*, Flamingo, London.

Prigogine, I. (1997) *The End of Certainty*, The Free Press, New York.

Rajchman, J. (2001) 'Out of the fold', in G. di Cristina (ed.), *Architecture and Science*, AD, Wiley-Academy, Chichester, pp. 35-37.

Schönwandt, W.L. (2008) *Planning in Crisis? Theoretical Orientations for Architecture and Planning*, Ashgate, Aldershot.

Teisman, G.R. (1992) *Complexe besluitvorming; een pluricentrisch perspectief op besluitvorming over ruimtelijke investeringen* [*Complex decision making: a pluricentric perspective on dicision-makijng regarding spatial investments*], VUGA, The Hague.

Van den Bergh, J. and Fetchenhauer, D. (2001) *Voorbij het Rationele Model: Evolutionaire Verklaringen van Gedrag en Sociaal-Economische Instituties* [*Beyond the Rational Model: Evolutionary Explanations of Behaviour and Social-Economic Institutions*], MAGW, NWO, The Hague.

Verma, N. (1998) *Similarities, Connections, and Systems: The Search for a New Rationality for Planning and Management*, Lexington Books, Lanham.

Von Neumann, J. (1966) *Theory of Self-Reproducing Automata (with Arthur W. Burks)*, University of Illinois Press, Chicago.

Waldrop, M.M. (1993) *Complexity: The Emerging Science at the Edge of Order and Chaos*, Viking, London.

Wolfram, S. (1984) 'Universality and complexity in cellular automata', *Physica D*, no. 10, January, pp. 1-35.

Wolfram, S. (2002) *A New Kind of Science*, Wolfram Media, Champaign, IL.

Zadeh, L. (1965) 'Fuzzy Sets', *Information and Control*, vol. 8, pp. 338-353.

Chapter 2
Being or Becoming? That is the Question! Confronting Complexity with Contemporary Planning Theory

Gert de Roo[1]

The concept of complexity is the unparalleled representative of a vision that portrays our reality as continuously evolving. Complexity is thus inextricably linked to dynamic processes of development and is therefore a qualification of a reality in which situations (including spatial situations) cannot be seen as unchanging, atemporal and independent of their context. With complexity, the meaning of a planning issue is sought not only in 'being' but also in 'becoming'.

Whilst planners advocate interventions in the physical environment in order to support the societal process in the future, they mainly base their choices on situations as they 'are'. In planning, the main concern is still the 'here and now' of a planning issue. What is more, the theoretical scope of planning is mainly limited to rationality and hardly considers time, development or progress. In this chapter we will take the view that planners must no longer close their eyes to the message that is inherent in the concept of complexity.

2.1 Introduction

Planning theory and complexity thinking are two different matters. It is therefore not easy to connect the two. Any attempt to do this anyway will undoubtedly invite numerous critical reactions. We need to be aware that, in relation to the broad academic discussion about complexity, contemporary planning theory is lagging behind.

In this contribution we will use systems thinking, among others, to link complexity and planning theory. From a systems theory point of view and using the concept of complexity we will show where current planning theory stands. Planning issues are interpreted nowadays from the perspective of open, network

1 Gert de Roo is Professor of Spatial Planning. He is Head of the Department of Planning and Environment, Faculty of Spatial Sciences at the University of Groningen in the Netherlands. He coordinates the Planning and Complexity thematic group of the Association of European Schools of Planning (AESOP).

systems in which actors share their perceptions, positions and interests. As such, these are issues ranging from 'complex' to 'very complex'. They can no longer be interpreted as feedback systems, let alone as closed systems. We have come to realise that only the very simple and 'straightforward' issues can be interpreted with closed systems. This also means that planning issues are far from equal and that each should be considered on its own merits.

Following Christensen (1985), different authors (De Roo, 2000/2001; Geurtsen, 1996; Van de Graaf and Hoppe, 1996; Minzberg, 1983; Stacey, 2001; Van der Valk, 1999) have proposed classifying planning issues according to their complexity. This classification according to 'the degree of complexity' makes it possible to connect issues, the type of approach and the consequences entailed. When an issue is judged to be of 'a higher degree' of complexity, the approach shifts accordingly from one that corresponds to a closed system to one that corresponds to an open, network system.

We consider this understanding to be a first step in connecting planning and complexity theory. However, this is just the beginning. Around the subject of complexity an academic debate has taken place that, for the most part, has remained out of sight of planning. This debate has produced a fascinating perspective of reality. This perspective is best expressed in a systems class that is still unknown to planning: the complex system. Characteristics such as adaptation, emergence, self-organisation and co-evolution are associated with this 'complex system'. These characteristics are directly linked to the theme of time.

These characteristics are not (yet) part of contemporary planning theory. This is curious, given the intrinsic objectives of spatial planning – intervening in the physical environment for the benefit of society and its development, and the wellbeing of society in the (near) future. Current planning theory is still, to a great extent, 'atemporal'.

2.2 From 'steady state' to 'unpredictable patterns'

It is becoming clear that planning theory is hardly aware of and is not keeping up with current developments in systems theory. Generally accepted is the following:

The first concepts in planning theory were based on the idea of closed systems with clear components between which there were direct causal relationships. These are unchanging systems that, in theory, can be fully known. We call this system class I (steady-state equilibrium, Kauffman, 1991). In the post-war period it became increasingly difficult to hold on to the idea of closed systems.

An alternative for closed systems was found in the idea of feedback systems, with the scenario approach as the best example of new amendments in planning. We call this system class II (oscillation between fixed states, Kauffman, 1991). However, the basic concepts of planning that are based on feedback systems were not free from criticism either. Network systems were introduced into the realm of planning to complement system class II, and became increasingly popular.

These network systems focus on the interaction between the actors, rather than on how the physical identity of the issue is represented. In this way, the attention shifts from an object-oriented and knowable reality to an intersubjective and perceived reality. We summarise these network systems here as system class III (no predictable patterns or stability, Kauffman, 1991).

Contemporary planning theory is attempting to ease itself away from the idea that reality can be made and managed. With this paradigm shift there is a strong interest in the experiences of network approaches. In planning theory, the rationality behind these approaches is called 'communicative'. It is these communicative rational approaches in planning that are attracting the attention of planning theorists at the beginning of the 21st century (cf. Allmendinger and Tewdwr-Jones, 2002).

2.3 The rise and fall of certainty

In the 1990s a tremendous shift in attitude took place within both planning theory and practice (Allmendinger, 2002). Essentially, this shift involved the defeat of a belief system that incorporated the idea that certainty can be achieved within planning processes. A period of several decades in which planners toyed with object-oriented planning approaches for a universally understood and true material world is coming to an end. Nevertheless, this idea that certainty is within reach has been fundamental to post-war planning and its dominance is represented by a technical or procedural-rational approach (Meyerson and Banfield, 1955; Paris, 1982): hence the belief in closed-systems thinking.

This belief in certainty cannot be seen solely as a heritage of the war period, with its need for precision and 'command and control'. There was also a desire within the various social-science disciplines to be as well defined and straightforward as Newtonian physics had proven to be (Bohman, 1991). However, what was more important for the rise of certainty as a belief system was its philosophical origin in neo-positivism, one of the later – and rather influential – philosophical approaches, in which we are willing to understand our material world as an absolute truth (see Figure 2.1). Obviously, if there is one truth there is also certainty to gain. The neo-positivistic methodology for gaining certainty was verification, which, at the time (early 1900s), was considered to be the ultimate test for grasping reality (Chalmers, 1976; Klee, 1999).

In post-war planning it was this straightforwardness that was appreciated: if we consider the facts known to us at the beginning of the planning process we will be able to predict and produce a desired outcome, based on well-defined, obvious and direct causal relationships connecting the various phases of the process of planning (Sagoff, 1988). This was considered to be a rational approach to planning (Meyerson and Banfield, 1955). However, with the rise of other

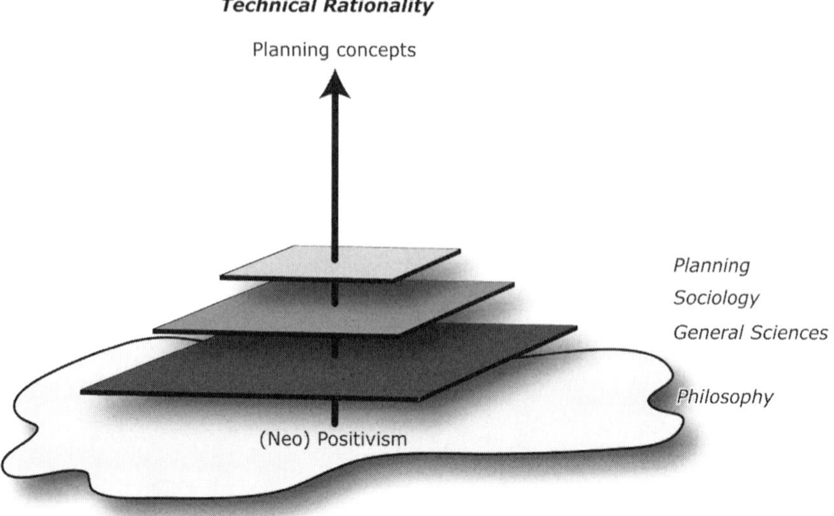

Figure 2.1 Early planning theory: The 'rational' approach emerges from neo-positivism

rationales in contemporary planning, we nowadays typify this particular rationale as functional (Friedmann, 1987), procedural (Faludi, 1987) or technical (Healey, 1983). Following a technical-rational approach, planners have tried to contribute to the progress and development of our society, creating and shaping a desired physical environment based on certainty, the possibility to predict our future and – in the end – to control this future, which is a planned future, with the planner as the expert showing us the way. This divine role for planners was legitimate because the powers given to them by democratically elected bodies were equally technical and functional, in anticipation of a population-wide consensus: it was functionality that was considered necessary in order to get things done.

Nowadays, most of us see this wonderfully straightforward understanding of our world (as represented by closed systems) as a utopia that cannot be: a reality where certainty prevails, with an environment we understand, know and fully control so that development and progress take place in a way that the planner appreciates. Over the years, numerous arguments have emerged in support of a somewhat critical attitude towards technical rationality in planning (March and Simon, 1958). A strong argument was that, although bounded rationality was acknowledged when considering new approaches such as scenario techniques and feedback systems, the results of planning processes remained disappointing. In retrospect, we can see numerous excuses – or modifications if you like – being made in an attempt to hold on to the technical-rational approach and its promise of certainty and control. Bounded rationality was among the most obvious excuses, making the same neo-positivistic assumptions and taking the position that a technical-rational approach had not yet fully matured (compared to Newtonian physics) in the case of the social sciences, which included planning and decision making. In addition, 'boundedness', such as a lack of time, money and energy, was an obvious excuse (Berry, 1974; Harper and Stein, 1995).

2.4 Accepting uncertainty

Thanks to the work of Faludi, critical rationalism was introduced into planning (Faludi, 1986). This work reflected upon the ideas of Karl Popper, who argued quite convincingly that we should be moderate in our quest for truth and certainty. His basic point was that the truth would never be found, which puts verification to the test as a method for establishing the truth. Falsification, Popper's alternative, is far less ambitious because it does not claim the truth or suchlike as a criterion for differentiating scientific statements from other statements, but rather being 'just'. Popper's method for testing hypotheses gave us a methodology for pursuing progress; however, this was not towards a single truth but for pursuing progress within the academic theoretical debate and in theory building. This 'critical thinking' did not make much difference to planning practice. Planning remained functional in its approach, with a positive attitude towards object-related interventions based on desirable procedures that would be generally applicable and independent of contextual influences.

Despite moderate ambitions and a growing sense of realism in planning, there was growing opposition to a modernistic attitude. In particular, radical social theory proved to be a valuable source of counterarguments. At the time – in the 1960s and 1970s – radical social theory was emphasising the importance of the socio-political context, with a particular interest in the contradictions of capitalism and the victims this socio-political context allegedly produced (Crook, 1991; Schönwandt, 2002/2007). It focused not so much on the conduct of planning and how to improve it, but on the state of our society and the way in which various interventions – not least through planning – conformed to the prevailing mode of production. As a result, radical theorists were suspicious of general applications, modes and theories. The downscaling of trust and faith in favour of technical rationality by critical rationalists, and the rise of radicalism – rejecting the existence of general principles independent of societal forces entailed a shift away from modernistic assumptions towards a post-modern attitude among a growing few. As such, planners were becoming susceptible to intersubjective orientations to and within planning.

Intersubjectivity became a serious issue within planning thought when planners discovered those philosophers emphasising intersubjective communication being as important as the traditional object oriented focus, in constructing a fair idea about reality. Among these were Habermas, Foucault and Derrida. Foucault is considered to be the founding father of discourse analysis, focusing as he does on storytelling, lines of reasoning, motives, attitudes and perceptions (Hacking, 1999). It was no coincidence that this new perspective was accepted at the moment that the Iron Curtain fell. It was as if radical theory and intersubjectivity were set free from their Marxist background. At the same time, object-oriented planning had reached a dead end when it came to identifying new developments that would push planning ahead. The momentum was present for change to take place.

2.5 Rationalising the communicative side of planning

This development drastically widened the scope of options for planners. Equally exciting was the way in which both planning practice and theory embraced this intersubjective communication and collaboration as a new perspective on planning. The enthusiasm with which not only the theorists but also the practitioners embraced approaches that are solely based on communication, participation and interaction between planning subjects emphasises how desperately planning society had been waiting for change.

The move towards these new approaches in planning opened the door to theoretical concepts such as social-constructivism (Hacking, 1999) and discourse analysis (Hajer, 1995) to enter mainstream planning thought. For planning thought, planning practice and practitioners this proved to be enriching in very many ways. A new rationality emerged based on 'the fundamental properties of social choice' (Weaver et al., 1985, p. 148). The terms 'social' (Van der Cammen, 1979), 'collective' (Elster, 1983), 'communicative' (Healey, 1992) and 'collaborative' (Healey, 1997) are used as a preposition to this rationale in planning.

In retrospect, one could consider the question of how to cope with the rather persistent lack of certainty to have been answered in a rather radical and resolute way: we are no longer looking for certainty as uncertainty is now going to be the way to go. If full certainty is a reality that does not exist and does not lead to a true and clearly defined world in which progress and development take place, could it be that it is worthwhile looking at uncertainty? In answering this question, object-oriented approaches, which were supposed to indicate an indisputably true world, are no longer the way ahead. Instead, within a network environment, the formulation of a shared perspective on our reality and its basic assumptions and implications, are considered essential steps to be taken.

In that perspective, planners no longer seek the means to maximise planning goals. Instead they have to act as mediators, advocates and guides for the actors involved in the planning process in order to optimise their interests. This means a shift from direct control towards self-regulation. More importantly, it means accepting that many planning issues are more complex than considered possible within a technical mode of planning. This is due not only to their physical situation – which, indeed decision making bodies can hardly oversee anymore – but it is also acknowledged that there are multiple stakeholders whose decision making powers, or powers to support or obstruct, have to be appreciated within planning processes.

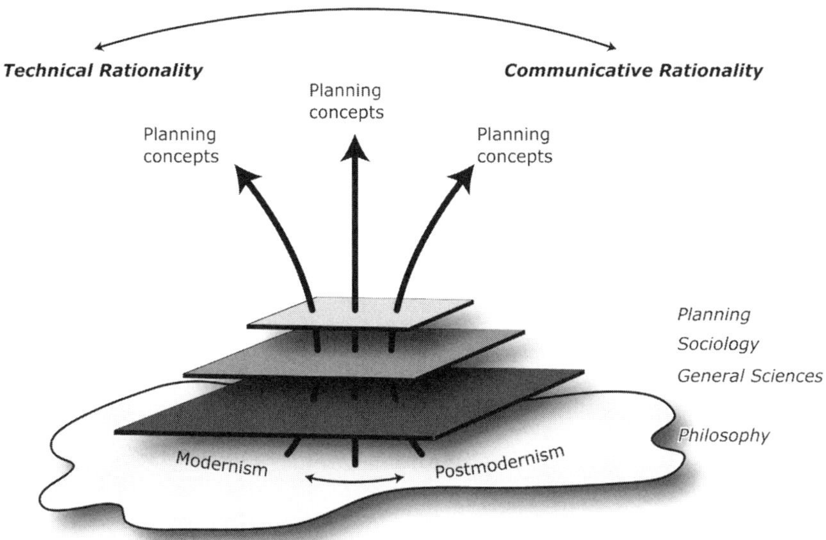

Figure 2.2 Contemporary planning theory extends between two extremes of planning thought: Technical versus communicative rationale

Planners who were ready for change moved away from a modernistic, technical rationale and embraced communicative, collaborative and participative approaches representing late- and post-modern alternatives. This shift, which revolutionised planning thought, did not stand alone but is part of a wider debate that runs through the various academic disciplines and has a strong footing in philosophy. In essence, the post-modern argument is that nothing is certain and that everything is subject to doubts, considerations and – in the end – nihilism (Harper and Stein, 1995). While a solely technical perspective on our reality would prove to be too good to be true, a post-modern view would leave us nothing but scepticism and is – in essence – rather fatalistic. The result is a schizophrenic reality, in which one view cannot exist alongside another.

2.6 Complexity in an atemporal planning environment

This schism in planning, which has created two separate worlds, overlooks the idea that reality is not black or white, certain or uncertain, but is likely to be various shades of grey. In this contribution we are seeking an argument that responds to the awareness that certainty and uncertainty go side by side, in both daily life and theory. We would like to pursue this idea by introducing complexity as an

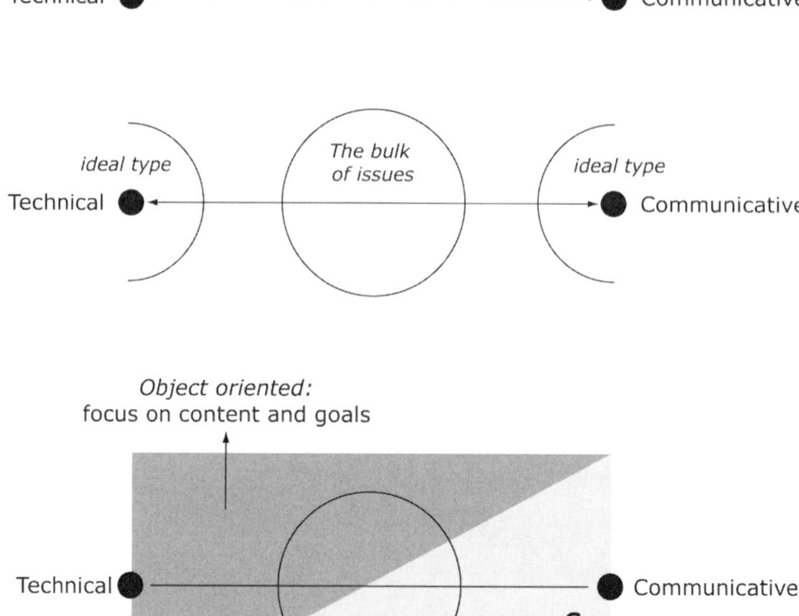

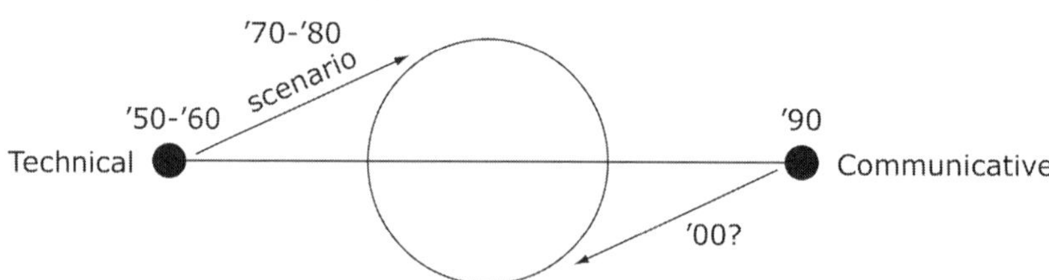

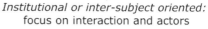

Figure 2.3 Between the two extremes in planning theory, an object-oriented view of the world and an intersubjective understanding of our reality go hand in hand

Source: De Roo, 2002; De Roo and Porter, 2007.

important notion in planning. In doing so we will make use of some particular assumptions made by contingency and systems theory, and use these as stepping stones to chaos and complexity theories.

In this respect we are acknowledging an abstract and philosophical mode of reasoning with regard to the notion of complexity that Christensen (1985) brought into the planning debate. Christensen introduced complexity as a phenomenon in planning that could help us to construct a view on planning that is not bounded (in a technical sense) but must cope with a reality comprising various degrees of complexity.

We can imagine a spectrum (Figure 2.2) with an orderly world with specific conditions at one extreme (technical rationality) and a highly complex and almost chaotic world with its own specific conditions at the other extreme (communicative rationality). From this line of reasoning, a reality begins to unfold that contains an ordered and a chaotic, uncertain world, as well as a world in between. This in-between world can be understood partly by building on both extremes (Figure 2.3) and by reflecting upon them, while appreciating that this world also has its own dynamic.

Both extremes on our spectrum, the technical versus the communicative rationale, can be seen as representations of a non-existent and therefore theoretical view of the world. These are positions on the spectrum where only one type of rationale, either technical or communicative, prevails. Anywhere in between we can pinpoint positions where both coexist. Or, to be more precise, when moving along the spectrum from a technical rationale towards a communicative rationale, the view of the world becomes less object-oriented and our understanding of reality becomes more intersubjective (Figure 2.3). And, indeed, it is also considered a move from orderly towards chaotic and uncertain situations, in other words, an increase in complexity.

A decline in direct causal relationships, increasing fuzziness of entities and unstable and interfering contexts results in an increasing need to consult each other about how to position ourselves in an uncertain world. Causality, entity and stability are some of the important mechanisms used by our brains to understand, to structure and to rationalise our orientation towards the material world. As such, these mechanisms are seen in the light of an object-subject orientation. Intersubjectivity welcomes mechanisms such as valuing, argumentation, agreeing, discourse and storytelling. In other words, when encountering uncertainty, communication and interaction with other subjects becomes desirable and this is likely to result in actions that are jointly agreed upon. This is rather crucial as intersubjective approaches become so widespread within a communicative mode of planning.

Other deductions can be made; for example, in a technical-rational decision making environment the focus will be on the individual parts of an issue, as it has to be assumed that the context is stable or does not interfere with the issue. This focus on the individual parts will help gain certainty about the issue and its proposed planning process, and this will result in goal maximisation: single and precisely defined outcomes are the upshot. In a communicative-rational decision environment, the opposite will be true. The focus will be on the context as it interferes heavily and inconsistently with the issue, with uncertainty as a consequence. The strategy here is to optimise the planning process while going through the various phases: an infinite number of options will emerge throughout the planning process.

Growing complexity due to a progression from orderly towards chaotic situations means that precisely defined outcomes will have to be substituted by an appreciation of an increasing number of options to select from during the planning process. It will mean a shift from goal maximisation towards process optimisation. From this perspective it is important to appreciate that, although the issue at hand is becoming more complex, the most suitable planning approach is not necessarily becoming more complex but different.

What does this mean for our understanding of planning? It enables us to merge two opposing belief systems – one representing order and the other representing chaotic, uncertain or very complex situations – in planning, as soon as we consider these systems to be extremes of the same reality (Figure 2.3). While embracing the communicative rationale in contemporary planning, we cannot abandon as obsolete the technical rationale in planning. Technical rationality, and the certainties it brings us, remains a necessity. In other words, while accepting uncertainties in planning, it still remains important to seek those certainties that do exist.

Another result of this line of reasoning is that, in focussing on both ideal types in planning, we managed to avoid tackling the 'confusing middle' in between the two extremes. However, scenario and contingency planning could, perhaps, be seen as ways of coping with the difficulties of this particular part of the spectrum. Nevertheless, the majority of planning issues are located here, 'in-between'.

By introducing a spectrum the two worlds will meet, as they are linked to each other by a phenomenon representing various degrees of both worlds. We have also argued that, as the degree of complexity of the planning issue increases, less attention is paid to object-orientation and the focus shifts to the intersubjective side of planning. As such, we have introduced complexity as a criterion for planning and decision making. This, however, is just one side of complexity – its atemporal side. The next step in our line of reasoning would therefore be to include time.

2.7 Chaos and 'out-of-balance' situations

In this chapter we refer several times to, and make use of, systems thinking. It was possible to link the different system classes to consecutive developments in planning theory. This systems thinking is part of what we call 'general sciences'. As such, systems theory is applied by the different scientific disciplines and where possible these are linked with each other. Bertalanffy (1968) is viewed as one of the founders of the so-called general systems theory.

The name Lorentz is inextricably linked to chaos theory (Lorentz, 1963). Whereas Bertalanffy assumes that systems flourish in states of equilibrium (steady state), Lorentz argues that systems that are out of balance – chaotic dynamic systems – reveal a very different reality. In chaotic dynamic systems, small differences can lead to very diverse results. These systems show a reality with great uncertainties but also with a wealth of possibilities.

Systems theory regards the system as a way of understanding reality on the basis of a collection of nodes (entities) that are connected by their (joint) actions and reactions. These entities interact in different ways with each other and the outside world, and we can therefore distinguish a variety of systems. Categorising these systems results in the system classes presented in Section 2.2. Chaos theory goes further by also considering the development of these systems in non-equilibrium situations and by confronting the systems with the factor of time. Chaos theory shows that, contrary to what we expect, the development of systems can be non-linear and dynamic.

Chaos theory presents us with an alternative way of understanding reality. This reality is not represented by stable entities but is a progressive process. Fundamental to this is the idea of how the world around us evolves from simple and straightforward conditions (an orderly world represented by closed systems) towards highly complex, chaotic situations that are highly unpredictable and susceptible to intervening interactions (a chaotic world with informal networks to help cope with it) that take place continuously at various levels (Gleick, 1987).

Instead of either accepting a knowable and predictable world, interpreted by means of a technical rationale, or accepting an uncertain, multi-interpretable world that can be dealt with by adopting a communicative rationale, this idea of an evolving process from order to chaos touches both worlds. It connects these worlds, because it considers this evolving process from one towards the other a necessity. It is an evolving process due to a growing degree of complexity or a shift from a univocal order towards diversity. How different this is from the Newtonian world, which is an orderly world in full balance that excludes any system change, and as a result denies any progress (see also Latour, 1993 and Dean, 2000).

This perspective, which is deduced from chaos theory, acknowledges a reality between the two opposing views, where development and progress are to be expected. If we consider this perspective on progress and development to be universal, it enables us to formulate at least a number of fundamental statements about planning. Planning is addressing a reality (the physical and social environment) that is evolving from simple and straightforward entities and interactions between them, to highly complex situations, fuzzy entities and interactions that are best represented by informal networks. Planning itself, as a practice and as a scientific discipline, will evolve too. We can see this, for example, in a move from a technical towards a communicative rationale.

If we consider that technical and communicative rationales are perspectives in planning that are positioned at extremes on a spectrum (and rather theoretical

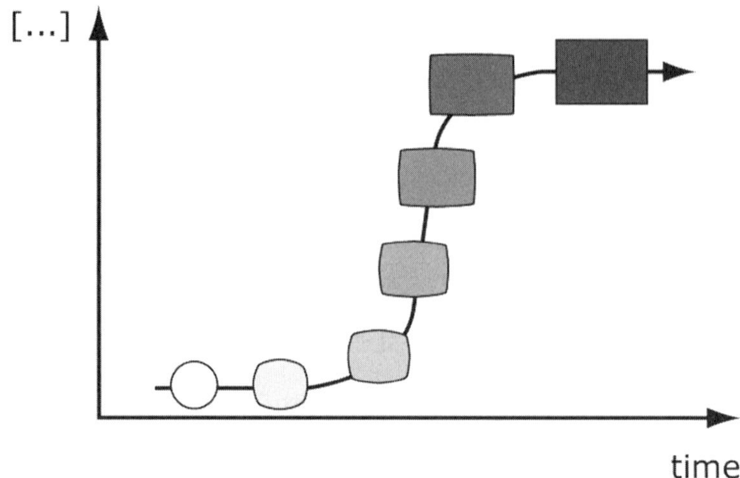

Figure 2.4 The complex system evolves in structure and function: Co-evolution

and ideal-type), it means there is something in between as well. Planning issues that are 'in between' will always contain aspects of both worlds, although varying in degree, depending on the circumstances, i.e. their complexity (see Figure 2.3).

We propose three assumptions, made from chaos and complexity theories, which together form an exegesis for development and progress. We can use the reasoning above, which is supported by chaos theory, as a first assumption that will help to explain change and progress. This first assumption represents the idea that an open system evolves, due to growing complexity, from order towards chaos. This assumption has its roots in chaos theory (Gleick, 1987; Prigogine and Stengers, 1984). As such, it represents a transition, seen also in planning, from orderly to highly complex conditions. An important aspect of this is therefore the idea that contemporary planning connects with this first assumption because it has evolved along the line of development from orderly (technical rational) to very complex (communicative rational).

The second assumption is that complex systems emerge 'at the edge of order and chaos' (Waldrop, 1992). This 'complexity thinking' supposes that, under such circumstances, these complex systems are visibly 'out of balance' and co-evolve (see Figure 2.4). The characteristics of a complex system are emergent and adaptive behaviour, and a large degree of self-organisation. Here, self-organisation means the spontaneous development of new structures as a result of feedback and feedforward mechanisms. This makes the complex system robust and flexible at the same time. The complex system does not just develop randomly but is path-dependent, i.e. development takes place under certain conditions that can be defined and that provide insight into the system and its development.

The third assumption is that new, orderly systems emerge from these systems at a higher level and that these will start to evolve – again, and in accordance with our first assumption – as complexity increases. Together, these three assumptions represent a non-linear, evolutionary process.

2.8 Complex systems and 'becoming'

Although the planner's world is still very much embedded in the first assumption, the second assumption builds upon it, since it focuses on the behaviour of complex systems, supposedly between the two extremes. According to complexity theory, in a complex environment, between order and chaos, there is an unstable world that is out of balance, but, nevertheless, there is a knowable reality. Research from various disciplines has revealed that complex systems tend to gravitate towards an area of complexity between order and chaos, never reaching the ultimate state of chaos, but evolving as 'coherent structures that propagated, grew, split apart, and recombined in a wonderfully complex way' (Waldrop, 1992, p. 226). To a greater or lesser extent, these complex systems are stable and predictable, and show behaviour that is to be expected under the conditions of our first assumption. However, there are also moments when complex systems are far from stable and they behave in a highly dynamic fashion.

Complex systems have the possibility and the flexibility to move between stable and unstable conditions, resulting in situations that allow the system to optimise 'the benefits of stability while retaining a capacity of change' (Phelan, 1995, p. 6). Systems in these circumstances must continuously co-evolve as they adjust to contextual influences and the adaptation of opposing systems. Phelan elaborates, 'A change in the environment may cause an "arms race" or evolutionary spurt until a local optimum is again at reach' (1995, p. 6). Byrne (1998, p. 14) suggests that this 'includes most of the social and natural aspects of the world, particularly interrelationships between the social and the natural'. In other words, an important part of our dynamic reality occurs 'on the edge of order and chaos', 'where the components of a system never quite lock into place, and yet never quite dissolve into turbulence either' (Waldrop, 1992, p. 12).

The second assumption with regard to complex systems affects planning because it points to those systems we can recognise in the physical environment that are both robust and flexible in the event of sudden contextual influences. Cities and infrastructure are examples of such systems. This understanding of complex systems is slowly affecting planning thought, as ideas based on mathematical propositions and modelling techniques are being used to address these 'complex systems'. This refers in particular to techniques such as autopoiesis (Luhmann, 1984; Kickert, 1993), cellular automata (Batty et al., 1997), non-linear dynamics and multiscalar modelling (Allen, 1997). These are not just newly developed out of chaos and complexity theories but also relate to game theory, systems theory, etc. These are considered to be strongly supported by complexity thinking, however. These techniques are becoming increasingly popular and are relevant to evaluation, simulation and scenario processes (Portugali, 1999), urban growth models (Allen, 1997) and GIS. They are methods that appreciate spatial systems as complex open systems, with adaptation, co-evolution and learning as important notions. In the words of Byrne (2003, p. 173), this is a rather essential ontological assertion to complexity theory.

Among the planners, the model builders are the frontrunners here (Allen, 1997; Batty and Longley, 1996; Batty, 2005). It is not particularly surprising that they are the first to be confronted with the newest developments in system, chaos and complexity theories. These developments demonstrate a strong interest in emergent, adaptive and self-organising systems behaviour. We can define these complex systems as systems class IV (capable of producing extended transients, Kauffman, 1991).

The way in which we view class IV systems differs fundamentally from the first three system classes mentioned above (see Section 2.2). In system class I, the system and its nodes and interactions are fixed. Although in system class II the nodes and interactions that represent the system are still fixed, the feedback causes the meaning of these to change. In system class III, the system again stays more or less unchanged, but the parts that make up the system – the nodes and interactions – do change. With all three system classes, the system itself unabatedly maintains its structure and function. With class IV systems this is no longer the case (see Figure 2.4).

These systems evolve, on the one hand, by transforming as an entity. But, on the other hand, the meaning that is conferred to the system also undergoes continuous change. We therefore do speak of co-evolution. A good example of such a complex system is a city (Batty, 2005). Cities develop as physical entities over time. They are very robust systems – even if a city burns down several times or has faced the consequences of an atomic bomb, it is very likely that the city will start again and apparently carry on developing further without too much difficulty. At the same time, cities are very flexible systems that continuously adapt to public needs and, where possible, create new needs, chances and opportunities. Cities were once citadels of safety, then market places, and were then transformed during the industrial revolution into important links in the production and consumption process. Today, a city is a place of creativity and knowledge, of communication and interaction, and of leisure and enjoyment.

It is characteristic of such complex systems that they are, on the one hand, robust and, on the other hand, flexible when it comes to internal and external influences. 'Class IV behaviour enables entities in the system to maximise the benefits of stability while retaining a capacity to change' (Phelan, 1999). These evolving forms of change – the becoming – we can call development and progress.

The third assumption tells us that a new order is likely to emerge from periods of change, chaos and transition when the system connects well with a stable

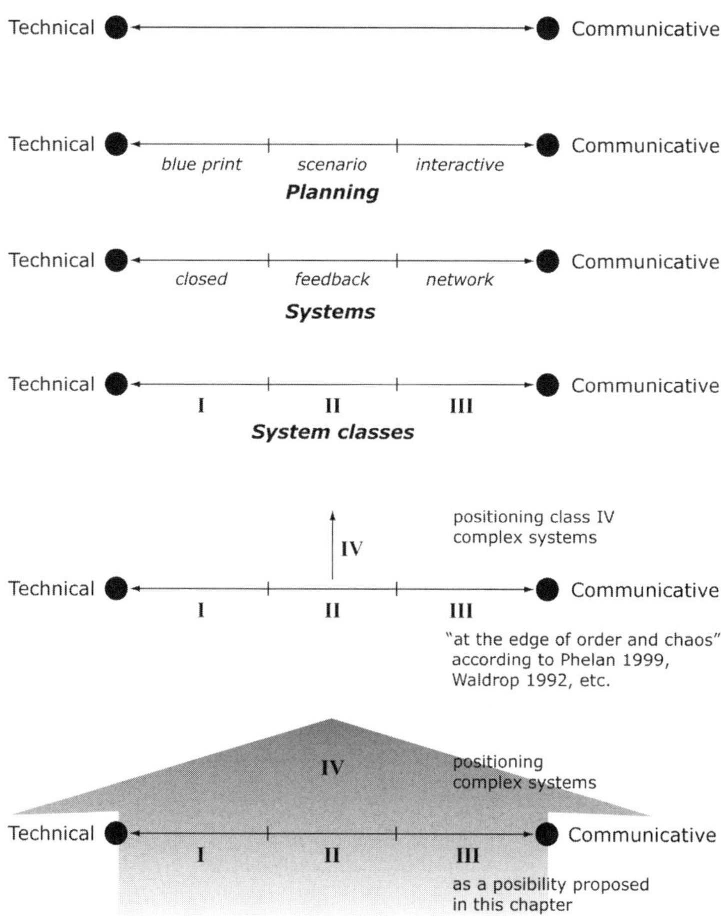

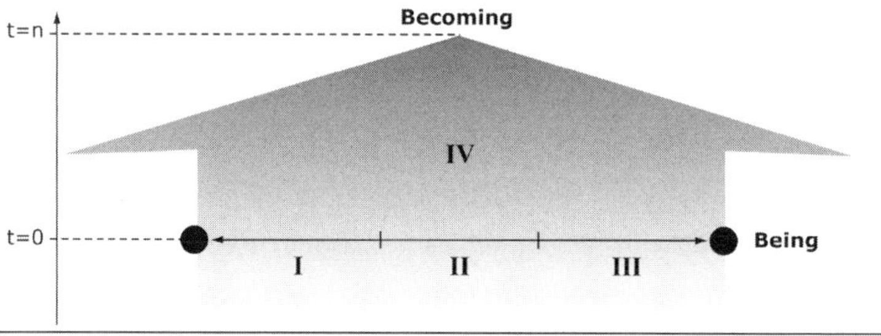

Figure 2.5 Possible relationships between class I, II, III and IV systems (for further explanation, see text)

contextual environment at a higher level, while adding new dimensions to this contextual environment. Paths developed into sand roads, which were suitable for horses to ride on. They were then transformed further first into brick and then tarmac roads, which were so welcome in the age of the car. These evolved further into district roads, roads connecting the city centre with its districts, ring roads and motorways connecting cities, countries and continents.

If we consider progress as a transition towards higher degrees of complexity, from which co-evolving and emergent systems arise, resulting in a new order at a higher level, this not only transcends but also connects the different academic disciplines, including planning, focusing as they do on the various aspects of the world around us.

2.9 Planning and complex systems behaviour

In the introduction (Section 2.1) we argued that complex systems fundamentally differ from the three systems that are recognised within planning (closed, feedback and network). A question remaining is about how these fundamentally different systems relate to each other. We believe that it makes no sense to see the complex systems as separate and with no connection whatsoever to the classic system descriptions.

By contrast, when looking at t=0 in complex systems we can imagine that, at that particular moment in time, three common systems exist in planning (Figure 2.5). If we look at the complex systems without including the time factor (becoming) we see in this 'fixed state' the traditional systems again (being), assuming that they are stable (in balance). In other words, as planners we have thus far looked at a frozen reality where the time factor has not played a serious part.

If we look at contemporary planning from this perspective, we are justified in concluding that the implicit assumption of planning activity is the 'fixed state' of structure and function, fact and value, and shape and meaning, within a planning situation. Evolving developments hardly play any part at all in the planning debate, planning activity and the way in which planning situations are viewed. In other words, time is not considered a significant factor in planning. With complex systems, this is precisely the crux of the matter: the changing processes of development and progress at different junctures. The question with which planning is confronted is therefore: is it a matter of being or becoming?

This is in no way a negative judgement. After all, we are not writing off traditional and contemporary planning when embracing complexity thinking. The opposite is true: we planners already have an extremely good command of part of complexity thinking. This refers to 'fixed state' at the t=0 moment, about which we already know plenty. At t=0 we have illustrated a world comprising various degrees of (atemporal) complexity. This conclusion also shows that the concept of complexity can very well be implemented within contemporary planning.

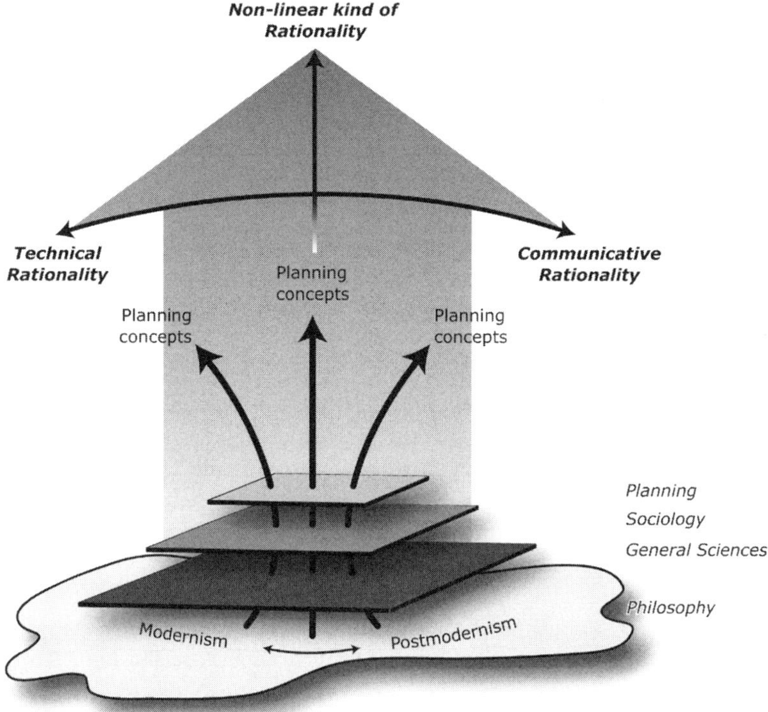

Figure 2.6 Beyond contemporary planning theory: The inclusion of non-linear development over time

It is inevitable that planning theory will develop further. Alongside the rationalities upon which it now focuses – technical and communicative rationality – the theoretical discussion will have to tackle a 'non-linear' or 'evolutionary' kind of rationality (Figure 2.6), in which time, development and progress play a role. This rationality will also have to serve as a guide for planner's activities. This discussion will influence the planning practice, the instruments of planning and the role of the planner. Once, the planner's role was limited to that of technician, later evolving into the role of mediator in planning conflicts. Now, the planner is also entering the picture as a trend watcher and transition manager.

2.10 Reflection

Theories of complexity and chaos represent discussions that cut through academic disciplines, bringing people together from various backgrounds such as economics, philosophy, physics and sociology. These are crosscutting discussions that bridge the various disciplines, as systems theory has done in the past. Although there are contributions from various disciplines, planners have rarely participated in the debate. If, however, planning as a discipline is to be considered a discussion in progress, which aims to grasp human interaction with and intervention in the physical environment, we believe this major and crosscutting academic debate on complexity and chaos cannot be ignored.

While the debate in contemporary planning seems to focus on a dichotomy between technical rationality and communicative rationality, we have introduced the argument that chaos, complexity, complexity thinking and complex systems are elements of discussions that might provide answers that it is worthwhile for planners to pursue. Additionally, chaos and complexity theories could shed an alternative light on the 'muddled' issues with which planners are so often confronted.

In their quest for certainty planners have stumbled upon rather persistent limitations, inevitably leading to an acceptance of uncertainty as a reality. This acceptance brought us the communicative rationale, which proved to be a major step forward in planning theory and practice. In addition, we have put forth three assumptions, the first of which represents a transition from order to chaos. This appears to be a mechanism in reality that explains – at least in part – progress and development. In this contribution we wish to emphasise the argument that, by considering this reality in terms of 'degrees of complexity', we are just one step away from considerations that are proposed by evolution-oriented understandings of reality, by complexity theory and by class IV systems – the 'complex systems'. These systems bring us, *inter alia*, non-linearity, emergence, adaptation, self-organisation and the inclusion of time.

References

Allen, P.M. (1997) *Cities and Regions as Self-Organizing Systems: Models of Complexity*, Gordon and Breach Science Publishers, Amsterdam.

Allmendinger, P. (2002) *Planning Theory*, Palgrave, Basingstoke.

Allmendinger, P. and Tewdwr-Jones, M. (eds.) (2002) *Planning Futures: New Directions for Planning Theory*, Routledge, London.

Batty, M. and Longley, P. (1996) *Fractal Cities: A Geometry of Form and Function*, Academic Press, London.

Batty, M. (2005) *Cities and Complexity: Understanding Cities with Cellular Automata, Agent-Based Models, and Fractals*, The MIT Press, Cambridge.

Beauregard, R.A. (1989) 'Between modernity and postmodernity: The ambiguous position of us planning', *Environment and Planning D: Society and Space*, vol. 7, pp. 381-395.

Berry, D.E. (1974) 'The transfer of planning theories to health planning practice', *Policy Sciences*, vol. 5, pp. 343-361.

Berting, J. (1996) 'Over rationaliteit en complexiteit' ['About rationality and complexity'], in P. Nijkamp, W. Begeer and J. Berting (eds.), *Denken over complexe besluitvorming: een panorama* [*Thoughts about complex decision making: an overview*], SDU Uitgevers, The Hague, pp. 17-29.

Bohman, J. (1991) *New Philosophy of Social Science: Problems of Indeterminacy*, Polity Press, Cambridge.

Byrne, D. (1998) *Complexity Theory and the Social Sciences: An Introduction*, Routledge, London.

Byrne, D. (2003) 'Complexity theory and planning theory: A necessary encounter', *Planning Theory*, vol. 2(3), pp. 171-178.

Chalmers, A. (1976) *What is This Thing Called Science?*, University of Queensland Press, St. Lucia.

Christensen, K.S. (1985) 'Coping with uncertainty in planning', *Journal of the American Planning Association*, vol. 51(1), pp. 63-73.

Crook, S. (1991) *Modernist Radicalism and its Aftermath: Foundationalism and Anti-foundationalism in Radical Social Theory*, Routledge, London.

Dean, A. (2000) *Complex Life: Nonmodernity and the Emergence of Cognition and Culture*, Ashgate Publishing, Aldershot.

De Roo, G. (2000) 'Environmental conflicts in compact cities: complexity, decision making, and policy approaches', *Environment and Planning B: Planning and Design*, vol. 27, pp. 229-241.

De Roo, G. (2001) 'Complexity as a criterion for decision making; a theoretical perspective for complex (urban) conflicts', paper presented at the 1st World Planning School Congress at the College of Architecture and Urban Planning, Tongji University, July 2001, Shanghai.

De Roo, G. (2002) 'In weelde gevangen: van ruimtelijk paradijs naar een leefomgeving in voortdurende staat van verandering…' ['Caught in heaven: from a spatial paradise towards a state of continuous change'], inaugural lecture, Faculty of Spatial Sciences, University of Groningen, Groningen.

De Roo, G. (2003) *Environmental Planning in The Netherlands: Too Good to be True: From Command-and-Control Planning to Shared Governance*, Ashgate Publishing, Aldershot.

De Roo, G. and Porter, G. (2007) *Fuzzy Planning: The Role of Actors in a Fuzzy Governance Environment*, Ashgate Publishing, Aldershot.

Elster, J. (1983) *Sour Grapes: Studies in the Subversion of Rationality*, Cambridge University Press, Cambridge.

Emery, F.E. and Trist, E.L. (1965) 'The causal texture of organizational environments', in F.E. Emery (ed.), *Systems Thinking*, Penguin Books, Harmondsworth, pp. 241-257.

Faludi, A. (1973) *Planning Theory*, Pergamon Press, Oxford.

Faludi, A. (1987) *A Decision-Centered View of Environmental Planning*, Pergamon Press, Oxford.

Friedmann, J. (1987) *Planning in the Public Domain: From Knowledge to Action*, Princeton University Press, Princeton.

Friend, J.K. and Jessop, N. (1969) *Local Government and Strategic Choice*, Pergamon, Oxford.

Fuenmayor, R. (1991) 'Between systems thinking and systems practice', in R.L. Flood and M.C. Jackson (eds.), *Critical Systems Thinking*, John Wiley & Sons, Chichester, pp. 227-244.

Geurtsen, A. (1996) 'Situatie-afhankelijke informatievoorziening, een onderzoek naar het verduidelijken van de realtie tussen situatie en informatievoorziening' ['Situation dependent assessability of information, a research to clarify the relation between situation and assessability of information'], Drukkerij Elinkwijk, Utrecht.

Gleick, J. (1987) *Chaos, Making a New Science*, Viking, New York.

Hacking, I. (1999) *The Social Construction of What?* Harvard University Press, Cambridge.

Hajer, M.A. (1995) *The Politics of Environmental Discourse: Ecological Modernization and the Policy Process*, Oxford University Press, Oxford.

Harper, Th.L. and Stein, S.M. (1995) 'Out of the postmodern abyss: Preserving the rationale for liberal planning', *Journal of Planning Education and Research*, vol. 14, pp. 233-244.

Healey, P. (1983) '"Rational method" as a mode of policy information and implementation in land-use policy', *Environment and Planning B: Planning and Design*, vol. 10, pp. 19-39.

Healey, P. (1992) 'Planning through debate: The communicative turn in planning theory', *Town Planning Review*, vol. 63(2), pp. 143-162.

Healey, P. (1997) *Collaborative Planning: Shaping Places in Fragmented Societies*, Macmillan, Basingstoke.

Holland, J. (1998) *Emergence: From Chaos to Order*, Addison-Wesley, New York.

Innes, J.E. (1995) 'Planning theory's emerging paradigm: communicative action and interactive practice', *Journal of Planning Education and Research*, vol. 14(3), pp. 183-189.

Innes, J.E. (1996) 'Planning through consensus building: A new view of the comprehensive planning ideal', *Journal of the American Planning Association*, vol. 62(4), pp. 460-472.

Kauffman, S. (1995) *At Home in the Universe*, Oxford University Press, New York.

Kickert, W.J.M. (1993) 'Autopoiesis and the science of (public) administration: Essence, sense and nonsense', *Organization Studies*, vol. 14(2), pp. 261-278.

Klee, R. (ed.) (1999) *Scientific Inquiry: Readings in the Philosophy of Science*, Oxford University Press, New York.

Kosko, B. (2004) *Fuzzy Thinking: The New Science of Fuzzy Logic*, Flamingo, London.

Latour, B. (1993) *We Have Never Been Modern*, Harvester Wheatsheaf, Hemel Hempstead.

Lim, G.C. (1986) 'Toward a synthesis of contemporary planning theory', *Journal of Planning Education and Research*, vol. 5(2), pp. 75-85.

Lorentz, E.N. (1963) 'Deterministic nonperiodic flow', *Journal of Atmospheric Sciences*, vol. 20, pp. 130-141.

Luhmann, N. (1995) *Social Systems*, Stanford University Press, San Francisco.

Meyerson, M. and Banfield, E. (1955) *Politics, Planning and the Public Interest: The Case of Public housing in Chicago*, Free Press, New York.

Minzberg, H. (1983) *Structure in Fives: Designing Effective Organisations*, Prentice Hall, New Jersey.

Moore Milroy, B. (1991) 'Into postmodern weightlessness', *Journal of Planning Education and Research*, vol. 10(3), pp. 181-187.

Paris, C. (ed.) (1982) *Critical Readings in Planning Theory*, Pergamon Press, London.

Phelan, S.E. (1995) 'From chaos to complexity in strategic planning', paper presented at the 55th Annual Meeting of the Academy of Management, August 6-9, Vancouver.

Phelan, S.E. (1999) 'A note on the correspondence between complexity and systems theory', *Systemic Practice and Action Research*, vol. 12(3), June 1999, pp. 237-246.

Portugali, J. (1999) *Self-organization and the City*, Springer-Verlag, Berlin.

Prigogine, I. and Stengers, I. (1984) *Order Out of Chaos*, New Science Press, Boulder.

Sagoff, M. (1988) *The Economy of the Earth: Philosophy, Law and the Environment*, Cambridge University Press, Cambridge.

Scheff, T.J. (1967) 'Towards a sociological model of consensus', *American Sociological Review*, vol. 32, pp. 32-46.

Schönwandt, W.L. (2002) *Planung in der Krise? Theoretische Orientieringen für Architektur, Stadt- und Raumplanung* [*Planning in Crisis? Theoretical Orientations for Architecture and Planning*], Kohlhammer Verlag, Stuttgart.

Schönwandt, W.L. (2007) *Planning in Crisis? Theoretical Orientations for Architecture and Planning*, Ashgate, Aldershot.

Scott, J. (1995) *Sociological Theory; Contemporary Debates*, Edward Elgar Publishing Limited, Cheltenham/Lyme.

Stacey, R.D. (2001) *Complexity and Creativity in Organizations*, Berrett-Koehler Publishers, San Francisco.

Urry, J. (2003) *Global Complexity*, Polity Press, Cambridge.

Van de Graaf, H. and Hoppe, R. (1996) *Beleid en politiek; Een inleiding tot de beleids- wetenschap en de beleidskunde* [*Policy and politics: An introduction in the arts and science of policy*], Dick Coutinho, Bussum.

Van der Cammen, H. (1979) *De binnenkant van de planologie* [*The inside of spatial planning*], Dick Coutinho, Bussum.

Van der Valk, A.J.J. (1999) 'Willens en wetens: Planning en wetenschap tussen wens en werkelijkheid' ['Deliberately and knowingly: Planners and science between desire and reality'], inaugural lecture, Wageningen University, Wageningen.

Von Bertalanffy, L. (1968) *General Systems Theory: Foundations, Development and Applications*, Braziller, New York.

Waldrop, M.M. (1992) *Complexity: The Emerging Science at the Edge of Order and Chaos*, Penguin Books, London.

Weaver, C., Jessop, J. and Das, V. (1985) 'Rationality in the public interest: Notes towards a new synthesis', in M. Breheny and A. Hooper (eds.), *Rationality in Planning: Critical Essays on the Role of Rationality in Urban and Regional Planning*, Pion, London, pp. 145-165.

Chapter 3
Dealing with Society's 'Big Messes'

Jens-Peter Grunau and Walter L. Schönwandt[1]

It is often said that we live in an increasingly complex world with increasingly complex problems. Among other things, it is the job of fundamental research to uncover the nature and implications of this complexity as it pertains to planning. This is also relevant because many people – this is especially true of politicians as well as individuals who are affected by planning – often complain that plans and concepts do not function properly. These people complain that at times our plans fail to achieve their goals. That they sometimes fail to meet the needs of those who are affected by plans. That planning often fails to meet the complexity of a planning problem head on. Or, in the context of higher education, that our schools fail to provide an adequate education to future generations of planners. It is therefore essential that we do not limit our thinking to actual, complex problems in planning and stop there. Rather, we must also think carefully about the process of planning itself. With this in mind, we have created a 'guide' for dealing with complex problems. Our guide is composed of a number of explicit steps and it is based on a theoretical planning model. It is useful both in practice and for pedagogical purposes. As such, it aims to put theory into practice.

3.1 Introduction: Different models for planning

The history of planning theory is full of different models for planning. Some of them have changed and developed over time. Some have become fashionable and then vanished again. Others have had more staying power.

We are all familiar with some of these various models and so-called 'turns'. They include everything from formal systems to simplistic slogans and self-styled Kuhnian paradigms: rational choice theory, 'planning is communication', 'planning is power', telling stories, 'muddling through', the garbage can model, post rational models, the argumentative turn, behavioural turn, cultural turn, design oriented turn, institutional turn, political turn, scientific turn, sociological turn, etc. (see also Lindblom, 1959; March and Olsen, 1986; Schönwandt, 2002).

---

1 Dr Jens-Peter Grunau, is General Secretary of the European Network of Construction Companies for Research and Development (ENCORD). Prof. Dr Walter Schönwandt is from the Institute for the Foundations of Planning, Faculty for Architecture and Urban Planning, University Stuttgart, Germany.

For those who are not familiar with the details of the discussions in planning theory, we will elaborate a bit on the history. The discussion can be summarised in three consecutive generations of planning models. The first generation of planning theory was embedded in an instrumental or technical rationality point of view. The second generation focused on a communicative and participative understanding of planning. The third generation can be summarised under the term of 'turn to content'.

The criticism of the first generation is widely known and published in works by Lindblom, Rittel, Forester, Healy, Innes, and so on. In contrast to the rational planning theories of the first generation, the second generation states that every planning description includes aspects of the cognitive world of the describer, that every description of facts is theory-driven and that all planning knowledge is socially constructed.

In principle it is not possible for humans to understand, describe, or act on anything without doing so on the basis of some cognitive process and from some cognitive viewpoint: there is no vision from nowhere. Everything that we see, think, plan, say, and do is influenced by our perceptions and experiences. We see the world as if through a pattern or mould of our own making into which we then try to fit our experiences of that world. Since there are always a great many people involved in planning, it follows that there will always be manifold viewpoints and stances on issues rather than a single, 'true' matter of fact. And in the planning process, one has to work with and talk about these different viewpoint – thus making the essential role of communication obvious.

In planning theory, the realisation that knowledge is subjective has resulted in a critique and almost abandonment of the 'rational' planning model. This is in part because – at least implicitly – the 'rational' model assumed that a planning situation can be described in terms that are purely 'objective' and do not take into account the experiences of individual subjects.

The third generation incorporates this perception while eliminating some weak points of the second generation. These deficits e.g. include, that it is not *explicitly* stated which aspects, topics or methods are needed in successful planning and how these *explicitly* relate to each other, what interdependencies exist between them.

The second generation also ignores a key difference between the conceptual content of planning and topics like participation and communication: 'communication' is important, but no more important than the question of what a given act of communication is *about*. It is true that some advocates of the turn to communication – Habermas is a prominent example – understood that the content of communication, which is to say knowledge, must form an important part of any discussion about communication. However, the mainstream of the contemporary discussion on communication in planning theory often ignores this aspect.

The shortcomings of a collaborative/communicative approach to planning with which we are concerned can be described as follows: there is a difference between the conceptual contents of a planning task on the one hand and, on the other hand, issues such as 'communication' and 'discourse', meaning, the historical, social,

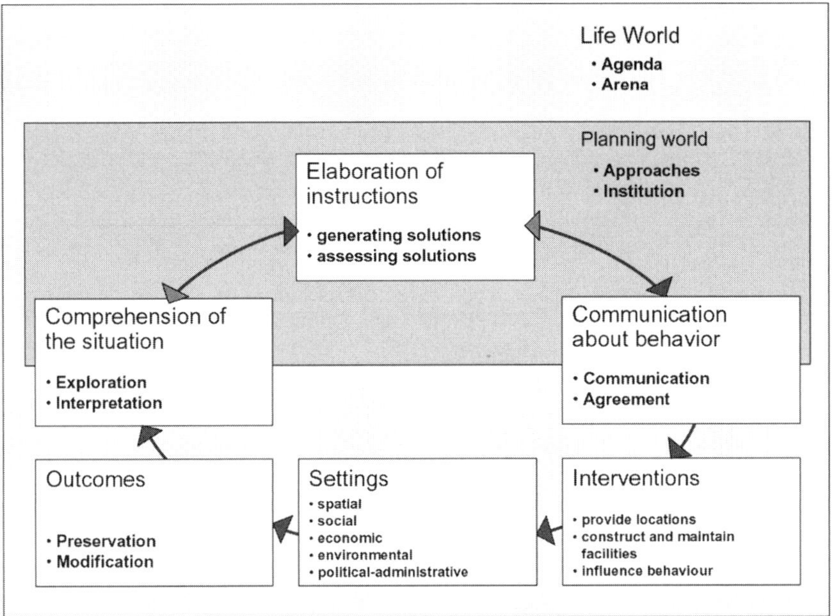

Figure 3.1 Definition of a problem

psychological, etc. conditions that make it possible to process and convey this content in the first place. These two issues – 'content' and 'communication' – are often at least implicitly and incorrectly assumed to be identical. Above all else, the word communication here refers to the aforementioned conditions that make it possible to create and process the content, rather than the content itself. In this context, 'communication' is similar to 'transport'. That is because the word 'transport' similarly leaves unanswered the question of what it is that is being transported. 'Communication' and 'discourse' *influence* the processing of conceptual contents, yet they are *not* to be *equated* with the contents themselves.

That is why the third generation of planning models – on which this chapter is based – also advocates a 'turn to content' as logical enhancements of the first and second generation of planning models (for more details see Schönwandt, 2002).

3.2 Our framework

There is no way to avoid using some model or framework when planning and solving complex problems. Everybody uses some kind of a model, some way of organising what we see and what should be done. Some do it consciously, others unknowingly. Hence, the choice is not one between using and not using a model, but rather which model to use and how to use it.

We adapted a systems theory model for our purposes that is in part based on the work of Claus Heidemann (1992) from Germany and Mario Bunge (1983, 1996) from Canada. This model enables us to work on diverse problems ranging from 'classic' problems in urban and spatial planning and architecture to political and economic problems.

Our framework enumerates and details the steps of planning, places them in methodical relation to one another, and integrates some of their many aspects. It helps us to handle complex problems and facilitates the search for many and various kinds of solutions. In short, it makes the complexity of planning tasks more transparent and manageable.[2]

At this point, it should probably be clear to most readers that we see planning as a task that involves solving complex problems rather than a simple application of pre-established and routine solutions. In our approach, planning situations always pose some kind of a problem, and these problems are always more or less complex. The following paragraph provides a brief indication of how we define problems (see Figure 3.1), as well as how we define complexity in respect of complex problems.

We are presented with a situation that is in some respects deficient, that falls short of what is wanted in some way. A faulty situation – such as, for example, a street – is prone to traffic jams, a neighbourhood has too few grocery stores, life in a city is too expensive, etc. In the very abstract and reduced definition of a problem we labelled this 'big mess a(-)'. We want to rectify this situation, want to change the 'big mess' into something different, something better, something desired: a 'goal b(+)'. And of course the 'big messes' and the desired goal are subjective and thus socially constructed.

The problem lies in the fact that we do not always know what the appropriate measures to take are. We do not immediately know how to ameliorate the situation at hand. The 'measures' are unknown.

3.3 Complexity

The nature of complexity seems to be hard to capture distinctly. McGlade and Garnsey (2006) state, 'However, despite its fashionable status and evident popularity, there is little consensus on just what is meant by the term. In fact, complexity has the unenviable distinction of meaning "all things to all people" and is characterised by imprecise and general ambiguous usage'.

2 A more detailed description of our framework can be found in the book *Planung in der Krise* [*Planning in a Crisis? Theoretical Orientation for Architecture, City and Spatial Planning*] (Schönwandt, 2002).

In the psychological literature which we refer to, complexity in the context of problems has been examined and described extensively by various authors (Dörner, 1989; Von der Weth, 2001). In his book *Die Logik des Misslingens* [*The Logic of Failure*], Dörner postulates the following as main features of complexity: number of variables, interdependence, change and opacity (Dörner, 1989). Von der Werth extended this list to include time pressure, a plurality of goals (i.e. resulting in potential various alternative actions) and novelty (Von der Weth, 2001). Pavard and Dugdale (2000) outline non-determinism and non-tractability, limited functional decomposability, the distributed nature of information and representation and emergence and self-organisation as characteristics of complexity. These notions can be integrated in the above mentioned points of Dörner and described as follows:

i. *Variables* A large number of variables are present, all of which are important and deserve close scrutiny. The more variables are present, the higher the degree of complexity will be. For example, in spatial planning this implies the following: The interests of all those involved must be taken into account and innumerable components such as, e.g., laws must be considered. In the construction of a new street, city planners must consider all sorts of variables, including: the use of space, the encroachment on living space, construction and maintenance costs, number of trucks per day, noise pollution and so forth. Whereas the mere existence of a large number of variables does not in itself define complexity, it clearly becomes relevant if the large numbers are combined with the aspects mentioned below.
ii. *Interdependence* The complexity of a situation increases if the variables are dependent on or linked to one another and are in addition connected by interwoven feedback effects. According to Dörner, it is this interdependence of different variables that 'force us to take a good many features [of a problem] into account simultaneously and has the consequence that we [...] can hardly ever do only one thing at a time' (Dörner, 1989). Every planning process, especially in spatial planning, is embedded in a larger social, ecological, economic, political, and administrative setting. And this larger setting must be taken into consideration. For example, the construction of a new bridge in Dresden, the so-called 'Waldschlösschen' Bridge, is supposed to help prevent traffic jams (Boltz, 2005). However, it also has more or less far-reaching side effects, contextual interferences, that must be taken into consideration. The route over this bridge decreases the distance between two highways considerably: taking the bridge can shorten some drivers' commute by 11 kilometres. However, this could also lead to an increase in traffic, which might result in traffic jams on narrow access ramps and an increase in noise pollution. Hence, the construction of this bridge has the potential to reduce the quality of living space.
iii. *Change* When a system has components and demands that change with the process of planning, we consider the system to be dynamic. Some systems

also have an internal dynamic, implying, they change even without the planner interfering. The reason for this is usually the interdependence of different variables, such as when the system consists of positive and negative feedback loops. This can put pressure on planners to predict future developments quickly. Spatial planning itself is a long-term process and its effects often cannot be felt until far into the future. So, for example, the situation changed in the course of the debate over the Waldschlösschen Bridge: Dresden was designated a UNESCO World Heritage Site, which then had negative consequences for the construction efforts, to the effect that that status would be lost if the bridge were to be built. The dynamics in the system also results in the challenge that it seems hard to deal with the situation by decomposing the problem into functionally stable parts that stand alone. Even decomposed parts still need to be seen within an interwoven system.

iv. *Opacity* A planning process is said to be opaque when some of its aspects are hidden from view, inaccessible, or simply unknown. Even in cases where the variables generally are known, there is still a question about which features are really at hand. Hence, we distinguish between opacity of circumstances (where actual conditions are unclear), opacity of variables (where the number and configuration of variables is unclear), as well as opacity of rules (where it is unclear what rules apply to a given situation) (Strohschneider and Von der Weth, 2002). Opacity is often also an attribute of spatial planning. For example, the planners responsible for the Waldschlösschen Bridge could not have known exactly how those who opposed building this bridge would behave. Nor could they have known exactly what budgetary changes would be implemented.

v. *Multi-sided* In planning, a wide range of possible goals and solutions may contradict one another. Plans tend to have more than one goal. For example, spatial planning often tries to achieve economic, ecological, and aesthetic goals at one and the same time. It often happens that many of these diverse goals do not agree with one another, that they contradict each other. In the case of the Waldschlösschen Bridge, UNESCO had goals that ran orthogonal to those of traffic planners, and this caused the project to come to a standstill.

vi. *Novelty* Complex situations are made up of many aspects that are at least in some respects novel and are therefore difficult to handle using routine measures. The problem is not just to build a bridge; rather, it is to come to terms with a new and complex constellation of circumstances.

We propose a framework to deal with complex problems that is based on some key assumptions. For example, we assume it is possible to design a general model for planning that represents the process of solving complex problems in broad strokes. This requires that there be certain recurring structures that obtain in many different complex problems. It also requires that these structures are not unique and specific

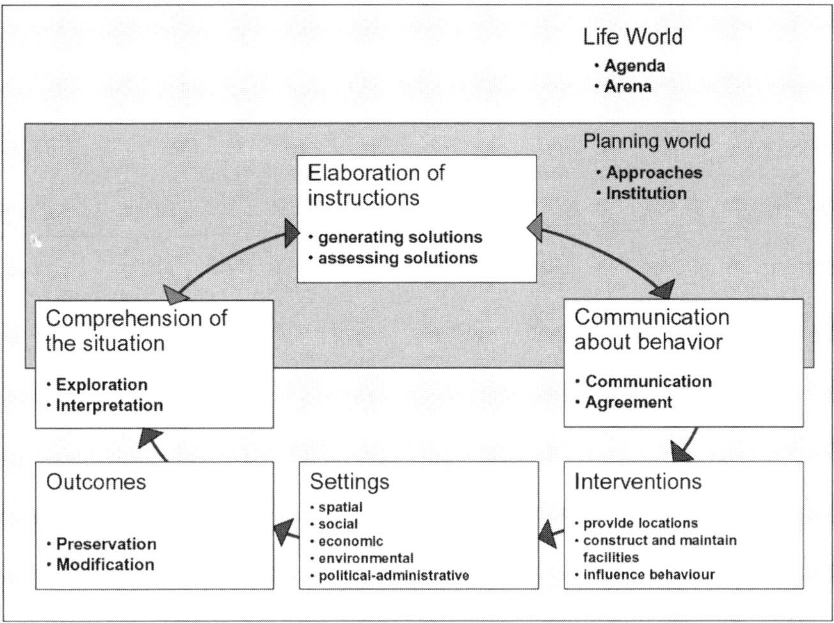

Figure 3.2 A model for planning

to the problem – at hand – that they can be transferred from one complex problem to another. At the same time, we must be able to explicitly describe this model to students and other planners. If we are going to use this model as a way to teach the 'art' of solving complex problems, it must be possible to understand the model on a level that goes beyond mere intuition and tacit knowledge.

3.4 '5-28-52-x' model

Our model is composed of several levels. The first of these levels is made up of around 28 components, including: defining the problem, finding solutions, deliberating on positive and negative effects of alternatives, describing those who are involved and what their interests are, planning for the implementation of solutions, etc. Figure 3.2 gives a brief overview of the model at the level of 28 components (for more details see Heidemann, 1992).

The second level is made up of well over 52 components. Beyond that, there lie even more components and aspects, including a large variety of individual methods such as communication, participation, creativity methods, project management, etc. All of these make up components of a larger problem-solving cycle that ranges from the definition of a problem to finding solutions to implementing these solutions to evaluating the solutions and their implementation. Various paradigmatic approaches to problem solving as well as the 'professional community' of problem solvers forms the backbone of this cycle. Finally, this cycle in its entirety, with all of its various components, is embedded in a larger environment complete with all its social, ecological, economic, political, and administrative aspects – emphasising the socially constructed aspect of problem solving once again.

The sketch above is intended to give only a rather general sense of some of the many relevant aspects that are involved in all planning and problem solving. Despite the large number and diversity of components and aspects that obtain in the planning process, experience shows that a handful of broad themes can serve as the foundation of most planning processes. As in many other areas, the 20/80 rule also seems to apply here: a few themes influence the largest part of the planning process. These themes are the 'big messes', 'concepts', 'causes', 'measures' and 'approaches', and we have named them the 'key five'. They set the scope and our view of the problem at hand, the methods we use to solve the problem, as well as the solution(s) we end up implementing. Hence, the power to define these 'key five' tends to confer the power to define and determine the outcome of a planning process.

As a consequence of what has been said so far, in our work we begin by focusing on these 'key five'. In the pages that follow, we provide a brief overview of these five themes, focusing most of our attention on the 'big messes' and describing 'causes' and 'measures' as one area in an effort to keep this chapter short. At the same time, we will also introduce and outline some alternative approaches to planning and then identify what we believe their shortcomings and disadvantages are. We end with a brief description of how we have adapted our model to make it more useful in a pedagogical context. We will also report on our preliminary experience when putting this model to use in a classroom setting.

3.5 'Big messes'

Clearly, it is difficult if not impossible to solve a problem that we do not understand. Hence, one of the first and most important steps among the 'key five' is to understand the problem. This will then help us to find solutions. We begin to understand a problem by defining the 'big messes' – situations that are deemed wanting or deficient in some way, situations that have the potential to cause suffering or harm and that ought therefore to be altered.

'Messes first'

If we look at what these big messes actually consist of, we often find they are amazingly trivial and easy to solve. However, if we look at how many planners actually go about solving problems we see that many of them do not start by looking at the 'big messes'. Interviews with practitioners have revealed that as many as 80 per cent do not start the process of finding solutions by first looking for the underlying 'big messes'.

The inclination to forgo first taking a close look at the 'big messes' is not surprising. As practising planners, we are sometimes inclined to look for immediate or prompt solutions to problems. This is in part because we believe that doing so is above all else what others expect from us: we are expected to find solutions that can be implemented quickly and easily. Or it is expected that planners take on the role of being mediators of communicative and participative processes – also taking the focus away from working on the content to sometimes merely moderating the process of communication. Such a mindset also fits particularly well with the tenor of our times, in which so much is oriented towards quick, short-term successes. Hence, we tend not to be accustomed to a precise, detailed, and time as well as energy-consuming investigation of some situation, some 'big mess'. Moreover, traditional pedagogical techniques and working methods (such as we find at our institutions of higher learning) train us to think that the most important aspect of planning is the presentation of attainable goals as well as quick, neat solutions.

But is it really possible to find a solution without first understanding the problem or making others aware about how to consider their 'common' problem without acknowledging the problematic state of affairs head-on? If the state of affairs in need of improvement – the 'big mess', as we have termed it – is not clear and well-understood, then planning is in danger of descending into mere actionism, of doing things simply for the sake of doing them. In these cases, the risks are serious and manifold:

i. ineffective measures may be proposed that do not actually solve the problem;
ii. valuable resources such as time and money may be wasted;
iii. or, a plan might result in a situation that differs from the problem but does not really represent an improvement over the past.

These points should suffice to convince readers that planners are well advised to begin the planning process by first defining the state of affairs in need of improvement – the 'big mess'. Readers will permit us to further illustrate the importance of focusing on the 'big messes' at the beginning of a planning process with the following example:

Imagine you are asked to solve the problem of traffic density in London. What are the big messes? Are the roads too narrow, or the cars too numerous? Might the problem lie in the fact that too many people work in London, or does London attract too many tourists? Are the cars just too big, or is driving perhaps too cheap relative other modes of transportation?

The relevance of also knowing the 'big messes' seems clear because solving a problem that remains poorly understood requires pure luck rather than careful planning. In most cases, a problem that is not well understood will persist despite the best efforts of planners. Hence, knowing the 'big messes' helps us reduce mindless and useless actions that needlessly consume resources without actually solving the problem at hand.

Even once the 'big messes' are defined, different people might nevertheless perceive the negative situation in different ways. Some might actually see advantages in the big mess. It follows that the 'problem' situation is always socially constructed rather than objective. Thus, it is neither right nor wrong but 'valued' negative of positive. The definition of big messes therefore brings with it a great deal of power and control. Whoever decides how a big mess is defined also directs and constrains the future direction of problem solving. That is because the definition of problems – which happens right at the beginning of a planning process – immediately suggests some possible avenues to a solution while simultaneously eliminating many others.

We proceed from the assumption that effective planning requires knowledge of the negative situation in need of improvement. It follows that the solution of complex planning problems consists in a meaningful sense of the precise understanding and identification of a negative situation. However, our research has shown that, in actual practice, planning often proceeds differently: the stage of working out a sufficiently precise definition and identification of a negative situation is often omitted.

Here is a sketch of four common procedures we find are commonly used in practice:

i. preconceived solutions that may have been successfully applied to some problems in the past are applied to the new problem at hand, regardless of whether the new problem resembles the old one or not;
ii. well-known methods are used to solve a problem, regardless of whether they fit the actual problem at hand or not;
iii. goals are defined right from the start, regardless of whether these goals really have anything to do with the 'big messes' or not, and;
iv. theories, such as the 'Central Place Theory' are applied, regardless of their applicability to the particular problem at hand.

Procedure: Proposing solutions directly

Often, measures or solutions are directly and immediately proposed. Such a measure might include the construction of a park or some other place in a neighbourhood that is intended to improve communication among neighbours and encourage them to identify with their surroundings. In carrying out this measure, alternative or supporting measures, such as encouraging a formal process for neighbours to help one another with their everyday problems, courses at schools to help students better integrate into society at large, etc., are often overlooked.

Or, to take another example, in Stuttgart a bridge was built over a multi-lane downtown highway. However, it was never explained exactly which negative situations this bridge was supposed to ameliorate. Clearly there is the desire to traverse from one side of the street to the other. But what exactly is the negative situation? Are we trying to make the museum district more accessible to pedestrians from the downtown area? Are we trying to counteract the tendency of a federal highway to break the city up into autonomous pieces? The questions are endless. So now there is a bridge which may indeed be very well designed, but whether its functionality in exactly this place and according to this design makes much sense remains to be seen.

Or, to take a third example, in 2006 the following various planning tasks of regional importance were proposed to the Rhine/Main region around Frankfurt:

i. it was proposed to create, run, and maintain facilities for sport, leisure, and relaxation as well as cultural facilities of super-regional importance;
ii. it was proposed to create organisations that would induce a 'collective and cooperative effort' to plan and manage regional traffic, as well as market standards for and the promotion of economic development.

But it had never been stated what negative situations these measures are supposed to ameliorate. As such, it is not clear that the proposed solution – the creation of an organisation, for example – will even help to improve the negative situation in question. On the contrary, it may even be possible that the newly created organisations will only compete for resources with existing organisations that are already in part responsible for dealing with these and similar problems, which, in turn, could lead to the creation of new and as of yet unforeseen negative circumstances.

Procedure: Methods

The planning process always involves – either implicitly or explicitly – adopting some method or another. So, for example, in spatial planning the planning process often begins with the application of some 'conventional' method for gathering data about, for example, the population, economy (e.g. unemployment), traffic (e.g. commuters), infrastructure, etc. Doing so can seriously restrict how we approach the problem at hand. That's because we now artificially limit ourselves to working on those aspects of a problem that can be 'read' off of the data we previously decided to gather. Hence, it is not only the content of the available data that determines the spectrum of what can be 'read' from the data. The manner in which we choose to process data in the context of a planning question also determines what information can then be extracted from the data and what information is irrevocably lost. For example, the level at which we decide to aggregate a given data set often determines how much and what kind of information is lost in this context. In practice, this often means that if we combine two separate data sets into a single, aggregate data set, we lose much of the detailed information contained in each one of the two separate data sets. The methodological rule that results from this is well known: it is easy to combine separate data sets but it is often impossible to disaggregate, or separate them again without incurring a substantial risk of failure.

A simple example will suffice to make the point more concrete: it is not possible to calculate, e.g., the price of diesel fuel from information about the average price of all the different kinds of fuels that are available in Germany's gas stations. This is true even though we had to know the price of diesel fuel when calculating this average in the first place.

The literature on spatial planning is replete with suggestions on which conventional kinds of data to gather at the beginning of a planning task. It should therefore be clear that, even when simply gathering data, we are not working absent a method. Methods are and will continue to be the main tools in our conceptual toolbox. But each and every method has a more or less circumscribed domain of application and is not well suited for every situation and task. To put it in somewhat more provocative terms: we cannot do without methods, even though every method leads us down a path that results in a restricted worldview.

Procedure: Striving only for goals

It is not uncommon for planners to proceed simply by specifying what goals they wish to achieve, without giving a thought to what negative situations all of this is supposed to ameliorate. There is no question that we cannot make progress and reach a destination without subjective, socially constructed goals in mind. But without defining the negative situation that is to be overcome, our search for a solution will resemble a blind and meandering journey through conceptual nebulae.

If we focus exclusively on goals in our planning and tacitly assume that doing so can spare us the trouble of having to define the negative situation that is to be overcome, it will be difficult at best to find a conclusive solution. If we proceed exclusively by defining our goals, then it may happen – under extraordinarily good circumstances – that eventually we do indeed achieve our goals. However, the still undefined problems may remain and continue to exert a negative effect on the situation well into the future.

A 'city of short distances' could for instance be considered as such a goal. If we operate exclusively with this goal in mind – that is, without first ascertaining if this goal is an appropriate solution for the implicitly assumed problem – then our planning measures will often be ineffective. Other, typical goals that are formulated without taking a problem or negative situation into account include:

i. 'preserving the traditional industries of a region';
ii. 'safeguarding local amenities';
iii. 'encouraging a culture of innovation';
iv. 'ensuring the appreciation of existing industrial sectors';
v. 'strengthening the division of labour in an economic region'.

Procedure: Theories

Sometimes a planning task proceeds from the decision – be it conscious or otherwise – to apply a given theory or thesis. For example: Work on regional planning often relies on the so-called 'Central Place Theory' when determining the placement of infrastructure throughout a region. This theory is widely accepted and has many well-tested domains of application. However, like any other theory, it is not well-suited for *everything*. If, for example, we were to determine the placement of a regional hospital according to this theory we would have to base our decision about where medical facilities are most useful on demographic data. This may well be the best way to proceed when thinking about providing people with basic care. However, things look rather different if we want to maximise the accessibility of specialised medical knowledge. Nowadays, most people seek out expert physicians when undergoing medical procedures that are either difficult or that can be planned well in advance. For example, spinal or tropical illnesses are referred to specialised hospitals and not just the nearest available hospital. Due to this change in contemporary medical practice, Central Place Theory can no longer function unquestioned as it once did – while planning practitioners and administrative groups sometimes still base their actions on this thinking. Furthermore, it is an open discussion how well this theory can be applied to find solutions for planning problems in connection to eastern Germany (and soon perhaps other parts of Germany as well) where planners find themselves having to take more and more measures to deal with a shrinking population. Can the Central Place Theory help us formulate plans on how to dismantle rather than build infrastructure?

In any case, the Central Place Theory often continues to play an important role in regional planning in Germany. Here – as with any theory – it is indeed very much a possibility that the application of an individual theory diverts our attention from the core of the particular problem we are trying to solve. In some cases, a theory makes it all but impossible to find an adequate solution to a given problem in spatial planning.

Conclusion

Above we have presented a brief overview of four approaches in planning and problem solving, as well as a brief discussion of why we find portions of each to be questionable.

As we have stated, we are convinced that sustained attention to negative situations ought to play a more central role in planning. If a planning task commences with a definition of what negative situation ought to be ameliorated, then it almost always follows that the aforementioned conventional tools, disciplinary goals, disciplinary methods, as well as disciplinary theories and hypotheses can no longer be given free and unfettered application.

What are the concrete implications of this? Beginning with the definition of a negative situation requires that appropriate methods and theories are only sought *ex post facto*. This requires a degree of practice, as well as a self-assuredness that 'somehow it will all work out in the end'. This can have significant effects which are all too easy to understand from a human perspective, because starting with the 'messes first' often creates a certain degree of uneasiness and uncertainty in the beginning of a planning task, as one to face problems without the familiar 'conceptual toolbox' in hand, so to speak. Or, to put a sharper edge on the point, we can imagine someone immersed in the full complexity of a given problem finding himself without any familiar tools at hand. Such a person finds himself in a void of nothingness, confronted by the 'horror vacuums'.

Our goal was therefore to develop a procedure that can help planners avoid this 'horror vacuums' by supplanting the familiar methods with a conceptual scaffolding that, at one and the same time, underlie and supersede those traditional methods. We hope that our work will help planners reduce the uneasiness associated with abandoning their conceptual toolbox by offering them a solid theoretical framework that can help them reach well thought out and consistent solutions, in so far as this is possible.

3.6 Concepts/terms

When dealing with one of the 'big messes' in particular or with planning more generally, we never confront the world 'as such'. Rather, our experience of the world is always already mediated by more or less abstract descriptions of that world. All such descriptions are made up of concepts (or terms) that are joined to propositions by way of relations. In the context of this chapter, we will restrict our focus to the concepts.

Why are concepts important? In planning, we are always confronted with the task of defining key terms. For example, imagine a group of planners who are asked to work out a plan for the 'sustainable urban development' of some part of London. Most professionals in the field would, if asked, have some ideas to contribute to the project. But in order for those ideas to function as genuine contributions to the project, the participants must first be able to engage in meaningful communication. For example, if the planners engaged in this project could not agree to a shared understanding of what is meant by the words 'sustainable' and 'urban development', they would not get very far in finding a solution to their problem, as the problem is devoid of its proper content. Concepts are important because they function as the bearers of knowledge.

Moreover, the content of concepts used in planning often vary from person to person, especially if they have different professional backgrounds. The meaning of terms is therefore subjective, which can and often does lead to misunderstandings. Meanings are established by convention, not empirical fact. Accordingly, the use of individual terms in the context of a particular planning problem is never true or false, but only relevant/irrelevant, useful/useless, etc. This accounts for some of the difficulty we face in communication.

In contrast to this difficulty, the ambiguity and polysemy of linguistic utterances also has some positive, generative features: different definitions and interpretations of individual terms and concepts shed light on some of the different aspects of a given problem. Sometimes, it is enough to change the definition of a term: certain problems can be eliminated wholesale without doing anything further.

For example: the European Union legislated the minimum quality of its drinking water by stipulating how many parts per million of various pollutants it may contain. Unfortunately, the use of fertilisers by farmers has polluted the local drinking water in several places to a degree where it no longer meets the minimum health requirements as they were defined by the EU. The question now is what we should do to solve this problem. An obvious solution would be to pass laws and measures to reduce the pollution from farmers seeping into the ground water. But the EU has actually begun thinking of an alternative strategy to solve this problem: simply re-defining the acceptable level of pollutants in Europe's drinking water will re-establish the legal quality of Europe's drinking water. Needless to say this solution may only be a solution in the narrowest sense of that word, and we will have to keep a close eye on any negative health effects that may ensue.

3.7 Causes and effects

Some people do not stop with the claim that planning often fails adequately to consider the negative side effects concomitant with some of its solutions. They go further and claim that planning is also totally ineffective, that is overly academic, and that it is simply not in a position to solve actual, real-world problems.

This brings us back to the importance of providing an adequate and convincing explanation of what caused a certain problem to arise in the first place. Having done so, we are then in a position to outline measures that will work against the negative causes which brought about the problem and that will strengthen the positive causes that are serving to mitigate the effects of the problem at hand. Of course, if we fail to apply these measures in the correct places or in an effective way then most likely the problem will persist into the future.

If we do not know, or, worse yet, refuse to acknowledge the causes that led to the 'big mess' in the first place, it will be hard if not impossible to do much about it. The negative situation will continue to exist, or, failing that, it has the potential to arise again and again. Hence, the relation between cause and effect – the relation that explains what brought about the problem in question – is at the very core of every planning process.

That having been said, it should not be assumed that the connection between the causal relation and the suggested measures functions in any way like a 'solution machine'. Rather, each individual planner must work proactively to assemble all the relevant pieces into a coherent picture of what is going on, weigh the different aspects one against the other, and then, as is usually the case, exercise to a considerable degree his personal creativity in the search for plausible candidate solutions (see also Meyerson and Banfield, 1955).

Using our framework, planners can find a large variety of solutions that partly go beyond the confines of their own professional background and really take aim at the problem itself rather than just trying to cure some of its symptoms. In order to do this, we put a strong emphasis on systematic, visual representations of the causes and effects, the measures, their consequences, and their subsequent and of necessity subjective assessment. Doing so provides a sort of 'map of the arguments' that can then serve as a basis for further discussions and that can be used in the effort to develop additional measures and steps in the solution of a problem.

3.8 Approaches

The last of the 'key five' are the 'approaches'. The underlying and paradigmatic approaches of all those involved in the planning process are essential to each of the previous components described above, as those approaches significantly influence how those people view the planning problem as well as its solution. These approaches include the philosophical pre-suppositions and transdisciplinary knowledge of each participant, as well as the specific professional knowledge that each participant brings to the table during the planning process.

There is no way to get around these individual approaches, as everybody cannot help but make use of them. They are like our own individual 'thinking hats'. They are not generated by the problems themselves. Rather, they are something that each of us always already brings to a planning situation. This means that other planners might see the problem and its various solutions quite differently, depending on the unique character of their own, idiosyncratic approach.

Depending on our approach, for example, we would have a different view on whether or not the state should engage in the construction of public housing projects: an advocate of social justice would probably demand that the state play a strong role and see the state's involvement in the construction of public housing projects as indispensable. An advocate of a more liberalistic economic world view, on the other hand, would most likely argue that free markets are best equipped to run the housing market and would therefore demand a reduced role for the state. It goes without saying that both planners would probably act rather differently and that it would therefore be helpful were they to reflect on their own approaches to a problem and try to better understand the context of their own ideas and actions.

Approaches also serve as an exceedingly useful tool in planning. It is often possible to discover new solutions by adopting a new, different, perhaps even opposing approach or direction in one's thinking. Doing so is also extremely helpful when we are trying to interpret and understand the actions of other actors who are involved in the planning process. Finally, being aware of the different approaches that are out there and the concepts and ideas that result from them helps to keep planners from limiting themselves to an overly narrow view of a given problem.

This, in turn, serves to extend the scope of possible solutions they can devise. In short: approaches have a significant influence on the planning process, how we view planning problems, and how we devise solutions to those problems.

3.9 Application of the planning model in pedagogy and practice

The following paragraphs briefly outline how we have applied the planning model in pedagogy and practice. Going from model to lecturing might appear to be a break in the line of reasoning. But this is actually one of the key aspects of our work, as we did not want to limit ourselves to theorising and coming up with ideas without a direct, useful and practical implication. So the 'translation' of our framework into a university course or the use of the framework in real-world planning projects also serves as a test, if our concepts actually work.

Some may ask 'is it really that easy', while others ask 'are you not demanding too much from practitioners and your students'? To close this chapter, we will provide a brief answer to the question of how we teach our framework and the ways in which we have put it into practice outside the confines of a university.

In what follows, we will therefore provide the methodological repertoire we use to apply the planning model described above in both practical and pedagogical circumstances – but due to the countless connections that obtain between all of the themes, what follows is of necessity a sketchy and greatly simplified treatment of the framework that we have developed.

Pedagogy

We have designed several courses to teach our method for solving complex problems in the context of several PhD theses, regular research at the Institute for the Foundations of Planning, as well as a joint research project with psychologists at the 'Hochschule für Technik und Wirtschaft' [Polytechnic] in Dresden, the latter of which was sponsored by the German Research Foundation (DFG). The courses that resulted from these collaborations and experiences are strongly centred on a 'problem-based' approach to learning, in which a series of question lead students through our framework and line of reasoning as they are introduced to various content modules and engage in peer reviews, face to face interactions and also include online elements.

In the context of our courses, several aspects of our planning model were 'translated' into concrete actions intended to solve complex problems. We created such a methodological repertoire as a list of questions and themes that have been used for teaching purposes at the Faculty for Architecture and Urban Planning at the University of Stuttgart for a number of years now. In the context of the DFG-Research project, central aspects of this methodological repertoire are being subjected to further research as well as being actively restructured.

Our course of study offers a systematic education that qualifies students to work on complex problems in planning. Our goal is to educate planners who can integrate many aspects of a planning task, from the initial stages of developing a plan to its implementation and, eventually, evaluation. As complex problems in planning often require the integration of disparate kinds of specialised knowledge from various domains of inquiry our pedagogy does not focus on imparting students with a set canon of expertise. Rather, we focus on training our students in structural and methodological thinking to help them deal with complex tasks of many different kinds.

The central goals – which we derive from the above-sketched '5-28-52-x Model' – of our training include, among others:

i. a precise definition of the problem at hand, as well as the goal to be reached;
ii. the quick and conclusive discovery of well-founded solutions;
iii. to keep everyday, lived experiences – including political power and the worldview of planners, for example – in mind when developing concrete solutions to planning problems;
iv. to theoretically as well as methodologically penetrate individual themes (such as assessment procedures, participation procedures, etc.) and steps (such as prognostication, the generation of ideas, evaluations, etc.) of the process involved in working through a given planning task, and to then apply what has been learned;
v. to acquire the psychological, communications theoretical, and semiotic skills needed to better understand and acknowledge the subjective use of concepts, the situated knowledge that under-girds them, as well as the goals and motives of all the various people involved in a planning task.

As we have already mentioned above, the steps enumerated above cannot encompass all the relevant aspects and tasks of concrete planning process. However, they can be understood as central steps that overlap from one planning task to another and therefore have to be worked out in almost every situation. In addition they can also be understood as basic 'building blocks' that form the conceptual 'framework' of a planner.

Evaluation and outlook

The outlined courses have received positive evaluations from participants and outside experts. In addition, the value of our research for practicing planners is currently being reviewed by experts with many years of professional experience in the field. In the context of a half-standardised interview process, practicing planners who work in various domains of planning will assess the practical relevance of our conclusions and methods.

The following questions will be central to the review process:

i. Are those aspects of the planning method that have yielded positive effects applicable to practical, real-world problems?
ii. How are these aspects of our method most effectively communicated and imparted to practicing, mid-career planners in the context of a professional training program?
iii. Is it possible to transfer our method to the problem of grasping and evaluating a real-world, practical planning process with relative ease and economy?
iv. Are our methods well suited for controlling and steering the direction of a particular project?

Based on the results of this review process, we will further develop our model of planning. In doing so, we will methodically develop well-founded methods to help planners in their day-to-day work. From a more psychological point of view, we will also work out a cognitive process model that clarifies and explains the connection between systematic ways to deal with conceptual systems on the one hand and an improvement of the deliberative process among planners on the other. Such a clarification and explanation will be essential for imparting competence in dealing with complex problems on the ground and will therefore support the practical work of professional planners.

Our model has been practically implemented in various projects. For example, we where able to provide input to a project of the Swiss Scholl & Signer office for planning in Zürich, the so-called By-pass Basel railway system, which includes rails from the DB, SBB, and the SNCF. The planning task involved the construction of new railway lines in the Basel region, the need for which resulted from tunnel construction in the Lötschberg and the Gotthard. In addition, our model was also implemented in various urban planning projects, including some in Budapest, Milan and a collaboration with regional planning offices in the Southern Rhine and the Upper Rhine/Bodensee regions.

3.10 Summary

In this chapter, we have sketched a model for planning and detailed some aspects of that model that serve as the basis for a 'guide' to help planners solve complex problems. On the basis of our research and practical experience, we are in a position to say that:

i. The use of our method helps introduce a greater measure of order into the planning process. This helps to ensure that relevant steps in the planning process are not left out. It also helps to better delegate and organise responsibility in projects that require teamwork.
ii. The application of our method ensures a more precise definition of the problem at hand.

iii. On the basis of this precise definition of the problem, more effective, well-founded, and applicable solutions can be worked out.
iv. Acknowledging the subjective use of propositions and concepts, as well as the underlying planning assumptions, results in more precise and diversified solutions.
v. And, in working out possible solutions to a problem the basic conditions of planning – especially issues of power and politics – are taken into greater consideration.

References

Adis, A. and Schönwandt, W.L. (2004) 'Grundbausteine des planungswissens' ['Basic building blocks of planning knowledge'], in Akademie für Raumforschung und Landesplanung (ARL) (ed.), Handwörterbuch der Raumentwicklung, Hannover.

Boltz, F. (2005) 'Informationen zum verkehrszug Waldschlösschenbrücke' ['Information about the traffic concept Waldschlösschenbrücke'], *Elbtal: Kurier*, 2-8.

Bunge, M. (1983) *Treatise on Basic Philosophy, Vol. 5, Epistemology I: Exploring the World*, Reidel, Dordrecht/Boston.

Bunge, M. (1996) *Finding Philosophy in Social Science*, Yale University Press, New Haven/London.

Dörner, D. (1989) *Die Logik des Misslingens: Strategisches Denken in komplexen Situationen* [*The Logic of Failure: Strategic Thinking in Complex Situations*], Rowohlt, Reinbek.

Dörner, D. and Schaub, H. (1995) 'Handeln in unbestimmtheit und komplexität' ['Acting in uncertainty and complexity'], *Organisationsentwicklung*, vol. 14(3), pp. 34-47.

Funke, J. (1992) *Wissen über Dynamische Systeme. Erwerb, Repräsentation und Anwendung* [*Knowledge about Dynamic Systems: Acquisition, Representation and Application*], Springer, Berlin.

Grunau, J. (2008) 'Lösen komplexer probleme: theoretische grundlagen und deren umsetzung für lehre und praxis' ['Solving complex problems: theoretical foundations and their use in education and practice'], Der Andere Verlag, Tönning, Lübeck und Marburg.

Grunau, J., Hemberger, C., Saifoulline, R., Schönwandt, W. and Von der Weth, R. (2006), 'Mentale modelle bei komplexen aufgaben in der regionalplanung' ['Mental models in complex tasks in regional planning'], 45, Kongress der Deutschen Gesellschaft für Psychologie, Nuremberg.

Grunau, J., Heberling, G., Scholl, B. and Schönwandt, W. (2003) 'Abschlussbericht forschungsprojekt: Planerausbildung mit fachübergreifenden internetbasierten lehrmodulen' ['Final report of the research project: Education of planner with transdisciplinary web-based learning modules'], ISL, IGP, Karlsruhe, Stuttgart.

Grunau, J. and Schönwandt, W. (2006) 'Solving complex problems', Second World Planning School Congress (WPSC), Mexico City.

Grunau, J. and Schönwandt, W. (2006) 'Problems first', Third Meeting AESOP Thematic Group Complexity, Cardiff.

Heidemann, C. (1992) 'Regional planning methodology: The first and only annotated picture primer on regional planning', Discussion Paper, Institut für Regionalwissenschaft, Karlsruhe.

Kuhn, T.S. (1962/1981) *Die Struktur wissenschaftlicher Revolutionen* [*The Structure of Scientific Revolutions*], Suhrkamp, Frankfurt am Main (fifth edition).

Lindblom, C. (1959) 'The science of muddling through', in J.M. Stein (ed.) (1995), *Classic Readings in Urban Planning*; McGraw-Hill, New York, pp. 35-48, original in *Public Administration Review*, vol. 19(2), pp. 78-88.

March, J.G. and Olsen, J.P. (1986) 'Garbage can models of decision making in organizations', in J.G. March and R. Weissinger-Baylon (eds.), *Ambiguity and Command: Organizational Perspectives on Military Decision Making*, Pitman, Marshfield, pp. 11-35.

Maurer, J. (2002a) 'Eines planers geschichten' ['Stories of a planner'], in S. Strohschneider and R. von der Weth (eds.), *Ja, mach nur einen Plan...Pannen und Fehlschläge: Ursachen, Beispiele, Lösungen* [*Yes, Make a Plan...Glitches and Failures: Causes, Examples, Solutions*], 2, Vollständig überarbeitete, erweiterte und aktualisierte Auflage, Huber, Bern, pp. 109-129.

Maurer, J. (2002b) 'Über die methodik der raumplanung' ['About the methodology in spatial planning'], in S. Strohschneider and R. von der Weth (eds.), *Ja, mach nur einen Plan...Pannen und Fehlschläge: Ursachen, Beispiele, Lösungen* [*Yes, Make a Plan...Glitches and Failures: Causes, Examples, Solutions*], 2, Vollständig überarbeitete, erweiterte und aktualisierte Auflage, Huber, Bern, pp. 182-192.

McGlade, J. and Garnsey, E. (2006) 'The nature of complexity', in E. Garnsey and J. McGlade (eds.), *Complexity and Co-Evolution*, Edward Elgar Publishing Limited, Cheltenham, pp. 1-21.

Meyerson, M. and Banfield, E.C. (1955) *Politics, Planning, and the Public Interest*, The Free Press of Glencoe, New York.

Neisser, U. (1979) *Kognition und Wirklichkeit* [*Cognition and Reality*], Klett-Cotta, Stuttgart.

Pavard, B. and Dugdale, J. (2000) 'An introduction to complexity in social science', GRIC-IRIT, Toulouse, October 20, 2007, available at http://www.irit.fr/ COSI/training/complexity-tutorial/ complexity-tutorial.htm.

Schönwandt, W.L. (1986) *Denkfallen beim Planen* [*Fallacies in Planning*], Vieweg, Braunschweig.

Schönwandt, W.L. (2002) *Planung in der Krise? Theoretische Orientierungen für Architektur, Stadt- und Raumplanung* [*Planning in a Crises? Theoretical

Orientation for Architecture, City- and Spatial Planning], Kohlhammer, Stuttgart.

Schönwandt, W.L. and Voigt, A. (2004) 'Planungsansätze' ['Approaches in Planning'], in *Handwörterbuch der Raumentwicklung*; Akademie für Raumforschung und Landesplanung (Hrsg.), Verlag der Akademie für Raumforschung und Landesplanung, Hannover, pp. 769-776.

Simon, H.A. (1973) 'The structure of ill-structured problems', *Artificial Intelligence*, vol. 4(3), pp. 181-201.

Strohschneider, S. and Von der Weth, R. (eds.) (2002) *Ja, mach nur einen Plan... Pannen und Fehlschläge: Ursachen, Beispiele, Lösungen* [*Yes, Make a Plan...Glitches and Failures: Causes, Examples, Solutions*], 2, Vollständig überarbeitete, erweiterte und aktualisierte Auflage, Huber, Bern.

Von der Weth, R. (2001) *Management der Komplexität: ressourcenorientiertes Handeln in der Praxis* [*Management of Complexity*], Huber, Bern.

Chapter 4
Complexity in Spatial Planning Practice and Theory: The Case of Kiruna Mining Town

Kristina L. Nilsson[1]

The relation between planning practice and theories of critical realism and complexity is discussed in this chapter. It is a critical and reflective exploration of how complexity is managed in local planning practice. Using a case study of a northern local Swedish authority with a multi-complexity situation – Kiruna Mining Town – the chapter studies hierarchy, power relations, uncertainties, chaos, actor-network and self-organisation.

4.1 Introduction

Planning practice is often confronted with numerous tasks and requirements. These situations are caused by both global and local changes, and with requirements of more sustainable development and greater participation of local communities. This interconnected and multi-dimensional context makes contemporary planning both complicated and complex. Complexity refers to uncertainties and unpredictable outcomes when different natural, technical and social conditions are integrated with actions and reactions from various actors and stakeholders and when a great number and a variety of elements and time dimensions interact in society as a whole and in planning in particular. Planning administrations and planners have to manage and improve methods to handle the growing complexity in planning practice.

An informative example of the highly complicated and complex context of planning is the small town of Kiruna, located in Northern Sweden. Kiruna is a mining town located in a subarctic region, with harsh climatic conditions, at the tree line in the Swedish mountain area. The state-owned LKAB (Luossavaara-Kiirunavaara Aktiebolag) iron-ore mine is the main industry, together with space technology and tourism. There are several processes of spatial planning going on, caused by the necessity to relocate or rebuild one third of the built environment.

---

1 Dr Kristina L. Nilsson is Professor in Architecture at Luleå University of Technology in Sweden.

This relocation is the result of an interest from the mining company, LKAB, to extend the mine underneath the existing town in order to exploit the iron-ore deposits located there. The historic and current mining activities have already lead to mine subsidence too risky for the urban area and for existing infrastructure.

The feasibility of the current relocation scenario proposed by LKAB is based on today's exceptionally high iron-ore prices. The local spatial planning administration is dependent for their planning decisions on the prognoses from the mining company of future number of staff, together with the estimated rate of continued mine subsidence. The existing town is a national heritage site surrounded by high natural environmental qualities; national road, railway and airport infrastructure; as well as pastures for the reindeer of the Saami people.[2] The vision for the spatial planning process is to contribute to sustainable development and to create an open deliberative planning process for all actors and stakeholders.

These combined conditions result in a complex context for the spatial planning situation in Kiruna. Various elements of the basic planning data remain uncertain, including the global demand of iron-ore, the size of housing market development, whether or not the state will finance the new railway track, and development of other industry and commerce besides the mining company, etc. It is also a physical uncertainty how fast the rock will crack and to what extent mine subsidence can be tolerated by current infrastructure and buildings. There are also unpredictable social elements, including how the inhabitants and businessmen will act and react as an effect of coming changes. Together with all these issues specific for this mining community there are common planning issues for an expanding community, including urban density, height of building structure, street grid, types of public transport system. Furthermore, all these factors are interdependent of one another in a non-linear way, as is the case in complex systems (Merry, 1995).

This chapter concerns what practical problems the planning practitioners meet in complex conditions, and the theoretical and practical challenges researchers meet when looking at the Kiruna case through a scientific perspective of complexity and critical realism. What can we learn when we study the integration of space, time and causalities? While it is not possible in the scope of this chapter to delve in-depth into the theories, we do present a condensed basic presentation of the perception of critical realism and complexity used in the analysis.

4.2 Planning and reality

Theories of critical realism have been brought into play in this case study in analysing and understanding a complex society and planning practice. From a meta-theoretical or philosophical perspective of *critical realism* (Bhaskar, 1979/1989; Sayer, 1992/2000; Archer et al., 1998) 'reality' can be understood through observing the events affected by mechanisms in society. Reality is, from this

2 The Saami people are Sweden's indigenous people in Lapland.

view, not transparent; it has power and mechanisms that cannot be observed, but can be identified indirectly through what it causes in the world. Bhaskar (1979) argues that scientific work deals with investigating and identifying context and no context respectively. This will be made between what we can observe, what 'really' occurs, and the underlying causal mechanisms producing global and local affairs. While there may be indications that causal chains exist, we cannot be sure of a causality, which in turn produces complexity (1979). 'Reality' must then be searched for behind the observable; behind what we can scrutinise and experience with our empirical studies.

With a critical realist method the attention is directed to the mechanisms that produce the events (Sayer, 1992). 'Reality' is assumed to include several domains. One is the 'domain of reality', which consists of mechanisms. The other one is the 'domain of events' generated by the mechanisms. The third is the 'empirical domain', where the occurrences can be observed. Scientific work consists of investigation and identification of connections, or when there are no connections between what one can experience, what actually occurs and the underlying mechanisms that produce the events in the world (Bhaskar via Danermark et al., 1997).

The scientific perspective of critical realism holds the view of an existing reality beyond our concepts of reality. One way to make this possible is to analyse scientific *intransitive* objects. From this point of view the knowledge of *reality* is based on our theories and concepts of reality, which generate *transitive* objects. This transitive dimension is socially defined and changing. The view of knowledge of reality as being socially produced, not only socially defined, is what distinguishes social science from natural science. This knowledge is also different from what you could call a naive realism – objectivism – from where a view of a correct and objective representation of reality is seen. Advocates for critical realism also imply that this knowledge is also different from the view of constructivism and relativism, which is seen to over accentuate the transitive side (Danermark et al., 1997, pp. 282-285).

The research approach of critical realism could be a useful way to understand the current complexity of society, where a growing number of institutions, actors and stakeholders are involved in complex combinations of relations. In complex spatial planning situations these social conditions have to be managed together with an amount of various underlying data and uncertain events, or, when spatial, causal and time dimensions are interlinked to each other. One important element of critical realism for the study of spatial planning is the view that space exists *a priori*: spatiality is always concrete and real. This differs from most social sciences that have a non-spatial dimension. Sayer argues that space is a necessary dimension of all material phenomena, social included, in that they have spatial extensions and spatial exclusivity and sometimes a limited variety of forms (Sayer, 2000, p. 129). Spatial planning, and handling future changes to be implemented in reality, needs a decision for one solution that has as great benefits for as many as possible. Critical realism seems to offer an inclusive theoretical foundation for approaching planning for 'complex' urban developments (Kain, 2003).

4.3 Planning and complexity

In meta-theoretical terms complexity theories have ontological and epistemological implications which make them an essential part of the realist programme of scientific understanding and inquiry (Byrne, 1998, p. 7). Jessop explains complex situations in the following way: 'Intensification of societal complexity which flows from growing functional differentiation of institutional orders within an increasingly global society with all that this implies for the widening and deepening of systemic interdependencies across various social, spatial, and temporal horizons of action' (Jessop, 2001). However, since the real world is infinitely complex, it is also inevitably analytically inexhaustible.

Chaos and complexity theories are wide and developed by various scholars. In this short basis for the analysis Merry (1995) with his introductory book *Coping with Uncertainty: Insights from the New Sciences of Chaos, Self-Organization, and Complexity* gives us an overview of the main complexity approach. Chaos theory can be described in the following way: 'A great complexity can end up in chaos as a time in transition between orders; a temporary period of uncertainty, unpredictability, and disorder accompanied by great difficulty to end the uncertainty, disarray, confusion, tension, conflict and disruption' (Merry, 1995). Chaos can also be understood as irregular, uncertain and unpredictable forms in which many things change, or shortly explained, unpredictable change. When a system is in a chaotic state there is particular patterned order in the way it changes as a whole, but the future behaviour of its individual components is totally unpredictable. Chaos, seen from a complexity theory perspective, is not deep chaos, but is considered as a natural, inescapable essential stage in the transformation of all life forms. From the perspective of complexity theories, chaos is instead a form that can be turned to creativity and innovation. Out of chaos come forth 'the fertile variety of forms of existence and life in the universe' (Merry, 1995, p. 11).

A social system always has a period of great instability on its way to a new order. It meets decision points on which its future will depend as a variety of possible paths are opened up. In complexity theory these points of choice are named *bifurcations*, that is, points of forking or branching. When a system reaches a bifurcation point it is faced with the possibility of choosing from different paths. Each path may lead in a completely different direction and open the possibility for diverse ways of self-organising itself (Merry, 1995, p. 50). Byrne (1998) notes that at the bifurcation point very small differences in control parameter values determine which path the system will follow.

A system has the potential to spontaneously and unpredictably develop new forms and structures by itself. This kind of self-organisation provides a way for a system to develop itself out of chaos. However, processes are always continuous, which means that the world as a whole and the human world is complex in itself. Such an understanding, of complexity, continuity and flows, will lead to a better understanding, but as well to an intensification of uncertainty and difficulties of adaptation of the systems (Merry, 1995, p. 55).

Equilibrium is a condition when systems are stable. Although, advocators for complexity theory state that urban governance is not concerned with maintaining an equilibrium and stable environment. In systemic terms, cities are necessarily complex and evolving away from equilibrium. Cities are systems with an evolutionary character (Byrne, 1998).

4.4 Relocation of the mining town Kiruna

Empirical data for this chapter is based on the planning activities concerned with the relocation of a third of the town of Kiruna. This analysis forms a part of a larger research project (in progress) which concerns complex planning problems. The investigation is carried out as a single case study (Yin, 1994) and in an *intensive* methodological way (Danemark et al., 1997, p. 237). This *intensive* method combines interviews, together with an analysis of documents, records, plans and available statistics. Kiruna provides an extreme case. However, the type of complexity, with interconnected occurrences and multi-dimensional context filled with uncertainties, exists in most urban planning situations, the difference being that these types of factors are not generally included in the same process. The Kiruna example provides a particularly obvious case upon which it is possible to draw and generalise conclusions.

Kiruna is a small town, with approximately 20,000 inhabitants, located in the very north of Sweden (Kiruna, 2008). The town was established in 1905 with the purpose of mining iron-ore. During the 100 years of operation the mine's production has fluctuated in relation to market conditions. In March 2004 LKAB (2007b), the mining company, informed Kiruna's local authority about increased mine subsidence, caused by earlier mining. They also reported their future plans for extensive mining activities which will mine the ore-body that continues underneath the existing town. Both these occurrences threaten the existing urban structure and will result in the relocation of at least one third of the town.

The investigation focuses on the on-going spatial planning processes for drastic changes. The expansion of the town is directly dependent on the ore mine and its fluctuating market value. Today's high global price of iron has initiated the interest from the mining company to expand the mine. If the high profit from the mining continues the mine will be extended and parts of the existing town must successively be moved to a secure ground. The local planning administration has a process of comprehensive planning in progress, based on the assumption to move or rebuild a large part of the built environment. The existing railway and the main European road, from the Baltic Sea on the east side coast to the Norwegian coast at the west side, have to be moved away from their current locations, as they suffer from deformation zones. Because of this, there are also on-going planning processes for the new railway line as well as where to place the new part of the main road.

The existing town has a recognised status as a cultural heritage site, because of its unique grid plan and its collection of buildings of high architectural value. In addition, the urbanisation is surrounded by values of other high national interests such as environmental values, plenty of unexplored mineral findings, national road, railway and airport infrastructure, of as well as important pasture areas for Saami people's reindeers. When Kiruna was established 100 years ago it was designed and realised as a model town. The current comprehensive plan is based on a political vision of a future model town, as a conception of a sustainable city. The various functions in the town are expected to be integrated to reach good living conditions in an ecological, social and economical fashion for all its inhabitants (Kiruna, 2006). All these interests of the territory and space are often overlapping and interrelated and sometimes also contradictory. It is also complicated as to how all these various interests are evaluated and prioritised in relation to one another.

In Kiruna, the major changes are planned in cooperation with several important actors and a manifold of agents. There are both actors, which have active roles in the processes, and stakeholders, who have stakes but perhaps do not act. Instead, there can be agents acting as representatives for the stakeholders. These actors and stakeholders are competing for the territory in, around and even below the existing town. The main actors have to act within the frame of respective national legislation. Additionally, all activities must be managed according to the principle of sustainable development as outlined in the UN agreements of Bruntland, the Rio-declaration and Habitat-agenda.

The local authority of Kiruna is, by the planning monopoly and Planning and Building Act, responsible for developing a comprehensive plan for the relocation. This planning instrument aims to address and integrate all sector interests. The national infrastructure of main roads are managed and financed by the National Road Admininstration and is regulated by the Road Act. The railway lines are managed and financed by the National Railway Adminstration and is regulated by the Railway Act. The iron mine is a state-owned company LKAB (Loussvaara-Kiirunavaara Aktiebolag). The mining is regulated by the Mineral Act and Environmental Code. Other national authorities are engaged in the planning processes as well.

The County Board and the National Heritage Board are responsible for managing heritage values in an appropriate way. Heritage values are regulated by the Ancient Monument Act as well as by Planning and Building Act. The Swedish Board of Agriculture, through the County Board, is responsible for the Saami people and the reindeer commercial interests. The Swedish Civil Aviation Administration is responsible for the airport. Furthermore, all the plans must be assessed according to the Swedish Environmental Code.

The greatest stakeholder group in the development of future employment and living environment is the local community of Kiruna as well as non-governmental organisations. The extreme situation in Kiruna is clearly demonstrated by the way the Swedish Government 2006 gave the national Board of Housing and Planning (Boverket) a mission to 'coordinate the stately interests in the assignment to advise how general interests should be considered in the best way for planning' of Kiruna (Regeringskansliet, 2006). In addition, the National Heritage Board has received a governmental mission on how to handle the cultural heritage values.

There is a wide time span between the different activities. On the one hand there is a long term vision. The town has existed for 100 years. The local authority will look both backwards at the old model town and look forward the same length of time. This is the reason why the planning administration and the leading politicians have worked out a vision for the future 100 years. Moreover, representatives from the mining company estimate where the extraction of iron-ore will be in 100 years. On the other hand, there is a short term reality of the location of the new railway line, which had to be decided in 2006. This was not more than two years after the mine subsidence became known. And the railway must be physically rebuilt before 2012.

As presented above, there are various parallel planning processes in the preparation for Kiruna's urban development. The processes are managed in different modes according to regulating legislations, but also according to different professional traditions and perspectives from the officials involved. Kiruna has a limited planning administration, which is proportional to its small number of inhabitants and earlier minor planning activities. The local authority planning can be interpreted as incremental, since the planning complexity and problems are divided, limited, and addressed step-by-step in decision making (Lindblom, 1979). The experts from the National Railway Administration have thoroughly examined and professionally evaluated different alternatives for the new direction of the railway track. This can be characterised as rational planning (Etzioni, 1973). In 2005 the National Road Administration initiated a planning seminar for leading local politicians and officers, creating a dialogue with most of the actors. This can be characterised as communicative planning (Healey, 1997). The mining company LKAB (LKAB, 2007) submitted a plan for a new site of the town to the local authority in 2007, which was at that time alternative to the local authority plan. LKAB management have, during all planning, successively given the local planning administration basic data. The company's approach can be considered as negotiative planning, since the partners give their bid, from which they then negotiate over decisions.

Uncertainties are one part of the complexity in the Kiruna planning process. The main uncertainty is the global price of iron-ore, which directly influences the scale and rate of the mining activity. The scale of relocation and rebuilding of the town is related to the rate of mining. Another uncertainty is the efficiency of mining activity, which will influence the number of employees and their need of new apartments. There are also uncertainties concerning the development of the region, which will also influence the size of the Kiruna townscape. For example, new and faster transport routes can shorten commuting distances and enlarge the working region. Similarly, new types of vehicles can change the conditions for both railway and main roads and shorten commuting times. Market driven housing politics makes it difficult to predict the demand and type of sites and houses.

There are several issues of special strategic importance for the shape of the new town. These include the new infrastructure grid and implementation of new techniques for public transports within the town and the new localisation of the railway track and the main European road. In general, new railway tracks are very costly, long-lived and cause barrier effects. This issue is very important for the ore transportation. The ore trains constitute approximately 95 per cent of the rail transportations and only 5 per cent of the rail transportations are for private travel, hence the localisation of the new track in direct connection to the mining area. This in turn, makes a longer distance between the main track and the plans for a travelling centre close to the new city centre. In the sustainable urban vision (Kiruna, 2006), the importance of close connection between the railway station and the city centre is explicit, with the aim to entice increased travel by public transports.

Low transport energy use is also an important sustainability aspect. The professional proposal of the shape of the new town was to concentrate the urban structure in order to produce as short distances as possible. This would create a dense town shape in order to promote walking and bicycling. Unfortunately, such a shape will hinder future mining activities, as the mining company suggests the new structure to be developed in a northwest direction. The company's proposal will, however, cause a narrow and long stretched shape of the town.

The planning processes provide great problems and challenges for politicians and the local planning administration in Kiruna. As presented above, there are manifold and often overlapping and contradictory interests in terms of land-use. This, together with major global, regional and local uncertainties, expectations of a long term sustainable development, and tight deadlines, makes for a very complex situation. The complexity is based on the large amount and variation of factors interwoven as a multi-dimensional web. A web consisting of all the unpredictable components, with the variety of technical, environmental and social conditions must be integrated with various actors values and perspectives and the stakeholders' wishes. This produces a myriad of dilemmas to manage. And the new urban structure must be realised in a suitable shape that is functional for the local community, sustainable where possible, as well as the interests of the mine.

4.5 Managing complex planning

In this section the case of Kiruna planning is analysed using complexity theories. First, we can measure the spatial dimensions of Kiruna from a complexity perspective (Byrne, 1998). This is not a way to search for boundaries, but to analyse space at various scales. Kiruna town is the main locality in the study. Bugguely et al. (via Merry, 1998) assert 'the locality as a method' and this approach has grown from an attempt to address the complexity of spatially intersecting causal processes. The first scale of analysis in this method is the neighbourhood, although this is not present in this study of comprehensive planning. The region could be illustrated by the entire Kiruna local area, which in this case is extremely large with its 19,371 km^2 (Kiruna, 2008). This equals approximately half the size of Switzerland. The local authority consists of the main town Kiruna and many small settlements and a large 'fjell' area with a very small number of inhabitants. There is a working region partly around the town of Kiruna, where people commute from the nearest settlements. The other wider part of the working region is the nearest town Gällivare/Malmberget, another smaller mining town. There are daily commuting activities between Kiruna and Gällivare/Malmberget, despite the 120 km between the two points.

In the study we have strived to find the integrated systems in Kiruna, because human and social systems are difficult to understand by reducing them to isolated fragments. The systems have been analysed to find the interdependence between the pieces, which has shown the unpredictability in the systems. Some pieces have been regular and predictable and others have been chaotic and unpredictable. There is, as Merry (1995) describes it, interplay between order and disorder, regularity and chaos, predictability and unpredictability.

Hierarchy

Hierarchy can be seen as a type of official linear system. In Sweden there is a highly decentralised policy with regional and local authorities being granted considerable autonomy e.g. imposing tax on private income. The national government does, however, provide the framework and structure for local government activities. In principle, the local authority has a planning monopoly. That means that the planning authority primarily has the task to plan the use of land and water within a legal framework that is supervised by national government. It is in the local comprehensive plans that these intentions are set out. The planning monopoly is granted, however, under certain restrictions. Although the Planning and Building Act gives the local authorities responsibility for use of the land and water within its area, the local authority must consider the interests of the state when making their plans. Overall, this means that Kiruna local planning administration has the planning power in the design of the comprehensive plan.

Iron-ore mining was the key reason for the establishment of Kiruna town in the very north 100 years ago. The mining company LKAB is still the main industry and the main employer. When the company is wealthy the inhabitants are well-to-do. Today, the high price of iron-ore makes the company good profits and makes it a powerful actor. When the company became impatient with progress of the local municipality's comprehensive plan, the company developed an alternative plan for the town's relocation. With this plan the company has demonstrated their power to steer ideas for the future development of the town. This engagement caused a non-linear development in the system that caused a chaotic situation, because the local community did not know who was responsible for the relocation plans.

The local community has political power by voting in elections every fourth year. In addition they have formal possibilities to comment on the proposed plans through obligatory consultations. Surprisingly, the local community is inactive in relation to the proportion to the great changes proposed for the town. The town has, for the last 100 years, been dependent on the state, represented by the mining company together with the local administration. The population has, for generations, been dependent on the company and the state and the local administration. Today there is very little community debate considering the enormous scale of changes planned for the town. It seems that the community continues to trust in the state to plan for the public good.

However, even if the local authority has formal power over the planning, in this case the mining company holds the *de facto* power over the town. The state authorities for planning, railway and road have the obligation to protect the general interests for the population. The state also has to provide maintenance for this part of the country, given the areas high unemployment. At the same time the state has to support the economical progress of the mining industry. These sometimes competing obligations and powers poses several dilemmas. In a realistic perspective the mining company has the power over the local authority, even if the local authority has the official power through the planning monopoly. Altogether this illustrates a reality that is non-linear because it does not follow the formal linear hierarchy.

Uncertainties

Uncertainties are significant parts of the complex context in Kiruna. The main uncertainty consists of the global price of iron-ore, which directly influences the amount and rate of future mining activity. The scale, rate and timing of relocation thus depend on the future demand of iron-ore. Another uncertainty is the efficiency of the mining, which influences the number of employees and demand for new residential areas. Additionally, with market driven housing politics it is hard to predict the demand and type of sites, houses and homes.

There exists also a vagueness concerning how the region can be developed and how such a development can influence the development of the town. For example, new and faster transports will shorten commuting distances, which may, in turn, enlarge the working region. If new types of vehicles are developed, that may change the railway and main road which will drastically shorten the commuting time? Will people live in the central town, in surrounding settlements or at the countryside, in the fells or along the near riverside? Uncertainties can be managed by visions and scenarios. Kiruna local administration has presented a vision, but this vision is very general and rhetorically formulated.

Chaos, non-linearity and interdependencies

In 2004 the mining company proclaimed the news of increased rapid cracking ground under the existing urban structure. The local planning administration knew that according to the Planning and Building Act a new comprehensive plan had to be carried out. The aim of the plan has been to investigate how to relocate the new parts of the town: in which direction, the density area and shape. The planning officers, however, seem to be paralysed as to what way should they handle all risks and uncertainties, and as to where to start. The leading politicians were even more paralysed in this context of chaos and were unsure how to manage all these uncertainties in a democratic way. The planning administration began to plan in a linear order; they organised a comprehensive planning group and set up a program for a comprehensive plan. The main planning issues have been considered on different planning levels. It took a long time before the local planning administration presented the first plan proposal for the development of the transformation.

During this time, the leaders at the mining company became impatient when the local planning administration took considerable time to present proposals for the physical re-location of the new part of the town. The company hired two consultants, one architect and one infrastructure planner, who presented a speculative proposal with winding streets along the mountain slopes, and tropical gardens and an in-door skiing hill under a glass roof. The visionary and well illustrated proposal was attractive to the local community. However there were some contradictions. The local planning administration had suggested that the new parts of the town be located to the east of the existing town, and the company's proposal located these to the north-west. Some of the company's planned buildings were proposed on a slope where the company had previously informed the local authority that it was not possible to erect any structures. Additionally, no one had promised to finance the gardens and ski slopes or the glass roof.

All of these occurrences caused a chaotic situation in the local authority administration. Neither the politicians nor the officials were prepared for this. The plan proposal from the mining company made the local community extremely confused. Was this plan the current one? Where was the one the local authority had carried out? Who was responsible for the real planning proposal for the direction and shape of the future Kiruna? Was it the mining company with its economical power? Or was it the local authority planning administration? The chaos consisted of a great quantity of uncertainties in the basic data, as well uncertainties as how to manage the situation and what type of processes to design. The small group of planning staff was not experienced in dealing with planning issues of such a scale and complexity and under such tight deadlines.

Chaos develops in non-linear systems that are interdependent with each other. The mining company and the local authority are connected through a non-linear system, and while there are no formal links there are dependent relationships for both parts. Interdependency deals with the relationships between objects and the way they affect one another. In this case there is an obvious relationship between the mining activities and the proposed urban changes. All organisations in Kiruna are indeed interdependent on one another. The mine is the reason as to why the town is located in the place it is and a mine is not mobile, as are many other industries. A mine must be located where minerals are. Hence, the mine is itself the cause of the relocation of Kiruna town. The mining company is the greatest employer in the town. On the other hand, the company is dependent on a well organised town, with state social services that provide good living conditions, medical services, child-care and elderly-care, as well as commercial services. The mine is also dependent on a local authority that administrates these factors.

Actor-network perspective

The Kiruna case can also be analysed from an actor network theoretical (ANT) perspective (Latour, 2005). The ANT concept relies on a social science approach, where the social is seen as a movement during a process of assembling agents. Such an analysis of Kiruna assembles the persons as agent groups, which are representing each main actor. The current main actors, as previously presented, include the mining company, the local authority of Kiruna, the National Railway Administration and the National Road Administration. These authorities can be seen as actors, yet they cannot act as individuals, but must act in an assembled way as representatives for the organisation. Conversely, the local community is a heterogeneous group and cannot be seen as one common actor.

There are networks on three levels in the entire planning process of Kiruna. First, there is a network at a high national level called the delegation of Malmfälten (Malmfälten is the name of the mining region with the two main towns of Kiruna and Gällivare/Malmberget) with the Minister of Enterprise, the CEO of LKAB, the heads of National boards of planning, railway and road, and the governor of Norrbotten County. On a lower level there is a group with the county board, a management representative from LKAB and the heads on the regional level of railway and road administrations. Thirdly, there is a network of the civil servants from the same authorities as presented above, together with officers at the local planning administration.

These networks have been organised in a formal way to discuss and address the on-going activities on all levels and to discuss joint requirements. However, we cannot see that the networks have succeeded in producing any joint vision that could be interpreted as a regime, governance model, or a driving force for the development of the region and the town.

Self-organisation

The way in which the mining company initiated its own proposal to speed up the planning process can be interpreted as a type of self-organisation of the chaos. One of the company leaders expressed the situation; 'We wanted to start a discussion and show the possibility to build the new part of the town in the north direction' (A quote from an LKAB manager). This initiative caused a new type of chaos connected to non-linear relations. But, as previously argued, non-linearity is not the same thing as interdependence. Non-linearity is related to proportions between the incorporated conditions, which as example can express a disproportion between cause and effect. Small causes may lead to large effects and large causes may have small effects (Merry, 1995). As noted earlier, the local authority has, by the Swedish constitution, a planning monopoly, which means that the local authority is both responsible for and is the only part that is allowed to adopt plans. That is to say, the small urban design proposal from the mining company caused a lot of irritation in the local planning administration, and a lot of uncertainties among the local community. Moreover, it undermined the possibility to build up a trustful relation between the actors.

Another form of self-organisation concerns the local community. The local authority administration has the assignment to organise their work in a proper way. There was a chaotic atmosphere just after the news of the mine subsidence, since people close to the first deformation zone were fearful for their future property value and possibility to continue living where they were. They were unsure if they could sell their houses if they had to move earlier or if the company would have to provide compensation because of unstable ground. When should they move, and where, since new housing areas were not yet planned? Surprisingly, the local community has organised itself in relative quietness.

Reporters from the world press visited Kiruna and wrote about the relocation of the town, a relocation that upset people all over Sweden. Despite this, the local community knows that the locality is dependent on the mining industry; a wealthy mining company gives a wealthier town. When the town was located there 100 years ago the company took care of the local community. Even if they do not do so to the same extent today, people seem to be self-confident enough to trust that either the formal planning bodies or the company is able to manage present and future problems.

However, as Merry (1995, p. 55) notes, continuous and increasingly frequent processes of self-organisation mean that the locality as a whole and the human world are growing ever more complex. The self-organisation of the planning activities caused uncertainties for those who were actually responsible for carrying out the plan. The type of self-organisation of the local community caused other uncertainties for the planning administration. How was the planning administration to get the local community interested and more actively involved in the planning processes, given that the local community is expected to approve democratic decisions? This causes other forms of complexity and leads to an intensification of uncertainties and difficulties in adapting the plans for the shape of the new urban structure.

Time variables

In Kiruna the main physical variables concern the various directions of the proposed relocation of the new part of the town: will it be to the north, north-west, or east of the current town? Each direction has social variables in types of housing, of which detached luxury houses, terraced middle cost houses or unpretentious apartment blocks will dominate. The time variable consists of each ten year zone, based on the measured speed of mine subsidence. In this way we can identify the reality of dimensional space with the range of possible directions. Each direction can be defined by values of the categorical variables. In addition, the time variable is influenced by changes in the surrounding society, in turn influenced by globalisation.

Each of these variable aspects can be considered in a multi-dimensional space. Analysing events in 'a contingency table' will show samples of reality that can occur. A contingency table is a table where a sample of elements is cross-classified with respect to two or more qualitative variables (Everitt and Dunn via Byrne, 1998, p. 73). We can cross-classify the events in Kiruna in three main variables in a three-way table, including the physical dimension, the social dimension and the time dimension. In this table we can observe the relationship between the dimensions in each cell. All together the table can capture a manifold of variants, which demonstrates the complex situation at hand. The way to analyse the conditions in the form of a contingency table can perhaps provide a way to make more conscious decisions in bifurcation choices. Byrne refers to Cartwright (cited in Byrne, 1998, p. 146) who emphasises that chaotic systems can be predictable only on an incremental or local basis. These local plans for adaptation can have incremental strategies. Cartwright means that comprehensive planning in chaotic systems is too unpredictable because of the cumulative effects of various basic data.

Another time dimension analysed is the inextricable connection between the town of Kiruna and the mining company and the relation to past time, present time and future time. The mining company LKAB is constituted by the collective memory and experiences of the local community. LKAB is at the same time the self-evident future and horizon of expectations for the local community. Coincidently, there is a will to be free from the powerful company, just as youngsters wish to be free from their parents when they are growing up. This love-hate relationship between the town and the company links the past time, present time and future in a non-linear way. That is to say, the past time gives opportunities for the present time when future plans are made. But at the same time, the future plans raise new questions to be asked of the past. And these questions are successively reinterpreted and at the same time give new opportunities for the future.

Despite the system thinking, Byrne declares that we have the possibility of qualitative representations of alternative futures in forms of both literary and pictorial representations (Byrne, 1998, p. 167). These qualitative perspectives seem to have similarities to scenario techniques. The scenario technique implies successive alternatives; in each alternative there are always new choices to take. This, in turn, seems to have similarities to bifurcations; when a system reaches a bifurcation point it is faced with the possibility of choosing from different paths. Kiruna local planning administration has tried to meet some of the uncertainties by working out a political vision together with some scenarios. However the scenarios and their implications are too general for the assessment of the consequences. Otherwise scenarios are a way to get knowledge as basis for more conscious choices and management of uncertainties. As Batty (cited in Byrne, 1998) notes, we understand cities as highly complex dynamic systems.

4.6 Complexity reflected in a critical realistic view

In this section the Kiruna case is considered from the perspective of critical realism. With a critical realistic method the focus is on the mechanisms that produce the events. As presented earlier, reality is assumed to include several domains: the 'domain of reality', the 'domain of events' and the 'empirical domain'. The investigation is made in the visible empirical domain, where the findings are collected. Analysis of documents and interviews has provided the material for this. The first interpretation is made with the aim to understand the domain of events, that is to say which events have caused the occurrences. To find mechanisms in the invisible domain of reality requires even deeper interpretation of the events, that is to say, to search for mechanisms, which strengthen and empower future actions.

From the empirical domain we can identify three main events. One is the global demand for iron-ore which provides the basis for the company's economical assessment of the rate of extension of the mine. The second is the parallel planning processes. The third is the local community's reaction or lack of reaction to the on-going planning processes and the new image of the town. The mechanisms that produce the events have been searched for beyond the invisible.

The global demand for iron-ore is being driven by technical and industrial development. The production of new technological products increases the demand for metals. There is strong economical development in the eastern part of the world, particularly in China and India. The Chinese building boom has increased the global demand for iron-ore and steel and is causing iron-ore prices to rise. This higher market price makes it profitable to expand an iron-ore mine on the other side of the globe, and worthwhile to bear the costs to move an existing town in Kiruna. However, the mechanisms of global prices are not stable and predictable over time, which may cause complex conditions with great uncertainties of future events. Sudden changes can initiate chaotic situations.

The mechanism that is causing the events of planning processes, is the desire of the same local community that will be affected by changed situations, and their methods to estimate the future. Plans are a way of producing strategies to manage uncertain future events. Planning processes are influenced by both linear and non-linear hierarchies between the actors and stakeholders involved. These conditions will also cause complex context and chaotic situations when the different lines tangle.

> In Freire's view, empowerment was about giving people tools for knowledge and understanding so that they could act. The radical end of urban governance, in a complex world, consists in a commitment to the rationality of complexity and the maintenance of collective mechanisms. These mechanisms are for the development of understanding based on that rationality and for the implementation of projects based on collective will (Byrne, 1998, p. 154).

The inhabitants of Kiruna react to events that will affect their situations and daily life. According to complexity theories, these can be caused by the mechanism of self-organising out of chaotic situations. However, surprisingly, the inhabitants have in this case self-organised themselves into calmness and trustfulness, despite the changing and uncertain conditions.

Kiruna planning administration, as well as other Swedish local authorities, has the ambition to cooperate with the local community in the comprehensive planning process. There is great uncertainty about how to involve the public in the on-going processes. On the one hand, the public seems to avoid the complex issues of the unpredictable future. On the other, the public seem to enjoy living in Kiruna despite the harsh climatic conditions. Many stay in Kiruna even though the miners today could live with their families in other places around the country and fly in to Kiruna for working periods, as do employees working on oil platforms at sea.

The urban transformation of Kiruna town is the main spatial dimension of the case study. The spatial dimension is related to the time dimension in the past, the present and the future. During this entire time there have been and will be several events based on the same main realities that are present in and around the town, which have caused different types of occurrences. The town has been located in this place for the past hundred years, with the urban qualities of that time. The planning events occurring in the present time are there to prepare for the future time. Nevertheless we can see that the events in the present time are not following causal chains. This is the reason for the complexity in the present time. It is also the reason for the complex context when qualities from the past time, as for example cultural heritage sites, will meet the requirements and qualities of the future. This future's lack of causal chains makes it challenging for the planners.

These reflections have been a way to illustrate a number of theoretical and practical challenges the planners and the planning researcher meet when looking at the Kiruna occurrences in a scientific perspective of complexity and critical realism.

References

Albrechts, L. (2002) 'Planning and Power', paper presented at the XVI AESOP congress, July 2002, Volos.

Archer, M., Bhaskar, R., Collier, A., Lawson, T. and Norrie, A. (eds.) (1998) *Critical Realism: Essential Readings*, Routledge, London/New York.

Bhaskar, R. (1979) *Philosophy and the Human Sciences*, Harvester Press, Brighton.

Bhaskar, R. (1989) *Reclaiming Reality. A Critical Introduction to Contemporary Philosophy*, Verso, London.

Byrne, D.S. (1998) *Complexity Theory and the Social Sciences: An Introduction*, Routledge, New York.

Danermark, B., Ekström, M., Jakobsen, L. and Karlsson J.C. (1997) 'Att förklara samhället' ['To explain the society'], Studentlitteratur, Academia Adacta, Lund.

Etzioni, A. (1973) 'Mixed-scanning: A third approach to decision making', in A. Faludi (ed.), *A Reader in Planning Theory*, Pergamon Press, Oxford.

Hall, T. (1992) *Urban and Regional Planning,* Routledge, London.

Healey, P. (2007) *Urban Complexity and Spatial Strategies: Towards a Relational Planning for our Times*, Routledge, London/New York.

Jessop, B. (2001) 'The governance of complexity and the complexity of governance', paper available at www.comp.lancaster.ac.uk/sociology/soc024rj. html, Department of Sociology, Lancaster University, Lancaster.

Kain, J.H. (2003) *Sociotechnical Knowledge: An Approach to Localised Infrastructure Planning and Sustainable Urban Development*, Department of Built Environment and School of Architecture, Chalmers University of Technology, Göteborg.

Kiruna Kommun (2006) *Fördjupad översiktsplan för Kiruna centralort: Samrådshandling* [*Deepening of the comprehensive plan for Kiruna town*], Kiruna kommun, kommunkontoret, Kiruna.

Kiruna (2008) http://www.kommun.kiruna.se/web2/ny_web/NyaKirunaweb/ index. html.

Latour, B. (2005) *Reassembling the Social: An Introduction to Actor-Network-Theory*, Oxford University Press, Oxford.

Lindblom, C. (1965) *The Intelligence of Democracy: Decisionmaking through Mutual Adjustment*, Free Press, New York, Collier-Macmillan, London.

Lindblom, C. (1979) 'Still muddling through', *Public Administration Review*, vol. 39, pp. 517-525.

LKAB (2007a) *Nya Kiruna [The New Kiruna*], available at http://www.lkab.com/ ?openform&id=74C2 and http://www.lkab.com/__C12570A1002EAAAE. nsf/($all)/ 0395C011B 79D31FEC1257125004C3CF0/$file/NyaKiruna.pdf.

LKAB (2007b) *Future Plans*, available at http://www.lkab.com/ ?openform&id=7492.

Merry, U. (1995) *Coping with Uncertainty: Insights from the New Sciences of Chaos, Self-Organization, and Complexity*, Praeger Publisher, London.

Regeringskansliet (2006) *Uppdrag att följa utvecklingen av fysisk planering och byggande i Malmfälten* [*Task to follow the development of spatial planning and building in Malmfälten*], Miljö- och samhällsbyggnadsdepartementet, Stockholm.

Sayer, A. (1992) *Method in Social Science: A Realist Approach*, Hutchinson & Co. Ltd, London (second edition).

Sayer, A. (2000) *Realism and Social Science*, Sage Publications, London.

Yin, R.K. (1994) *Case Study Research: Design and Methods*, Sage Publications, London/New Dehli (second edition).

Chapter 5
Complex Systems, Evolutionary Planning?

Luca Bertolini[1]

Coping with uncertainty is a defining challenge for spatial planners. Accordingly, most spatial planning theories and methods are aimed at reducing uncertainty. However, the question is what should be done when this seems impossible? This chapter proposes an evolutionary interpretation of spatial planning as a way of exploring this challenge. It is based on the notion of spatial systems as complex systems and seeks further inspiration in fields where this thinking has been developed in more detail – most notably evolutionary economics. The main normative implications are the need to find a workable fit between planning innovations and local conditions – because of path-dependence – and the need to enhance the resilience and adaptability of the spatial system – because of unpredictability. An ongoing societal dialogue which covers different views on the means and goals of planning and an experimental attitude towards policies are required to identify appropriate interventions.

5.1 Introduction

There is a deep-seated tension between planning's constitutive orientation towards the future and the future's intrinsic uncertainty. Finding ways of dealing with this tension, or reducing uncertainty, is a central challenge for planners and a core objective of planning theories and methods. What should be done, however, when it appears impossible to reduce uncertainty, as in a seemingly increasing range of situations? This chapter explores how an evolutionary interpretation of planning, based on the recognition that social systems are complex systems, might help. The focus is on spatial planning as a combination of transportation and land use planning. Nevertheless, the essence of the argument could be extended to other planning fields. The chapter firstly deals in more detail with this key planning predicament. Secondly, it discusses how an evolutionary interpretation of planning might help address it. Finally, the thus defined 'evolutionary planning' is compared

1 Luca Bertolini is Professor of Urban and Regional Planning at AMIDSt, the Amsterdam Institute for Metropolitan and International Development Studies, University of Amsterdam, The Netherlands.

with emerging planning interpretations and approaches, including those derived from applications of complexity theory to planning.

5.2 Planning and the future

Concern with the future is perhaps the characteristic that most distinguishes planning from other activities, professions and disciplines. Myers (2001, p. 366) remarks that: 'The future is the only topic that other professions have ceded to planners as relatively uncontested turf'. However, the ground the future provides to planners is not, and cannot be a firm one, as the future is by definition uncertain. Myers (2001, p. 365) further articulates the problem by observing that: 'Two difficulties constrain planners' role in shaping the future. First, the future consequences of planning actions are not knowable with much certainty […] Second, […] decisions about the future require agreement among a great many stakeholders'. Finding ways of dealing with such fundamental uncertainty and disagreement about goals and means is a, if not *the*, central task facing planners.

The ideal, rational approach to this task is that of choosing desirable goals, identifying the most effective and efficient means to achieve these goals, and acting accordingly (Simon, 1957; March and Simon, 1958; Simon, 1969). It requires the ability to predict alternative possible future states of a spatial system, and to identify and control the variables that would lead to a preferred state. The practice of spatial planning rarely if ever conforms to this rational ideal. Endemic disagreement and uncertainty about goals and means impedes that. In the real world decisions rather resemble a process of mutual adjustment between different, competing views on goals and means, as conceptualised in the incremental approach to decision making (Lindblom, 1959; Lindblom, 1968; Braybrooke and Lindblom, 1970). The incremental approach has, however, also been criticised, most notably for its risk of aligning with the views of the most powerful and conserving the status quo at the expense of weaker interests and basic innovations. The mixed-scanning approach to decision making (Etzioni, 1967) has attempted to overcome both these critiques by proposing a model of the decision making process that combines 'fundamental' decisions to set basic directions, and 'incremental' decisions to prepare and work out those fundamental decisions. Mixed-scanning seems to many a better characterisation of how decision making processes in spatial planning are and should be. However, it also raises questions about the precise nature of and relationship between fundamental and incremental decisions, and about the mechanism through which they are generated and interact with each other and the context.

We believe that the conceptualisation of spatial systems as complex systems, and of spatial planning as evolutionary can help in this latter respect. As more extensively argued in other parts of this book, complex systems are constituted by an indefinite (and indefinable) number of components and relationships. Because of this characteristic, future states of the system cannot be predicted (or just partially), and relevant variables cannot be identified and controlled (or insufficiently). Hence, improvements in complex systems cannot be just achieved in the ideal, rational way. Also a purely incremental approach is, however, at pains with complex systems, as it neglects another of their fundamental characteristics. This is path-dependence, or the fact that the accumulation of incremental changes in the past fundamentally limits the scope of changes in the future, with a constant risk of suboptimal outcomes, and even to the point of system collapse. A mechanism of improvement that seems to better suit the characteristics of complex systems is evolution, or the process of variation in the features of the system and selection by its environment. Evolution does not require the previous identification of goals and means (other than those intrinsic to the system's environment), the prediction of future states, or the identification and control of relevant variables. At the same time, evolution seems to have been able to cope with many of the crisis that a combination of fundamental change in the environment which the path-dependence of the system inevitably leads to. Evolution is, of course, an established way of describing and explaining change in natural systems. It is, however, being increasingly employed in other fields. In the social sciences it is especially evolutionary economics that has elaborated on these ideas. Following the reasoning so far, it seems thus interesting to explore how the conceptualisations of evolutionary economics, and of evolutionary thinking in general, can help shed light on the challenges of spatial planning. This is what the rest of this chapter attempts.

5.3 Looking for answers: Complexity systems and evolutionary economics

Evolutionary thinking has its origins in the natural sciences but has been increasingly applied to social sciences and most explicitly to economics (Nelson and Winter, 1982; Dosi and Nelson, 1994; Van den Bergh and Fetchenhauer, 2001; Boschma et al., 2002), with a more recent but growing focus on policy implications (Metcalfe, 1994; Rammel and Van den Bergh, 2003; Witt, 2003). Underlying evolutionary thinking in social sciences is the recognition that social systems are complex systems. Because of this complexity, social actors cannot just behave rationally. A set of further assumptions characterises the various streams of theoretical and empirical work. At a micro level, it is posited that different actors can react differently to similar system-wide perturbations, depending on the specificities of the local context and on their individual features (such as attitudes resulting from past experiences). Individual decisions and actions eventually cumulate into system developments that are (a) path-dependent – as earlier experiences largely determine the response to new stimuli – and (b) unpredictable – as even small, local differences can have major, global consequences due to self-reinforcing mechanisms. At macro level, and related to this, the assumption of (a single) equilibrium as the system's 'natural' state is questioned, and attention is directed instead towards far-from-equilibrium processes of change.

A focus on evolutionary economics can help further develop the argument. While different interpretations exist within the field, the basic principles are aptly captured by the notion of microevolution introduced by Nelson and Winter (1982; see also Nelson, 1995; Hall and Soskice, 2001). According to Nelson and Winter, irreducible uncertainty, the existence of transaction costs and the difficulty of change in the short-term mean that firms tend to follow proven ways of conducting business, rather than consider each time all the possible alternative courses of action. Nelson and Winter call these proven ways of doing business 'organisational routines'. On the other hand, the evaluation of current routines can lead firms to implement adjustments and even substitutions. The results of such a 'searching process' are also uncertain. Furthermore, because past experiences influence both existing routines and the search for new ones, different firms will have different routines and try different alternatives, resulting in a variety of economic behaviour. Eventually, the actual performance of a firm will be the major incentive for maintaining or changing a routine. Such performance is dependent on the characteristics of the environment in which the firm operates (most notably constituted by the market, but also by other institutions). Operational routines that fit the environment have more chance of surviving than those that do not. Because of this role in selecting successful behaviour Nelson and Winter call the firm's environment, in analogy with biological evolution, 'selection environment'. The selection environment is not a static entity either, as it will also change as a result of the accumulation of firm-specific processes. In this sense, there is 'co-evolution' between the market, other institutions, and individual firms.

The resulting economic reality is one characterised by continuous successions of disturbances and adaptations which preclude the attainment of a stable equilibrium. Relatively stable periods dominated by quantitative, incremental change are alternated by much more unstable periods dominated by qualitative, radical change – or 'transition phases' – eventually leading to a new equilibrium. Continuous change means that previously successful organisational routines may become less efficient or effective, or even have unexpected consequences. There is no once-and-for-all, optimal routine. Furthermore, the nature of the process underlies the incremental nature of change, and the difficulty of more than marginally altering an existing routine. Because of such 'path-dependence' the risk that firms become 'locked-in' in a non-optimal routine is therefore always present (David, 1985; Arthur, 1989). The implication is that marginal change will not suffice beyond a certain threshold and that coordinated change will be required. However, because it is uncertain which new routines will be able to break the impasse, firms should be stimulated to explore a diversity of new routines. It is precisely such diversity that makes the economic system 'resilient' and 'adaptable' that is capable of continuous performance in the face of changing, uncertain circumstances.

More recently, evolutionary economists have been trying to apply their insights to policy (Metcalfe, 1992; Rammel and Van den Bergh, 2003; Witt, 2003). While this avenue of reflection is still relatively underdeveloped, some principles which deal with policy goals and means on one side and the policy process on the other side have been identified. With respect to policy goals and means, the core principle is that of the need to maintain and increase the *diversity* of organisational routines (Rammel and Van den Bergh, 2003). Since every successful organisational routine is only a temporary solution to changing selective conditions, developing and maintaining a diverse repertoire of alternative options increases the possibility that altered conditions can be successfully met. Diversity gives thus the system an evolutionary advantage, at least in the long term. In this respect, the problem with an excessively strong reliance on market selection mechanisms, as well as conventional narrow policy selection approaches such as those based on cost-benefit analysis, is that they tend to emphasise short-term efficiency at the expense of long-term viability. In the face of this, the aim of an evolutionary approach to policy making should, according to these authors, be to stimulate the generation of diversity through innovation and to ensure that the selection process does not impair diversity-generating mechanisms. There is however, they also observe, an inevitable trade off between maintaining a diversity of organisational routines and achieving short term, local optima, because the former would have to include organisational routines that are less efficient in the present context. A balance between short term efficiency and long term viability needs therefore to be found.

With respect to the policy making process, the distinctive contribution made by an evolutionary approach is the notion that the knowledge of all the actors involved changes during the course of the process (Witt, 2003). In other words, actors can and do *learn*. This is true for both positive knowledge (means-goals relationships) and normative knowledge (values, interests), and for both policy makers and actors affected by policies. Intersubjective learning is necessary because some degree of shared positive and normative knowledge is a condition for collective action. Finding ways of enhancing and acknowledging learning processes of policy makers and those affected by policies is thus, in this view, a crucial condition for successful collective action.

5.4 Evolutionary planning?

How can the above conceptualisation can be applied to the issue of how to cope with irreducible uncertainty in planning? With reference to spatial planning, existing transport and land use policies can be seen as 'organisational routines'. The broader socio-demographic and economic context – as embodied by actors and institutions in the spatial political arena – can be seen as the 'selection environment' in which existing policies must continuously prove their worth and the searching process for fitter policies takes place. As policies, in turn, also affect the selection environment, there is 'co-evolution' between environment and policies. The analogy with evolutionary economics further suggests that there is no universally valid, optimal set of policies. While it is important to learn from practical experience elsewhere and from theoretical models, the value of a solution can only be appreciated in a specific, continuously evolving local situation. Understanding the unique set of opportunities and constraints determined by a given historical development and local configuration of factors – that is, 'path-dependence' – is therefore essential.

However, because of the limits to predictability, only actual engagement with the policy selection environment (the actors and institutions in the spatial political arena) can provide such understanding. This engagement, for-real or simulated, amounts to a 'policy experiment' of a sort (Szejnwald Brown et al., 2004).

Recognition of the unpredictability of the outcome – particularly in the long term – should also result in recognition of the need to look for ways of improving the ability of the spatial system to react and perform in the face of unforeseen (and unforeseeable) change. A transport and land use system capable of performing in the face of unpredictable change would, in the first place, be capable of continuing to function in the face of change. In other words, it must be a 'resilient' system. Secondly, it would be a system capable of changing itself in response to change in the socio-economic environment. In other words, it must also be an 'adaptable' system. As the requirements of resilience and adaptability might be contradictory, finding an optimal balance between them lies at the heart of the task (Holling, 1973; Walker et al., 2004). The identification of this optimal balance can, however, only partly be accomplished beforehand and will also require actual engagement with the selection environment (actual actors and institutions in the spatial political arena, or possibly some simulation thereof), or 'policy experiments'.

The interpretation of planning following from the above can be summarised in three core-principles:

i. The first principle is that the spatial system changes in an evolutionary fashion. Defining, interrelated features are the occurrence of transition phases, the existence of path-dependence and the unpredictability of future states.
ii. The second, related principle is that land use and transportation policies need to find a fit with local conditions (because of path-dependence) and enhance the resilience and the adaptability of the system (because of unpredictability).
iii. The third and final principle is that 'policy experiments' (real or simulated) are essential for the identification of successful policies.

These three core principles will be examined in more detail in the next sections. Developments in the Amsterdam region in the post-war period will serve as an illustration (for a more in-depth discussion of this case see Bertolini, 2007).

5.5 The first principle: Features of evolutionary change

There are three defining features of evolutionary change identified by both the economics literature cited above and evolutionary work in other fields. The first is that it alternates periods of incremental, quantitative change and periods of radical, qualitative change, or system transition phases. The second defining feature is that change in the spatial system is path-dependent. In other words, existing system characteristics fundamentally limit the scope for change. The third and final defining feature is that change in the spatial system is, to a significant extent,

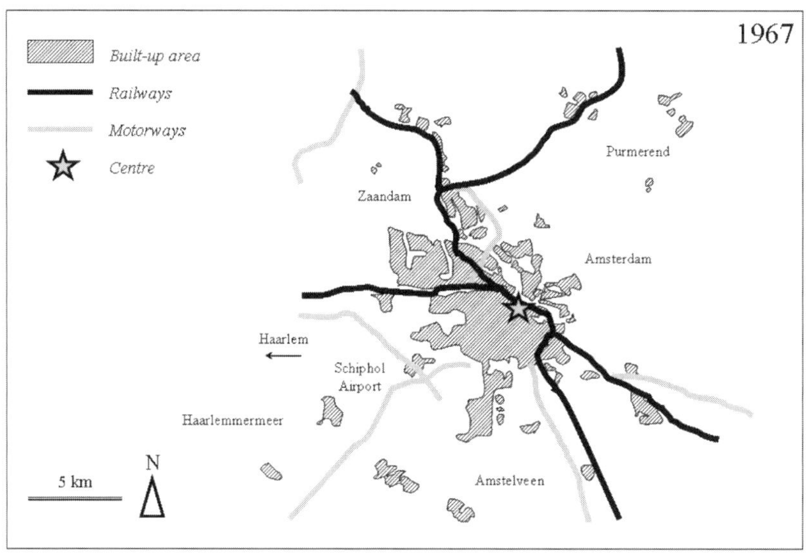

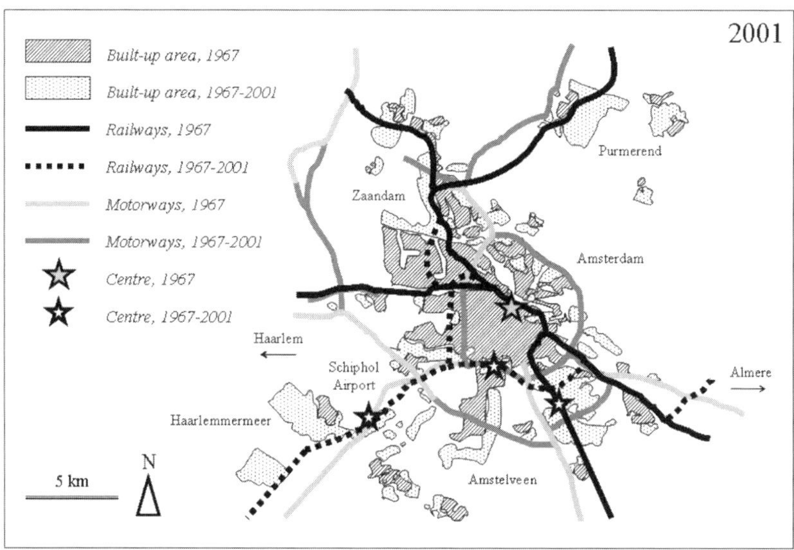

Figure 5.1 Changes in the built-up area and the infrastructure in the Amsterdam region, 1967-2001

Source: Adapted from Jansen, 2003.

unpredictable. As a consequence, interventions in the system will always also have significant unexpected effects.

All these three characteristics can be illustrated by means of developments of the Amsterdam spatial system in the second half of the past century. Next to more stable periods and incremental change, there were several instances of instability and more radical change. Massive migration by middle-class families from the city to the suburbs, their substitution by successive waves of foreign immigrants, and the emergence of new urban lifestyles in the city resulted in a major socio-demographic transition. Also the urban economy underwent radical change as traditional industrial activities were supplanted by business and financial services, leisure and tourism, and logistics, following a deep crisis in the 1970s and 1980s. Socio-demographic and economic change was accompanied by a fundamental reorganisation of the transport and land use structure, as a strongly radial transportation system which was focused on a single centre transformed into a complex multi-modal network supporting multiple centralities (Figure 5.1).

Both path-dependence and unpredictability characterised the changes sketched above. Spatial path-dependence, the second defining feature of evolutionary change, was most evident in the failure of repeated attempts to carry out a radical transformation of the physical fabric of the historic city centre. In the end, only policies which refrained from such radical morphological alterations were implemented. This is epitomised by the failure of a far-reaching, top-down approach to the transformation of the historic city centre, and the shift to a much more cautious, bottom-up approach as described in Box 5.1.

In the 1960s far-reaching urban renewal and infrastructure plans for Amsterdam were proposed. Population growth was to be accommodated in new expansions on the urban periphery and in 'growth centres' in the region; service growth was to be concentrated in an enlarged and restructured city centre; and new road and underground railway infrastructure was to be developed to link the new concentrations of population, jobs and services. Both the city council and the city planners backed these plans, and implementation started. However, and unexpectedly, it was met with forceful public resistance, in particular to the envisaged radical transformation of the historic city. Years of political turmoil followed, until a new and fundamentally different policy course emerged. 'Urban renewal' was traded for 'building for the neighbourhood': incremental, housing-led adaptation of the historic city without displacement of the existing inhabitants. On the transport side, development of new, heavy infrastructure was traded for improvement of the existing tram system, introduction of more hierarchy in the existing road network, imposition of a restrictive parking policy, and creation of new cycling routes.

Box 5.1 The late 1960s and early 1970s, a transport and land use policy transition dissected

Sources: Le Clercq, 2002; Dienst Ruimtelijke Ordening Amsterdam, 2003; Dijkstra et al., 1999; Honig, 1996; Poelstra, 2003.

5.6 The second principle: Policy implications of path-dependency and unpredictability

How did spatial planning cope with these developments? In which sense can successful transport and land use policies be characterised as evolutionary? The focus will first be on the policy implications of path-dependence and then on those of unpredictability.

The policy implication of path-dependence is that successful policies need to find a fit with the unique set of opportunities and constraints for change determined by a specific historical development path and local combination of factors. The issue of path-dependence is a wide-ranging one, cutting across multiple aspects and different layers of economic, social and cultural trends. This paragraph will have to limit itself to no more than a reference to morphological aspects. The fact that successful policies (that is, policies that have achieved their declared goals) have found a fit with the existing urban morphology, rather than ignoring it, is taken as evidence of the acknowledgment of path-dependence. The failure of attempts to radically transform the city centre and the success of more morphologically (but not necessarily economically or socially) conservative land use and transport policies there, are the clearest illustrations of this in Amsterdam (see Box 5.1).

The second policy implication of evolutionary change is that, due to unpredictability, spatial policies need to increase the resilience of the spatial system, that is its ability to *keep functioning* in the face of unexpected change. In Amsterdam, the shape of the infrastructure networks seems to have had this characteristic. The combination of motorway and railway radials and tangents shown in Figure 5.1 was able to support a wide variety of developments across the whole period. These importantly included both developments before and development after transition phases, thus developments that could not be anticipated when the infrastructure was conceived and laid down. Examples of these developments are the sharply shifting foci of economic and social activity from one to multiple centres (Figure 5.1); changes in the transport systems (as in the shift from a freight to a passenger function, and from just a national to also a local scale: see Bertolini, 2007); or radical policy shifts as the one described in Box 5.1.

The third and last policy implication is that, due to unpredictability, there is also a need to increase the adaptability of the system, that is its ability to *react* to unexpected change. The fact that policies that were not resilient in the sense discussed above needed to be adapted in order to succeed can be seen as illustration of this point. The most poignant example seems, once again, to be the radical change of course of transport and land use policies in the 1970s (see Box 5.1). Such policy adaptation has been an essential condition for the development of the new, quite successful policy mix that – at least as far as the historic city of Amsterdam is concerned – has been considered viable up to the present day (whether this will also hold for the future is, of course, a different matter).

5.7 The third principle: Identifying policies through experiment

The central contention made above is that a spatial system capable of supporting change is also one capable of continuing to function in the face of change. In other words it must be a resilient system. Secondly, a spatial system capable of supporting change must be able to adapt itself in response to changes in the socio-economic environment. In other words, it must also be an adaptable system. The above characterisation of the Amsterdam case illustrates both some of the workings of resilience and adaptability, and context specific ways (that is, ways that take account of path-dependence) of achieving them. But how have the policies behind these results been identified? In this respect, the Amsterdam case seems to suggest that there are limits to a purely 'rational choice' (in the sense of Simon, 1957) approach to achieving resilience and adaptability. The present, resilient transport network morphology is, for instance, the result of a very long chain of decisions and actions, which sometimes contributed unconsciously or unwillingly to the final result, rather than being the product of one piece of long-range planning (details in Bertolini, 2007). Also the ultimately successful land use and mobility management policy transition described in Box 5.1 emerged after a protracted period of conflicts and contradictions, rather than through a rational process of goal and means selection, and many effects were not anticipated. In both cases there seems, however, to be more at play than just incremental mutual adjustments between competing views. The outcomes were far form being just a confirmation of the status quo and the then powerful interests. How can these processes be then interpreted?

A possible answer lies in the third core principle of evolutionary planning, the idea the 'policy experiments' are essential for the identification of adequate policies. A reference to Christensen's (1985) characterisation of how to cope with uncertainty in planning can help articulate this idea further.

According to Christensen planning problems can be characterised in terms of the uncertainty about goals and the means of achieving them (what she terms 'technology').[2] If there is agreement on goals and the technology is known 'programming' can take place. If no agreement can be reached on goals, 'bargaining' needs to take place. If not enough is known about the technology, 'experiments' should be carried out. The existence of both disagreement about goals and uncertainty about technology results in 'chaos', and 'order' must somehow 'be discovered'. This last, 'chaotic' situation is particularly irrelevant here. Situations of this type seem by no means atypical in planning. They are, arguably, even characteristic. But what is exactly 'chaos'? And, more importantly,

2 In the following, and as in Christensen (1985), the term 'technology' will be used in the broad sense of a 'means to achieve goals'. In this respect a transportation system is a technology, as is a zoning regime, or a marketing campaign. Furthermore, the term is inclusive of the economic, social and cultural institutions that identify the context in which a technology is developed and applied.

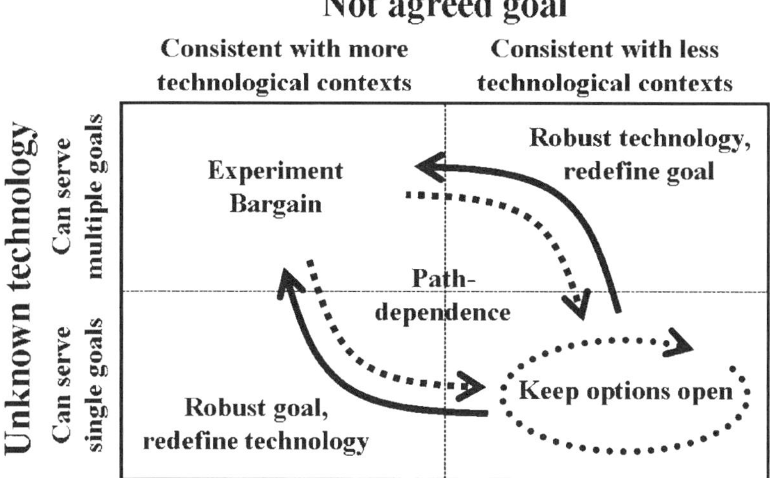

Figure 5.2 Coping with irreducible uncertainty in planning

what exactly does 'discovering order' mean? Figure 5.2 sketches a possible, evolutionary interpretation.

In Figure 5.2, the bottom right quadrant – disagreement about goals and uncertainty about technology, or 'chaos' – of Christensen's typology is blown up. The starting point is the observation that even when there is no agreement on the goals, a distinction can be made between goals that are not agreed but that are consistent with different future technological contexts and goals that are not. For instance, a goal as 'accommodating the growth of the urban economy' might not be shared by all actors but will remain meaningful irrespective of how the technological context will develop. On the contrary, a goal as 'accommodating the growth of a specific economic sector in a specific location' is not only a goal that not everybody will share but is also much more dependent on a specific technological context (for example, a location which is central in a railway dominated transport system will not necessarily be so in a car dominated system). By analogy, even when nothing is known about the technology, a distinction can be made between a technology that only has the potential to serve limited goals (as, for instance, a transportation system connecting a limited number of places in a limited number of ways) and a technology that has the potential to serve more goals (as a transportation system connecting more places in more ways).

If goals are not agreed *and* only relevant in a limited range of future technological contexts, and technologies are unknown *and* can only serve limited goals, options should be kept open, thus preserving the adaptability of the system. With reference to the illustrations above, an irreversible choice for 'accommodating the growth of a specific economic sector in a specific location' should not be made, acknowledging that other sectors and other locations could later emerge. The same would apply, on the technology side, to 'a transportation system connecting a limited number of places in a limited number of ways' (as apparently was in Amsterdam the system being first proposed in the 1960s; see Box 5.1). By contrast, when goals are not agreed *but* are consistent with more technological contexts, and when technologies are unknown *but* can serve many goals they are, at least potentially, *robust* goals and technologies and should be further explored. With reference to the illustrations above, even if not everybody agrees, a goal as 'accommodating the growth of the urban economy' should be acknowledged, as it is likely to continue to play a role in whatever technological future. The same applies to the technology 'a transportation system connecting more places in more ways', because it is likely to be able to serve more goals (as was apparently the case in Amsterdam with the much more articulated system that emerged at the end of the policy transition described in Box 5.1). However, because of the limits to predictability, only real-life (and possibly simulated) bargaining and experimentation – or 'policy experiments' – will tell how relevant this potential robustness is. If it is, policies should be developed further to allow implementation, as they are likely to improve the resilience of the system. If it is not, options will have to be reopened. In the course of this continuous, negotiated and experimental process, the opportunities for and constraints on policy intervention set by local conditions (or path-dependence) can be also appreciated and policies can be modified to take account of them (as happened in the policy transition sketched in Box 5.1).

5.8 Evolutionary planning and complexity

The evolutionary interpretation of planning sketched above – which in the following we will call for simplicity 'evolutionary planning' – is neither the only nor the first to try and address the challenges of irreducible uncertainty. In order to identify what the possibilities for cross-fertilisation or even integration between different interpretations and approaches, some of them are compared below. While the overview is not exhaustive, the planning interpretations and approaches discussed share a fundamental feature. They focus on ways to cope with *irreducible* uncertainty. In that, they are different from more traditional planning interpretations and approaches that rather focus on ways of *reducing* uncertainty, that is on finding a consensus on *one* view of the future. They include more operational methods such as Adaptive Management and Adaptive Governance (AM: Holling, 1978; Walters, 1986; AG: Dietz et al., 2003), the Strategic Choice Approach (SCA: Friend and Hickling, 2005), and Robust Decision making methods for long-term policy analysis (RDM: Lempert et al., 2003). They also include the more conceptual, emerging applications of complexity theory to planning discussed elsewhere in this book and in other contributions (CT: Teisman, 1992; Portugali, 1999; De Roo, 2003; Alfasi and Portugali, 2004; Teisman, 2005; see also Innes and Booher, 1999; Byrne, 2003).[3] These will serve as terms of reference for the rest of the discussion.

The central challenge of planning in the face of irreducible uncertainty is to 'acknowledge deep uncertainty *and simultaneously* provide operational policy recommendations' (Lempert et al., 2003, p. 19, emphasis added). 'Evolutionary planning' as conceptualised in this chapter seeks a solution in the identification of robust measures – to enhance the resilience of the system – and options which can and should be left open – to enhance the adaptability of the system. The focus on the identification of robust measures (and conversely, on options to leave open) is shared with the SCA and RDM. The SCA has a robustness index for the purpose, 'a "robust" action being seen as one which is preferable to others in that it leaves open a wider range of acceptable paths for the future' (Friend and Hickling, 2005, p. 60). RDM are methods to 'frame arguments about near-term policy actions that hold true for the full range of plausible futures and that are acknowledged as useful and valid by all concerned parties' (Lempert et al., 2003, p. 44). It connects this search for robust actions to the need to enhance the 'adaptivity' of the system, that is, of 'identifying, assessing, and choosing among near-term actions that shape options available to future generations' (Lempert et al., 2003, p. 59). The other interpretations, methods and approaches cited above are implicit rather than explicit about the relationship between the acknowledgement of irreducible uncertainty and the need to identify robust policy measures.

A second feature of evolutionary planning is that, in line with Christensen (1985), it distinguishes between uncertainty about goals and uncertainty about means. A similar distinction is also made in RDM, SCA, and AG. The aim of RDM is to 'seek robust [...] strategies that perform "well enough" by meeting or exceeding selected criteria across a broad range of plausible features *and* alternative ways of ranking the desirability of alternative scenarios' (Lempert et al. 2003, p. 45, emphasis added). The SCA distinguishes between 'uncertainty about guiding values' (analogous to uncertainty about goals) and 'uncertainty about the working environment' (analogous to uncertainty about means).[4] AG 'involves making tough decisions under uncertainty, complexity, and substantial biophysical constraints *as well as* conflicting human values and interests' (Dietz et al., 2003, p. 3 of download version, emphasis added). This distinction is less explicit in the other interpretations, methods and approaches. However, it is analytically important as it highlights two distinct planning challenges. The first is how to reach agreements

---

3 For more examples of, and an ongoing discussion of, applications of complexity theory to planning, readers are advised to visit the site of the thematic group 'Planning and Complexity' of the Association of European Schools of Planning (AESOP) at www.aesop-planning.com.

4 The SCA also identifies a third type of uncertainty, namely 'uncertainty about related decisions' which accounts for organisational and institutional aspects. This is a dimension of uncertainty also explicitly recognised by De Roo (2003) and Teisman (1992, 2005), and implicitly rather than explicitly addressed in this chapter.

about goals and the other is how to reach agreement about how to achieve goals? Each challenge points to a different sort of planning action, namely 'bargaining' and 'experimenting' respectively. However at the same time, evolutionary planning – such as RDM, the SCA, and AG – recognises that the two types of challenges and actions cannot be separated in practice. This is why it focuses on situations where both apply (the 'chaotic' quadrant in Christensen's typology). The concept of 'policy experiment' has been introduced to try and capture this idea of bargaining while experimenting, experimenting while bargaining. In this double emphasis, evolutionary planning, RDM, the SCA, and AG are distinct from collaborative planning (Healey, 1997) and similar 'communicative' interpretations of land use planning, where the emphasis tends to be on coping with uncertainty about goals, or bargaining. They are also distinct from emerging transportation planning approaches such as transition management (Kemp and Rotmans, 2004), where the emphasis is rather on coping with uncertainty about means, or experimenting.

In more abstract terms, evolutionary planning recognises the need to distinguish between, and link, what Mannheim (1940, 1949) would call substantive and functional rationality, and what Faludi (1973, 1984) would call theories in planning and theories of planning, or the questions of 'what to plan' and 'how to plan' (see also De Roo, 2003). The identification of the overarching goal of planning as that of enhancing the resilience and adaptability of its object is about substantive rationality ('what to plan'), and it is shared with AM and AG. The characterisation of the planning process as a continuous search for robust measures and options that need to be left open is related to functional rationality ('how to plan'), and it is shared with the SCA and RDM. The importance of distinguishing between the substantial and functional dimensions of planning is that arguments about 'what to plan' (what are robust interventions?) and 'how to plan' (how to identify them?) can be assessed and developed according to their own merits and internal logic. The importance of linking them is that different types of knowledge and rationality, both substantive and functional, can thus be tapped into, can meaningfully interact, and can potentially reinforce each other.

Evolutionary planning is conceptual rather than operational, it is an interpretation rather than an approach, or method. It shares this feature with Complexity Theory applications and in this way it is different from operational methods as the SCA and RDM, while AM and AG occupy a middle ground. This offers both advantages and disadvantages. The obvious disadvantage is that it cannot be readily or directly applied. An advantage is that it can serve as an interpretative and assessment framework of more diffuse, less formalised planning processes. The above discussion of the Amsterdam case is one illustration. It is a relevant characteristic: a lot of planning cannot be clearly defined with recognisable content borders, a beginning and an end, and a finite number of actors, issues and arenas, as for instance implied by SCA and RDM. This is an argument that is also made forcefully by CT thinkers (e.g. Teisman, 1992; Portugali, 1999; De Roo, 2003; Alfasi and Portugali, 2004; Teisman, 2005; see also Healey, 1997).

Evolutionary planning draws inspiration from the natural sciences. This is a final feature, and one shared with AM, AG, and CT applications. All these are based on concepts which have been originally developed in order to understand natural phenomena, and consider them potentially relevant for understanding of social phenomena. Importantly however, this belief is grounded in more than vague associations between natural and social phenomena. The point of departure is rather the observation that, at a meta-systemic level, there are fundamental parallels between natural and social systems in that both are characterised by many components and relationships which are at least partly indefinite and of which full knowledge can never be acquired. Because of this, both are only partially predictable and controllable (uncertainty is to a significant extent irreducible). Order emerges from within rather than being imposed from the outside. Some understanding of how this happens is an essential precondition if attempts at influencing development of the system (that is, planning) are to succeed.

5.9 Conclusion

Dealing with the irreducible uncertainty (and welcome openness!) of the future is an essential task of planning. Both disagreement about goals and lack of knowledge concerning the means need to be addressed at the same time, as disagreement and lack of knowledge are irreducible to a considerable extent. Classic planning methods and theories have not yet dealt adequately with this fact. A number of emerging planning interpretations, methods and approaches seem to be deliberately building on it instead. This chapter has outlined one such possible interpretation. The point of departure was the conceptualisation of spatial systems as complex systems. Further inspiration was sought in evolutionary theories and methods, as originated in the biological sciences and introduced and further developed in the social sciences and most notably economics. Evolutionary theories and methods have not entered yet the realm of planning theory, at least not explicitly. The case for planning practice might be a different one, because if the argument of this chapter is accepted, it follows that successful plans must have already had, *de facto* if not literally, an evolutionary dimension. Establishing whether this is the case, that is further exploring and testing the principles advanced here against past experiences, is therefore an obvious line of research which could follow on from this discussion. A second direction of work, and one which is also a form of research, is to try and apply these insights to current planning issues. Doing so might allow some of the more operational methods discussed in the last section to be integrated in the interpretation.

References

Alfasi, N. and Portugali, J. (2004) 'Planning just-in-time versus planning just-in-case', *Cities*, vol. 21(1), pp. 29-39.

Arthur, W.B. (1989) 'Competing technologies, increasing returns, and lock-in by historical events', *The Economic Journal*, vol. 99, pp. 116-131.

Bertolini, L. (2007) 'Evolutionary transportation planning? An exploration', *Environment and Planning A*, vol. 39(8), pp. 1998-2019.

Braybrooke, D. and Lindblom, C. (1970) *A Strategy of Decision*, Free Press, New York.

Boschma, R., Frenken, K. and Lambooy, J.G. (2002) *Evolutionaire economie. Een inleiding* [*Evolutionary economics: An introduction*], Coutinho, Bussum.

Byrne, D. (2003) 'Complexity theory and planning theory: A necessary encounter', *Planning Theory*, vol. 2(3), pp. 171-178.

Christensen, K.S. (1985) 'Coping with uncertainty in planning', *APA Journal*, vol. 51(1), pp. 63-73.

David, P.A. (1985) 'The economics of QWERTY', *American Economic Review*, vol. 75(3), pp. 332-337.

De Roo, G. (2003) *Environmental Planning in the Netherlands: Too Good to be True: From Command-and-Control Planning to Shared Governance*, Ashgate, Aldershot (first published 1999 in Dutch).

Dienst Ruimtelijke Ordening Amsterdam (ed.) (2003) *Stadsplan Amsterdam: Toekomstvisies op de ruimtelijke ontwikkeling van de stad, 1928-2003* [*City plan Amsterdam: Future visions of the spatial developments of the city, 1928-2003*], Nai Uitgevers, Rotterdam.

Dietz, T., Ostrom, E. and Stern, P.C. (2003) 'The struggle to govern the commons', *Science*, vol. 302(5652), pp. 1907-1912.

Dosi, G. and Nelson, R.R. (1994) 'An introduction to evolutionary theories in economics', *Journal of Evolutionary Economics*, vol. 4(3), pp. 153-172.

Dijkstra, C., Retisma, M. and Rommerts, A. (1999) *Atlas Amsterdam*, Thoth, Bussum.

Etzioni, A. (1967) 'Mixed scanning: A "third" approach to decision making', *Public Administration Review*, vol. 27(5), pp. 385-392.

Faludi, A. (1973) *Planning Theory*, Pergamon, Oxford.

Friend, J. and Hickling, A. (2005) *Planning Under Pressure: The Strategic Choice Approach, Third Edition*, Elsevier, Amsterdam (first edition 1987).

Hall, P.A. and Soskice, D. (2001) *Varieties of Capitalism: The Institutional Foundations of Comparative Advantage*, Oxford University Press, Oxford.

Healey, P. (1997) *Collaborative Planning: Shaping Places in Fragmented Societies*, Macmillan, Houndmills/London.

Holling, C.S. (1973) 'Resilience and stability of ecological systems', *Annual Review of Ecological Systems*, vol. 4, pp. 1-23.

Holling, C.S. (ed.) (1978) *Adaptive Environmental Assessment and Management*, John Wiley & Sons, Chichester.

Honig, R. (1996) 'Railinfrastructuur in Amsterdam: Trein, metro, sneltram' ['Rail infrastructure in Amsterdam: Train, metro, tram'] *PlanAmsterdam*, vol. 2(9-10), pp. 1-26.

Innes, J.E. and Booher, D.E. (1999) 'Consensus building and complex adaptive systems: A framework for evaluating collaborative planning', *Journal of the American Planning Association*, vol. 65(4), pp. 412-423.

Kemp, R. and Rotmans, J. (2004) 'Managing the transition to sustainable mobility', in B. Elzen, F.W. Geels and K. Green (eds.), *System Innovation and the Transition to Sustainability*, Edward Elgar, Cheltenham, pp. 137-167.

Jansen, A. (2003) 'Co-evolutie van infrastructuur en verstedelijkingsstructuur' ['Co-evolution of infrastructure and urbanisation'], MA Thesis, University of Amsterdam, Amsterdam.

Le Clercq, F. (2002) 'Planologie en mobiliteit in Amsterdam' ['Planning and mobility Amsterdam'], in H. Knippenberg and M. van Schendelen (eds.), *Alles heeft zijn Plaats: 125 jaar Geografie en Planologie aan de Universiteit van Amsterdam, 1877-2002* [*Everything has its Place: 125 years of Geography and Planning at the University of Amsterdam, 1877-2002*], Askant, Amsterdam, pp. 399-419.

Lempert, R.J., Popper, S.W. and Bankes, S.C. (2003) *Shaping the Next One Hundred Years: New Methods for Quantitative, Long-Term Policy Analysis*, RAND, Santa Monica.

Lindblom, C. (1959) 'The science of muddling through', *Public Administration Review*, vol. 19(2), pp. 79-88.

Lindblom, C. (1968) *The Policy-Making Process*, Prentice-Hall, Englewood Cliff.

Mannheim, K. (1940) *Man and Society in an Age of Reconstruction*, Routledge & Kegan Paul, London.

Mannheim, K. (1949) *Ideology and Utopia*, Harcourt Brace, New York.

March, J. and Simon, H. (1958) *Organizations*, Wiley, New York.

Metcalfe, J.S. (1994) 'Evolutionary economics and technology policy', *The Economic Journal*, vol. 104(425), pp. 931-944.

Myers, D. (2001) 'Introduction', *APA Journal*, vol. 67(4), pp. 365-367.

Nelson, R. and Winter, S. (1982) *Evolutionary Theory of Economic Change*, Harvard University Press, Cambridge.

Nelson, R. (1995) 'Co-evolution of industry structure, technology and supporting institutions, and the making of comparative advantage', *International Journal of the Economics of Business*, vol. 2(2), pp. 171-184.

Poelstra, H. (2003) 'Eerst infrastructuur, dan beleid' ['First infrastructure, then policy'], in Dienst Ruimtelijk Ordening, Gemeente Amsterdam (ed.), *Stadsplan Amsterdam, 1928-2003* [*City Plan Amsterdam, 1928-2003*], Nai Uitgevers, Rotterdam, pp. 118-129.

Portugali, J. (1999) *Self-Organization and the City*, Springer, Berlin.

Rammel, C. and Van den Bergh, J.C.J.M. (2003) 'Evolutionary policies for sustainable development: Adaptive flexibility and risk minimizing', *Ecological Economics*, vol. 43(2-3), pp. 121-133.

Simon, H. (1957) 'A behavioral model of rational choice', in H. Simon (ed.), *Models of Man*, Wiley, New York, pp. 241-260.

Simon, H. (1969) *Sciences of the Artificial*, MIT Press, Cambridge.

Szejnwald Brown, H., Vergragt, P.J., Green, K. and Bechicchi, L. (2004) 'Bounded socio-technical experiments (BSTEs): Higher order learning for transitions towards sustainable mobility', in B. Elzen, F.W. Geels and K. Green (eds.), *System Innovation and the Transition to Sustainability*, Edward Elgar, Cheltenham, pp. 191-219.

Teisman, G. (1992) *Complexe besluitvorming. Een pluricentrisch perspectief op besluitvorming over ruimtelijke investeringen* [*Complex decision making. A pluricentric perspective on decision making on spatial investments*], VUGA, The Hague.

Teisman, G. (2005) *Publiek management op de grens van chaos en orde. Over leidinggeven en organiseren in complexiteit* [*Public management at the border of chaos and order. About leadership and organisation in complexity*], Sdu Uitgevers, The Hague.

Terhorst, P. and Van de Ven, J. (2003) 'The economic restructuring of the historic city centre', in S. Musterd and W. Salet (eds.), *Amsterdam Human Capital*, Amsterdam University Press, Amsterdam, pp. 85-101.

Van den Bergh, J. and Fetchenhauer, D. (2001) *Voorbij het Rationele Model: Evolutionaire Verklaringen van Gedrag en Sociaal-Economische Instituties* [*Beyond the Rational Model: Evolutionary Explanations of Behaviour and Social-Economic Institutions*], NWO/MaGW, The Hague.

Walker, B., Holling C.S., Carpenter S.R. and Kinzig, A. (2004) 'Resilience, adaptability and transformability in socio-ecological systems', *Ecology and Society*, vol. 9(2), art. 5.

Walters, C. (1986) *Adaptive Management of Renewable Resources*, Macmillan Publishers, New York.

Witt, U. (2003) 'Economic policy making in evolutionary perspective', *Journal of Evolutionary Economics*, vol. 13(2), pp. 77-94.

Chapter 6
Complexity in City Systems: Understanding, Evolution, and Design

Michael Batty[1]

As we learn more about the world and reflect on its meaning, an overwhelming sense of inadequacy in our ability to both understand and change it has developed. In many disciplines, the idea of 'complexity' as a coherent perspective for organising our knowledge has come to the fore. These 'complexity sciences' first evolved from ideas associated with dynamic systems through ideas about chaos, non-linearity, disruptive technologies, emergence and surprise. Recently they have begun to infuse areas as diverse as postmodernism and management. Cities and planning have not escaped this force, indeed in some respects they are in the vanguard of these developments.

In this chapter, we will sketch how this movement has evolved. Throughout we make a key distinction between the evolution of cities and the processes used in their planning and design, first fashioning complexity around the notion of the city as a system but then moving to examining how problems of their design and planning reveal a rather different type of complexity. We conclude with speculations about fostering change in cities in the light of this complexity. We propose a somewhat less invasive, more sensitive bottom-up style of physical planning that is in stark contrast to the institutionalisation of planning and its practice which still dominates most developed societies.

6.1 The argument, a message

> ... there is a fundamental law about the creation of complexity [...] [which] states simply this: *all* the well-ordered systems that we know in the world, all those anyway that we view as highly successful, are *generated* structures, not fabricated structures (Alexander, 2002, p. 80).

A very simple definition of a complex system is 'a system that is composed of complex systems'. This recursion makes considerable sense when we ponder systems such as economies and cities for their elements – individuals – clearly

---

1 Michael Batty is Barlett Professor of Planning at University College London, Centre for Advanced Spatial Analysis, London, UK.

have the same order of complexity as any aggregation into groups or institutions while any disaggregation into constituent parts moves quickly into physiology and psychology. Artefacts that we build to give physical representation to cities can also be so partitioned into their component parts blurring into the material world which has its own logic and structure. In the past, we have tended to see these different levels as being systems in their own right which can be partitioned easily and conveniently from the rest of the world. But it is increasingly clear that although such an assumption might have been useful in making initial progress, as soon as this science came to be applied to human affairs, such assumptions of independence between levels are no longer tenable.

In the last 30 or so years, the complexity sciences have developed to make sense of such systems, and in doing so, have begun to fashion a theory and method which is rapidly gaining credence in the social sciences and beyond. In the mid-20th century, the prevailing view of society was one which treated social structure akin to the way machines functioned. This was not very surprising given the advances in science and technology of the previous two centuries but the metaphor of the city as a machine ignored self-determination and was only barely applicable in the most cursory ways to social problems. In the early 21st century, it is clear that a radical shift in metaphor is taking place to thinking of cities and societies as organisms, as biological rather than physical systems, echoing the quote from Alexander (2002) which introduces this chapter. This is also a switch from thinking of cities as being artefacts to be designed to thinking of them as systems that evolve, that grow and change in ways that might be steered and managed but rarely designed from the top down. This also reveals a shift from an emphasis on structure and form to one of behaviour and process and it mirrors the slow march from the physicalism which dominated city planning a generation or more ago to a serious concern for social process.

At the same time, these changes in perspective have been paralleled and sustained by a profound move in western societies from top-down, centralised structures of government and management to much more decentralised organisations which suppose that effective action comes from the grass roots, from the bottom up. This accords closely with the notion that cities grow from the bottom up, the concerted action of millions of individuals and agencies that generate structures of complexity that are virtually impossible to manage, control or redesign from the top down. At the same time, the development of technologies that enable much larger fractions of the population to gain access to information than hitherto, has given added impetus to the notion that systems evolve and grow from the bottom up, the world wide web being the seminal example. We continually need to be reminded of course that Adam Smith's (1776) view of the emergent modern economy in his *Wealth of Nations* published over 200 years ago was in similar vein. The 'hidden hand' of coordination which he argued enabled the economy to grow and function without falling apart, became the cornerstone of general equilibrium theory which is the classical edifice on which contemporary economics is constructed.

No one would pretend that cities and societies only grow in competitive and uncoordinated fashion from the bottom up for individuals act in groups, they form institutions with governments of various kinds acting in top-down fashion but at different levels. The complexity paradigm simply changes the focus from top down to bottom up, emphasising that actions are as much local as global but with structure and order emerging as much, if not more, from the bottom up. In fact the leitmotiv of the complexity sciences is that the order we observe 'emerges' from actions and decisions where individuals and agents respond to their environment and each other, competitively and collaboratively from the bottom up. Here we will sketch this logic for cities and their planning. We will begin by describing the development of a systems perspective 50 years ago, indicating how it was found wanting in important ways. The systems approach espoused the notion of the city as a machine and planning as its controller but it took the move from thinking of systems as physical entities to biological to generate the kind of insights that complexity theory is now bringing to our world.

After a sketch of this history, we will define the rudiments of complex systems and complexity theory, following this with some pertinent examples relating to urban structure at micro and macro levels. Our argument then veers towards the design of better cities, to planning and the problems that it attempts to alleviate. We then show how planning needs to respond to the ways in which cities evolve and change such that new styles need to be fashioned from the bottom up. This leads to the notion that in the solution of urban problems, far fewer interventions at much more appropriate entry or 'leverage' points are required, echoing many clichés from the past which as Anderson (1972) has argued, are widely applicable to the complexity sciences: 'less is more' and 'more is different'.

6.2 The systems approach

The notion that there might be a general theory applicable to the structure and behaviour of phenomena forming the subject matter of many different disciplinary perspectives is an old idea. But apart from some philosophic speculation, little was done in articulating such a theory until the early 20th century when enough momentum had been reached in the biological and engineering sciences to make such a quest feasible. Various physical processes in engineering and biological processes in the life sciences involved the transmission of 'information' rather than 'materials' and the fact that such diverse systems seemed to manifest a common structure arranged as an ordered hierarchy of parts and their interactions, quickly led to the notion that it was only the material composition of such systems that marked their difference. In fact, the idea that such systems had more commonalities than differences suggested that they were simply different realisations of some more general system based on the transmission of information, an idea that has developed very rapidly in the last half century with the convergence of computers and communications.

By the mid-20th century, 'general system theory' fashioned using biological analogies by von Bertalanffy (1968) and 'cybernetics' based on communication and control as articulated in engineering, principally by Weiner (1948), marked the beginnings of a perspective on science that came to be called the 'systems approach' (Churchman, 1968). This theory was attractive to the softer sciences, particularly those where their subject matter had developed in more *ad hoc* ways. Consequently through the 1950s and 1960s, the social sciences (with perhaps the exception of economics) and various professional fields from management science to urban planning each developed their own variety of systems approach as a basis for underpinning their structure and practice. Systems were conceived of as having subsystems tied together by interactions, thus invoking the idea of a network, but recursively ordered invoking the idea of hierarchy. Processes acting through subsystem interactions kept such systems in balance, in equilibrium, with the controller a special subsystem responsible for coordinating all the others. The behaviour of such a system was largely considered to be ordered with the controller acting to restore balance if the system should move away from its implicit goals or targets.

Cities were extremely suggestive artefacts for such a theory. Its components were individuals or groups tied together spatially and economically through transportation and socially through various friendship networks. Some of the key problems of the 1950s and 1960s manifested themselves in terms of congestion and the need to ensure effective transport, and the first steps towards rudimentary simulation models based on land use-transportation linked to the way populations created demand and supply for such uses were built with this image of the city as an interacting system in mind (Lowry, 1968). The idea that systems could be controlled or 'planned' to meet certain goals or targets was a natural extension of such logic. The goal of minimising interactions between home and work, for example, linked these transportation based models to optimisation procedures being developed in operations research and some rather neat solutions were revealed to exist if cities were conceived in this way.

The problem of course was that casting most urban problems into such narrowly defined domains was simply not sensible or feasible and much of our understanding of cities and their planning remained beyond the systems approach. In Britain, for example, the approach sustained by developments in planning theory and method, was popularised in various texts such as McLoughlin's (1969) *Urban and Regional Planning: A Systems Approach*, Chadwick's (1971) *A Systems View of Planning*, Faludi's (1972) *Planning Theory* and so on. Intellectually too, it was clear that what had emerged was a rather narrow view of the way systems behaved: most systems were not in quiet and passive equilibrium but in turmoil much of the time while the idea of evolution to new conditions implying different structures and behaviours simply lay beyond this kind of thinking.

Yet there were the seeds of a more sophisticated view right from the beginning and this was bound up with the working cliché of the systems approach contained in the mantra 'the whole is greater than the sum of the parts'. The argument implied by this gestalt was that system structure 'emerged' from the parts but that this was not simply a process of adding up the bits to get the whole. The processes themselves generated emergence and in this sense, general systems theory alluded to a dynamics that was well beyond anything that it actually specified. Simon (1962) anticipated this in an early statement of complexity which Alexander (1964, 2002) drew on his discussion of systems that grow from the bottom up. His focus was on design as evolution culminating in his recent magnum opus *The Nature of Order* but it was Jane Jacobs (1961) who really broached the question head on in her *Death and Life of Great American Cities*. She argued that the mechanistic way in which cities were conceived and planned was entirely counter to the diversity that made up vibrant and living cities, with the result that post-war urban planning (and modern architecture) were killing the heterogeneity and diversity that characterised urban life.

Following Weaver's (1948) threefold characterisation of science as dealing with problems of simplicity, problems of disorganised complexity, and problems of organised complexity, she argued that urban problems could not be treated like the first two. These in fact were the methods of classical and contemporary science respectively but she argued that the problems of cities needed to be treated as ones of organised complexity, the subject of the life sciences. In a way, this was a profound and insightful critique of the then emergent systems approach. It implied that cities should not be treated like machines but like living systems with the implication that life, hence city form, emerges from the bottom up following the Darwinian paradigm. Indeed, almost as soon as the systems approach was articulated, its limits became evident in that thinking of cities as systems in equilibrium with planning aimed at restoring this equilibrium, clearly conflicted with innovation, competition, conflict, diversity and heterogeneity, all hallmarks of successful city life. This led to the new paradigm that we will now elaborate.

6.3 The complexity sciences

Our preliminary definition of a complex system as being composed of complex systems certainly illustrates a recursion to an infinite regress or infinite expansion but it still ducks the question of what a complex system actually is. We first need to be clear about the fact that complex systems can never be precisely defined which lies at the basis of any attempt to understand such complexity. We can demonstrate this through the notion of variety, defining a system in terms of a number of components, say n, and the number of states, say m, which each component can take on (Ashby, 1956). The simplest demonstration is to compute the number of combinations of states when a state can exist or not given by the combinatorial:

$$(6.1)\quad C = \sum_{k=1}^{n} (n!/k!(n-k)!).$$

In Greater London for example, there are something in the order of 4.9 million building blocks and this formula counts the total number of different urban forms – arrangements of these blocks – when they are switched on or off. This varies through all combinations from the city composed as one block at one extreme to all 4.9 million as one at the other. This number is enormous, many orders of magnitude greater than the 10^{69} atoms in the universe. This might seem fanciful but all we are envisaging is all realisations of a city composed of any combinations of blocks up to this total number of buildings.

This number of combinations could be elaborated in countless ways and although it can be reduced simply by introducing constraints on what is feasible and what is behaviourally acceptable, it is still huge and to all intents and purposes infinite. This is one of the key challenges of complexity theory: understanding, grappling, and managing this sort of combinatorial explosion. Ashby (1956) calls this number of combinations variety and he makes the essential point that to control such a system, one needs as much variety in the controller as in the system. In theory, this means that to control such a system, we need as many elements in the control as there are states the system can take on. In fact, we can sometimes design good controllers that take account of the structure of such a system for it is most unlikely that the system can exist in all of these combinations with equal probability. The structures of the systems we deal with are hardly random and the trick for designing good controllers (or good plans) is to exploit this structure. Ashby refers to this as the law of requisite variety (Chadwick, 1977).

Coping with infinite variety is only one aspect of complex systems. Given such orders of magnitude, it is impossible to imagine that this kind of variety could be generated in any top-down fashion. In Alexander's introductory quote, it is impossible to envisage that such variety can be created by anything other than a bottom-up generative system. Life itself is the best example of such variety and most of us would now agree that the kind of diversity we see around us could only be generated by genetic variations that are consistent with neo-Darwinism. The corollary to this is that there is no way one might 'fabricate', in Alexander's terms, such complexity. Thus evolution from the bottom up is a hallmark of complexity and this too is consistent with the idea that order and structure emerge from actions and interactions in such systems. Generative systems are in fact central to simulating complexity and recent developments of agent-based models in cellular environments which have been quite widely developed in urban science of late are good examples of how complexity science is beginning to influence empirical work. Indeed Epstein (2007) argues that generative approaches are becoming central to social science with good theory being demonstrable by growing social structures from the ground up. Page (2005) captures this in the cliché that: 'if you didn't grow it, you didn't show it'.

If magnitude and bottom-up evolution are crucial to complex systems, so too is dynamics. All that we have said about complexity implies that dynamics is central to their development, hence their form and structure. In fact in the development of urban simulation models from the 1960s, temporal dynamics was always in mind in that static structures in equilibrium although appearing as reasonable approximations to urban structure, were widely regarded as first approximations. Equilibrium was in some senses regarded as a convenience. The development of dynamic urban models began with Forrester (1969) who simply used ideas from systems dynamics where feedback – positive and negative were central – to model inner cities and although his models were criticised for being non-spatial, he demonstrated the power of exponential and logistic growth. After that there was fascination with the notion that dynamic systems need not progress smoothly but could generate discontinuities such as catastrophes and chaos while notions about how systems admitted novelty and surprise from the bottom up began to develop using ideas from bifurcation theory (Wilson, 1981). Much of this kind of theorising did not lead to operational urban models while the development of cellular automata and agent-based models came from rather a different source as we will sketch below (Batty, 2005). Nevertheless the idea that cities could and should not be treated as being in equilibrium, began to penetrate the field pushing it towards the burgeoning sciences of complexity.

The context then is that complex systems have too many variables and too many interactions to be handled by traditional methods that seek to simplify and progress through parsimonious models. Phase spaces in which their realisations or solutions exist are effectively infinite and cannot be traversed. Such systems are thus unpredictable in the sense of classical science, but despite this, such systems are intrinsically temporal in that their dynamics is what makes them complex. As might be expected with such uncertainty, there is no widespread agreement as to precise definitions but there is a general consensus that there are quite well defined characteristics that such systems necessarily display. Durlauf (2005), himself a mild sceptic of complexity theory, identifies four key features which such systems must portray to be seriously considered as complex. He states these as *non-ergodicity*, *phase-transition*, *emergence*, and *universality* and these provide a brief but useful primer on what a complex system is as we will now explain.

Systems which are ergodic are those whose dynamics are predictable in that they are well behaved and often converge to some stable equilibrium. In fact this criterion was stated by Harris (1970) as a key requirement for good urban models despite the fact that real cities only appear to be stable at spatial scales where micro-change is averaged away. Durlauf in fact has a much more precise definition of *non-ergodicity* which he defines as systems that lack any kind of probable behaviour over the long term. This means that such systems can be characterised by exogenous shocks that affect long term behaviour. Such shocks are often said to generate path-dependent behaviour where historical accidents in the form of initial conditions or unpredictable shocks determine the long term behaviour and structure of the system. Endogenous change through positive feedback can also generate such unpredictability in that feedbacks can trigger surprise or novelty as new varieties of behaviour emerge. Such systems can also ‘lock in’ on end states which are generated through such feedbacks. In economic terms, path-dependence through positive feedback is sometimes called increasing returns. In social systems, this is often captured in the cliché that 'the rich get richer and the poor get poorer'.

This kind of dynamics can also lead to turbulence which characterises qualitative change in the form of *phase-transitions*. Such transitions occur often abruptly implying some form of threshold which if a system reaches or breaches, leads to qualitatively different structures and behaviours. A classic example in the physical sciences is water turning to ice or to steam which involves dramatic changes in structure at very specific temperatures, freezing and boiling points respectively; or in spatial systems, percolation through porous media which occurs once a certain level of network penetration becomes possible as threshold densities are reached. Novel change is thus triggered by small events. Another way of saying this is that complex systems have 'tipping points' where unusual sets of conditions come together and fire the system in one way or another. Gladwell's (2000) popular exposition of these phenomena are suggestive of such complexity in the social world. Furthermore, the rates of change and their turbulence imply intrinsic non-linearity in temporal behaviour which again limits predictability. Finally phase-transitions are also associated with qualitative changes such as that generated often endogenously within the system such as the development of disruptive technologies or dramatic switches in human behaviour and preferences.

In one sense, both non-ergodicity and phase-transitions are consistent with the notion of *emergence*. Usually emergence comes from the action and interaction of system components at lower levels in the absence of any higher level coordination functions but it can in fact happen at any level. In another sense, emergence is also akin to self-organisation, the generation of spontaneous order from the parts for which the mantra – the whole is greater than the sum of the parts – is central and essential. Such organisation depends not only on evolution but on co-evolution which reflects competition and conflict between system entities with such processes essential to the kind of positive feedback that leads to innovation, novelty, and surprise. In a way, the kinds of mutation that characterise genetic processes in human and animal populations reflect such spontaneity with the emergence of ever higher orders. Recent developments in fact suggest that the survival of the fittest, the term associated with Darwinian theory, must be dramatically qualified when dealing with human and social systems.

The last feature is *universality*. This is a characteristic defining the degree of order in a complex system and as such it is measured by a number of different signatures that show how the order in such system is manifest at different spatial and temporal scales. According to Durlauf (2005), a property of universality exists 'if its presence is robust to alterative specifications of the microstructure of the system'. This means that if the system exists under different realisations of its components, either in the past, present or future, then the system is universal in that there is no doubt that we are dealing with the same system. This is a rather weak condition which is probably more applicable to models of the systems than systems themselves but the way we recognise systems in fact is through this property. A much more specific definition is that the system has invariant properties in time and space. If it is quite clear when we examine the system at different times and spatial scales that the system is the 'same', then it is universal. In fact complex systems in very different fields might show the same structure and it is this that makes such complexity universal. This is no more or less than saying that analogies between systems that differ radically in material terms, can be very similar in more fundamental, informational terms.

A good but narrow example of universality relates to self-similarity of spatial structure. Cities exist in space in that they are structured around points of economic exchange, traditionally markets which form a hierarchy of types and sizes. This hierarchy although differentiated by size shows similarities at different scales in terms of the way cities of different sizes depend on each other. Central place theory suggests as much and this hierarchical order is also consistent with scaling of the city size distribution. In terms of spatial structure, cities distribute their resources in space in such a way that their networks of distribution fill space efficiently, moving goods and people along dendritic networks which fill space the most economically. These networks exist in the same form with the same space filling properties at different scales and through different times in terms of city growth. The whole idea of the fractal city which has a structure that manifests itself in the same morphology at different scales is entirely consistent with this kind of universality. In fact one of the key signatures of universality is the self similarity that is contained in scaling associated with fractals with measures of density and fractal dimension providing some meaning to this kind of theory (Batty and Longley, 1994).

6.4 Exemplars of complex systems

There are many signatures of complexity revealed in the space-time patterning of cities (Batty, 2005) and here we will indicate three rather different but nevertheless linked exemplars. Our first deals with generative systems which build order and pattern from the bottom up which necessarily involves generation in space but also through time. Were we to order the size of the components that are used in constructing cities physically, this would follow a rank-size rule with most components being very small in size with the least number of components being the largest in size. One could argue that most of the action – the decisions – would be associated with the smallest components and that this is indicative of the fact that most decisions are made from the bottom up. Imagine a large number of individuals who fall into two groups based on those who wish to live in a red house and those who wish to live in a green house, and let us assume that the initial distributions of houses are randomly coloured as either red or green. Now each individual is quite tolerant and would gladly live in an area where the number of houses which were painted in a colour different from their preference was the same as their personal preference. But if the number of their neighbours with a personal preference for a different coloured house began to dominate, they would be uncomfortable and would think about moving to a neighbourhood that had a more preferable balance.

Of course in real life, they would probably not move but repaint their houses and the situation would be a lot more messy. But it is easy to imagine that it is not the colour of their house but the political or social attitudes of their neighbours that is the issue (despite the fact that the colour of one's house is not as unimportant as one might think!). Now let us see what happens when we set up a simple rule for making decisions about such a situation and let us imagine that if a person in a green house finds themselves living in a neighbourhood with a majority of red houses, they will conform – not move – by painting their own house red. A symmetric situation exists for a person living in a red house in a neighbourhood dominated by green houses. In fact we could complicate this situation by some sort of tit-for-tat iteration in house painting but eventually we imagine that some sort of balance would take place through a combination of house painting and moving. If we implement this model on a fine lattice of cells in which we start with a random distribution of reds and greens as houses at points on the lattice, using the rule that if a person in a house whose colour is not in the majority in the cells around their house repaints their house to the majority colour, then the situation moves rapidly to extreme segregation as we show in Figure 6.1.

This is Schelling's (1969, 1978) model, first demonstrated nearly 40 years ago, which contributed to his winning the Nobel Prize for Economics in 2005. Essentially it is a perfect demonstration first, of how order emerges from randomness using simple but plausible rules of behaviour and second, of how an undesirable state implying extreme segregation and thus extreme preference emerges from rules that show only mild preferences for segregation. It is perhaps the classic model of ghetto formation and how individual actions can lead to unusual and perhaps surprising outcomes. It is also a very good example of cellular automata in that it reveals that specific actions in highly localised neighbourhoods generate global order of a kind that is surprising and cannot be anticipated from the basic rules. The models described by Elisabete Silva (Chapter 11) follow these ideas where spatial pattern and order emerge from the bottom up.

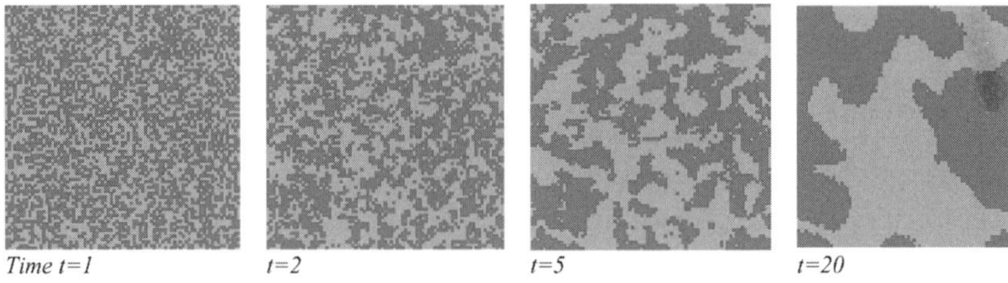

Figure 6.1 Order from randomness: Emergence of extreme segregation from local cellular automata rules implying a mild preference for living amongst one's own kind

In fact, this style of modelling also forms the basis of the field of artificial life (Langton, 1989) which builds on John Conway's early demonstration that such automata could sustain a great magnitude of patterns, some of which emerge spontaneously from a random soup, like life itself (Gardner, 1971). Schelling's model demonstrates many features of complex systems and that is why it is so powerful. First there is the idea that fragile equilibria exists which, when perturbed, moves rapidly to a stable equilibrium – the random starting pattern of red and green cells is not an equilibrium but imagine a checker board distribution of alternative red and green cells with a single dual cell perturbation of this pattern. The whole system would then unravel into the kind of clusters shown in Figure 6.1. Moreover such a fragile equilibrium is a tipping point in Gladwell's (2000) terms, ready to flip the system into a new state: very little change in two cells, in this example, leads to massive change in a much larger proportion of cells, a phase-transition reminiscent of percolation. Changes are clearly emergent, generated from the bottom up, and in this sense are unexpected. Such change is also based on positive feedback in which local changes in pattern, one cell at a time, build up to the tipping point in any local neighbourhood.

Our second example deals not with locations but with networks which link locations and thus introduce notions of movement or transportation. Just as a lattice represents an idealised representation of locations, a graph built from arcs connecting nodes is an idealised form of network. These simple models enable us to study the properties of networks in analogy to the properties of graphs which focus on their connectivity. Imagine a world where people are linked into tightly organised clusters, reminiscent of the sorts of links one might find in small villages which can then be generalised to a landscape of small villages, essentially a landscape of clusters. The clusters have dense connectivity but because transportation in such a world is limited by how far one can walk to work in a day, villages are spaced at something like six miles from one another. The linkages between people in different villages are much less than within a village and this world thus resembles something akin to the settlement landscape of Western Europe in medieval times. If we measure these properties of connectivity, we see that the connectivity of each cluster is much higher than the whole network. In short this is an inward looking world where travel between the clusters is difficult, thus representing some limit on its economic development. We show such a world in Figure 6.2(a) where we measure the average path length of each cluster separately, and then we compare this to the total average path length of the whole network. Each cluster has an average path length of one, much greater than the overall connectivity which has a path length of about three. Imagine a change in technology such as that introduced by steam power as in the Industrial Revolution. Fast links are established between some of the villages and we show three such links in Figure 6.2(b). When we recompute the average path length, the clusters still remain about the same but the overall network connectivity increases dramatically with the average path length falling from about three to about two.

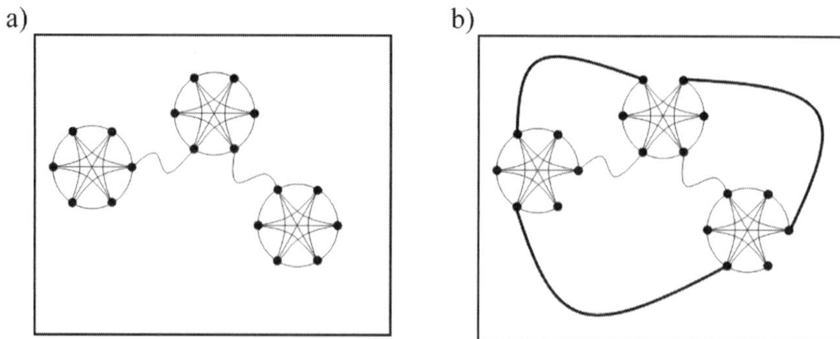

Figure 6.2 Evolution of a 'small world' due to technological change

Note: Here the network in (a) has low connectivity despite the presence of several clusters with high connectivity. In (b) because of the addition of only three long distance links, the network connectivity dramatically improves with the local clusters remaining largely unchanged. This is the best of both worlds and is referred to as a 'small world'.

This is what Milgram (1967) first defined as a small world: a network which has the benefits of high local density but also relatively short overall paths where people can connect up to one another. In cities, technical change is necessary to build networks which connect people and goods at different levels and bypass (at high speeds) lower level links. Indeed the very fact that cities still build bypasses and beltways is tantamount to saying that they are attempting to increase their efficiency by reinforcing their small world properties. In fact, a useful way of looking at cities is by measuring the connectivity of their transport networks at different scales and using such measures to assess their efficiency.

Small world properties of networks also indicate how such systems evolve from the bottom up. In a sense, this can be seen as an optimal process for generating structure. Like patterns generated from cellular automata, it is a process of efficient space filling without connecting everything in sight. Indeed, there are some who argue that many systems evolve in this way to an efficient threshold and that everything from brains, to nervous systems, to arterial transport in the body and the city are small worlds (Watts, 2003). Friendship networks too are small worlds with such nets bound together by critical links – weak ties in one sense but strong in another. We do not have time here to demonstrate in detail how a small world emerges from one which is highly clustered and then loses its qualities as more and more network links are built. But in essence, there is a threshold of connectivity where the benefits of high local cluster density/connectivity are retained in the presence of low overall average paths through the graph. As more links are built, the local cluster density and the overall connectivity of the network converge. If one were to argue that the cost of links is fixed, then a clear trade-off can be measured between connectivity and cost and it becomes clear that there is a point where adding more links leads to less and less improvements in connectivity. In short, thresholds can be defined which indicate optimal points of investment in the network, and there are strong links to percolation theory (Batty, 2005). There is a good example in London at present which suggests that adding some key links which have not evolved spontaneously, could make very dramatic improvements in travel: so called Cross-Rail, a high speed link from the west of the CBD to the east, is a case in point.

There have been some dramatic advances in this kind of network thinking in the last decade. Although the temporal dynamics of network evolution is still in its infancy, it is now quite clear that the structural properties of networks are important properties of complexity. Barabasi (2003) for example has demonstrated that many naturally evolving networks such as the internet have scale free properties which imply that the most connected nodes get richer as networks evolve and the poor get poorer. This is also consistent with the small world properties and these have important implications for how robust networks are to breakdown or attack and how strategies to leverage networks can be built. There are links to spatial epidemiology and thus to public health vaccination strategies in the preventing the diffusion of disease. Many of these ideas in cellular automata and network science tie together in the spatial domain through ideas that have been developed for several years in fractal geometry (Batty and Longley, 1994).

Our third example involves ideas about how systems evolve in time. There are many growth models which encompass the idea of positive feedback, the simplest being Malthus's model (Banks, 1994) where population change is proportional to population itself, leading to exponential growth (or decline). Many variants exist in which such growth models might be capacitated in some way, reaching limits posed by crowding where the growth rate embodying positive feedback is countered by a crowding constraint involving negative feedback. Let us begin by stating this model for the change in population:

$$(6.2)\quad dP(t) = \lambda P(t)[1\text{-}P(t)/\hat{P}(t)]dt$$

where $P(t)$ is the population and $\hat{P}(t)$ is the maximum population permissible at time t. If we assume that $P(t) = Z, \forall\ t$, then the change equation can be integrated from $t = 0$ to ∞ and it produces the classic logistic form given as:

$$(6.3)\quad P(t) = Z/[\eta\text{-}1)\exp(\text{-}\lambda t)]$$

where $\eta = P(\mathrm{t})/Z$. When there is no effective bound, that is, when Z , then the equation generates exponential growth:

$$(6.4)\quad P(t) = P(0)\exp(\lambda t)$$

which is Malthus's equation. All these are standard results.

The logistic appears to be relevant to population growth in human populations in capacitated spaces such as individual cities or countries but over longer periods, there is little doubt that the capacity limit varies, usually upwards. In fact capacity measured in population terms belies a variety of other influences that although incorporated by this measure, involve technological change. As building technology has developed, the capacity (which reflects density), increases. The socio-economic types of population occupying cities also change while employment as well as resident population is an important measure of size. This too relates to how much time people spend in cities living or working at high densities. If population capacity is thought of as a generic measure of resource, then basic technological change – agricultural, industrial and post-industrial and in disaggregate terms, mechanical, energetic, electronic, biophysical, medical and so on – is easy to reconcile with this model where growth through new technologies can occur in spurts. The simplest way to build this in is simply to add a baseline capacity over different periods. Once population reaches a certain level, let us say ψZ, this marks the start of a new growth process where the clock t is reset to 0. This resetting of the process occurs when:

$$(6.5)\ P(T) = \psi Z + P(T\text{-}1)$$

where T is the current time when this condition is met and T-1, the time when it happened previously. The logistic model can now be written as

$$(6.6)\ P(\tau) = \{\ \psi Z + P(T\text{-}1)\}\ \{Z/[(m\text{-}1)\exp(-\lambda\tau)]\}$$

This simply displaces the logistic in time rather than resetting the capacity per se although there are many variants of the function that can achieve this effect.

We show such an effect in Figure 6.3(a) where the logistic is displaced when:

$$(6.7)\ P(T) = 2^{-1} Z + P(T\text{-}1).$$

In Figure 6.3(b), we show the overall envelope produced by this process which implies that the growth process receives a number of shocks or kick starts. With 1/2, this means that when the growth process reaches the inflection point – that is, when growth just begins to increase as a decreasing rate, an innovation occurs that resets the process that projects it back to the point where positive feedback with increasing returns, dominates.

The process here has all the elements of complexity: phase-transitions or thresholds at which innovation occurs and pushes the system into a new regime, novelty and surprise in a process that is in reality likely to be fairly random in time (for we never know when such a shock might occur), and a sense that the usual state of the system is far-from-equilibrium. One of the features that this process implies is that growth is dominated by continual discontinuities or innovations, 'perpetual

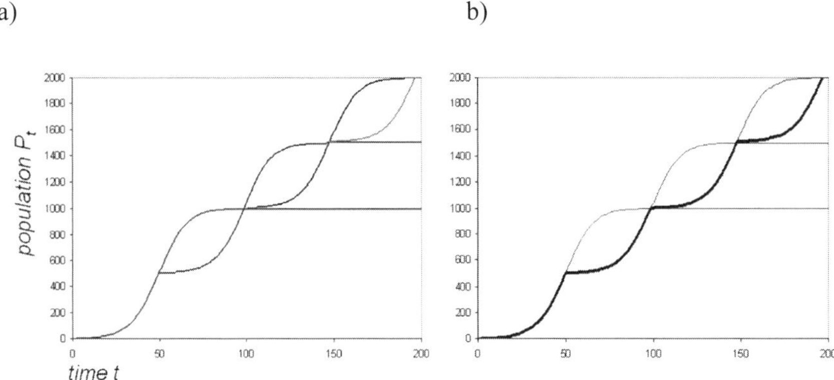

Figure 6.3 Population growth with changing resources due to innovation

novelty' as Arthur (2005) refers to it. Growth is only 'locked in' to an equilibrium between the discontinuities. Over time, these changes might be considered to be a perpetual series of 'avalanches' in the sense used by Bak (1999) in his discussion of self-organised criticality or punctuations in the sense used by Eldredge and Gould (1972). A much more complete and powerful model which mirrors similar growth profiles has been developed by West, Brown and Enquist (2001) for biological populations. This has been generalised to human populations by Bettencourt et al. (2006) who show that this kind of growth behaviour characterises some cities such as New York where there appear to be spurts in growth due to new land being released which in turn are influenced by changes in technology, attitudes towards high buildings, transportation innovations, and perhaps even changes in preferences to live at ever higher densities. The West-Brown-Enquist model differs from our simple model here in that pure population change is articulated as a scaling function of population; in its non-capacitated form, change in population is a scaling function where $dP(\mathrm{t})/\mathrm{dt} \sim P^{\beta}$ and it is this scaling that enables the model to generate many other effects from hyper-exponential growth leading to singularities and to exponential decline. It also maps this kind of growth model onto many other relationships that we observe for urban systems which are scaling, implying different economies of scale.

6.5 Evolution, planning and design

So far we have considered cities as complex systems where the idea of a city is as a comprehensive entity. When we act in making plans about cities, or consider any other forms of decision making which take place either in cities or with city development in mind, then perspectives change and with this so does the way we construe complexity. Our perspective here will be that of planning the city in expert-professional terms, more akin to designers but we will also broach complexity in other ways – from top-down controllers which imply a management perspective, from the perspective of the citizen, and from a more general, somewhat detached social science perspective. We do not have time to elaborate how each of these approaches manifests its own complexity but we will provide some simple signposts which let us put the complexity of physical planning and design in context.

From our perspective of cities as complex systems, a key consideration already raised is the notion that cities manifest a variety that has to be met by a controller requisite to the task in hand. This 'requisite variety' implies that any system of control, which here largely means keeping the system within certain targets, predicates some sort of system that has the same variety or diversity of the city itself. From all that has been said, the notion of a top-down controller is simply impossible given the degree of complexity that modern cities manifest and thus any successful control must probably operate from the bottom up. In fact, as cities in large part develop this way, bottom-up control makes logical sense; the way development takes place by successive and often incremental adjustments, even in terms of grand plans, implies control of some sort at the most basic level. This is not to say that higher level controls do not have some function for there is a hierarchy of control as Simon (1962) implies. As we learn more, we intervene less and the notion of finding critical leverage points in complex systems – tipping points as Gladwell (2000) refers to them – is quite consistent with this kind of bottom-up design. This implies that as we learn more, we intervene less because 'less means more' and 'more means different' (Anderson, 1972). An excellent example of this is based on identifying critical points within a network – weak links that in fact act in strong ways to cement the system together for relatively little cost but provide great added value.

From the perspective of the planner who identifies with the planning system, then, the system itself is complex in terms of its bureaucracy. Getting things done is usually the focus of this complexity in that planning is seen as being centric, or top down. Over the last 50 years such systems have been gradually hollowed out to the point where planning as a bureaucracy is often said to be part of the problem rather than the solution. Thirty or more years ago, Rittel and Webber (1973) articulated this in their definition of 'wicked problems', problems that were so interconnected that any thing one might do to alleviate or try to solve them, usually made them worse. It is in this sense then that planning is seen to be part of the problem. Wicked problems fight back and they resist solution. Wicked problems are unique and have no definitive formulation. Often the problem and the solution are the same thing, they have no stopping rule, it is hard to tell when a solution has been reached, there is no agreement about a solution, and no ultimate test that establishes whether a solution is optimal or has actually ever been reached. Such problems generate 'waves of consequences' such that there is never any end to these chains and thus problem-solving goes on forever until the problem changes out of all recognition or is deemed no longer relevant. In essence, every solution to a wicked problem is another wicked problem.

These characteristics in fact are those that imply complexity both in the methods of problem solution as well as the object of problem solving itself.

From the perspective of social science in general, identifying the city as the object of complexity or in terms of the process of changing it through planning and control, are equally narrow in conception. Cities are regarded as organisational, social structures that are changed through decision making of various kinds and it is this nexus of decisions across all scales and through all times that forms the web of complexity that is basic to the social sciences. There are many similarities to features of the complexity sciences that pervade the social sciences and to an extent this is reflected in both the substance of its inquiry as well as its methods. In these terms, there is some convergence of terminology and ideas. These are key themes that echo throughout these many perspectives such as those based on ideas about networks in particular and agents and agency in general (Bryne, 1998; Cilliers, 1998).

What all these approaches suggest is that planning, design, control, management – whatever constellation of interventionist perspectives are adopted – are difficult and potentially dangerous. If we assume that social systems and cities like biological systems are generated through a process of tinkering, through trial and error mutation which increase fitness and reduce error in the phylogeny, then interventions are potentially destructive unless we have a deep understanding of their causal effects. As we have learned more, we become more wary of the effects of such concerted action. In a sense, if the development of cities is really like the evolutionary process in biological populations, then we are inevitably wary of fine tuning such evolutionary processes. We are scared of evolution, we find it complex, and we are reluctant to disturb something we do not understand at all well.

We do not have a good answer to any of this although there is rapid progress in the notion of evolutionary design, particularly in inanimate systems where there are an increasing number of analogies between the evolution of animals, plants and machines. In one sense, social evolution has been characterised in similar ways in the past but it is only recently that formal design has begun to draw on this tradition. In terms of physical planning Alexander (1964, 2002) was one of the first to exploit the evolutionist paradigm but more recently his work on generative design using pattern languages has been paralleled by other generative approaches in the social sciences based on individual and agent-based modelling (Epstein, 2007). In fact in design, there are many new approaches revolving around generative systems, for example those based on shape grammars (Stiny, 2006), on cellular automata (Batty, 2005), and on evolutionary geometry (Watanabe, 2002).

A concept that emerges quite naturally from such purposive bottom-up actions is the idea that to explore good planning and design in cities, computer models should be set up in a laboratory-like context in which the focus is on exploration of different patterns which attempt to reach different goals, laboratories in which models are available in wide area mode, across the web in a form that many people can experiment with. The notion that many people collaborating is likely to produce better design than the few is based on recent thinking about collective action through the 'wisdom of crowds', to coin a popular phrase (Surowiecki, 2005). To illustrate these notions, we can use a cellular automata model as a laboratory in which the user works with a model of urban development where there are default rules relating to how one type of development relates to another. These are rules that are based on the type and density of different land use activities in different locations/cells which in turn influence what development takes place or is removed in adjacent cells as the city changes. The model also has rules that govern the life cycle of different land use activities which in turn influence their effect on other land uses at different points in their life cycles.

If one begins with a pattern of development – the 'physical' initial conditions – the user can change the default rules to those that might pertain to different goals – plausible or not – which in turn might reflect different ideals. As the simulation proceeds, development rules do not change but they can be altered by the user to imply a sense of learning. The model we will illustrate, *DUEM* – the Dynamic Urban Evolutionary Model – was developed by Xie (1994) and set up in laboratory context for such exploration by Batty, Xie and Sun (1999). What we show in Figure 6.4 is a branching tree of possibilities from four initial sets of conditions. The uppermost branch simply represents the development of the city in its default state with the rules set to reflect existing development process. But at each branch the rules are changed and a different path is taken. These bifurcations illustrate the incredible variety of solutions that such a model can generate with literally millions of possibilities: in fact an uncountable number and it is this style of theorising and thinking that generative social science strives for which is the hallmark of dealing with complexity. Although we have had little time to develop this here, we speculate that this is the style of simulation that living with complexity requires and that such laboratories for exploration, for growing cities in this way to meet planning ideals, must become the norm in post-industrial societies driven from the bottom up.

6.6 Conclusions and next steps

Our focus on complexity has many echoes in the other contributions to this book in terms of concepts, the focus on bottom up as opposed to top-down action and problem-solving, and the idea that planning and design are not really so very different from evolution and prediction. In fact in the last section, we argued that prediction, design and understanding are all of one piece. If we take the essential message of modern Darwinism that design is evolution, that the evolutionary process is the only process that leads to optimality in systems that grow from the bottom up, then planning must be subsumed in our theories and models. The fact that it has remained separate from the way we have tried to understand cities and make predictions in the past is part of the problem. Complexity science forces us to a more holistic view.

Several other features that we have introduced support the need for holistic theory and practice. There is little doubt that time and dynamics has come firmly onto the agenda and that we no longer think of cities as being in equilibrium. In hindsight, it is somewhat remarkable that we ever thought we could get away with the idea that we could encapsulate all our knowledge into equilibrium models because the whole point of planning is to generate change. Yet the notion that such equilibrium was non-optimal was a simplification in itself that gave planning a starting point for action. If the city is never in equilibrium as we now accept, if it is far-from-equilibrium as its social physics reveals, then this in itself casts doubt on the idea of intervention as the system may still be on course for some kind of optimality. Once again, we are drawn to the notion that intervention in complex systems must be treated with extreme caution.

The complexity sciences communicate a message to all functions and agencies that exercise control, management, planning, policy-making and perhaps design, and that is that the most effective intervention is based on small scale change which enables a system to meet its own goals. Slight changes in direction are thus preferred to radical top-down restructuring whose implications might be far reaching and completely unpredictable. This suggests broadening the remit of physical planning but there is only so far one can go. Better to set up mechanisms like the simulation laboratory sketched out above which enables stakeholders to participate in ways that are tempered by dialog and discussion and to let those affected see the consequences of their actions. Intervention is a serious matter that requires serious tools for tracing its potentially far-reaching and unanticipated implications.

What we have sought to do in this chapter is to sketch how complexity theory is beginning to inform our understanding of the physical development of cities. The growth of complexity theory as a major paradigm for science admits unpredictability and uncertainty, ambiguity and pluralism, and without being entirely relativist, it does throw doubt on the certainty of theory and science that has dominated our thinking about cities and about planning hitherto. The generic use of complexity language in articulating social affairs, policy, management and decision making is beginning to infuse our thinking. We are now much more comfortable with using the language of science with its physical metaphors involving diffusion, mobility, liquidity, fluidity and so on as useful characterisations of the complexity of the social world we have to deal with. We have had little time here to deal with the way these currents are beginning to mesh with globalisation and the modern information economy but these are being dealt with elsewhere in this book. There is now a very positive sense in which each of these perspectives is contributing to a new paradigm which is based on its own rhetoric in which 'the whole is greater than the sum of its parts'.

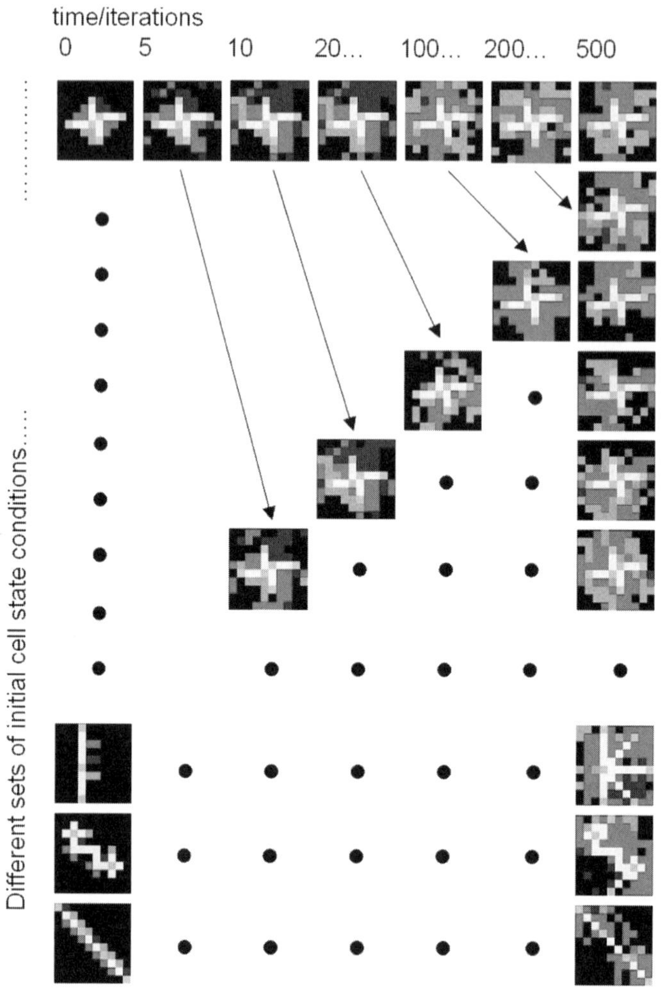

Figure 6.4 Generative predictions and designs in a cellular automata lab

Notes: Each row represents a different configuration and set of land use states in a 10 x 10 cellular space. The CA rules are then applied and each simulation is run for 500 steps giving the final cellular spaces in the last column of each row. However in the first case, after 5 steps, some of the rules are changed and the model is run for another 500 steps. The rules are then changed for the original initial conditions after 10 steps, 20 steps, 100 steps and 200 steps and in each case the model is run up to 500 steps. This gives a crude picture of the kind of variety that can be generated combinatorially as the user explores the enormous phase space of possible solutions in true generative fashion.

References

Alexander, C. (1964) *Notes of the Synthesis of Form*, Harvard University Press, Cambridge.

Alexander, C. (2002-2005) *The Nature of Order*, Books 1-4, Center for Environmental Structure, Berkeley.

Anderson, P. (1972) 'More is different', *Science*, vol. 177, pp. 393-396.

Arthur, W.B. (2005) 'Out-of-equilibrium economics and agent-based modelling', Santa Fe Institute Working Paper, viewed March 7, 2007, available at http://www.santafe.edu/~wbarthur/documents/OutofEquilPaper-SFI.pdf.

Ashby, W.R. (1956) *An Introduction to Cybernetics*, Chapman and Hall, London.

Bak, P. (1999) *How Nature Works: The Science of Self-Organized Criticality*, Springer-Verlag Telos, New York.

Banks, R.B. (1994) *Growth and Diffusion Phenomena: Mathematical Frameworks and Applications*, Springer-Verlag, New York.

Barabasi, A.L. (2003) *Linked: How Everything is Connected to Everything Else and What It Means*, Plume, New York.

Batty, M. (2005) *Cities and Complexity: Understanding Cities with Cellular Automata, Agent-Based Models, and Fractals*, The MIT Press, Cambridge.

Batty, M. and Longley, P.A. (1994) *Fractal Cities: A Geometry of Form and Function*, Academic Press, San Diego.

Batty, M., Xie, Y. and Sun, Z. (1999) 'Modelling urban dynamics through GIS-based cellular automata', *Computers, Environments and Urban Systems*, vol. 233, pp. 205-233.

Bettencourt, L.M.A., Lobo, J., Helbing, D., Kuehnert, C. and West G.B. (2006) 'Growth, innovation, scale and the pace of life in the city', Santa Fe Institute Working Paper, Santa Fe Institute, Santa Fe.

Byrne, D. (1998) *Complexity Theory and the Social Sciences: An Introduction*, Routledge, London.

Chadwick, G.F. (1971) *A Systems View of Planning*, Pergamon Press, Oxford.

Chadwick, G.F. (1977) 'The limits of the plannable: Stability and complexity in planning and planned systems', *Environment and Planning A*, vol. 9(10), pp. 1189-1192.

Churchman, C.W. (1968) *The Systems Approach*, Dell Publishing, New York.

Cilliers, P. (1998) *Complexity and Postmodernism: Understanding Complex Systems*, Routledge, London.

Durlauf, S.N. (2005) 'Complexity and empirical economics', *The Economic Journal*, vol. 115, pp. 225-243.

Eldredge, N. and Gould, S.J. (1972) 'Punctuated equilibria: An alternative to phyletic gradualism', in T.J.M. Schopf (ed.) *Models in Paleobiology*, Freeman, Cooper and Company, San Francisco, pp. 82-115.

Epstein, J. (2007) *Generative Social Science: Studies in Agent-Based Computational Modelling*, Princeton University Press, Princeton.

Faludi, A. (1972) *Planning Theory*, Pergamon Press, Oxford.

Forrester, J.W. (1969) *Urban Dynamics*, The MIT Press, Cambridge.

Gardner, M. (1971) 'On cellular automata, self-reproduction, the Garden of Eden and the game "Life"', *Scientific American*, vol. 224(2), pp. 112-117.

Gladwell, M. (2000) *The Tipping Point: How Little Things Can Make a Big Difference*, Little, Brown, New York.

Harris, B. (1970) *Change and Equilibrium in the Urban System*, Fels Center for Government Working Paper, University of Pennsylvania, Philadelphia.

Jacobs, J. (1961) *The Death and Life of Great American Cities*, Random House, New York.

Langton, C. (ed.) (1989) *Artificial Life*, Addison-Wesley, Redwood City.

Lowry, I.S. (1968) 'Seven models of urban development', in G. Hemmens (ed.), *Urban Development Models, Special Report 97*, Highway Research Board, Washington.

McLoughlin, J.B. (1969) *Urban and Regional Planning: A Systems Approach*, Faber and Faber, London.

Milgram, S. (1967) 'The small-world problem', *Psychology Today*, vol. 1, pp. 61-67.

Page, S. (2005) 'Agent based models', Center for the Study of Complex Systems, University of Michigan, Ann Arbor, viewed March 7, 2007, available at http://www.cscs.umich.edu/~spage/palgrave.pdf.

Rittel, H. and Webber, M. (1973) 'Dilemmas in a general theory of planning', *Policy Sciences*, vol. 4, pp. 155-169.

Schelling, T.S. (1969) 'Models of segregation', *American Economic Review, Papers and Proceedings*, vol. 59(2), pp. 488-493.

Schelling, T.S. (1978) *Micromotives and Macrobehavior*, W.W. Norton and Company, New York.

Simon, H.A. (1962) 'The architecture of complexity', *Proceedings of the American Philosophical Society*, vol. 106(6), pp. 467-482.

Smith, A. (1776) *An Inquiry into the Nature and Causes of the Wealth of Nations*, vol. 1, The Online Library of Liberty, 2005, viewed March 7, 2007, http://oll download.libertyfund.org/EBooks/Smith_0141.02.pdf.

Stiny, G. (2006) *Shape: Talking about Seeing and Doing*, The MIT Press, Cambridge.

Surowiecki, J. (2005) *The Wisdom of Crowds*, Anchor, New York.

Von Bertalanffy, L. (1968) *General System Theory: Foundations, Development, Applications*, George Braziller, New York.

Watanabe, M.S. (2002) *Induction Design*, Birkhauser, Basel.

Watts, D.J. (2003) *Six Degrees: The Science of a Connected Age*, W.W. Norton and Company, New York.

Weaver, W. (1948) 'Science and complexity', *American Scientist*, vol. 36, pp. 536-544.

West, G.B., Brown, J.H. and Enquist, B.J. (2001) 'A general allometric model of ontogenetic growth', *Nature*, vol. 413, pp. 628-631.

Wiener, N. (1948) *Cybernetics: or Control and Communication in the Animal and the Machine*, MIT Press, Cambridge.

Wilson, A.G. (1981) *Catastrophe Theory and Bifurcation: Applications to Urban and Regional Systems*, University of California Press, Berkeley.

Xie, Y. (1994) 'Dynamic urban evolutionary modelling', Unpublished PhD Thesis, State University of New York, Buffalo.

Chapter 7
Emergence, Spatial Order, Transaction Costs and Planning

Chris Webster[1]

This chapter considers the way in which cities organise themselves through the interaction of a multitude of interacting individual plans. It starts by interpreting the paradoxes of modern state-organised urban planning as a disjunction between the way cities actually function and the way planners and planning systems have typically assumed they function. It asks what theories of social order are consistent with the understanding of a city as a complex self-organising system and calls for a re-engagement with classical social scientific theories of emergence. Following strands of modern heterodox economics, a link is made between transaction costs and various forms of order. The remit of urban planners is identified not so much as prescribing spatial order as improving public domain order – order over resources characterised by unclear property rights. Historical theories of emergent social order are reviewed, focusing on the synthesising contribution of Friedrich von Hayek. Hayek's view of the price system as an emergent social phenomenon giving rise to the division of labour in society is – amongst others – brought to bear on the question of organising cooperation in the city.

7.1 Introducing complexity and the aims of urban planning

This chapter builds on the complexity discussion in planning by exploring the relationship between the distribution of knowledge in society, the division of labour, the division of land and the organisation of collective action in cities. Cities evolve and spatial patterns emerge as a result of multiple interacting plans. Government spatial plans are just one kind of urban plan that helps redistribute value throughout society. An analogy with thermodynamics is set up in which the economic plans of individuals have the effect of reducing unrealised gains from trade. Transaction costs feature in the economy like physical barriers in a thermodynamic system, preventing gains from trade. The interventions of government planners have the

1 Chris Webster is Professor of Urban Planning and Director of Research in the School of City and Regional Planning, Cardiff University, at Cardiff, UK. He leads the Cardiff University Spatial Analysis Research Group. He is also Director of the UK Centre for Education in the Built Environment (CEBE).

effect of modifying transaction costs and redirecting the gains from trade brought about by individual plans. Planners need to endogenise the planning function in their analysis of the city. Their plans do not work in the way that is typically taught in planning schools. Their plans work by interconnecting with private plans. Some tools used by planners have the tendency to reduce transaction costs, clarify property rights and establish order that is lacking. Simple rules are better at doing this – like clear and strongly enforced prohibitions of development. Other tools, such as prescriptive plans, can often add to the complexity of urban development processes, increasing uncertainty and transaction costs and preventing many opportunities to realise gains from trade in the division of land.

The stated aims of urban planning found in text books, journal articles, legislation and policy documents are deceptively unproblematic. Few would want to argue with the idea that the economic plans of individuals, firms and governments need to be coordinated and that there is a special sense in which this so for plans that use land resources. The fact that just about every economic decision has implications for the plans of others and that part of this interconnectedness arises through physical spill-over effects adds to the compelling argument for spatial planning. But scratch the surface and much of the rhetoric is deeply problematic. There are good arguments for planning, but they are more complex than those typically rehearsed. Planning is all about order. We plan, presumably, because we think that our planning produces superior order to that which might prevail without our plans. In countries with well established urban planning laws the idea that cities are highly adaptive complex systems capable of ordering themselves in many important dimensions, has been obscured over time. The intellectual understanding of spontaneous ordering processes has been lost, especially and ironically, among academic urban planners, whose scholarly endeavours tend to focus on an ever more sophisticated understanding of government-imposed spatial order. The failure to ask more generic questions about urban order weakens the academic and practicing planning community. The weakness is exposed in planning's paradoxical quests. Urban planners seek to design the informal; to manage spontaneity; to redistribute with growth; to predict the unknowable; to aggregate the irreconcilable; and to solve the irresolvable. Complexity is at the heart of these paradoxes. Cities are self-organising systems but we act as though we can shape them with prescriptive plans. This misses a fundamental insight from complexity science and from classical social science – complex systems are governed by simple rules (Wolfram, 2002; Kasper and Streit, 1998). To attempt to control them by complex rules is to risk losing control.

The work of American essayist Jane Jacobs unifies most urban planners everywhere. And yet Jacob's vision of vitality, spontaneity and informality sits awkwardly with the planner's predisposition towards centrally planned, prescriptive order. This is so in our science as well as our purposing. Our purpose has often been at odds with our science. In anticipating the future we have extrapolated the past. In seeking to reproduce the great urban morphologies of history we have designed rather than grown new spaces. Participatory processes designed to measure and aggregate diverse preferences have led to plans dominated by the interests of powerful groups. Stringent controls over building design have led to uniform mediocrity. Such tensions have meant that our science, technology and method has often shaped our purpose. Participation, plan making, development control and regulations have become ends in their own right. Planners have often lost site of the underlying social purpose of planning, their purpose becoming defined by what they do.

7.2 The scientific basis of planning

The science of planning has gone through several paradigm shifts over the past century and the scientific input to planning analysis and practice has waxed and waned over the decades (Batty, 1994; Webster, 2004). In principle, the science on offer has got better. The mechanistic systems modelling of the comprehensive land use planning era was underpinned by cybernetics. This gave way to catastrophe theory, chaos theory and now to complexity theory, the advances being made possible by increasing computational performance. Catastrophe and chaos ideas never made much of an impact on the scholarship of urban planning, but cybernetics was a more general paradigm that deeply influenced the purpose and methods of planning and still does. Complexity as a paradigm rather than a specific set of theoretical propositions, seems to have the potential to do the same. It is in line with the current philosophical predisposition towards holism and offers thinking tools and methods that address the interrelationships implicit in the notion of sustainability. The complexity paradigm is good news for cities. Complexity is the science of emergence and is much better aligned than was cybernetics, to the phenomena with which urban planners concern themselves. But the link remains awkward and undeveloped, largely un-influential in the practical realm of planning. Planning remains ambiguously positioned as the art of managing complex urban dynamics with a mixed set of tools, many of which are very unsuited to the job. Meanwhile, under the influence of a more general de-scientification of society, description in planning has become discourse; forecasting has become fabrication of the future; prescription has become pragmatic; models have become just one type of metaphor. Not all of this is bad, especially where it gets us away from the illusion of certainty and control. There is no doubt that more sophisticated tools, informed by complexity ideas, are needed in urban planning, for example, to model complex pedestrian, house price, migratory and commuting movements. A more urgent agenda, however, is to reconstruct the social science of planning.

Much of urban planning is one way or another still heavily predicated on cybernetic notions of control. The extension of cybernetics into policy arenas was a natural step in the climate of post war interventionism – Keynesianism in the UK, with its equivalents elsewhere (Webster, 2006). The UK's highly sophisticated spatial planning system is the last institution of the post war welfare state not to have shed its Keynesian roots. The state ownership of one of the crucial means of production in the built environment – the right to initiate land development – remains unchallenged. It sits awkwardly with an understanding of the city (and society more generally) as a self-organising system. It is pertinent to ask, therefore, what theories of social order are consistent with the idea of complex cities?

7.3 Institutions, transaction costs and self-organisation

Over the last two to three decades, there has been a resurgent interest in heterodox political economy in spontaneous order; emergence; decentralised decision making; local-global interactions; incomplete information; heterogeneous agents; and the influence of rules and rights on resource allocation . These developments go by various names: neo-institutionalism; heterodox economics; new institutional economics; transactions costs economics; property rights economics; economic sociology; and so on. One thing that can be said about all these strands is that they take us back to a social science that is altogether more simple and significant than that which dominated most of the 20th century. Together, they construct a unified social science bridging, as many of the classical economists did, sociology, economics politics and philosophy. They spurn the dryness and explanatory weakness of neo-classical economics (but not all of its tools). A strong unifying theme is the explanatory power of transaction costs. In economics, this amounts to a shift in focus from the discovery of prices that exhaust gains from trade to the barriers that inhibit gains from trade. It is a shift that suddenly makes economics useful once more and reunites it with sister social sciences. An emphasis on the barriers to productive exchange means an emphasis on institutions (which reduce the barriers) and the new paradigm has much to say, therefore, about how rules govern the emergence of order and about the efficiency of different institutions. This should be of great interest to a subject whose preoccupation is with institutions that govern the allocation of a society's fixed factor of production – land.

A general proposition in this literature is that order emerges as individuals seek to avoid the costs involved in co-operating for mutual gains. One of the first systematic attempts to develop an urban theory based on this premise is Webster and Lai (2003). Its under girding thesis is that five kinds of urban order (patterns) emerge as individual agents seek to avoid the costs of transacting: institutional order; organisational order; proprietary order; spatial order; and public domain order. The pressing role for urban planners is not so much in the fourth of these but the fifth. The design of physical and institutional solutions to govern resources over which property rights are ill-defined (public domain resources) is a crucial societal function. By contrast, the only place where spatial order can be designed is in a command economy. In any normal economy, based largely on voluntary exchange, the probability of achieving a specific spatial order by imposed plan is very low. Only where there is unitary ownership, such as the master planning of a site under single (private or public) ownership, can imposed spatial pattern be realised with some certainty. Even then, however, the spatial order of economic activities and land uses cannot easily be controlled. The use of even the smallest of spaces takes on a complex and unpredictable life of its own once constructed.

Cities evolve and grow by the exchange of property rights over land and buildings and various separable attributes of both. A transaction of rights implies, under normal circumstances, a mutual gain from trade (otherwise why trade?). The evolution of a city may thus be viewed as an entropic system in which gains to trade are progressively being diminished. Unrealised gains from trade – rent gaps – are like energy boundaries in a thermodynamic system. They exist due to barriers preventing dissipation of surplus value (stored energy). The barriers are physical in the natural science analogy. In an economy they are transaction costs. Physical distance, conventions and laws that fail to define clear rights, technological costs and legal costs all raise the costs of exchange and present the realisation of gains from trade. The externalities and public goods problems that form the conventional justification for urban planning are problems because they are unmarketable resources over which property rights are unclearly assigned. The cost of enclosing these resources and assigning clear ownership prevents their spontaneous redistribution. Institutions have the effect of reducing the costs of exchange, removing barriers and increasing the value of total social product. The traditional focus of urban planning, however, often seems not to be to help the urban system maximise gains from trade but to maximise conformity to a plan. This would be a fine thing if plans were made with complete information and optimal. But there is no guarantee of this as the discussion in the next section argues. The conventional focus is changing, however. The UK will shortly have a 'planning gain supplement', which like American-style impact fees, aims to price new development per unit according to a roughly estimated average social cost. It will be a tax price set by governments in their capacity as monopoly suppliers of development rights and a very imperfect pricing mechanism therefore. However, as an institution, it should reduce uncertainty-related transaction costs and thereby ease the flow of value. The UK planning system has recently had its biggest overhaul since its inception in the 1940s (Webster, 2005a) but it has a long way to go to align itself with the reality of complex urban dynamics.

7.4 Theories of emergent social order

Theories of spontaneous order should occupy a central place in the intellectual lexicon of planners and in the curricula of planning schools. In many ways they form a natural social scientific underpinning for planning in post-Keynesian mixed urban economies. Prominent among such theory is the work of Austrian born economist Friedrich von Hayek. Intellectual sparring partner to his Cambridge colleague John Maynard Keynes, Hayek lost in the battle of ideas that shaped the reconstruction of western Europe after the second world war, but was rehabilitated with a Nobel Economics prize in 1974. He went on to influence the 1980s Thatcher revolution and it is his legacy not Keynes' that in Britain and many other countries, continues to reshape the boundaries of the modern state.

One of Hayek's fundamental insights was that knowledge is dispersed throughout society (Hayek, 1945). Individuals each have their own subjective knowledge that uniquely equips them to be productive in combination with the subjective knowledge of others. Only an individual owner of a particular resource (house, home, labour, factory) can truly evaluate the net benefits of taking a new job, shopping at a new centre, moving home, expanding a business, selling a business, redeveloping an old building, renting out a piece of land and so on. That being so, attempts to co-ordinate the actions of individuals through centralised planning on the basis of centralised 'objective' knowledge, are likely to fail in many important respects. In the 1930s and 1940s Hayek anticipated the failures of central planning that brought about the collapse of the command economies several decades later (Hayek, 1935, 1948). His argument with Keynes and the post war socialist project was not over the ends of socialism but over the means by which it sought to achieve them. Specifically, planning would founder, he warned, because of the twin problems of incentive alignment and information. Attempts to foster the advancement of material production and social harmony through collective ownership of the means of production would fail because agents would not have the incentive to invest resources they own (including their own labour) and because of the impossibility of obtaining centrally, sufficient and meaningful information.

The argument was not about whether planning was needed or not. Since no-one can live as an island, even the simplest of households have to make economic projects – to exchange certain goods and skills for others. The question is how should the multitude of economic projects that make up society and economy be coordinated? Hayek, following von Mises before him, saw the price system as a simple but sophisticated institution that had emerged in parallel with modern human civilisation, underpinning it and shaping it into what it is. In particular and importantly, the price system (and the rules governing any specific instance of it) underpins the division of labour. Without an agreed set or rules about how prices function, exchange possibilities are very limited. The specialisation of knowledge and skill in a bartering economy does not run very deep. The price system permits an increasingly specialised division of labour.

It also permits an increasingly specialised division of land. The use of land under a bartering system remains as unspecialised as the division of labour. The knowledge specialisation facilitated by prices includes specific knowledge about how to make land more productive. Much of this knowledge has to be discovered. It is discovered locally and is locally specific. To try to replicate the process of spontaneous discovery by substituting centrally amassed objective knowledge for decentralised subjective knowledge and by substituting central land use planning for decentralised land use planning (voluntary transactions) has produced some outstanding planning failures over the last 50 years (Hall, 1982; Webster, 2005b).

Hayek's views on spontaneous social order are also views on emergence. For him, spontaneous order meant social regularities and conventions that result from human actions but not a specific action. In this, he synthesised a long tradition of theories of emergent social order (Barry, 1982; Klien, 1997). These are briefly summarised in the following.

Social scientists of the classical and medieval tradition understood the idea of emergence better than many of their 20th century successors. The Scottish Enlightenment produced the first major synthesis but academic discussion was underway well before the 18th century. Luis de Molina (1535-1600) was part of the Spanish school of Salamanca, an important theological city on the Portuguese border. Theologian philosophers from as early as the 13th century had been grappling with questions about social order and economics and the apparent autonomy of individual economic agents working to the plans of an omniscient and omnipotent God. One of Molina's insights was that a 'just price' emerges from interactions of agents demanding and supplying a commodity, not from the technical process of production. In Britain, Sir Matthew Hale (1609-1676), a prominent judge of the Commonwealth under Oliver Cromwell and then Lord Chief Justice under King Charles II, laid some of the foundations for the Scottish enlightenment view of spontaneous order. In particular, he saw common law as an emergent phenomenon that was superior to deliberately constructed law built upon *a priori* theories. Truly effective law, he argued, was discovered not made. In this, he presented an antithesis to his contemporary Thomas Hobbes, who saw the state as an agency for making laws to promote the welfare of its subjects. Bernard Mandeville (1670-1733) published in his *Fable of the Bees*, an early version of Adam Smith's *invisible hand* theory: individual agents acting selfishly give rise to the social good. His encouragement to act selfishly probably obscured the significance of his insight, which was later improved upon by Josiah Tucker (1712-1799), Dean of Gloucester – a town just up river from the great English trading port of Bristol. In a pamphlet urging against going to war for the sake of trade, Tucker anticipated Smith's views on the self-organising powers of open markets and the destructive effects of centralisation, including monopolies. He also made the emergence argument more palatable – we can see societal patterns of cooperation as arising from the self-centred acts of individual agents without having to urge selfishness.

David Hume (1711-1776), Adam Ferguson (1723-1816) and Adam Smith (1723-1790) crafted the basis for modern ideas on spontaneous social and economic order. Hume argued that socially beneficial rules emerge to lower the costs of trading. Like Hale's common law, rules governing rights and obligations over property help improve stability in society and promote growth and wellbeing, although they were not designed for that purpose by their inventors. Ferguson similarly saw that institutions that oil the wheels of society are discovered by trial and error. Society's successive waves of enlightenment ages, he suggested, were stumbled upon without orchestration or conscious planning. Smith's contributions to his own particular enlightenment wave are well known. *The Wealth of Nations* (1776) painted a picture of a self-regulating and spontaneous order emerging from individual impulses and actions on the precondition of a three-fold minimum ordering rule set: the rule of law, private property and freedom to contract. These three institutions ensure that individuals retain the fruits of their knowledge and thus have the incentive to invest their resources in ways that benefit others (through exchange).

Carl Menger (1840-1921), a principal influence on Hayek, saw language, religion, law, organisations, the state, markets and money as emergent phenomena. Language emerges to reduce the costs of communication; moral systems evolve to reduce the costs of social interaction and economic transaction; money evolves to reduce the costs of exchange. Menger and the so called Austrian School of economics that he inspired, argued that social science should be founded on the study of individual agents. The methodological individualism of Menger was stronger and more well reasoned than Smith and the Enlightenment philosophers. Only individuals can value things because knowledge is personal and subjective. We must therefore look for explanations of social regularities in the *composite effects* of many individual actions. His explanation for the emergence of money illustrates this well. Individuals need to exchange their resources with those of others in order to prosper. Only individuals can evaluate any particular exchange possibility. In a bartering system, successful exchange depends on the rare double coincidence – two individuals valuing each others' goods approximately equally. This limits exchange and wealth creation. Some individuals will realise that it is in their interest to make indirect exchanges, acquiring goods valued highly by a large number of people. This way they can store value, make more exchanges and become richer. As they do, others imitate, accumulating commodities that other people want. Less saleable goods are gradually exchanged for more saleable goods and the most saleable of all eventually become money. Money is therefore an emergent social institution, evolving by trial, error and competition.

7.5 Spontaneous order, the price system and urban planning

Hayek's notion of emergent order was a synthesis and elaboration of these and other historical contributions. He should not be understood, however, to be antithetical to all forms of planning, as should already be clear (Lai, 1999). The challenge Hayek poses to planners is to consider which kinds of transactions cannot be effectively governed spontaneously by the price system. David Hume understood the problem 250 years ago. He described the coordination problem that became the subject of welfare economic theory in the 20th century:

> Two neighbours may agree to drain a meadow, which they possess in common; because it is easy for them to know each other's mind; and each must perceive, that the immediate consequences of his failing in his part, is, the abandoning of the whole project. But 'tis very difficult, and indeed impossible, that a thousand persons should agree in any such action; it being difficult for them to concert so complicated a design, and still more difficult for them to execute it; while each

> seeks a pretext to free himself of the trouble and expense. And would lay the whole burden on others. Political society remedies both these inconveniences (Hume, 1739, p. 538).

Some goods cannot easily be priced because of collective action problems. In Hume's example, rights to benefits from the meadow are collective while rights to wealth given up to finance its improvement are individual. The misalignment makes it difficult for a price to emerge. Hume's argument – that collectively consumed goods need to be organised by political society – was a foundational one for the expansion of the national and municipal state during the 20th century, including its expansion into land use and spatial planning. The static nature of the interventionist argument (particularly as formalised by economists Arthur Pigu and Paul Samuelson) was exposed by Ronald Coase in one of his two Nobel prize winning essays 'The Problem of Social Cost' (1960). Coase showed that collective action problems in society are problems of unclear property rights. Many can be solved by the clarification of rights, and changes in the way in which rights are allocated can move contested resources in and out of the public domain. In his other Nobel prize winning essay – 'The Nature of the Firm' (1937) – containing ideas formulated while he was an undergraduate at the London School of Economics, Coase highlighted a fundamental variable governing the evolution of property rights in society – transaction costs. Hume, in the quote above, noted that *political society* (a particular type of organisation) needed to remedy the land resource allocation problem faced by the imaginary neighbours. Coase's insight was that it is transaction costs that determine the emergence of organisations.

It was economist Steven Cheung who explicitly extended the argument to governments, but nothing need be added to Coase's original formulation to make his 1937 paper a theory of all organisations, be they firms or governments. Organisations form because individual transactions are costly – involving the costs of searching for exchange partners, making and policing contracts and so on. If the costs of cooperating within a firm (dubbed 'hierarchy' by transaction-costs economist Oliver Williamson) are lower than those of cooperating in the market place then a firm will form. Coase asked why, if this is true, does society not grow into one big firm. His answer was that at some point the cost of organising cooperation within a firm gets too high and it becomes more efficient to transact with the market. Rising organisational costs at some point exceed market transaction costs saved and firms and functions within them break up, out-source, shrink or stop expanding. The same may be said of government organisations and agencies delivering particular functions like urban planning. Deconstruct urban planning into its multiple component functions and it becomes clear that the rationale for delivering those functions within or without the market changes over time.

If an entrepreneur were to discover a mechanism for collecting contributions from Hume's neighbours and to invent a contract that clearly assigns rights and responsibilities to them and also to the capitalist who lends money for the drainage project and to the engineer who manages it once built, then it may be that the project can be priced by the market. The question arises, which form of organisation can more efficiently and fairly deliver the collective action? The answer will depend on the relative performance of different organisations (firm, government, hybrid) in organising the various transactions that constitute the land reclamation project (Williamson, 1999). If the *political society* comprises only the neighbours, then the differences may not be great, although a private entrepreneur is likely to be more successful in organising finance and ongoing management. If it is a much wider society with many other responsibilities, then its information handicap and incentive problems will disadvantage it against the market solution. Crucial to the division of labour between private and public sector actors are the costs of gathering information and creating and sustaining multi-lateral agreements and contracts. As these transaction costs change over time, with changes in technology, legal instruments and preferences, the boundaries between public and private domains and between state and market change. To truly understand the nature of the self-organising city, therefore, urban planners need to endogenise the planning function in their analysis. That is to say, they need to see themselves as just one of the many different kinds of agents who plan the city. One reason why they seem to find it difficult to do this is their rigid distinction between public and private benefit. The market is not generally viewed as a benevolent institution that confers social benefits on society. This leads to the idea that it is only public plans that protect the public good and that their function is fundamentally different in purpose to private plans. This is incorrect.

7.6 Multiple interacting plans

Spatial patterns emerge through the complex interaction of many plans. One of the unfortunate outcomes of the professionalisation of urban planning during the last century has been the profession's view of itself as the only provider of urban planners and plans. Nothing could be farther from the truth. Anyone who invests in land and buildings, be they a householder extending a home or an industrialist redeveloping a factory site, has to coordinate with a multitude of other economic agents. All have economic plans and each plan has the potential to change the path of urban evolution. All types of development require coordination and planning. Public sector planners have just one among many types of coordinating roles – coordinating between agents who have unclear rights over shared resources (streets, the air around a polluting factory, views, parks, city centre precincts, redeveloped dockland environments and so on). If property rights are clear, such that all interested parties can coordinate among themselves, then planning can be left to the market. In reality most cities are planned by the private plans of individual agents. They coordinate locally via the price mechanism and as a result, land rights change, subdivide and combine yielding new uses and improvements. Most discernible patterns in cities (housing market areas, industrial clusters, service quarters, specialist shopping areas, financial and entertainment centres)

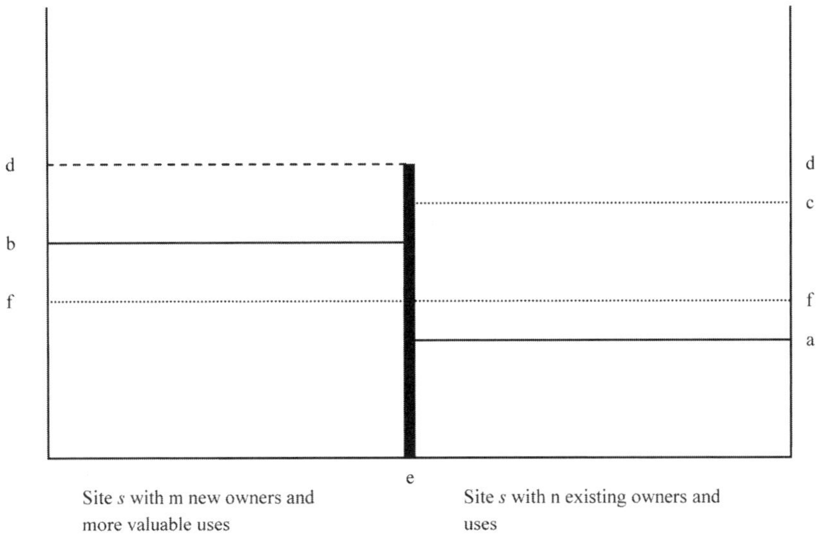

Figure 7.1 Plans, transaction costs and the distribution of value

emerge spontaneously. Individual agents seeking only to meet private goals end up meeting the needs of many others and creating a city that benefits an entire citizenry.

Public sector urban planners are most benefit to society when they proactively seek opportunities to remove barriers to land transactions that yield net gains for all parties to the transaction, including third parties (neighbours and more dispersed consumers of externalities). Figure 7.1 illustrates this. The figure is not a conventional economics graph – the horizontal dimension does not represent a quantity but is drawn to continue the analogy with entropy in a thermodynamic system. The height of the two horizontal lines *a* and *b* represent different valuations of a piece of land. This is like different levels of energy in a thermodynamic system – different temperatures in different rooms of a building, for example. The barriers to redistributing heat in a building are physical – the walls separating rooms for example. The barriers to redistributing the differences in the valuation of a tradable resource are the costs of transaction. In the absence of transaction costs, value naturally flows from one agent to another as they exchange goods and money for mutual gain. There is a natural entropy in the economy as value differences disperse along chains of transacting agents. Heat in a building spreads from warmer to cooler rooms. Potential gains from trade dissipate through economic exchange. Potential (unrealised) gains from trade are like free energy in a thermodynamic system – the energy in the system that can be converted into work. Gains from trade in land can be converted into welfare-raising land development. Entropy in the land economy drives what I have already termed the division of land.

Imagine that David Hume's meadow, 250 years on, is now on the edge of city and under the ownership of *n* owners in a variety of established uses. The aggregated market value summed across each owner's property is *a*. Then imagine that an entrepreneur, community activist, capitalist or entrepreneurial government planner sees an opportunity to redevelop the area and creates a project that combines the skills of house builders, commercial developers, engineers, architects, financiers, civic associations and so on. The project is organised by a legal entity *q* (a development firm, individual capitalist or partnership organisation for example). The project's objective is to combine ownership of the site by purchasing from *n* owners, prepare the site, design and construct the buildings and then subdividing ownership to *m* new owners in a variety of new and more valuable uses. The estimated aggregated market value of the finished project is *b*, which becomes the ceiling price bid by *q* – the maximum *q* will pay to secure the rights from existing owners. If each of the properties of the *n* owners were on the market, then the aggregated floor price for the site would be *a* – the minimum that owners are prepared to accept to give up rights to the site. However, a coincidence of economic projects is unlikely – all existing owners having plans to relocate at the same time as an entrepreneur having plans to redevelop. This means that the floor price of the existing users will be higher than the market price. They will need compensating – for the expense of relocating assets, for inconvenience, for temporary accommodation, for legal representation to ensure a good deal, for the costs of searching for alternative locations and so on. These are all costs that will have to be born if the transactions between *n*, *q* and *m* are to take place. Assume for now that the benefits and costs of the project are entirely contained within the trading parties, i.e. there are no third party benefits or costs.

Now consider various outcomes from this coordination problem.

1. *No site consolidation transaction costs:* At the market value of the existing properties the potential (aggregated) gains from trade are *(b-a)*. If the existing users all had their properties on the market at aggregate price *a*, then individually or collectively they might have negotiated (via and agent) with *q* on the sale price. Depending on the relative market power, the gains from trade *(b-a)* might have gone entirely to the existing owners, entirely to *q* or split between them, say at *f*, with *(b-f)* going to buyer *q* and *(f-a)* to the sellers.
2. *Transaction costs exceed gains from trade:* If the various compensation costs above the market price aggregate to *c*, the urban planning project of agent *q* will not go ahead. The floor price, including transaction costs exceeds the ceiling price. Transaction costs have prevented the realisation of gains from trade.
3. *Transaction costs <= gains from trade:* If the coordination costs are less than or equal to *(b-a),* then the transaction will go ahead. The market can deliver this urban plan.

4. *Total benefits > private benefits, transaction costs <= private gains from trade:* If the project yields benefits to third parties, call them *t*, (neighbours and more dispersed agents), equal, for example, to *(d-b)* and transaction costs < *(b-a)* then the market will deliver this plan, including its social benefits without the input of a government plan.
5. *Total benefits < private benefits, transaction costs <= private gains from trade:* If the project imposes social costs to third parties through negative externalities then the private gains from trade exceed the social gains from trade. Say the value of third party costs is *(b-f)*. Without regulation, the private plan would go ahead but the net gains from trade are reduced to *(f-a)*. Note that if an institution was in place that allowed value to flow from *q* to affected third parties *t*, then the plan would still yield net benefits to society. *q* could compensate *t* by *(b-f),* exactly compensating them for the social costs imposed; the residual gains from trade to be shared by the private transacting parties is *(f-a),* which is sufficient to induce a transaction so long as the transaction costs are < *(f-a)*. If a government planner sought to prevent the transaction (for example, because it failed to conform to a zoning plan or agreed density or use pattern) then all would be worse off (apart perhaps from the planner). This is equivalent to increasing transaction costs (thick black line) to a prohibitive level.

Instead of expending profession expertise on implementing institutions that raise transaction costs, government plans should be creating new solutions to urban development and regeneration problems that lower the costs of private plans and allow greater amounts of value redistribution. Of course, if the third party costs are unquestionably high – for example the loss of a highly valued natural or built environment – then an appropriate response may indeed be to prohibit development. Few who know the Balearic island of Minorca – local residents, visitors, investors and land owners – would want to see the island's pristine south coast fall to the coastal sprawl that has overrun most of mainland Spain's south coast. Where the dispersed public interest is as clear as this, a strong proscriptive policy has the effect of reducing transaction costs. The simple rule is effective in imposing order in the development industry – prohibiting certain private plans from taking effect. Where a preservation rule prohibits development from a land resource of less obvious social value, as is the case with London's greenbelt, for example, then the simple rule will not be as effective at ordering the complex process of urban growth. The policy will be contended and a policy that should have reduced the costs of individual development plans ends up increasing them by high uncertainty and administrative costs. The illustration in Figure 7.2 makes the point that cities evolve under the influence of individual economic plans. Each plan is made at a point in time and interacts with many others. Because they are each shaped by specific configurations of local and subjective knowledge, they interact in space and time in unpredictable ways. Potential gains from trade diffuse over space and time as agents perceive rent gaps and invest in them to realise

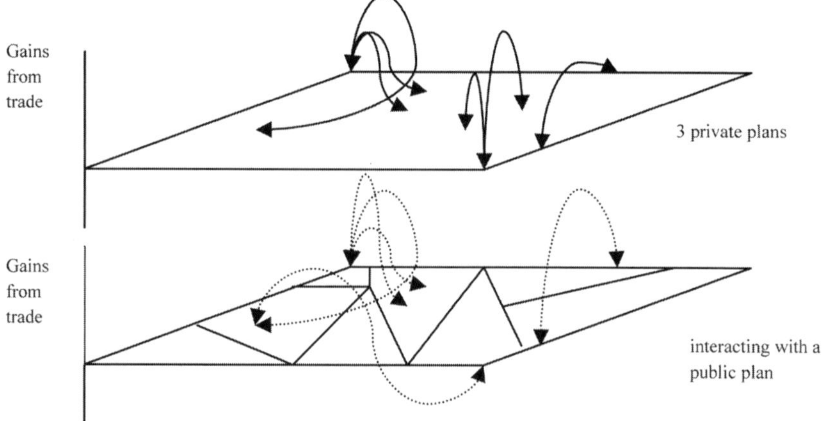

Figure 7.2 Gains from trade in three private plans modified by a public plan

the gains. Government plans that specify detailed land uses, densities, spatial strategies, infrastructural investment and regeneration proposals are just one kind of plan amongst many. They work by the effect they have on the economic plans of individuals and firms – by assigning and attenuating property rights over land and by changing the costs of the transactions that constitute those private plans. Their impact is to modify the redistribution of value brought about by private plans. The upper half of Figure 7.2 represents three private plans: respectively involving transactions between four, three and two agents. The height of the linking arrows represents the value of gains from trade achieved by the plans. The lower half of the figure represents a government land use plan (the polygons), which interacts with the private plans in unpredictable ways, changing the flows of value between agents co-operating in the private plans. The four-way cooperation remains intact in the diagram. The three-way cooperation disappears, for example because the public plan has prohibited development in a part of the city. The two-way plan remains but the value of the transaction has been reduced, for example because the public plan has reduced the value of the land being transacted. The reassignment of property rights by the government plan induces an additional private plan which has positive private gains from trade but negative total gains when social costs are accounted for, because of unanticipated effects of densification, for example.

Each of the arrows in Figure 7.2 is a time-space specific flow of value and these three dimensions – time, space and value of individual transactions influence the total value of the private plan. They also influence the value of other private plans and indeed the value of a public plan. It is the spatial and temporal sequence of these interactions that yields spontaneous urban order. The public plan cannot control it but it can participate in it.

7.7 Conclusion

Like the division of labour in society, the division of land emerges hand-in-hand with the specialisation of knowledge. The more specialised knowledge, labour and land become, the greater the interconnectivity in society, the more numerous are the economic transactions that sustain it and the more complex and unpredictable the trends and patterns of growth. Individuals and households plan the transactions that sustain and improve their wellbeing. The numbers of economic plans governing the life of an individual in the course of a single day are numerous. As individual plans are made, firms, governments and other organisations form. An academic will generally find it less costly to pool the property right to her own labour with those of others – becoming employed by a university – than to organise the delivery of teaching and research via many separate market transactions. Organisations, like land use patterns are emergent social phenomena. The plans of organisations and individuals have to be coordinated to work. This happens in two ways: in a decentralised way via the price mechanism and via centralised control. How the two approaches should be balanced is one of the big social questions of our time. In a 1945 paper, Hayek argued that the central theoretical problem of all social science is to discover how civilisation can advance 'by extending the number of important operations which we can perform without thinking about them' (Hayek, 1945, p. 88). One of the greatest insights that the complexity paradigm, specifically the idea of emergence, can bring to the scholarship of cities and city planning is the understanding that cities can be shaped more effectively by incentive than by spatial design. We should be asking questions such as what kinds of rules can be devised and crafted into the DNA of urban dynamics that will help cities spontaneously become more sustainable, liveable, just and wealthy? The difference between this position and that of cybernetics and centralised spatial planning is that we need not be so concerned with plan optimality or conformity to the plan. Rules can be deemed to work if the outcomes are good – or better than the outcomes that can be envisaged with alternative rules. Cellular automata (CA) models of emergent cities might be more use as a metaphor than as a decision support tool. Our task might be framed as discovering rules that govern spontaneously evolving cities in a way that maximises the private and social value of individual plans. This would move the intellectual project of urban planning on and at the same time root it back in a centuries old tradition of classical social science.

References

Barry, N. (1982) 'The tradition of spontaneous order', *Literature of Liberty*, vol. 5, pp. 7-58.

Batty, M. (1994) 'A chronicle of scientific planning: The Anglo-American modelling experience', *Journal of the American Planning Association*, vol. 59, pp. 7-16.

Coase, R.H. (1937) 'The nature of the firm', *Economica N.S.*, vol. 4(16), pp. 386-405.

Coase, R.H. (1960) 'The problem of social cost', *Journal of Law and Economics*, vol. 3, pp. 1-44.

Evans, A.W. (1991) 'Rabbit hutches on postage stamps: planning, development and political economy', *Urban Studies*, vol. 28(6), pp. 853-870.

Hall, P. (1982) *Great Planning Disasters*, University of California Press, Berkeley.

Hayek, F.A. (1935) *Collectivist Economic Planning*, Routledge, London.

Hayek, F.A. (1945) 'The use of knowledge in society', *American Economic Review*, vol. 35(4), pp. 519-30, and in F.A. Hayek (1996) *Individualism and Economic Order*, UCP, Chicago, pp. 77-91.

Hayek, F.A. (1948) *Individualism and Economic Order*, University of Chicago Press, Chicago.

Kasper, W. and Streit, M.E. (1998) *Institutional Economics*, Edward Elgar, Cheltenham.

Klien, D. (1997) 'Convention, social order and the two coordinations', *Constitutional Political Economy*, vol. 8, pp. 319-335.

Lai, L.W.C. (1999) 'Hayek and town planning: A note on Hayek's views towards town planning in *The Constitution of Liberty*', *Environment and Planning A*, vol. 31(9), pp. 1521-1710.

Webster, C.J. (1994) 'GIS and the scientific inputs to urban planning: prediction and prescription', *Environment and Planning B*, vol. 21(2), pp. 145-157.

Webster, C.J. and Lai, L.W.C. (2003) *Property Rights, Planning and Markets: Managing Spontaneous Cities*, Edward Elgar, Cheltenham.

Webster, C.J. (2005a) 'The new institutional economics and the evolution of modern urban planning: insights, issues and lessons', *Town Planning Review*, vol. 76(4), pp. 471-501.

Webster, C.J. (2005b) 'Editorial: Diversifying the institutions of local planning', *Economic Affairs*, vol. 25(4), pp. 4-10.

Webster, C.J. (2006) 'The battle for ideas that shaped British planning', *Proceedings of the International Symposium on Epistemological Understandings of Spatial Policy and Rural Change: Experiences from Korea, the US, the UK and Asian Countries*. Seoul National University, May 25, 2006, pp. 31-59.

Williamson, O.E. (1999) 'Public and private bureaucracies: a transaction cost economics perspective', *Journal of Law and Economic Organisation*, vol. 15(1), pp. 306-342.

Wolfram, S. (2002) *A New Kind of Science*. Wolfram Media Inc., Champaign, IL.

Chapter 8
Spatial Planning Processes: Applying a Dynamic Complex Systems Perspective

Menno Huys and Marcel van Gils[1]

In this chapter we argue that the concepts of co-evolution and complex adaptive systems derived from complexity theories, offer useful additions to contemporary conceptualisations of complex dynamics surrounding planning processes. In particular, they offer an improved understanding of how dynamics are actually generated in the social and physical realities in which planning processes are intervening, by explicating the role of interactions between elements involved in the planning process and interactions resulting from interventions in the physical and social system. This, then, allows for the development of a realist approach for understanding the planning process at hand, which can serve as a basis for the creation of more effective management. Despite the assumption that planning processes remain largely unpredictable, it is argued that this does not necessarily leave the planner helpless. Planning still matters, but it implies a specific set of tasks when confronted with dynamic complex settings. In this chapter it is argued that the main task for the planner in such contexts is first of all to acknowledge and understand the mechanisms of co-evolution at work. Second, it is about facilitating the creation of the necessary conditions that allow for an optimal circulation of knowledge and information through the planning process and the social and physical system it intervenes in. Planning becomes essentially a matter of creating the right connections, based upon a sophisticated and flexible understanding of the situation at hand.

8.1 Introduction

In this chapter it is argued that we have a need for concepts based upon a dynamic complex systems perspective to increase our understanding of the physical and social dynamics in which humans try to interfere via planning processes. This, then, can help to improve the management of these processes (Hajer and Wagenaar, 2003; Teisman, 2005). In order to do so, we first sketch the central concepts used

1 Menno Huys is PhD researcher at the Faculty of Technology, Policy and Management, Delft University of Technology, The Netherlands. Marcel van Gils is strategy consultant at Strategy Works/Academy in Rotterdam, The Netherlands.

in this chapter. The focus is on complex *planning processes*. These processes are defined as conscious attempts to intervene in the social and physical realities in order to facilitate the spatial development that is desired and deemed necessary by the actors involved. In these planning processes different actors come together. These actors often have different goals with regard to a specific spatial issue. As most actors do not possess the resources to achieve outcomes on their own, they need to collaborate with others. As such, actors start to form all kinds of formal and informal interactions. Hanf and Scharpf (1978) introduced the concept of *mutual dependency* to describe this phenomenon; actors need each other's resources in order to achieve their interest and/or find solutions for their problems. The resulting planning processes consist of webs of interrelations between actors, converging around a specific spatial issue.

Generally speaking there are two ways theorists deal with the challenge of understanding complex dynamics. The first group departs from the idea that they can understand dynamics with help of meta-theories. The second group is departing from the interpretative side; for them analysing the planning practices of the actors involved is the best way to understand what is happening (Walby, 2004). In this chapter we adopt the first line of reasoning and aim to offer meta-theoretical understanding of how dynamics are generated. Within the meta-theoretical line of thought, several theories and conceptual frameworks have been developed to understand planning processes. In this chapter we shortly present several major perspectives that have been identified by a variety of scholars. This overview is meant to embed the dynamic complex systems perspective that we propose. It allows us to indicate the main differences between the dynamic complex systems perspective and more traditional static perspectives. Next we shall illustrate how such a perspective can improve our understanding of the real world in which planning process interfere, which serves as a solid ground for discerning intervening strategies. The chapter is structured in the following way.

Section 8.2 presents an overview of the more traditional static perspectives and introduces the dynamic complex systems perspective. Section 8.3 presents two concepts, known as Complex Adaptive Systems (CAS) and co-evolution. Section 8.4 explores the implications of the dynamic complex system perspective for the management of spatial planning processes. We conclude this chapter with a discussion (Section 8.5) about the promises and dangers of theoretical concepts regarding complex dynamics for spatial planning processes and the roles that planners can play in these settings.

8.2 Introducing a dynamic perspective in spatial planning

Throughout the years many scholars have tried to understand complex dynamics surrounding planning processes. These dynamics are the result of many interactions among crucial actors. Interactions have been the central object of study in a long history of systems thinking. System theorists use the image of a system to help them understand reality (Hick, 1991). Senge states that: 'System thinking is a discipline for seeing wholes. It is a framework for seeing interrelationships rather than things, for seeing patterns of change rather than static snapshots' (1990, p. 68). A system view helps in gaining insight in the interrelationships that underlie dynamic situations. It offers a broad research focus wherein as many of the relevant actors, interactions and effects (of the interactions) are taken into account as possible. Systems can be defined as sets of elements that are interconnected together and which form properties of the whole rather than of its consistent parts (Checkland, 1981). Generally speaking a classic, static perspective on systems has been evolving from reductionist, via holistic towards expansionist strands. the next section presents a short overview of different streams in the classic, static perspective.

Evolution of the classic, static perspective

Traditionally planning and policy processes[2] have been conceptualised as being linear of character. The linear model, better known as the phase model or rational comprehensive model, is originally derived from Laswell (1951). During the 1960s and early 1970s the approach was dominant in spatial planning; it was assumed that planning processes would follow a logical and ordered sequence of phases: Problem definition, information gathering, and selection of possible interventions, decision making, implementation and evaluation. During the first phases of preparation all relevant costs and benefits with regard to the issue were gathered. Next alternatives were developed and the best available option (in terms of costs and benefits) was selected for implementation. The planning process was seen as a rational, balanced and objective problem solving process. The well-known blueprint planning method is based on this rational perspective, which breaths the legacy of the survey before plan ideal once introduced by Geddes at the start of the 20th century (Faludi, 1973). The perspective has been heavily criticised for its assumptions. Policy processes would not unravel in neat and orderly ways and people seemed not to be the rational beings they were assumed to be. Amongst others, Lindblom's incrementalism (1959) and Simon's bounded rationality (1979) offered modifications to this rational view of the planning process. Still however, the political dimension remained largely ignored within the rational perspective, since its ideal was to take planning out of politics.

Gradually scientists and practitioners acknowledged that the rational approach did not suit very well in planning situations characterised by interactions between actors. As a consequence several more politically sensitive perspectives emerged, like the policy streams model.

2 In the remainder of this chapter we shall only use the term planning processes. For us policy-making processes form an important part of the planning process, which is broader and also deals with implementation.

The policy streams model (Kingdon, 1984) is based on the garbage can model (Cohen et al., 1972)[3] and depicts the process as consisting of three streams: A stream of participants *(i)*, of problems *(ii)* and solutions *(iii)*. The model is *holistic*, in the sense that it shows that several processes are unravelling at the same time (multi-process), with their own logics and dynamics. At certain moments the three streams are coming together and a policy window opens. The windows can be regarded as opportunities where the problems are linked to solutions and decision makers (Kingdon, 1984). The strength of Kingdon's approach is that he conceptualises policy processes from a holistic point of view (i.e. the sum of the process is more then the actions of single actors). He also acknowledges that there is always much about these processes that remains unpredictable. He argued that if one can specify the initial conditions in a process, and if one has good information about those conditions, then one can predict outcomes more reliably than if one does not know the initial conditions (Kingdon, 1995). Hence, he accepts the unpredictable dynamics of the process, but he believes it is possible to discern the initial starting conditions. In the model it is assumed that policies and plans can be traced back to their origins in retrospect. Evenly important for our purposes, he does not offer the analytical tools for understanding the dynamics from an interactionist point of view.

A different strand of theories aimed to develop a more sophisticated understanding of the actual interactions that generate dynamics. So-called network theories started to question the imminent rationality of actors in processes and the rationality of interactions. Network theorists describe processes in terms of circularity, feedback and networks. Processes are marked by decisions which are the crystallisation of a round of decision making, and which are also the starting point of a new round (Teisman, 1992). The round concept has mingled with (policy) network theories. In the network perspective processes consist of networks of actors that are mutually dependent for achieving their goals (Kickert et al., 1997; Koppenjan and Klijn, 2004). Several networks can co-exist at the same time and the interactions of actors within and between these networks generate dynamics. Plans are seen as the result of conflict, bargaining and coalition formation among groups of actors. In literature there are several applications of types of networks of actors, e.g. advocacy coalitions (Sabatier and Jenkins, 1993), issue networks (Heclo, 1978), discourse coalitions (Hajer, 1995), communities of practice (Wenger, 1998) and epistemic communities (Haas, 1992). The rounds/networks models look at the dynamics by focusing on the interactions between actors in the planning. The network theories are *expansionist* since they focus very much on contextual interactions. The network theorists start to recognise that interactions might not be rational or linear. The theorists open up the idea of non-linearity, which means that due to chains of interactions the outcomes of interactions are no

3 The garbage can model stresses the anarchical nature of organisations as 'loose collections of ideas' as opposed to rational 'coherent structures'. Organisations discover preferences through action, rather than act out of preferences (Cohen et al., 1972, p. 2).

longer predictable. The non-linearity is mainly due to the fact that people cannot control extended chains of interaction. Network theorists state that non-linearity can be reconstructed and cause and effect can still be found in retrospective (in line with Kingdon's opinion on knowing the initial conditions).

The amount of alternative conceptualisations (in terms of phases, streams and networks) has however not been able to deal with the inherent unpredictability of the dynamics surrounding planning processes. Emerging events and outcomes have largely remained unpredictable and unexplained. Cause and effect relations of lots of these outcomes have never been found. A lack of understanding about dynamics in planning processes is an explanation for why we often get surprised by unanticipated outcomes and unintended effects. Recently evolutionary economics (see Chapter 5) and complexity and chaos theories have entered the field of spatial planning. These theories shed new light on how inherent non-linear dynamics are generated (see for example De Roo, 1999; Innes and Booher, 1999). In the following section we introduce two concepts (co-evolution and Complex Adaptive Systems) derived from theories on dynamic complex systems (often labelled complexity theories) to present a different view on non-linearity. This allows us to develop a more sophisticated understanding of the mechanisms at work that shape the dynamics. This, then, can serve as a basis for the creation of management strategies in the quest for effective spatial planning processes.

Towards a dynamic complex systems perspective

Dynamics in complex systems depend on the number of actors in a system and the diversity and interdependency among these actors, as well as the interdependency between the system and its environment (Checkland, 1981). In early system thinking there was a strong belief in linear cause-effect relations and the predictability of developments (rational view, in line with Lasswell). Systems could be understood by reducing them to their basic building blocks and by looking for mechanisms through which these interacted (De Roo, 1999; Innes and Booher, 1999). However, in the operation of dynamic social systems linear relations were difficult to find. Moreover, plans that were implemented worked out in unpredictable and sometimes even perverse ways (Innes and Booher, 2001). Different system theories revisions emerged in which circularity and feedback where introduced (parallel to development streams, rounds model). The theories do however not have answers to seemingly more fundamental unpredictability in and around planning processes.

In this section the concepts Complex Adaptive Systems (CAS) and co-evolution will be introduced to outline the dynamic complex systems perspective. The concepts CAS and co-evolution have their roots in different theories and scientific disciplines. Whereas CAS thinking originates from systems thinking, co-evolution has its roots in biology, evolutionary economics and environmental science (Kauffman, 1993). The concepts will be used to explore a meta-theoretical view on fundamental unpredictability.

8.3 CAS and co-evolution

Insights from the natural and physical sciences did lead to the emergence of an alternative view on social systems (Hwang, 1996; Kaufmann, 2000). Complexity theory, that is an amalgam of various concepts and theories from various natural and economic sciences, builds on and enriches system theory by articulating additional characteristics of complex systems (see Chapter 2). The system concept was rethought; new ideas about non-linear relationships and the relationship between the system and its environment emerged (Walby, 2004). Non-linear relationships here imply that there is no consistent relationship between cause and effect (also not in retrospective, see notion on non-linearity above). In other words, the same causes can produce totally different kinds of effect, even when the circumstances are more or less the same (Teisman, 2005). The adaptability of the complex systems and the way these systems evolved became the centre of the debate. A system that behaves like an organism can adapt and change in response to information it gathers from its environment, with which it is continuously interacting (Capra, 1996). Especially this notion of *contextual interaction* is seen as important for gaining insight in the dynamic behaviour of a system (parallel to the network perspective on systems). A system is constantly evolving as a result from perpetual and complex interactions among its parts and its contextual environment.

The importance of interrelations within the system and with the context has implications for our understanding of complex systems. The inherent unpredictability of dynamic complex systems results from the interactions among its elements and with the context. Dynamic complex adaptive systems are characterised by non-linearity and *ad random* fluctuations and influences coming from a contextual environment, to which the system as whole adapts (Axelrod and Cohen, 1999; Wagenaar, 2005).

The concept *co-evolution* is essential for understanding interactions. It means that actors evolve through each other (in an iterative and reinforcing way), resulting in a specific kind of interaction, which is the primary reason for evolution (Van den Bergh and Gowdy, 2000). Co-evolution is 'the way each element influences and is in turn influenced by all other related elements in an (eco)system' (Mitleton-Kelly, 2003, p. 7). There is no strict hierarchy of actors, levels or processes, and as a consequence all actors can have implications for other actors (Byrne, 2003; Walby, 2004). Influences can flow in all possible directions, the space of influence is strongly related to the resources actors have. Nevertheless even actors with little resources can have a large impact on the long run.

The concept of co-evolution replaces the notion of an actor having a simple impact on another actor (Kaufmann, 2000; Merry, 1999). A system has no hard boundaries, but it is separate from its environment, to which it adapts. Change needs to be seen in terms of co-evolution with all these other related systems (other planning processes, actors outside the planning process) rather than as an adaptation to a separate and distinct environment composed of a higher level. In addition Urry states, drawing on Latour, that there is no zoom going from macro structure to micro interactions, but many systems of connections or circulations that effect relationally at multiple and varied ways (Urry, 2005). In concrete planning situations this implies that local actors, like municipalities and environmental pressure groups or neighbourhood councils, do influence the global companies and do influence many other actors in their interactions (and vice versa; global actors influence local actors). In sum, co-evolution proposes that contextual interaction is not only interaction within a hierarchical frame; interactions can flow in every direction.

The actors in the system, like local citizens, governmental bodies and private companies are constantly searching for behavioural strategies to fulfil their needs and to survive in their competitive environments. Actors are interdependent to fulfil these needs and start interacting. Because of the actions of one actor, other actors respond. The central point is that all actors in the system display actions that influence the behaviour of the other actors to more or lesser extent, dependent on their degree of connectivity and interdependence. Due to the continuous (inter)actions a system becomes dynamic and highly unpredictable (because the actions of all actors can simply not be predicted). This means that little shifts in a strategy of one actor can reverberate through the system and cause a chain of reactions that can generate large effects for the system as a whole. Because the effects can never be predicted due to the complex and diverse interactions, different trajectories of future developments are possible. Even in relatively simple situations when the general pattern of the behaviour may be predictable, this implies that the details of how the system will behave cannot be predicted for any specific case or time. The character of the responses of an actor cannot be known, because this depends on the way the other actors react and other actions that influence the system at the same time. The reactions of individual actors are in turn constrained by the actors' current state (its resources, competencies, capabilities, position in the system, etc.) and the current state of the actor's environment (the behaviour of the other actors, but also the institutional, political and cultural context). Based on all this information the actor will make a series of critical decisions from several possible alternatives that will determine its response that may be more *intuitive* than purely rational.

We can illustrate this rather abstract argument with an example. When an airline lowers its ticket rates (a reaction in itself) this can cause a chain of reactions. Some actors, like other airlines and consumers, have a high degree of interdependency with the airline that lowers its prices and as a consequence they will immediately react and change their own behaviour. Hence, others come into a position in which they might respond, but we cannot predict whether they shall respond, and if so, how they shall respond. A possible response might be that other airlines can counter this by further reducing their prices. When the prices are lowering, a possible consumer response is that the demand shall grow. And when the demand grows, there may be scarcity of tickets and prices can be heightened. Other actors that are less interdependent and thus less connected and dependent on the actions of the airlines, like the private companies or the governmental bodies, do not have to respond immediately. But they might when certain effects emerge because of the airline behaviour that danger their own needs. When air traffic grows at high rates because of the new airline strategies, governments can increase certain taxes, if they want to discourage air travel. And if the airlines need to pay more taxes, they need more revenues, thus heightening the rates. Or governments may choose to lower the taxes further and as such create possibilities to lower the rates even further.

The main point of this example is to illustrate how a highly dynamic and unpredictable chain of actions and reactions can emerge from a relatively minor change in behaviour of one actor. In the end it is even possible that the whole aviation system changes. Such examples of complex chains of emerging interactions can be found in almost all planning processes that are surrounded with and have to deal with a diversity of actors, spread over different territorial levels and who are involved in different processes and networks. Moreover, these mechanisms explicate the unintended consequences of specific plans or policies.

For example, policies that are adopted by the actors can get dispersed and fragmented and it is not to say how the policies shall reverberate through the system. For example, when actors are confronted with a new public policy, they can adapt by changing their interaction patterns. When one actor changes its behaviour as a consequence of changes in his environment, this actor changes the environment of other actors in the system further. These actors adapt to the new circumstances, which changes the relations and the interaction patterns in a system (Axelrod and Cohen, 1999; Wagenaar, 2005). This means that it is possible that the nature of the relations can change when the environment changes (Stacey, 1996; Teisman, 2005). For example actors can intensify their interactions with certain actors, seek new interaction patterns, or abandon old ones. The actors constantly adapt, change the environment, and co-evolve. The way this co-evolution works out is however unpredictable. After actors interpret policies in their own way, they often react on them in their own way (Mittleton-Kelly, 2003; Wagenaar, 2004).

It is important to stress that the theories on dynamic complex systems offer us an alternative perspective to understand what is going on in and around interactive planning processes. They do not intend however to make the process more predictable. On the contrary, the assumption that emerging chains of events and interactions remain highly unpredictable lies at the core of these theories. However, as we shall argue in the next section (8.4), this does not necessarily leave the planner helpless. It only implies a specific set of tasks for the planner when confronted with dynamic complex settings.

8.4 Managing the planning process from a CAS/co-evolution perspective

Both CAS and co-evolution offer an alternative way of conceptualising the nature of interactions in complex settings, which helps us to understand the dynamics and unpredictability surrounding planning processes. In this paragraph we argue that the concepts allow us to develop a more sophisticated understanding of the mechanisms at work that shape the dynamics. This helps us to develop a *realist* perspective of the planning process that can serve as a basis for the creation of management strategies in the quest for more effective spatial plans and policies. We shall illustrate the possibilities by indicating how the dynamic complex system perspective offers a strong argument for the creation of a more deliberative planning process, an ideal to which most planning theorists adhere to (although differing in their expectations about the actual possibilities). Of course, this is a rather universal ideal, but as we shall argue, the real world understanding that the complexity concepts offer, create fruitful grounds for discerning realistic management strategies with regard to this Habermasian ideal. We start our elaboration with the argument that the dynamic complex system perspective offers at least three promises for the management of dynamic planning processes. After having done so, we turn to the more concrete management question about the role of the planner confronted with such dynamic complex planning processes.

The threefold promise of the dynamic complex perspective for planning processes

To start with, the CAS/co-evolution perspective does not leave us with a relativistic or nihilistic perspective on the management of planning processes, but with a realist perspective. The idea that developments in complex adaptive systems are non-linear and outcomes are by definition unpredictable has raised doubts about the (human) abilities to influence future developments in such complex systems (see for example Cilliers, 1998). The realist perspective offers a different view: It is to acknowledge that multiple futures are possible, but social actions can influence the possible futures that will actually come to pass (Byrne, 2003). All actors *can* influence the development of a system (including planners). This means that what we do (e.g. as planners) matters, and as such plans and policies (and related processes) that aim to regulate and intervene in a social system can have a (profound) influence on the kind of future that will come to pass. Hence, complexity cannot be controlled, but it can be understood and harnessed. By this we mean that some ways of dealing with complexity are more fruitful and more productive than others (Axelrod and Cohen, 1999). Instead of a risk, complexity can be an asset, or a source of productive inquiry and understanding.

Secondly, interventions in a system, be it policies or strategic behaviour, can have intended but also unintended (sometimes even perverse) effects. This helps to explain why many policies nowadays do have many unexpected effects (see 8.2). This insight has brought some authors to the conclusion that the complexity frustrates the traditional instrumental policy making practices (Teisman, 2005; Wagenaar, 2005, Hajer and Wagenaar, 2003). These traditional approaches are based on the mixture of static approaches (reductionist, holist and expansionist) in which dynamics are largely ignored. Simplification results fundamentally in wrong answers and policies will probably be counterproductive (Innes and Booher, 2003). The environment of a process changes, when the system becomes subject of plans or policies. Policy interventions can be seen as perturbations to the current state of a complex system. The actors adapt to this policy by changing their behaviour, not just by reacting the way the policy makers would like to see them react.

A third insight is that complex adaptive systems possess mechanisms that can increase the *variety of knowledge and information* that circulates through the whole system. This is the basis for increasing the intelligence of the system. This ideal is based upon the assumption derived from co-evolution, that, when interacting, actors exchange information with their environment. Based on this information actors adapt their behaviour. The idea is that if more information circulates through the system, both the individual actors and the system as a whole are better able to adapt to changing circumstances. Hence, it is about accessing an as wide as possible diversity of knowledge, and allowing this knowledge to spread over all levels and agents. As both actors and the system become more intelligent, insight in specific planning problems and solution types to these problems can increase. The main point here is that through the creation of a, as diverse as possible, circulation of knowledge and information, the system has the potential to become more intelligent. When relevant actors are well connected in the system and the information that is exchanged in these connections is taken seriously, distributional intelligence comes into the system, in which knowledge spreads over all levels and agents (Innes and Booher, 2003; Wagenaar, 2005).

This holds a promise for all those concerned with making the planning process more deliberative. The co-evolutionary perspective underlines the benefits for involving lay knowledge, a point already made by many proponents of increased participation (see for example Fung and Wright, 2001; Dryzek, 1990; Innes and Booher. 2003; Healey, 1997; Yanow, 2003). From a co-evolutionary perspective a deliberative or participatory planning process offers more possibilities for complex problem solving than less deliberative processes. Interaction is perceived to be essential for stimulating diversity and variety, which are both conditions for generating creative solutions to problems and hence for harnessing complexity. For example, by including local actors, like citizens, in the planning process, new knowledge and information is allowed to enter the process and the system as a whole. This knowledge is local and practical and usually not available to the formal planners and policy makers. By increasing participation, the diversity of knowledge and information that circulates within the policy process and within the system as a whole is enhanced. More knowledge means more possibilities for the actors involved to produce, appreciate and select productive intervention strategies, problem understandings, and ranges of possible solutions.

As such, the complexity concepts presented in this chapter offer a renewed argument for the much older claim for deliberative planning. At first sight, this may look like a rather naïve belief in the possibilities to actually create such an intelligent system. Therefore we would like to stress once more that the main value of the complexity perspective lies in its potential to offer a realistic and sophisticated understanding of the interaction patterns that cause enormous dynamics. It allows us to recognise the variety and frequency of the interaction patterns within the process and between the process and its environment (other actors/processes) and the nature of the interaction patterns. Co-evolution teaches us that in order to understand the dynamics, the interactions with actors and networks surrounding the process should be taken into account. Moreover, in order to understand the potential for improvements, the nature of these interactions should be understood. The result is a realistic understanding of the dynamics and also a realist perspective on the possibilities to make the system more intelligent. Or in other words, it allows us also to judge what possibilities there are to make the system more intelligent.

So far we have argued that from the dynamic complex system perspective, planning still matters, but that the planner has a specific task. In the next section we further elaborate on the changing role of the planner.

Planning as making right connections

As argued in the former section, the idea that all actors can influence the development of the system in unforeseen ways means that all actors should be taken seriously in the policy process. The diversity of actors, that have an interest or are affected, should be taken into account in the planning process. In order to capture this diversity, and reap the benefits of it, the system must be made well connected. These connections do not only refer to linking the different actors, but to linking the *relevant* networks and processes. By making connections formal and informal, networks and linkages are created, which allow information to travel through systems in all directions. The strength of the interactions and the way actors shall adapt depends on how well an individual agent is connected, what the nature of these connections is, and what the individual characteristics and competences of an actor are. Connecting as such is not the whole art; it is about connecting the actors that already do have interdependency relationships (because the resources are spread in and around planning processes). Of course, what is relevant remains a rather arbitrary question, which always involves practical judgment of the planner.

Moreover, it is not only about creating the right connections but it is also about creating connections that improve the circulation of relevant knowledge and information through the system (this refers to nature of the connections). Theories of consensus building and deliberative democracy (based on Habermasian norms), offer some insights in the conditions that are needed for the establishment for fruitful information exchanges (see for example Habermas, 1980; Innes and Booher, 2003). The linkages should in essence be deliberative and participative. All actors should have the possibility to influence each other in order to capture the diversity and all actors should take this full diversity seriously. This does not mean that actors cannot behave strategically. They can, but they are also aware of the necessity that they share their information with the other actors, because the actors are mutually dependent. If the design of the linkages can add to the flow of knowledge through the system and it helps actors to learn (gather information and act upon this) this could mean that the system gets more robust in the future. Of course, the specific possibilities to make such types of connections depend on the specific situation at hand. Through applying a co-evolutionary lens this specific situation can be adequately understood and the planner can develop intervening strategies based upon this. Moreover, such strategies can also be made in collaboration with the other actors in the system, since such choices are also improved by an increase in distributed intelligence. The main task for the planner is then first of all to acknowledge and understand the mechanisms of co-evolution at work in order to create the necessary conditions that allow for an optimal circulation of knowledge and information through the system. Whether this intelligence will actually be used is another matter. This depends on the willingness of actors to actually share their information, and their willingness to learn.

In sum, the concepts of co-evolution and CAS offer a different perspective on the role of the planner. There are the promises that planning still matters and that management should especially be about creating the necessary conditions that allow for an optimal circulation of knowledge and information through the system. The role of the planner is then to create the right connections.

8.5 Conclusion

In this chapter we have argued that the concepts complex adaptive systems and co-evolution offer useful insights for understanding and dealing (or managing) with the dynamics of social and physical realities that planning processes intervene in. The dynamic complex systems approach makes valuable additions to existing approaches for conceptualising dynamics surrounding planning processes, like the rational comprehensive models, the streams models, and the rounds/network model. It allows us to develop a more sophisticated understanding of the mechanisms at work that shape the dynamics that surround the planning process. This understanding, then, can serve as a basis for the creation of intervening strategies in the quest for effective and legitimate spatial plans and policies.

We have argued that complex adaptive systems possess mechanisms that can increase the *variety of knowledge and information* that circulates through the whole system. This is the basis for increasing the intelligence of the system. Planning is about creating fruitful linkages between actors and networks (on different levels and processes), in order to develop a system of distributed intelligence. The ideas of complex adaptive systems and co-evolutions show that it is important to recognise and deal with the diversity of actors within and between systems by making the system well connected. This perspective is complementary to many insights already used in collaborative planning theory (Innes, Booher, Healey), deliberative policy-making (Hajer, Wagenaar) and public administration and organisational management (Hanf, Scharpf, Teisman, Koppenjan, Klijn). A main difference is that unpredictability is now perceived as inevitable, resulting in a more realistic and less ambitious perspective on the possible merits of such deliberative processes and the role of the planner in shaping such processes.

Next, complexity insights add to the contemporary understanding by offering concepts for understanding the logics and the consequences of interactions in a complex system. Understanding these conditions offers ways forward for designing management strategies that are more tailor-made instead of universal. Furthermore, the complexity concepts allow for a more fluid conception of the planning process vis-à-vis network theories. By allowing more room for acknowledging changes in constellations within and between networks of actors the complexity perspective is less static and more fluid. Conditions defined at the start of the process are not seen as frozen entities, but as constantly evolving and changing and hence it is important to adopt a flexible scope (instead of a rather static scope).

If we are able to successfully apply some ideas of complex adaptive systems and co-evolutions in practice than complexity theoretical notions can offer an important additional perspective to the contemporary toolbox for understanding social and physical dynamics surrounding planning processes. This, then, allows us to develop effective strategies to manage complex planning processes in the future. In order to fulfil these promises however, and in order to legitimise the use of complexity theoretical concepts in the social sciences, we have need for empirical proof. Up until now the application of complexity notions in planning studies has remained largely metaphorical (Chettiparamb, 2005). If we want to make more grounded comments on the management of dynamic planning processes (like large infrastructure developments), we need proper operationalisation of co-evolution that can be applied in practice. Capturing the dynamics descriptively in terms of co-evolution between different actors and processes in the way proposed in this chapter might contribute to this and further validate the assumptions about management in complex dynamic settings.

References

Axelrod, R. and Cohen M. (1999) *Harnessing Complexity: Organizational Implications of a Scientific Frontier*, Free Press, New York.

Bourdieu, P. (1998) *Practical Reason*, Stanford University Press, Palo Alto.

Byrne, D. (2003) 'Complexity theory and planning theory: A necessary encounter', *Journal of Planning Theory*, vol. 2.

Capra, F. (1996) *The Web of Life*, Anchor, New York.

Checkland, P. (1981) *Systems Thinking*, Wiley, Chichester.

Chettiparamb, A. (2005) 'Metaphors in complexity theory and planning', *Planning Theory*, vol. 5(1), pp. 71-91.

Cilliers, P. (1998) *Complexity and Postmodernism*, Routledge, London.

Cohen, M., March J. and Olsen, J. (1972) 'A garbage can model of organizational choice', *Administration Science Quarterly*, vol. 17, pp. 1-25.

De Roo, G. (1999) *Planning per se, planning per saldo: Over conflicten, complexiteit en besluitvorming in de milieuplanning* [*Environmental planning in The Netherlands: Too good to be true: About conflicts, complexity and decision making*], SDU Publishers, The Hague.

Faludi, A. (1973) *Planning Theory*, Pergamon, Oxford.

Faludi, A. (1987) *A Decision Centred View of Environmental Planning*, Pergamon, Oxford.

Fischer, F. and Forester, J. (1993) *The Argumentative Turn in Policy Analysis and Planning*, Duke University Press, Durham.

Habermas, J. (1989) *The Structural Transformation of the Public Sphere: An Inquiry into Category of Bourgeois Society*, MIT Press, Cambridge.

Hajer, M.A. (1995) *The Politics of Environmental Discourse: Ecological Modernization and the Policy Process*, Oxford University Press, Oxford.

Hajer, M.A. (2002) 'Naar een samengesteld begrip van democratie: of hoe aan representatie nieuwe inhoud kan worden gegeven' ['Towards a composed concept of democracy: How to add new content to representation'], in G.M.A. van der Heijden en J.F. Schrijver (eds.), *Representatief en participatief; dubbele democratie* [*Representative and participative: double-democracy*], Ebruon, Delft, pp. 71-88.

Hajer, M. and Wagenaar, H. (2003) *Deliberative Policy Analysis: Understanding Governance in the Network Society*, Cambridge University Press, Cambridge.

Hanf, S. and Sharpf, F. (1978) *Interorganizational Policymaking*, Sage, London.

Healey, P. (2006) *Collaborative Planning, Shaping Places in Fragmented Societies*, Palgrave and Macmillan, New York (second edition).

Heclo, H. (1978) 'Issue networks and the executive establishment', in A. Kind (ed.), *The New American Political System*, AEIPPR, Washington.

Hick, M.J. (1991) *Problem Solving in Business and Management: Hard, Soft and Creative Approaches*, Chapman & Hall, London.

Holland, J. (1995) *Hidden Order: How Adaptation Builds Complexity*, Addison-Wesley, Reading.

Hwang, S.W. (1996) 'The implications of the nonlinear paradigm for integrated environmental design and planning', *Journal of Planning Literature*, vol. 11, pp. 167-180.

Innes, J. and Booher, D. (1999a) 'Consensus building and complex adaptive systems, a framework for evaluating collaborative planning', *Journal of the American Planning Association* (Autumn 1999), vol. 65(4), pp. 412-423.

Innes, J. and Booher, D. (1999b) 'Metropolitan development as a complex system. A new approach to sustainability', *Economic Development Quarterly*, vol. 13(2), pp. 141-156.

Innes, J. and Booher, D. (2003) 'The impact of Collaborative Planning on Governance Capacity', working paper IURD 2003-03, University of California, Berkeley.

Kauffman, S.A. (2000) *Investigations*, Oxford University Press, Oxford.

Kickert, W.J.M., Klijn, E.H. and Koppenjan, J.F.M. (eds.) (1997) *Managing Complex Networks*, Sage, London.

Kingdon, J. (1984) *Agendas, Alternatives and Public Policies*, Little, Brown, Boston.

Kingdon, J. (1995) *Agendas, Alternatives and Public Policies*, Little, Brown, Boston (second edition).

Lindblom, C. (1959) 'The science of muddling through', *Public Administration Review*, vol. 19(2), pp. 79-88.

Koppenjan, J. and Klijn, E.H. (2004) *Managing Uncertainties in Networks*, Routledge, London.

Lasswell, H. (1951) *The Political Writings of Harold D. Lasswell*, Free Press, Glencoe.

Merry, U. (1999) 'Organizational strategy on different landscapes: a new science approach', *Systemic Practice and Action Research*, vol. 12(3), pp. 257-278.

Mittleton-Kelly, E. (2003) 'Ten principles of complexity and enabling structures', in E. Mittleton-Kelly (ed.), *Complex Systems and Evolutionary Perspectives of Organisations: The Application of Complexity Theory to Organisations*, Elsevier, Amsterdam.

Rhodes, R.A.W. (1997) *Understanding Governance. Policy Networks, Governance, Reflexivity and Accountability*, University Press, Buckingham.

Sabatier, P. and Jenkins-Smith, H. (eds.) (1993) *Policy Change and Learning: An Advocacy Coalition Approach*, Westview Press, New York.

Senge, P. (1990) *The Fifth Discipline: The Art and Practice of the Learning Organization*, Currency Doubleday, New York.

Stacey, R. (2007) *Strategic Management and Organizational Dynamics: The Challenge of Complexity*, Prentice Hall, Harlow.

Simon, H.A. (1979) 'Rational decision making in business organizations', *The American Economic Review*, 69(4), pp. 493-513.

Teisman, G. (1992) *Complexe Besluitvorming; een pluricentrisch perspectief op besluitvorming over ruimtelijke investeringen* [*Complex Decision making; a pluralistic perspective on decision making about spatial investments*], VUGA, The Hague.

Teisman, G. (2005) *Publiek management op de grens van orde en chaos* [*Public management at the edge of chaos and order*], Academic Service, The Hague.

Urry, J. (2005) 'The complexities of the global', *Theory, Culture and Society*, vol. 22, pp. 235-254.

Van den Bergh, J. and Gowdy, J. (2000) 'Evolutionary theories in environmental and resource economics: Approaches and applications', *Environmental and Resource Economics*, vol. 17, pp. 37-57.

Wagenaar, H. (2004) 'Local governance, complexity and democratic participation', Conference on democratic network governance, October 20-21, 2004, Roskilde University, Roskilde.

Walby, S. (2004) *Globalization and Difference: Theorizing Complex Modernities*, Sage, London.

Chapter 9
The Awakening of Complexity in Conceptualisations of Space in Planning

Janneke E. Hagens[1]

> And then again, is the contrast between simplicity and complexity itself too simple a dichotomy? (Law and Mol, 2002, p. 1).

In this chapter we explore the roles of concepts of space in planning in understanding complex landscapes and in dealing with ambitions concerning these landscapes. We elaborate on the idea that concepts of space are a paradoxical combination of simplification and particularisation of complexity of space; moreover, a combination of a normal but surprising planning tool.

9.1 Introduction of conceptualisation of space in planning

In this section, we firstly introduce space, as landscape or environment, its position in planning and its diverse aspects. We subsequently present the role of conceptualisation of space as a way of dealing with complexity of space, along with the problems of inadequate understanding of space. We finish with an introduction to related perspectives on complexity.

Context: Making doubly complex space

While the position of space is so natural in planning, as start and result of many activities, planners often overlook its complexity. Dealing with space in planning is complex for many reasons. We here focus on two connected kinds of complexities: immeasurable ambitions related to space and the complex features of space itself.

Ambitions of planners make dealing with space complex. Spatial planners deal with space with the intention of remaking it; intentions are derived from policy targets and the complicated 'will' of planners. 'The spatial practice of planning is the gerundic of making space – travelling the dialectic distance between abstract and concrete space' (Perry in Campbell and Fainstein, 2003, p. 161). In redeveloping brownfields, connecting European railways, designing a flood plain or analysing a provincial territory, planners remake parts of 'concrete spaces' because they are driven by idealised images of 'abstract spaces'. In this way, actual

---

1 Janneke Hagens is consultant with NovioConsult, Nijmegen, The Netherlands.

space in planning is related to spatial ambitions (cf. planning as an expression of a 'will to order' in Jensen and Richardson, 2004, p. 56). When planners deal with space, they colour and construct space from a specific perspective and in a specific situation (cf. Jensen and Richardson, 2004; Hajer, 2004; Healey, 2004). Consequently, space in planning includes a mix of facts and fictions, which is hard to grasp in a clear way.

The complexity of actively dealing with space in planning, based on ambitions, corresponds to the challenge of representing space in general. Barnes and Duncan (1992, p. 3), for example, explain how representations of landscapes are influenced by 'local settings' and 'local interests'. These 'local' influences make space multi-interpretable: coloured and constructed, as mentioned above. Representations of space can be regarded as 'rhetorical devices', since 'constitutive' and 'not simply reflective' (p. 3). Likewise, Law and Urry (2004) argue that methods, in general, are never 'innocent', but 'political' and help 'to *make* realities' (p. 404).

Features of space make dealing with space in planning more complex; namely, space is difficult by nature. Space in planning is multifaceted and therefore hard to simplify. It includes complexities of both physical and social systems (see, for example, Kleefmann et al. in Hidding, 2006). Space encloses the positions and qualities of objects, people and functions, together with various natural and directed developments, patterns, movements and relations (cf. ibid.).

In short, ambitions of planners and the many-sided features of space make dealing with space, and understanding this process, doubly complex. Massey (1999) summarises this complexity in other words:

> ... space could be imagined as the sphere of the existence of multiplicity, of the possibility of the existence of difference. Such a space is the sphere in which distinct stories coexist, meet up, affect each other, come into conflict or cooperate. This space is not static, not a cross-section through time; it is disrupted, active and generative. It is not a closed system; it is constantly, as space-time, being made (Massey, 1999, p. 274).

Challenge: Conceptualisation of doubly complex space

Planners frequently deal with deliberately coloured and inherently complex spaces by using appealing concepts. Such *concepts of space* in planning are a common answer to complexity in Dutch and European planning. These concepts are a helpful tool in understanding, organising and communicating about spatial issues (cf. Zonneveld, 1991; Van Duinen, 2004). Concepts of space are consequently 'labelled packages' of specific spatial information about abstract and concrete spaces. Concepts of space refer to areas or land use functions in a metaphorical or schematic way. Some examples are Urban Network, Corridor, Ecological Network, Layer Approach and Green Heart. The actual meanings of these concepts in planning practice, in comparison to 'intended' meanings on paper, are created by their users in practice; therefore, the actual meanings depend, for example, on the task, responsibility, employer and culture of a user (Beunen and Hagens, 2007).

A main problem of using concepts of space is that the concepts often include knowledge of space that is inadequate for justifying a spatial planning situation. More specifically, planners often *perceive* our present spaces as relational, dynamic or networked, yet they subsequently or simultaneously *apply* traditional, essentialist, Euclidian approaches of spatial analysis (cf. the abyss 'between transcendence and immanence' in Hillier, 2005). The traditional approach represents space as static and measurable, while the relational move represents space as interdependent and multiple (Graham and Healey, 1999; Healey, 2004/2006; Van Duinen, 2004; Boelens, 2005; Dühr, 2005). The alternative geographical imagination, which we will for now call the relational approach, '…sees space as an inherent spatiality in all relations, whether social, ecological or biospherical, and […] understands place as a social construct, generated as meanings are given in particular social contexts to particular sites, areas, nodes of interactions, etc.' (Healey, 2004, p. 47). A relational approach seems to recognise important features of complexity of space such as 'folded conceptions of space' (cf. immeasurable ambitions) and 'non-linear' development (cf. complex features) (ibid., p. 48). This approach seems to correspond to the above-mentioned planning approach, which regards space as coloured and constructed by planners based on their specific situation and driven by ambitions.

According to some case studies of Healey (2004, and in Albrechts and Mandelbaum (eds.), 2005) actual practices are still weak in addressing and imagining relational complexity. Since a transformation towards a relational approach is not theorised from practice, it is argued that the relational approach is rather a prescriptive turn (Sandercock in Albrechts and Mandelbaum (eds.), 2005). Prior to defending or rejecting a relational approach, in theory and practice, we want to *explore* the potential turn towards a relational approach in more detail. Is a relational approach of conceptualisation of space promising on paper but still weak in practice? And if so, why? To answer this question, we firstly explore some critical theoretical viewpoints about why and how planners deal with relational complexity. Consequently, we combine various complexity perspectives with the activity of conceptualisation of space into a 'character-table' of concepts. Then, we further explore current ways of dealing with complexity of space in practice; that is, in our case, an example of conceptualisation of space in Dutch regional planning. This chapter ends with some reflection.

9.2 Featuring relational complexity

Opening to some complexity approaches

Planners use concepts of space to imagine the concrete and abstract spaces of, for example, brownfields, railways, flood plains or provincial territories. Complexity approaches can support our understanding about how planners conceptualise these spaces in a relational way. 'Complexity' is doing 'metaphorical, theoretical and empirical work within many social and intellectual discourses and practices besides "science"' (Urry, 2005b, p. 2); accordingly, we assume that some complexity approaches can be helpful in planning research about practices. Therefore, we have to enter the field of complexity approaches, which is made complex by the various scientific foundations and assumptions about knowledge and predictability. Thrift (1999) regards complexity theory as 'a scientific amalgam' and 'an accretion of ideas, a rhetorical hybrid' (p. 33). We focus on complexity approaches that take into account the qualities of the relational approach of space and planning. Planning theories have included rational and technical conceptions of planning, as well as contextualised and linguistic conceptions. In this 'cluttered landscape' of respectively positivist and post-positivist approaches of planning (Allmendinger, 2002, p. 29), the relational approach of space corresponds with some post-positivistic planning approaches. Following this relational line, we leave out the option of complexity theory as being one 'theory of everything' (Manson and O'Sullivan, 2006, p. 678), because spatial understanding is coloured and constructed (cf. Section 9.1). Additionally, we acknowledge that '... human-environment research pushes complexity research beyond its usual focus on stylized, "toy-like" models towards the messy reality of human decision making in the context of social and natural complex systems' (O'Sullivan et al., 2006, p. 613). Due to the 'messy reality' in planning, we differ from a positivistic complexity approach if this approach includes simplified models of merely non-relational aspects. Alternatively, we recognise that a relational approach is associated with:

> ... a growing awareness of the limitations of any and all tools for understanding complex systems. Indeed, there is no way to fully comprehend a complex system and therefore no way to intervene in them in a totally risk-free way – taking action always means taking a step into the unknown to some degree. An understanding of complexity requires an understanding of the limits to one's analyses. Such an understanding changes the way in which we regard these tools – not as accurate representations of reality, but as useful fictions to facilitate limited sense making. So complexity thinking is not only about the tools we use, but also how those tools are used (Richardson, 2007, p. 281; cf. Cilliers, 2005).

Within a relational approach of planning and space, conceptualisation of space can be regarded as a tool that has 'limitations', yet it is a 'useful fiction' (ibid.). We focus on a combination of two complexity aspects to understand how planners deal with complexity of space in a relational way with the help of concepts of space as tools. Firstly, we focus on *expectations* about the possibilities and outcome of dealing with complexity of space; that is, the likely reaction to complexity of planners who apply relational approaches to space. Secondly, we focus on relevant relational complexity *features* of space within a context of knowing limitations of tools.

The adventurous reaction

Planners have to think complexity before dealing with relational complexity. Or rather, planners have to think complexity in order to deal with relational complexity. Bauman's vision about people who deal with 'changeability, diversity and uncertainty' is useful in understanding how planners could react to complexity (in Bauman and Munters (eds.), 1998). The experience of complexity can result in two different feelings: adventure and nervousness (ibid.). On the one hand, we consider nervousness, or more optimistically 'caution', as a reaction of a traditional planner who wants to *control* complexity. On the other hand, according to Bauman (ibid., in reference to Richard Sennett) the crux of dealing with complexity is seeing the adventure of complexity and specifically being aware of this complexity; in contrast to managing or removing complexity, people should be concerned with ambiguity. In that case, *accepting* complexity is an essential step in dealing with relational complexity.

Relational features

Since space in planning is a complicated system with various relations between things and people, we compare it to a complex system in complexity thinking. Many features in complexity thinking correspond to the above-mentioned relational features of space (see Section 9.1). Relevant complexity approaches, mainly from the field of social science and geography, include diverse relational notions and metaphors such as openness, irreducibility, incompressibility, self-organisation, chaos, contingency, specificity, multiple components, multiple routes, dynamic interactions, emergence, dependency and instability (Thrift, 1999; Richardson et al., 2001; Law and Urry, 2004; Cilliers, 2005; Nowotny, 2005; Urry, 2005a/2005b; O'Sullivan et al., 2006; Manson and O'Sullivan, 2006). From these complexity approaches, we derive two specific features of relational complexity: connectivity and dynamics. These features are difficult to grasp yet relevant relational features of space in planning

i. *Space as connected arrangement* (cf. holistic arrangement): Space includes relations between different entities and their 'emergence' (cf. Thrift, 1999; Manson and O'Sullivan, 2006). In other words, space is not only greater than the sum of its parts, but 'there are [also] system effects that are different from their parts' (Urry, 2005b, p. 5, in reference to Jervis). Manson and O'Sullivan (2006) argue that thinking holistically is also paradoxically about reducing, or rather about balancing between holism and reductionism. In other words, understanding the lower entities is also necessary when thinking holistically. Furthermore, a focus on connectivity of space can help break the boundaries between the divisions of hard and soft approaches of spaces (cf. Law and Urry, 2004, in reference to Wallerstein and Prigogine). Likewise, when people consider space as a connected arrangement, they can more easily emphasise the interdisciplinary features of space in planning: combining people and place, nature and society, urban and rural areas; as well as going beyond political boundaries and spatial scales.

ii. *Space including dynamics:* In addition to connectivity, dynamic space incorporates different processes and interactions of social, physical and political aspects. Space consequently goes beyond static pictures. Dynamic space is like '... a world of avalanches, of founder effects, self-restoring patterns, apparently stable regimes that suddenly collapse, punctuated equilibria, 'butterfly effects' and thresholds as systems tip from one state to another' (Urry, 2005a, p. 237). These dynamics can to a certain extent explain the situations of past, present and future spaces.

Having more clues about the relational way of dealing with complexity of space, we now return to the question to what extent a relational approach of conceptualisation of space is promising on paper but weak in planning practice.

9.3 Joining complexity thinking and planning activities

Understanding a perspective on complexity of space can improve the understanding of an activity of conceptualisation of space. Figure 9.1 is a character-table of concepts; it brings together complexity perspectives, both traditional and relational, and planning perspectives on the activity of conceptualisation of space.

<table>
<tr><td colspan="4">Traditional features of space
Controlling a complex reality</td></tr>
<tr><td rowspan="2">Activity: problem-setting
analyses & debates</td><td>CATCHER</td><td>AUTHORITY</td><td rowspan="2">Activity: directions
designs & decisions</td></tr>
<tr><td>TYPIFICATION</td><td>CREATION</td></tr>
<tr><td colspan="4">Relational features of space
Accepting complexity in reality</td></tr>
</table>

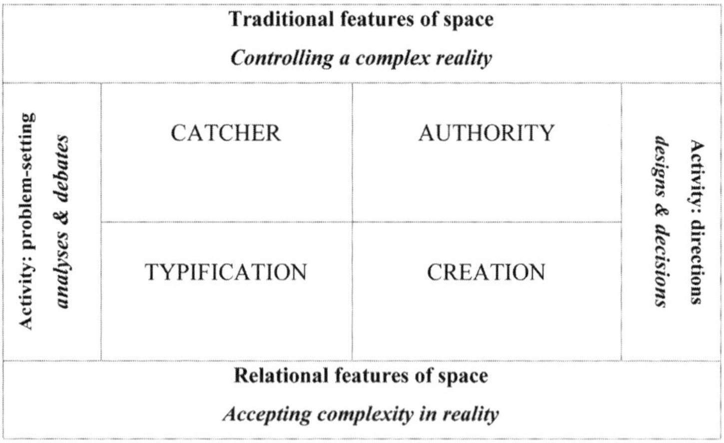

Figure 9.1 Different characters of concepts of space in dealing with complexity of space in planning

Complexity perspective – vertical

A complexity perspective of a user of a concept is based on a combination of a reaction to complexity plus the related type of spatial features. In Figure 9.1 an adventurous reaction to complexity goes together with relational features of space. In that case, complexity is *accepted*; it will be named and used, instead of reduced and managed. Reducing and managing complexity will arise from a traditional complexity reaction, which is based on a need to *control* complexity. These two perspectives are a view on how people can think differently about the 'same' complex issue. Perspectives are not directly strategies. Nevertheless, a perspective can have consequences for the value of following strategies in planning. In extreme form, somebody who accepts complexity may 'overestimate' complexity and argue that the world is entirely unpredictable. Planning strategies are then based on merely 'gut instinct' that abandons analytical procedures (Courtney et al., 1997, p. 68). A planner whose approach is to control complexity runs another risk. Then, in extreme form, '[u]nderestimating uncertainty can lead to strategies that neither defend against the threats nor take advantage of the opportunities that higher levels of uncertainty may provide' (ibid.).

Planning perspective – horizontal

The use of concepts of space is encountered in many planning steps. Here, we distinguish steps in 'problem-setting' and steps in 'directing' (cf. Zonneveld, 1991; Van Duinen, 2004). 'Problem-setting' involves identifying the actual and desired spatial situation, for example by analyses and debates. 'Directing' includes activities that will change a spatial situation, like design and decision making.

Characters

Depending on the complexity perspective of a user plus the kind of planning activity in which the concept is used, a concept in practice can be characterised as Catcher-, Authority-, Typification- or Creation-concept. Each concept has a particular 'character'. Using the table (Figure 9.1) can shed light on the effects and restrictions of a concept in a specific context. The categorised character of a concept tells about the possible impact of a concept. A character is not definite but an indication of possible impacts on that situation. We will explain the use of the table with three examples:

i. The Dutch Green Heart concept in contemporary planning, referring to a less urbanised area within the urbanised western part of the Netherlands, can be labelled as an Authority-concept. This category of Authority-concept tells us, for instance, about the *potential* of having obtained a fixed status (as controlling decisions, in a cautious way), together with the *risk* of lacking power to innovate (as accepting flexibility, in an adventurous way).

ii. A concept has usually *multi-functions* in practice, which makes a concept valuable yet ambiguous. The use of this character-table (Figure 9.1) can show the risk of a situation in which 'one' concept is used for different aims, by different people, but within one project. What are the consequences if, for example, Urban Network can be characterised as Typification-concept in one application and, meanwhile but unnoticed, as Creation-concept in another application? A concept is in this case describing both problem and solution, which could be misleading in communication between planners (see also Hagens, 2005).
iii. We stated before that some planners seek relational approaches of spaces but act traditionally. According to Figure 9.1, the justification of the use of a certain concept is in that case based on different characters. A *mix* of traditional and relational characters can be confusing if relational and traditional arguments are used in a contradictory way. This latter situation is, for example, observed in some uses of the Ecological Network concept (cf. Beunen and Hagens, 2007). In some studies the concept can be defined as a Creation-concept but in some policy documents as an Authority-concept. The first character refers to the design of flexible networks of functionally connected habitats. The second character refers to physical networks in a static and bordered way, which seems practical for implementation but does not fully justify the reality of landscape ecology.

A perfect character of a concept does not exist. The character-table is a *method* to better understand the different kinds of concepts of space and their impacts in practice. Catcher- and Authority-concepts have the potential to be comprehensive but rigorous; Typification- and Creation-concepts have the potential to be accurate but unclear. These characters confirm the dilemma and paradoxical challenge of simplification and particularisation of complexity by concepts. The efficiency of a concept depends on the reactions to complexity of space, as well as the degree of complexity of space (cf. De Roo, 2003) and the specific planning situation.

9.4 Illustrations of a regional planning document

Dutch background

In this chapter, we study conceptualisation of space in the regional spatial planning document of the Dutch province Noord-Brabant (2002). Noord-Brabant is one of twelve provinces of the Netherlands and is situated in the south of the Netherlands (see Figure 9.2). Dutch provincial governments have faced some challenges on spatial policy making and politics in recent years, which concern regional planning. Provincial governments are facing new and growing responsibilities of managing spatial developments. These responsibilities stem from the, disputed, national motto to 'decentralise' spatial planning tasks to regional and local level (as, for example,

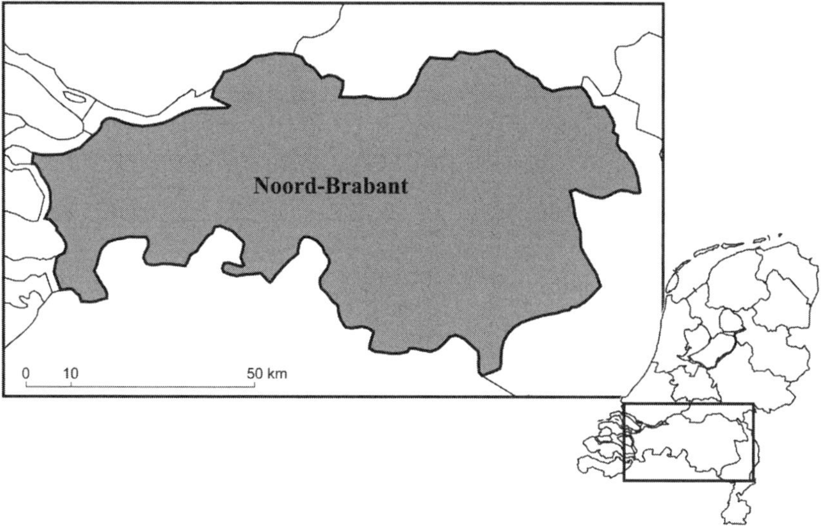

Figure 9.2 Province of Noord-Brabant, The Netherlands

stated in VROM, 2004; see also Dammers et al., 2004). Zonneveld and Verwest (2005) describe in more detail the current challenges of conceptualisation of space in Dutch national planning practice. Among other conclusions, they point to the importance of regional approaches in conceptualising urban developments, as well as creating concepts of space in planning that are related to specific areas (cf. Healey, 2004). In addition, they observe that, although in an undecided way, the strict distinction between urban and rural areas in conceptualisation has been left (cf. 'town and country as networks' in Hidding et al., 2000). These issues are signals of the need for relational approaches in practice; for example, they relate to 'specificity' of conceptualisation and 'dependency' between land uses. In that case, dealing with these planning challenges will be assisted by a relational approach of space. To what extent does the province of Noord-Brabant, as an illustrative example, already make use of relation approaches of conceptualisation of space? We study conceptualisations of space in their regional spatial planning document and assess the observations with the use of the character-table of concepts (Figure 9.1).

Conceptualisation in the vision

The regional planning document of Noord-Brabant (2002)[2] includes the main directions of the provincial spatial policies, presented as spatial future-image. The document starts with a Vision as a basis for policy directions. The motto

2 The following texts refer to this document, unless otherwise stated. The translations are made by the author.

of the document is 'Brabant Balanced'; in other words, 'Brabant in Balance'. One of the document's main statements is that Noord-Brabant is one of the most dynamic provinces of the Netherlands. On the one hand, these dynamics include a variety of economic, ecological and social-cultural *values*. Values mentioned are, for example, the province's geographical position with regard to transport, business, open space, a diversity of villages and city-landscapes, many recreation possibilities, skilled people and a strong social network. On the other hand, the dynamics are related to *threats*. People fear 'Randstad-features' (literally: Rim-city features) of uniformity, and urban spatial claims at the cost of valuable open spaces. This fear refers to similar developments in the adjoining Randstad-area, the most urbanised part of the Netherlands, located in the western part of the country. A story about Noord-Brabant in 2020 is additionally used to explain the desired future situation.

The 'dynamics' of Noord-Brabant are explained by some trends, such as economic growth and changing living preferences. These developments are illustrated by a few statistics about housing and land claims. Other complex trends, like globalisation and individualisation, are identified but less explained, neither in numbers nor in words.

We observe that both relational and traditional conceptualisation is used to present the values and threats of future Noord-Brabant. We identify some Typification-conceptualisation (as references to multiple developments) as well as Catcher-conceptualisation (as numbers about land claims).

Conceptualisation in five key principles

Based on the above-mentioned Vision, Noord-Brabant introduces five main principles to achieve Balanced Land Use. The first principle is based on the Layer Approach concept, presented and promoted by the Dutch Ministry of Housing, Spatial Planning and the Environment (see, for example, VROM, 2004). In some key descriptions (De Hoog et al., 1998; VROM, 2001), the Layer Approach is originally presented as a complete representation of a landscape. This representation includes three layers: surface-, infrastructure networks-, and occupation-layer. Each layer is characterised by its own specific dynamics, being development- or recovery-time. Furthermore, the Layer Approach stresses the importance of the connections between these layers. These connections are defined as consequences, possibilities and restrictions, of actions in one layer in relation to the other layers. Noord-Brabant uses the Layer Approach in its own way, by paying 'more attention' to the lower layers. This is a guideline that is also promoted in national documents in which the vulnerability of the surface layer is stressed. In the regional planning document of Noord-Brabant, this guideline is partly explained by describing the surface and infrastructure network layers; namely, by describing the aspects of nature, water, physical environment and infrastructure, together with their preconditions to succeed. These two layers and their dynamics are given attention, though merely in a separate way. Moreover, the third layer is not specifically described; especially the connection to the other layers is hereby neglected. Therefore, the connection between the three layers is a 'one way' relation; for example, the relation is expressed by the introduction of a hydrological test, based on the preconditions of the surface layer, for the assessment of new developments of the occupation layer. We observe that the Layer Approach in the document is used as a rather 'authoritative' concept, being a classical tool that promotes hierarchical thinking.

The following three principles in the document are about Efficient Land Use, Concentration of Urbanisation and Zoning of the Countryside. Efficient Land Use combines the values and threats that are mentioned in the Vision by suggesting 'multiple land use' and redevelopment instead of new sprawl. Concentration of Urbanisation is based on development in urban networks and protection of open space. The principle of Zoning of the Countryside is about agriculture, nature and recreation, which are planned by combining these functions in different 'zones' or 'main structures'. The practical distinction between urbanisation and the countryside pushes the principle of Efficient Land Use into the background. We argue that urban-rural issues are treated both holistically as well as separately: Multiple Land Use as Creation-concepts and Zoning as Authority-concepts. Whether this relational-traditional mix will result in confusing policy or not depends on the details of future applications of the principles.

The last principle of the Noord-Brabant document is about Thinking and Acting Beyond Boundaries. The document briefly states that physical systems and human activity take place 'beyond boundaries'. The document also mentions international and interprovincial cooperation. After that, the following text is mainly about territorial neighbours and Noord-Brabant's physical geographical position. We observe again a typical example of starting with relational thinking and continuing with traditional thinking. What are consequences for Noord-Brabant by omitting relational neighbours?

The document does not explicitly integrate the described five principles in the end, except for the integration of aspects in some maps and in the principle of Efficient Land Use. Therefore, the suggestion of 'balancing between holism and reductionism' (Manson and O'Sullivan, 2006, see 9.2), to achieve a total view of relations between parts, is partly achieved. The document mostly focuses on features of single parts. Is complexity only 'accepted' or 'controlled' on the lower level but not sufficiently dealt with on a higher level?

9.5 Reflection

The illustration of Noord-Brabant

We have used the document of Noord-Brabant to illustrate the current state of complexity-thinking in conceptualisation of space in planning. In line with other planning research (see Section 9.1), we underline the difficulties of presenting spatial relational features in contrast to traditional spatial features. The complexity features of connectivity and dynamics are two examples of hard to explain and hard to imagine aspects (cf. Dühr, 2005); meanwhile, these features include potential for relational thinking. Noord-Brabant starts including connectivity and dynamics of space in their analyses but does not finish it adequately. The feeling and awareness of relational aspects is present but not sufficiently developed to justify spatial problems; for example, the presented values and threats concerning the future of Noord-Brabant are superficially explained. Certainly, the rhetorical presentation of values and threats is in line with the political nature of the document. Nevertheless, some explanations of the relational dynamics *behind* the values and threats could be valuable, both as ethical principle in promoting and as deliberative principle in giving account for the politically defined values and threats. What are, for example, the expectations and risks of the economic, ecological and socio-cultural features of space? Following the missed relational opportunities in problem-setting, some relational directions are also missed in the document. The use of the Layer Approach by Noord-Brabant is a typical example; a consequence of the actual 'authoritative' interpretation is that 'creative' opportunities are overlooked, like innovative solutions rooted in the occupation-layer to protect the surface-layer.

Characters into consideration

The 'will to order' space is inherent to planning. Conceptualisation of space is in line with the urge to order and is *a* way of dealing with complexities of space. Understanding the context of the application of concepts of space in practice is valuable. The related spatial ambitions, the spatial issues themselves and the kind of planning activity in which the concept is used all influence the possible qualities of a concept in a specific situation. The addition of complexity perspectives to planning perspectives offers a more complete picture of the potential 'character' of a concept (see Figure 9.1). Knowing the kind of complexity features that are emphasised and the kind of complexity-drive from which planners operate shed other light on the use of concepts. For example, is an ambition of Balanced Land Use based on the urge to control complexity or on the adventure of accepting complexity? What about the complexity drives behind the concept of Zoning? The answer to these questions makes a difference in the progress and outcome of a concept of space; the result of a concept of space is partly influenced by the kind of complexity approach.

Breaking categories

A relational approach is promising on paper but still weak in practice; on paper it justifies complexity but in practice it risks not being, or rather not yet, understood. Conversely, a traditional approach of complexity risks oversimplification but is simple in practice. How to overcome this deadlock? Possibly, '…is the contrast between simplicity and complexity itself too simple a dichotomy?' (Law and Mol,

2002, p. 1). Similarly, is the contrast between traditional and relational complexity too simple? For now, these contrasts, and the categories of characters of concepts, offer an original view on conceptualisation of space. In future practice, the crux may be to integrate traditional and relational perspectives, along with knowing the different roots and limitations.

In future, we should combine questions from specific planning practices and insights from theories about complexities to better understand how to deal with complex spaces in planning by conceptualisation. Conceptualisation of space in practice is both to order and to justify complexities, taking into account the specific task and ambition of a planner: we have to find a balanced mix of controlling a complex reality and accepting complexity in reality.

References

Albrechts, L. and Mandelbaum, S.J. (eds.) (2005) *The Network Society: A New Context for Planning?*, Routledge, London/New York.

Allmendinger, P. (2002) *Planning Theory*, Palgrave, Basingstoke.

Barnes, T.J. and Duncan, J.S. (1992) *Writing Worlds: Discourse, Text and Metaphor in the Representation of Landscape*, Routledge, London.

Bauman, Z. and Munters, R.R. (1998) *Leven met veranderlijkheid, verscheidenheid en onzekerheid* [*Living with volatility, diversity and uncertainty*], Boom, Amsterdam.

Beunen, R. and Hagens, J.E. (2010) 'The use of the concept ecological networks in nature conservation policies and planning practices' Routledge, London.

Boelens, L. (2005) 'Fluviology: A new approach of spatial planning', inaugural lecture, University of Utrecht, Utrecht, available at www.urbanunlimited.nl.

Cilliers, P. (2005) 'Complexity, deconstruction and relativism', *Theory Culture Society*, vol. 22, pp. 255-267.

Courtney, H., Kirkland, J. and Viguerie, P. (1997) 'Strategy under uncertainty', *Harvard Business Review*, vol. 75, pp. 66-79.

Dammers, E., Verwest, F., Staffhorst, B. and Verschoor, W. (2004) *Ontwikkelingsplanologie: lessen uit en voor de praktijk* [*Developmentplanning: lessons out of and for practice*], NAi Uitgevers, Rotterdam.

De Hoog, M., Sijmons, D. and Verschuuren, S. (1998) 'Herontwerp van het laagland', in D.H. Frieling (ed.), *Het Metropolitane Debat*, Thoth, Bussum, pp. 74-87.

De Roo, G. (2003) *Environmental Planning in the Netherlands: Too Good to be True: From Command-and-Control Planning to Shared Governance*, Ashgate, Aldershot.

Dühr, S. (2005) 'Exploring cartographic representations for spatial planning in Europe', Faculty of the Built Environment, University of the West of England, Bristol.

Frieling, D.H. (1998) *Het Metropolitane Debat* [*The Metropolitane Debate*], Thoth, Bussum.

Graham, S. and Healey, P. (1999) 'Relational concepts of space and place: Issues for planning theory and practice', *European Planning Studies*, vol. 7.

Hagens, J.E. (2005) 'The networked world: The example of urban network in spatial planning', *A Greater Europe*, Vienna University of Technology, Vienna.

Hajer, M.A. (2004) 'Coalitions, practices and meaning in environmental politics: from acid rain to BSE', *Discourse Analysis in the Social Sciences: Theories and Methods*, Nethur, Utrecht.

Healey, P. (2004) 'The treatment of space and place in the new strategic spatial planning in europe', *International Journal of Urban and Regional Research*, vol. 28, pp. 45-67.

Healey, P. (2006) 'Relational complexity and the imaginative power of strategic spatial planning', *European Planning Studies*, vol. 14, p. 525.

Hidding, M. (2006) *Planning voor stad en land* [*Planning for city and countryside*], Coutinho, Bussum.

Hidding, M., Needham, B. and Wisserhof, J. (2000) 'Discourses of town and country', *Landscape and Urban Planning*, vol. 48, pp. 121-130.

Hillier, J. (2005) 'Straddling the post-structuralist abyss: Between transcendence and immanence?', *Planning Theory*, vol. 4, pp. 271-299.

Jensen, O.B. and Richardson, T. (2004) *Making European Space: Mobility, Power and Territorial Identity*, Routledge, London.

Law, J. and Mol, A. (2002) *Complexities: Social Studies of Knowledge Practices*, Duke University Press, Durham.

Law, J. and Urry, J. (2004) 'Enacting the social', *Economy and Society*, vol. 33, pp. 390-410.

Manson, S.M. and O'Sullivan, D. (2006) 'Complexity theory in the study of space and place', *Environment and Planning A*, vol. 38, pp. 677-692.

Massey, D. (1999) 'Space-time, "science" and the relationship between physical geography and human geography', *Transactions of the Institute of British Geographers*, vol. 24, pp. 261-276.

Noord-Brabant, Province of (2002) 'Streekplan Noord-Brabant 2002: "Brabant in balans"' ['Regional plan Noord-Brabant 2002:" Brabant in balance"'] (Partially Revised December 3, 2004), Province of Noord-Brabant, 's-Hertogenbosch.

Nowotny, H. (2005) 'The increase of complexity and its reduction: Emergent interfaces between the natural sciences, humanities and social sciences', *Theory Culture Society*, vol. 22, pp. 15-31.

O'Sullivan, D., Manson, S.M., Messina, J.P. and Crawford, T.W. (2006) 'Space, place, and complexity science', *Environment and Planning A*, vol. 38, pp. 611-617.

Perry, D.C. (2003) 'Making space: planning as a mode of thought', in S. Campbell and S.S. Fainstein (2003), *Readings in Planning Theory*, Blackwell, Malden, pp. 142-165.

Richardson, K.A. (2007) 'Complex systems thinking and its implications for policy analysis', in G. Morçöl, *Handbook of Decision Making, Public Administration and Public Policy/123*, Taylor and Francis Group, Oxford, pp. 189-222.

Richardson, K.A., Cilliers, P. and Lissack, M. (2001) 'Complexity science: A "gray" science for the "stuff in between"', *Emergence*, vol. 3, pp. 6-18.

Thrift, N. (1999) 'The place of complexity', *Theory, Culture and Society*, vol. 16, pp. 31-69.

Urry, J. (2005a) 'The complexities of the global', *Theory, Culture and Society*, vol. 22, pp. 235-254.

Urry, J. (2005b) 'The complexity turn', *Theory Culture Society*, vol. 22, pp. 1-14.

Van Duinen, L.B.J. (2004) *Planning Imagery: The Emergence and Development of New Planning Concepts in Dutch National Spatial Policy*, PrintPartners Ipskamp, Enschede.

VROM, Ministerie (2001) *Ruimtelijke verkenningen 2000: jaarboek rijksplanologische dienst* [*Spatial explorations 2000: Yearbook governmental planning service*], Ruimtelijk Planbureau (RPB), The Hague.

VROM, Ministerie (2004) *National Spatial Strategy: Creating Space for Development*, Ministry of Housing, Spatial Planning and the Environment, The Hague.

Zonneveld, W. (1991) *Conceptvorming in de ruimtelijke planning* [*Formation of concepts in spatial planning*], Planologisch en Demografisch Instituut, Amsterdam.

Zonneveld, W. and Verwest, F. (2005) *Tussen droom en retoriek: de conceptualisering van ruimte in de Nederlandse planning* [*Between dream and rhetoric: the conceptualisation of space in Dutch planning*], Ruimtelijk Planbureau (RPB), The Hague.

Chapter 10

Process and Transient Scenarios in Collaborative Planning: Managing the Time Dimension

Adele Celino and Grazia Concilio[1]

In collaborative planning the time dimension emerges and is created throughout the interactive process and it is intrinsically related to it. The chapter starts discussing an evolutionary approach to planning and then explores both the role played by the time dimension and the way time is conceptualised and managed by the knowledge actors involved in the collaborative planning process. Planning artefacts are analysed referring to both their evolving character and the mode they internalise the time dimension.

What frames should planning artefacts have in order to make such unique temporal dimension explicit? The chapter discusses the issue above and introduces the concepts of *process* and *transient scenarios* as evolving artefacts: the *process-scenario* is a scenario which evolves together with its related planning system and along with the planning action itself; the *transient-scenarios* are temporary images of the *process-scenario* and are linked together by the cognitive conditions explaining the *process-scenario* evolution. Finally the chapter presents some preliminary results of three different research experiences aiming at testing these concepts and defining some possible frameworks for the two scenario forms.

10.1 Evolutionary approach and time dimension

The complexity of spatial processes and phenomena, strongly related to human values and behaviours, to observation, interaction, and communication abilities and to the environmental processes can no longer be faced within a traditional view of both the planning process and the plan. Not only recently, these are asking for a deep epistemological and paradigmatic revision (Healey, 1996/1997; Forester, 1999; Scandurra, 2001). Some new approaches have been developed and tested

1 Adele Celino (Ing, docente a contratto) is from the Dipartimento di Architettura e Urbanistica, Politecnico di Bari. Grazia Concilio (PhD, ricarcatore) is Researcher at the Dipartimento di Architettura a pianificatzione at the Politecnico di Milano, Italy.

but the most of them are still failing in bridging the planning process and the plans to the highly evolving nature of spatial systems. The simple sequence:

'observation → analysis → action'

can no longer compete with the speed of changes: more and more observatory, analytical, and exploratory approaches need to be merged within a unique view of the planning action thus making the plan one of the possible means (it can no longer be the only one) through which the planning action is being explicated.

10.2 Towards anytime planning: An evolutionary approach

Even within participatory or collaborative approaches, planners are still asked to design plans considered sort of end-products of the planning process. The growing complexity of the planning tasks, particularly when dealing with spatial systems, makes the planners behave more and more as 'anytime planners'. Anytime planners are deeply aware of the operative limits of theoretical models and tools and try, throughout the planning action, to behave coherently with the dynamicity of the planning environments. It is not only the dynamics of spatial systems to ask for 'anytime planning'; it is also necessary due to the crucial uncertainty under which planning action is carried out within spatial systems: action can only have a step-by-step framework, sort of micro-decisions approach, in order to reduce the probability of processes irreversibility.

Anytime planning is well known in the domain of system control and autonomous agents and has been developed in order to overcome the infeasible strategy of always searching for an optimal plan when planning has to be carried out under time limit. In these domains anytime planners operate by producing a highly suboptimal plan first, and then improving it (Hawes, 2002; Ferrer, 2002; Likhachev, 2005); planning action is divided into planning steps, each one being relevant in terms of the learning opportunities offered to the following of the process.

The idea of anytime planning becomes crucial when considering the cognitive dynamicity and complexity introduced into spatial planning by collaborative and participatory approaches. Planning actions are giving rise to distributed knowledge arenas where it becomes crucial to manage knowledge consistently with the concept of knowledge ecology (Pór and Spivak, 2000; Malhotra, 2002; Davenport and Prusak, 1997).

We believe that collaborative planning arenas could be seen as 'large knowledge ecosystems'. As such, these systems incorporate the dynamic evolution of knowledge interactions between entities; hence the desire to conceptualise knowledge ecosystems supporting planning processes, decision making processes and evolutionary arenas of collaboration.

Components of knowledge ecosystems are, or need to be, involved in productive conversations enabling a continuous restructuring of a knowledge network. Knowledge flows, containing ideas, information and inspiration, cross-fertilise and feed components one each other, eventually supported by a technology network of knowledge bases, communication links, action scripts, sense-making and negotiation tools enabling plan re-generation throughout the planning action carried out by its components within the knowledge ecosystem.

When transferring the concept of anytime planning into the collaborative spatial planning domain two main activities appear relevant:

i. Exploration of the currently available portion of the action space. Decision making is not carried out considering all the possible action alternatives (i.e. the whole action space).
ii. Production of new portions of the action space or exploration of unexplored ones.

Due to the continuous acquisition and/or creation of knowledge and information taking place in anytime planning activities, decision making processes can be conceived as evolving exploration-creation of the action space. An evolutionary approach to planning becomes relevant: the exploration of the planning action space has a productive nature. New knowledge is produced and new opportunities for the planning action are envisaged which interiorise and are strengthen by both the knowledge flows and the organisational context (cognitive and organisational history) which created it.

Within an evolutionary approach a planning step does not represent an element of a predetermined planning sequence (as it is, for example, within the rational model), it is rather a sort of a temporary version of the plan (a portion of the action space) on which the knowledge ecosystem works within a more or less shared vision of the future. The shift from one step to the subsequent can be described as a cognitive transaction (Celino and Concilio, 2006a) and is carried out as a self-regulatory effort of the knowledge ecosystem. The cognitive transaction enables the regeneration of the plan. Referring to management theory this regeneration of plans can be described as rolling planning:

> Rolling planning is a procedure of continuous revision of intertemporal programs, such that the time horizon lying ahead at the time of each revision remains constant. [It is] considered by the theorists of planning as a suitable framework for coordinating short-term and long-terms plans, which combines the elements of planning and control (Kaganovich, 1996, p. 173).

In our vision the regeneration effort derives from the need to continuously coordinate short-term with long-term visions but it is the result of an anytime self-regulatory process (obviously including control) mainly based on the dynamics of the knowledge ecosystem being shaped by and shaping the planning effort. Moreover our idea of anytime planning combines the concept of rolling planning, modified as suggested above, with the idea that each planning step is also rich of the cognitive and organisational history of the knowledge ecosystem producing it.

10.3 The time dimension

A common predominant perspective on time is the objective one. Planners still widely assume (usually implicitly) that time acts as an external, single, universal 'container within which human life is played out' (Graham and Healey, 1999). According to this point of view time is a frame in which planning operates and suggests changes; it is a functional parameter in order to program and organise activities, interventions, and events. The planning process emerges as a temporal sequence of decisions first and events/actions then. Metaphors such as a line, cycle and clock (Orlikowski and Yates, 2002) used in many planning process remind the notions of sequence and linearity and suggest an homogenous, measurable (Starkey, 1989) and therefore predictable (Paulk et al., 1993) flow of time.

There are two critical issues in such a perspective. First, the time-lag between defining the problem, making decisions, and implementing plan activities reveals a serious situation: results and impacts, positive or negative, of implemented plan activities could only be accomplished on the long-term. Secondly, the spatial problems and the complex planning contexts are dynamic. As well, both the exogenous variables that affect the planning context and the positions of actors may be changing. Therefore, the interconnected aspects and variables of the planning processes are not static: they are changing as we are planning.

An objective perspective on time badly matches the socio-environmental domain characterised by a scarce linearity and continuity of environmental processes, the great diversity and dynamic nature of knowledge and interests involved, the instability and variability of decision making components both in temporal and spatial dimensions (Mathew et al., 1999; Innes and Booher, 1999). Goals and objectives in a specific planning situation may vary over time, as may vary the understanding of alternative solutions, thereby causing a shift in the subject-matter of planning.

A converse subjective idea of time focuses on the way actors perceive time in the situations (and consequently in the events) in which they are involved. Time exists only since it is socially (Orlikowski and Yates, 2002), historically, and locally created: it is heterogeneous, non-linear, and non-sequential. Times, as spaces, 'are effectively produced and created through social actions within and between places' (Graham and Healey, 1999). Nigel Thrift (1996, p. 2) asserts that:

> ... time is a multiple phenomena; many times are working themselves out simultaneously in resonant interaction with each other.

Therefore, planning has an important role in helping to frame the communicative and interpretive processes through which collective meanings of time are negotiated and maintained (Healey, 1997). Some efforts are made in order to introduce innovations with respect to time policies in cities (Bonfiglioli and Mareggi, 1997) and by widespread attempts to treat time and space in an integrated way through '24 hour city' strategies.

A third perspective considers that time is experienced intersubjectively through a process of temporal structuring; this point of view is supposed to constitute a bridge between the objective and subjective way of thinking about time (Orlikowski and Yates, 2002). Orlikowski and Yates (2002) propose a social, historical and local framing of time related to more or less stabilised structuring processes that actors, in their daily and collaborative action settings, activate. The recurrent interactions, activities, and practices help to produce and reproduce 'temporal structures' (Orlikowski and Yates, 2002), 'transient constructs' (Lanzara, 1999) or rhythms (Nandhakumar, 2002) that are individual or collective practices institutionalised through the reproduction of such practices. Under different conditions, individuals and groups reinforce or change their 'temporal structures', as well as introduce new ones. These 'temporal structures' change as actions change or as new actors participate to the interaction.

In collaborative planning, time put (objectively) constrains to the actors but these constrains are (subjectively) created during and along the interaction and action themselves. During interactions the temporal dimension affects cognitive transactions due to both the continuous mutual adjustment of the daily experience and actions and the continuous modification of the interactive structures activated. Actors modify the context: each change, also depending on interactions, modifies the existing context and creates a new arena for the next interaction. In such a way 'time in planning' is the time embedded in processes, in social interactions, in structures, in practices, in knowledge, and in environments that, therefore, could all be defined 'temporal structures'.

10.4 Towards temporal structured plans

What kind of frames?

According to the third way to manage the time dimension in planning, the planning artifacts (plans, scenarios, norms, regulations…), considered as temporal structures, must retain and maintain their evolving feature; in this way they could be used as a tool to facilitate the cognitive transactions enabling the organisational action and its anytime planning. Referring to this last goal, we can make the following reflection. Planning objectives are always aimed at something that should happen or should not happen in the future. Since the status quo view of the problem situation is not enough to create an overview about the situation; actors think about the past in order to act in the present and they use fragments of past experiences which are remembered for their explicit results. However, only looking to the past and making extrapolations for the future is dangerous and mostly wrong.

With the proposed third perspective on time we could transfer past experience into the future as soon as the future vision/scenario is being generated; in this way, the experience could be interpreted at a specific moment of the process, in the light of current events, interpretation, and actions. The interpreted past could not correspond to the planned past that is a past frozen in plans and procedures; on the contrary, it could be continuously interpreted in the light of the current situation.

But, what features should planning artifacts have in order to be considered temporal structures and to evolve together with on-going process of actions planning and implementation? What planning structures and contents are more suitable to facilitate the cognitive transactions between actors?

What we propose and introduce in this contribution are the operative concepts of *process-* and *transient-scenarios* as evolving, and therefore temporal, artifacts. The *process-scenario* is a scenario which evolves together with its related knowledge ecosystem and along with the planning action itself; the *transient-scenarios* are temporary images of the *process-scenario* and are linked together by the cognitive conditions determining the *process-scenario* evolution. Such scenarios are introduced and deeply analysed in the following paragraph.

Process- *and* transient-scenarios

Taking into account the temporal dimension in a process of scenario generation, and not only in the scenario itself, requires a dynamic representation of the scenario; indeed, such scenario representation has to be considered as a tool not only for the long term visioning/forecasting activities but also:

i. to make explicit (and then visible to the actors) the conditions (in terms of actors, positions, context…) and argumentations generating the transactions in order to stimulate deliberation and learning and,
ii. to explore the operability of the scenario.

We define a *process-scenario* as a scenario which evolves together with its related decision making system and along with the action itself; the modifications in the scenario represent the transactions from one action space to another. The *process-scenario* represents both the support and the outcome of the learning process taking place within the knowledge ecosystem. It is a sort of planning process history (Snowden, 2005, could call it a sort of self-narrative of the organisation) where the interconnected sets, sequences, cycles of transactions can be structured like a chain, not necessarily a linear chain, of different images of the scenario (the *transient-scenarios*); these transient images are linked together by the conditions and events explaining the *process-scenario* evolution.

Each cognitive transaction determines a regeneration of the *transient-scenario* and therefore an evolution of the *process-scenario*. *Transient-scenarios* are considered 'snapshots' of the *process-scenario*; they represent temporary images of the *process-scenario*, portions of the portion of the action space which the

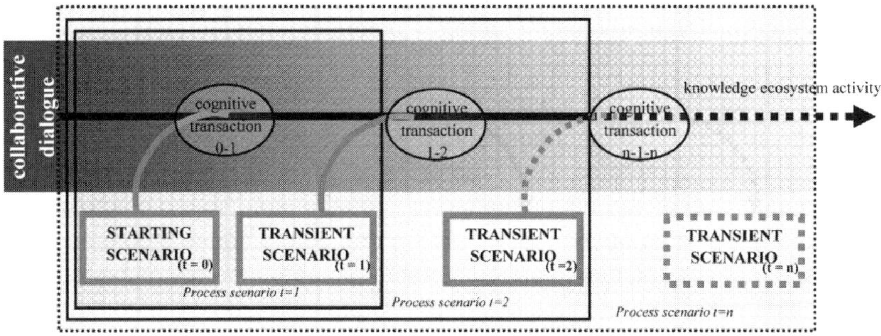

Figure 10.1 The process-scenario development and the role of transient-scenario

knowledge ecosystem is currently working on. They provide a representation of the organisational and interpersonal communication within the knowledge ecosystem, and make such representation available for subsequent regeneration and use in the context of anytime planning activities.

The role of *transient-scenario* is to mediate between the quasi-organisational memory (Celino and Concilio, 2006a) and the collaborative dialogue environment (Figure 10.1). Such *transient-scenarios* should be provided as mechanisms to augment and interconnect the components of the knowledge ecosystem so that information and knowledge can be created, organised, distributed, exchanged and applied within a knowledge network. In such a role, the *transient-scenario*:

i. takes a picture of 'current' knowledge; in structuring and connecting information and knowledge shared throughout the collaborative interactions, the *transient-scenario* captures the formative context[2] (Ciborra and Lanzara, 1994) of specific ideas, decisions, and actions;
ii. helps in focusing the actors' attention on particular aspects of the planning problem (Celino and Concilio, 2004);
iii. represents the set of transient constructs which are knowledge 'containers' (Lanzara, 1990) facilitating experimentations and changes;
iv. provides a temporary frame able to structure the information and knowledge for storage; in such a way, the *transient-scenario* connects the space for collaborative dialogues to the quasi-organisational memory so that all the argumentative content can be preserved and shared (Celino and Concilio, 2006a);

2 A formative context is here considered, coherently with Ciborra and Lanzara (1994), as a 'set of pre-existing institutional arrangements, cognitive frames and imageries that actors bring routinely and enact in a situation of action' (p. 70).

v. represents knowledge in a dynamic format (in a process-scenario pattern) through its modification, creation, and use along time.

Finally, the *transient-scenario*, as a snapshot of the *process-scenario*, gives a direction to the decision making process by linking the past to the future via the present state or situation. *Transient-scenario* conveys a sense of movement, direction and instability, stimulating search and exploration. Knowledge is embedded in the process and the process is used to structure knowledge (Celino and Concilio, 2004). Adopting the proposed temporal structures, the knowledge is stored in a 'process form'.

10.5 Preliminary results

The experiences described below are drawn from spatial planning experiences involving the authors as facilitators (Celino and Concilio, 2004/2006b; Celino et al., 2007).

The three experiences focus on processes through which actors, in their plan regenerating efforts, come to develop new practical knowledge about artifacts and tools, roles and routines, the work setting and the overall organisation in which they work.

The collaboration support system for the Gravina Natural Park

The first experience refers to the work carried out while designing the architecture of GraviCS, an information system supporting argumentative discussion and cognitive interaction for environmental scenario development (Celino and Concilio, 2004) in the preparation process for the Gravina Regional Natural Park, in Southern Italy. In this case argumentation, explaining the dynamics of the decision making process (Chung and Goodwin, 1998), represents the power engine of the *process-scenario.*

This experience focuses on the possibility to use argumentative-maps as means to explain, even partially, the evolution of the *process-scenario*. In GraviCS argumentative-maps (argu-maps) are planned to be automatically extracted from the texts collected in the system and produced by the users while working on the current portion of the action space: in such conditions they work on available solutions, evaluate them and build hypotheses for moving from one portion to an other one (Borri et al., 2005). When argumentations are relevant enough in contents to be shared in terms of acceptable level of consensus among actors a modification in the scenario is produced: a new image of it is produced and the argu-maps supply a synthetic although partial explanation of the modification. The subsequent images of the scenario are the *transient-scenarios*: the current *transient-scenario* and its decision rationale (Chung and Goodwin, 1998; Banares-Alcantara and King, 1997) give shape to the *process-scenario* (Figure 10.2).

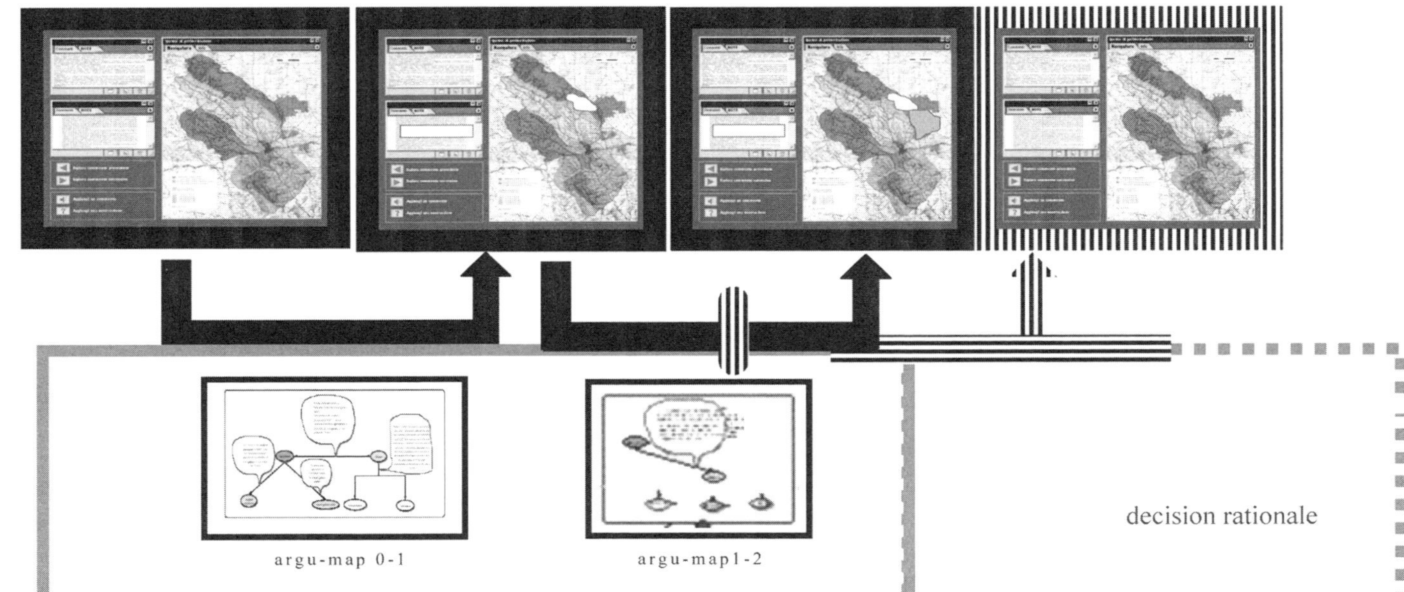

Figure 10.2 The evolution of transient-scenarios

Each *transient-scenario* takes a picture of the 'current' version of the park plan (the park boundary proposal, regulation proposal), all those argumentation and interaction activities not yet concluded into a new *transient scenario*. In managing *transient-scenarios*, the *process-scenario* contains not only knowledge created and manipulated in an organisational process (Huber, 1991; Casey, 1997) (repository of the content), but also:

i. the knowledge of the process itself in the form of process designs, case histories and lessons learned from past experiences by the participants (Kleiner and Roth, 1997);
ii. evolving content/knowledge (Lanzara, 1999) (repository of the process);
iii. information about the context (repository of context).

The structuring scenarios for the Veneto Delta of the Po River Park

This experience refers to the work carried out while developing the Long-term Social and Economic Plan for the Natural Park of the Veneto Delta of the Po River (Northern Italy) and represents an attempt made to manage knowledge in action by the use of 'structuring-scenarios' (Celino et al., 2007). They are long-term scenarios and do not converge towards one single and definite vision of the future; they point at structuring and modifying the interaction framework of actors who have to develop and manage an image of multiple possible futures.

The structuring-scenarios conceived as *process-scenarios* are made up of blocks of actions (called structuring-actions) aiming at coordinating and integrating the specific activities undertaken in the Po Delta area and the general activities to be carried out by the Park Agency. Structuring-scenarios have been conceived as meeting two main objectives:

i. to start a dialogue between the Park Agency and other local public/private actors;
ii. to provide a 'bin' where structuring-actions can evolve and be discussed.

These scenarios are wide and dynamic visions of what should be done, what actions contribute to further develop the scenarios themselves, what actors can be involved when developing and implementing them, and what are the possible impacts deriving from their implementation. Three structuring-scenarios have been defined with the help of some representative actors of the local community:

i. 'Towards a collective vision of the Park'
ii. 'Innovation'
iii. 'Network of agencies and Institutions'

Each structuring-scenario has been initially identified through its core goal and its title (the *transient-scenario* at $t=t_0$). These two elements already give an idea or 'suggestion' on its contents which are defined in an open way; they keep 'open' to new ideas, contents and actions (in this sense they are conceived as open-contents scenarios). The three structuring scenarios have been further regenerated, integrating different considerations coming from the experts' work and the outcomes of some questionnaires distributed among some local public/private institutions. Each structuring-scenario consists of three parts:

i. the description of the problem that the scenario means to address;
ii. the identification of the fields of intervention;
iii. the descriptions of structuring-actions.

The structuring-scenarios obtained in this way are 'open contents scenarios' (Celino et al., 2007), in the sense that contents (that is to say the structuring-actions and their descriptions defined for each scenario) are not introduced in the Long-term Social and Economic Plan as end-products of the planning activity; they are conceived as work-in-progress products to be supplied to the Park Agency as starting bases (the *transient-scenario* at $t=t_1$) or continuing to work and dialogue with local actors and agencies.

The transient constructs in the Torre Guaceto Natural Reserve

The Torre Guaceto experience refers to an on-going research activity aiming at defining an e-governance system's architecture able to sustain collaboration at the community level and to activate learning and innovation in complex organisational environments. The e-governance platform should provide the framework in which users collectively share and reflect on their individual knowledge and beliefs (Celino and Concilio, 2006b). In order to define such a platform we decided to capture the evolution of *transient-scenarios* throughout a decision making process emerged out of the institutional planning activity. The research traced the network of knowledge flows shaping the decision making process and analysed the knowledge infrastructure of complex and scarcely structured organisations shaping the evolution of *transient-scenarios*.

The observation of the Torre Guaceto decision making environment has been carried out analysing the contents modifications/development of the Land Use Norms (norms that are part of the Reserve Spatial Management Plan); such contents are prescriptions for biological olive tree cultivation and olive oil production. In particular, referring to the specific object of decision making as the *transient scenario*, it has been possible to observe how its contents evolve together with the cognitive frameworks acting on those contents.

The four schemas in Figure 10.2 visualise the main structures of knowledge flows (considered as a knowledge supply chain) and related knowledge actors determining the evolution along four *transient-scenarios* (Celino and Concilio, 2006b):

i. *Transient Scenario* 1, a preliminary version of the Norm for Olive Oil Production (NOOP) has been developed within the framework of the Land Use Plan for the Natural Reserve;
ii. *Transient Scenario* 2, a second version of the NOOP has been developed to facilitate the discussion among the Natural reserve Officers and the Torre Guaceto Agricultural Community each supported by their own consultants;
iii. *Transient Scenario* 3, a third version of the NOOP has been considered in forms of INTERREG project participation rules;
iv. *Transient Scenario* 4, a fourth version of the NOOP is currently being developed in form of Olive Oil Biological Producers Association.

The knowledge supply chain has been analysed coherently with a model developed by Bellantuono, Pontrandolfo and Scozzi (2006) and applied simplifying the analysis of each single flow by giving relevance to the interactive environment (collaborative, conflicting or neutral) in which the cognitive flows supplied any positive contribution to NOOP production.

Although still preliminary, the knowledge supply chain analysis enabled some relevant considerations regarding the conditions of interaction among knowledge actors, the evolution of the content at hand, the effectiveness of a dynamic definition of decision making protocols giving rise to different knowledge supply chains structures The more the organisational system evolves towards a collaborative one, the more in depth content is deliberated.

The Torre Guaceto System is currently being designed focusing on three main questions:

i. how to make the forms of interaction support flexible,
ii. how to manage 'evolving contents' that, due to their public character, have to be stored explicit, transparent and accessible as much as possible, that is they have to made open, and
iii. how to store the dynamic nature of the collective memory in all its dimension and levels.

10.6 Conclusions

After discussing the evolving nature of plans in anytime planning, this chapter analyses the idea of plans as temporal structures and suggests the use of *process* and *transient-scenarios* as planning artifacts retaining and maintaining the evolving feature of plans and facilitating the exploration of space actions. The concepts of *process* and *transient-scenarios* derive from experiences and observations carried out in the environmental planning domain; some of those experiences are above briefly described and refer to the processes producing future environmental scenarios.

Such experiences suggest a reflection on the temporal structures generated along the collaborative planning processes. They propose to shift attention to the temporal structuring that actors engage both in their everyday practices and in the interaction with other actors. The new focus stimulates an analysis and/or a representation of the temporal structures constituted through such interactions. The analysis of the temporal structures (see experience in Torre Guaceto) facilitates the exploration of the conditions under which people reinforce, adjust, or change their temporal structures, as well as introduce new ones; the representation of the temporal structures (see experiences in Gravina Natural Park and Delta del Po River Park) are expected to support the cognitive transactions described above and, consequently, learning processes.

References

Banares-Alcantara, R. and King, J.M.P. (1997) 'Design support systems for process engineering: III. Design rationale as a requirement for effective support', *Computers and Chemical Engineering*, vol. 21(3), pp. 263-276.

Bellantuono, N., Pontrandolfo, P. and Scozzi, B. (2006) 'Knowledge networks within supply chain to foster innovation', in *Proceedings of the 14th International Working Seminar on Production Economics, Innsbruck*, vol. 2, pp. 59-70.

Bonfiglioli, S. and Mareggi, M. (1997) 'Il tempo e la città fra natura e storia: Atlante di progetti sui tempi della città Rome' ['Time and city between nature and history: Atlas of projects on city times'], *Urbanistica Quaderni*, No. 12.

Borri, D., Celino, A., Concilio, G. and Deliddo, A. (2005) 'Argumentative support system in environmental scenario development', in S.E. Batty (ed.), *Computers in Urban Planning and Urban Management*, CASA, University College London, London, p. 217.

Casey, A. (1997) 'Collective memory in organizations', in J.P. Walsh and A.S. Huff (eds.), *Advances in Strategic Management*, JAI Press, Greenwich, CT, pp. 111-154.

Celino, A. and Concilio, G. (2004) 'Developing a collaborative learning support system for a natural protected area', lecture notes in Computer Science, Springer-Verlag, Heidelberg.

Celino, A. and Concilio, G. (2006a) 'Supporting collaborative learning in environmental scenario building through an argumentative system', *Knowledge Management Research and Practice*, vol. 4, pp. 240-249.

Celino, A. and Concilio, G. (2006b) 'Managing open contents for collaborative deliberation in environmental planning', in F. Malpica, A. Oropeza, J. Carrasquero, and P. Howell (eds.), 'Proceedings PISTA 2006', The 4th International Conference on Politics and Information Systems: Technologies and Applications, International Institute of Informatics and Systemics, Orlando.

Celino, A., Concilio, G., Cucurachi, E. and Deliddo, A. (2007) 'Scenari ambientali e contenuti aperti: il caso del Delta del Po Veneto' ['Managing knowledge in environmental future dcenarios: The case of Po Delta in Veneto Region'], in F. Trapani (ed.), *Urbacost: un Progetto Pilota per la Sicilia Centrale* [*Urbacost: a Pilot Project for the Central Sicily*], FrancoAngeli, Milan, pp. 257-270.

Chung, P.W.H. and Goodwin, R. (1998) 'An integrated approach to representing and accessing design rationale', *Engineering Applications of Artificial Intelligence*, vol. 11, pp. 149-159.

Ciborra, C.U. and Lanzara, G.F. (1994) 'Formative contexts and information technology: Understanding the dynamics of innovation in organizations', *Accounting, Management and Information Technology*, vol. 4(2), pp. 61-86.

Davenport, T.H. and Prusak, L. (1997) *Information Ecology: Mastering the Information and Knowledge Environment*, Oxford University Press, New York.

Ferrer, G.J. (2002) 'Anytime replanning using local subplan replacement', PhD thesis, University of Virginia, Charlottesville.

Forester, J. (1999) *The Deliberative Practitioner: Encouraging Participatory Planning Processes*, MIT Press, Cambridge.

Pór, G. and Spivak, J. (2000) 'The ecology of knowledge: A field of theory and practice, key to research and technology development', paper presented at the Consultation Meeting on the Future of Organizations and Knowledge Management of the European Commission's Directorate-General Information Society Technologies, May, Brussels, available at http://www.co-i-l.com/coil/knowledge-garden/kd/eoknowledge.shtml, viewed January 18, 2008.

Graham, S. and Healey, P. (1999) 'Issues for planning theory and practice: Relational concepts of space and place', *European Planning Studies*, vol. 7(5), pp. 623-646.

Hawes, N. (2002) 'An anytime planning agent for computer game worlds', in Proceedings of the Workshop on Agents in Computer Games at The 3rd International Conference on Computers and Games, University of Birmingham, Birmingham.

Healey, P. (1997) *Collaborative Planning: Shaping Places in Fragmented Societies*, Macmillan, London.

Healey, P. (1996) 'The communicative turn in planning theory and its implications for spatial strategy formations', *Environment and Planning B: Planning and Design*, vol. 23(2), pp. 217-234.

Huber, G.P. (1991) 'Organizational learning: The contributing processes and the literature', *Organization Science*, vol. 2, pp. 88-115.

Innes, J.E. and Booher, D.E. (1999) 'Consensus building and complex adaptive systems: A framework for evaluating collaborative planning', *Journal of the American Planning Association*, vol. 65(4), pp. 412-423.

Kaganovich, M. (1996) 'Rolling planning: Optimality and decentralization', *Journal of Economic Behavior and Organization*, vol. 29, pp. 173-185.

Kleiner, A. and Roth, G. (1997) 'Learning histories: A new tool for turning organizational experience into action', available at http://ccs.mit.edu/lh/ 21CWP002. html, viewed January 18, 2008.

Lanzara, G.F. (1990) 'Shifting stories: Learning from a reflective experiment in a design process', in D.A. Schon (ed.), *The Turn Reflective*, Columbia University, NY Teachers College Press, New York, pp. 285-320.

Lanzara, G.F. (1999) 'Between transient constructs and persistent structures: designing systems in action', *Journal of Strategic Information Systems*, vol. 8, pp. 331-349.

Likhachev, M. (2005) 'Search-based planning for large dynamic environments', PhD thesis, School of Computer Science Carnegie Mellon University, Pittsburgh.

Malhotra, Y. (2002) 'Information ecology and knowledge management: toward knowledge ecology for hyperturbulent organizational environmental environments', in, *Encyclopedia of Life Support Systems (EOLSS)*, UNESCO/ Eolss Publishers, Oxford.

Mathews, K.M., White, M.C. and Long, R.G. (1999) 'Why study the complexity sciences in the social sciences?', *Human Relations*, vol. 52(4), pp. 439-462.

Nandhakumar, J. (2002) 'Managing time in a software factory: Temporal and spatial organization of IS development activities', *The Information Society*, vol. 18(25), pp. 251-262.

Orlikowski, W.J. and Yates, J. (2002) 'It's about time: Temporal structuring in organizations', *Organization Science*, vol. 13(6), pp. 684-700.

Paulk, M.C., Curtis, B. and Chrissis, M.B. (1993) *Capability Maturity Model for Software*, vol. 1.1, Pittsburgh, PA, Software Engineering Institute, Carnegie Mellon University, Pittsburgh.

Scandurra, E. (2001) *Gli storni e l'urbanista. Progettare nella contemporaneità* [*Starlings and planners: Planning in the contemporaneity*], Meltemi, Rome.

Snowden, D.J. (2005) 'Narrative patterns the perils and possibilities of using story in organisations', available at http://www.kwork.org/Resources/narrative.pdf, accessed January 18, 2008.

Starkey, K. (1989) 'Time and work: A psychological perspective', in P. Blyton, J. Hassard, S. Hill, and K. Starkey (eds.), *Time, Work and Organization*, Routledge, London, pp. 35-56.

Thrift, N. (1996) 'New urban areas and old technological fears: Reconfiguring the goodwill of electronic things', *Urban Studies*, vol. 33(8), pp. 1463-1493.

Chapter 11
Complexity and Cellular Automaton: Exploring its Practical Application

Elisabete A. Silva[1]

This chapter explores the relationships between complexity and planning, focusing on experiences with Cellular Automaton (CA). It presents the results of using two Cellular Automaton models (SLEUTH and CVCA) in order to explore urban and environmental dynamics through time and space. The importance of these models is explored through quantitative and qualitative analysis. Sensitivity to local conditions, self-organisation, emergence, phase-transitions, DNAs, urban and environmental patterns, behaviour and decision making are explored using two very different metropolitan areas (the Lisbon and the Porto Metropolitan Areas). One of the most important results points to the idea that self-organisation plays an important role in the explanation of many of urban and environmental dynamics, and CA is capable of reporting these dynamics trough time.

11.1 Introduction: The application of complex systems using Cellular Automata

This chapter explores the implementation of some of the theoretical issues described in Chapter 17 of this book. It presents practical applications where it is possible to evaluate the use and importance of complex systems in order to understand the evolution of cities and the mechanisms that underlie urban growth.

This chapter discusses the issues where complexity and planning have a beneficial relationship, unveiling the benefits of applying complex systems theory to the understanding and planning of cities. It uses Cellular Automaton (CA) as an approach to incorporate complexity into the planning of metropolitan areas.

Therefore, it will demonstrate through the application of CA that 'complexity' and 'complicated' are not equivalent words. Complexity should be seen here as the study of 'complex systems' that goes beyond conventional systems of deterministic cause-effect relations (Batty, 1998/2007; Batty and Longley, 1994; Openshaw and Openshaw, 1997). Complexity here includes some attributes considered to be

1 Dr Elisabete A. Silva is University Lecturer in the Department of Land Economy, University of Cambridge, United Kingdom.

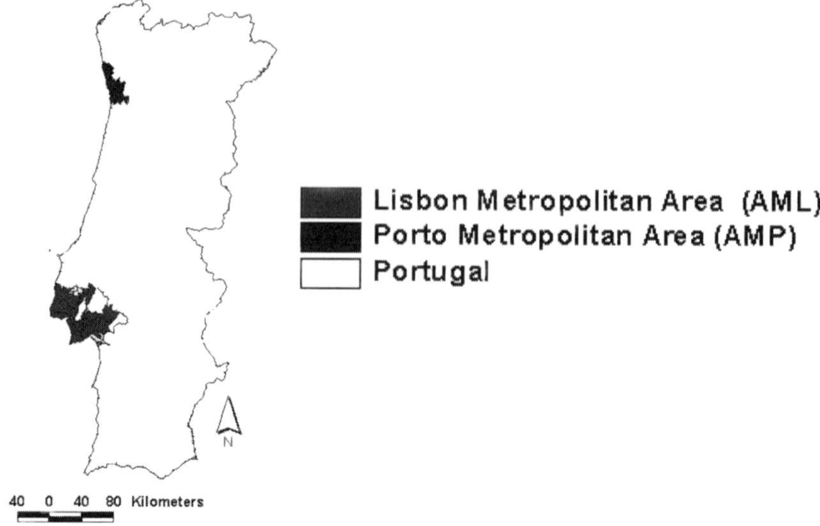

Figure 11.1 Location of the Lisbon and Porto Metropolitan Areas, Portugal

self-organising, able to adapt to their oppressing environment, and of revealing emerging properties.

The next points will exemplify the application of a new set of models that allows exploring complexity issues in a 'controlled' environment. As in a lab, a cellular model is a representation of the 'real world', in which dynamics are simulated in order to evaluate the self-organisation of urban and environmental cells that represent land cover types (Piyathamrongchai and Batty, 2007; Kocabas et al., 2007; Sudhira, 2004). In this 'controlled' environment the behaviour of land change is simulated in order to understand this change and to demonstrate some of the ideas proposed through the development of new theoretical concepts regarding – amongst others – phase-transitions and bifurcations and the development of DNAs (Webster, 1996; Liu Xiaping et al., 2007; Gazulis and Clarke, 2006; Silva, 2004).

This chapter is organised in five different main parts: the first part explores the idea of complexity and Cellular Automaton in order to understand urban growth as an evolution from the past into the future and the importance of past history and landscape characteristics in self-organisation of urban and environmental cells; the second part explores the development of the future simulations as scenarios resulting from different planning strategies; the third part assesses the different scenarios resulting from the future simulation; the fourth part discusses how important this is for the image and size of our metropolitan areas; the fifth part goes further and explores in the simulations the existence of phase-transitions and bifurcation; finally a conclusion wraps up the main ideas of the chapter.

11.2 Complexity and urban-environmental CA models

This chapter discusses complex systems theory using Cellular Automata (CA), through the use of CA models and its application to two metropolitan areas (Figure 11.1). Two computer models are used (the SLEUTH model and the CVCA model) and two case studies are explored (AML – Lisbon Metropolitan Area; AMP – Porto Metropolitan Areas – Figure 11.1). Although these two metropolitan areas are located in Portugal, they have very different topographic characteristics, population densities and planning strategies. These differences are fundamental to explore the adaptability of CA to local conditions and by doing so to contribute to the discussion of the importance of a complex system approach.

The Lisbon Metropolitan Area (AML) contains approximately 2.6 million inhabitants in an area of 2,957 km^2, which makes a population density of 893 people/km^2 (Lisbon is the capital of the country and main urban area). The Porto Metropolitan Area (AMP) contains a population of around 1,580 million inhabitants in a area of 1,573 km^2, and a population density of 1,005 people/km^2 (Porto is the second city of Portugal and the central nucleus of the AMP).

As mentioned, the models discussed in this chapter were applied to these two metropolitan areas in order to understand, among other things, the sensitivity of cellular automaton to local conditions, the capacity of these models to include the main elements that constrain the behaviour of cities and to simulate realistic images of these cities.

The two modes used were SLEUTH (developed by Clarke and Gaydos, 1998; Clarke et al., 2007) and CVCA (developed by Silva, 2000/2002; Wileden, Silva and Ahern, 2003; Silva, Wileden and Ahern, 2008). The application of these models to the Lisbon and Porto Metropolitan Areas were explored in several papers published during the last few years (Silva, 2000/2002/2004; Silva and Clarke, 2001/2002/2005; Gazulis and Clarke, 2006).

SLEUTH (the acronym for **S**lope, **L**and use, **E**xcluded areas of urbanisation, **U**rban, **T**ransportation, **H**illshade) is an Urban Cellular Automaton that simulates urban growth using a set of thirteen metrics and five indicators.

These metrics include computation of landscape characteristics such as: number of urban pixels, number of edges, number of urban clusters, mean cluster size, Leesalee (a shape index, a measurement of spatial fit between the model's growth and the known urban extent for the 'control' years, used for reference purposes), average slope, direction of urban growth, etc. Once these metrics are computed, besides a composite score that will allow synthesising these metrics behaviour (composite score), five indicators are outputted and allow characterising the behaviour of the system: the diffusion coefficient, the breed coefficient, the spread coefficient, the slope resistance, and the road gravity (Silva and Clarke, 2001). These metrics allow exploring a parameter space of five different layers: Slopes, Excluded of Urbanisation, Urban, Transportation and Hillshade. This parameter space is related to the number of 'layers' included in the model that characterise some of the variables analysed by the model.

CVCA is an acronym for environmental **C**ountervailing **C**ellular **A**utomaton. It uses a set of five decision rules (offensive, opportunistic, protective, defensive, and let it grow) in a parameter space that includes SLEUTH outputs of urban growth, and an adapted layer of environmental areas. In an interaction through time and space, landscape ecological strategies supported by a set of five landscape metrics (Edges, Area, Number of Clusters, Minimum Cluster Area, Mean Patch Size, Landscape Shape Index, Mean Nearest Neighbour Distance) directs growth to specific areas good to grow allowing the implementation of the five landscape strategies (resulting from the five decision rules) (Silva, Ahern and Wileden, 2008).

The five decision rules follow Ahern's (1998) Framework Method for landscape ecological planning that focuses on a set of possible, non-mutually exclusive planning strategies: *(i)* Protective Strategy (when the existing landscape supports the abiotic, biotic, and cultural ('abc') resource goals); *(ii)* Defensive strategy (when the existing landscape is already in a spatial configuration that is negatively impacting 'abc' resources); *(iii)* Offensive strategy (adopting a proactive action when the landscape is already deficient with respect to supporting 'abc' resources); and *(iv)* Opportunistic Strategy (since very frequently landscapes contain unique elements or configurations of elements that represent positive opportunities). It develops this using game theory and presents the model CVCA its computer application.

Cellular Automaton is particularly suited to simulate these dynamics. Several reasons can be pointed: the representation of space (a matrix), the representation of dynamics in space and time, the interaction of different elements that control the behaviour of the model through probabilistic systems. The results can be assessed in terms of the visual output, but also in terms of quantitative statistics.

The next point will explore some of the visual and quantitative outputs resulting from simulating the complex system that is the evolution of metropolitan areas through time. The first images report simulations from the past until the present, the second group of images build on present day data and propose a set of scenarios to the future.

11.3 Understanding the evolution of the metropolis through self-organisation

The self-organisation of cells representing urban growth can be seen in the evolution of the Metropolitan Areas of Lisbon and Porto from 1976 to 1997 (Figure 11.2). In both cases the system had to evolve through time, having as basic layers a set of 'control' years (years that are classified using Remote Sensing images and that are going to be used as calibration images between what is simulated and what was classified in the satellite images – four satellite images with four years of information regarding urban functions are used for that purpose), two road layers, and the slope layer (extracted from a digital terrain model) and 'excluded areas of urbanisation' layers.

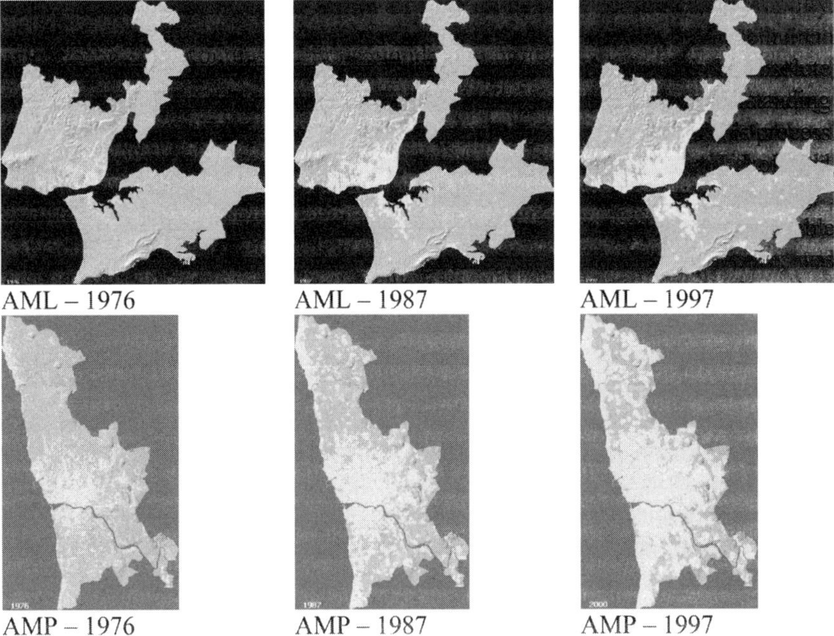

Figure 11.2 The urban evolution of the Lisbon Metropolitan Area (AML) and Porto Metropolitan area (AMP)

Note: The light grey cells represent urbanisation growth; the dark grey hillshade background was clipped to the administrative boundary of the Metropolitan Area.

The previous layers are used as basic information with which the model results will be compared. Each layer is a reference that the model needs to compare by accessing the degree of proximity between the simulated reality and the reality at these 'control' years that results from the satellite images and other cartographic information (i.e. the roads layer and for the agricultural and natural reserves layer).

Figure 11.2 presents a set of images for both metropolitan areas. In each image it is possible to see urban cells growing throughout the metropolitan areas at different intensities of urban growth and creating regional patterns that vary in shape and size. This urban evolution is perceived not only for one image but also through time, for multiple years. Those that are familiar with the Lisbon and the Porto Metropolitan Areas know that the simulations are very realistic. The analysis of these images allows seeing organic urban growth, as well as dispersed urban growth in the countryside. The intensity of the growth rates is also different, the number of light grey cells (urban cells) increase substantially during the 1990s. This is particularly visible in the Porto Metropolitan Area.

Table 11.1 The SLEUTH and the CVCA metrics

The SLEUTH metric

	AML Final Calibration	AMP Final Calibration
Diffusion	16	20
Breed	57	20
Spread	50	40
Slope	25	45
Roads	30	20

The CVCA metric

Landscape Metric	Value AML	Value AMP
Edges	35171	14964
Area	106460	24207
Num clusters	1134	708
MCS	93	34
MPS	577	275
LSI	9.9	7.7
MNND	1.6	1.5

The use of past data sets to calibrate the model simulations against existent ground data (the inputted layers resulting from the satellite images and from other cartographic information) are particularly important in Cellular Automaton (CA) and in many complex systems methodologies. Because these methodologies use CA as the base methodology to simulate self-organisation, they rely on the axiom that these are adaptive systems that require information as an important element for correct simulations. The only way to have the systems acquiring knowledge of it is through past simulations (the past is partially known to us, by maps, images, reports, etc).

While the visual images are very helpful to us, as a demonstration of the adaptability of these systems to local conditions and as a demonstration that complexity of urban dynamics can be simulated with a degree of certainty. The simulations are also important to calibrate the elements that control the behaviour of our systems (computation and knowledge of system dynamics made us opt for a set of well known and explored elements that control the behaviour of the urban system – roads, slope, spread, breed and diffusion. With time more elements will be included). Through a set of interactions, these five synthesis indicators pass from amorphous values starting at 'zero to 100' (from a parameter set where all values are at 0 intensity, to a parameter set where there will be a variation of numbers accordingly to the intensity of each cell) to reflect the nature of the system under study.

Table 11.1 presents these five synthesis indicator values for the Lisbon and the Porto Metropolitan Areas. As it is possible to see by the values of each indicator, the slope factor plays an important function in the Porto Metropolis. While in Lisbon it is the development of new nuclei being the main element controlling the growth of the metropolitan area.

Important for our analysis is the fact that these keys of numbers/indicators reflect the relative importance of each indicator in the present and future of each metropolitan area. For this reason it is possible to state that these are a kind of DNAs that characterise each metropolitan area (Gazulis and Clarke, 2006; Silva, 2004; Webster, 2004). The Lisbon Metropolitan Area DNA is 16, 57, 50, 25, 30 and the Porto Metropolitan Area DNA is 20, 20, 40, 45, 20 (see Table 11.1 for further explanation).

Similarly to what can be perceived for the SLEUTH metrics and its associated DNA values, can be stated for CVCA and its associated metrics. These metrics reflect the overall behaviour of the metropolitan area (individually per each cell it is possible to extract its equivalent individual value – except in the case of the Landscape Shape Index metrics). In the case of the LSI metrics (Landscape Shape Index) only one value is extracted for each metropolitan area. This overall indicator is important once it allows us to access the overall status of the metropolitan area, as well as comparing this LSI with other metropolitan area's LSIs.

11.4 The development of future scenarios and the inclusion of planning constraints in the Cellular Automata

While the future is considered uncertain, there is a probability of specific events to happen; the future evolution of a metropolitan areas is uncertain, but its inherent complexity can be predicted to a point of high probability of an event to happen particularly when speaking about built up human structures (and particularly if we consider the near future, i.e. the next 5 years).

The next paragraphs discuss the differences between the scenarios developed using CVCA and SLEUTH. A qualitative analysis of the visual image of the different scenarios is followed by a quantitative analysis of the number of urban pixels the specific scenario would generate. Afterwards, considerations about time evolution and the different paths each metropolitan area might experience conclude this point.

These simulations assume different scenarios. In the SLEUTH model we can develop trend scenarios of urban growth, or scenarios where the intensity and shape of urban growth can vary. In the case of CVCA, the goal is to interact five landscape strategies (protective, offensive, defensive, opportunistic, let it grow) with the urban growth proposed by SLEUTH. The resulting image will be of cells being set aside as protective, offensive, defensive, opportunistic cells in order to prevent urbanisation to happen in those specific cells. Only the strategy 'let it go' will allow urbanisation to happen.

Figure 11.3 presents the image resulting from the SLEUTH simulations for the year of 2025 for the Lisbon Metropolitan Area (AML) and the Porto Metropolitan Area (AMP). It is possible to identify in the images a different urban shape and size of urban growth in the case of having a scenario that protects the ecological and agricultural reserves (classified at the layer of excluded areas of urbanisation) or the one that includes countervailing CVCA strategies.

Looking at the simulations, it is possible to find a common point: the next decades will be of urban growth in the south margin of the AML, identified in the image with brackets and also called as 'Peninsula de Setubal' (this is also true when analysing the images resulting from the environmental model). While the north margin of the Tagus River will keep growing outwards, the speed and intensity of the urban growth in the south margin will overshadow the previous decades with more land being urbanised. The models predict that the heartland of the 'Peninsula de Setúbal' will experience the most intense growth of the Metropolitan Area of Lisbon. As it is possible to conclude, these models allow analysing visually and quantitatively how urban self-organisation will happen and with what kind of intensity of growth.

Another municipality that is worth mentioning is Azambuja (identified with a dotted arrow in the image). In the past decades this was discussed as one of the possible locations for a new international airport. However, while this is very close to the municipalities of Azambuja, no information regarding this infrastructure was included in the model. Nevertheless the model presents future impacts of this infrastructure in the areas surrounding the proposed site (fast rate of urban cells in the last year of 1998) as the model increases the speed of the proposed new urban cells for that central area of the municipality of Azambuja. The importance of emergence, is worth mentioning here, because, this case study clearly demonstrates that emergence exists once a deterministic model could not propose intense growth for an area very far away from the main urban centres.

In terms of quantitative analysis it is very important for researchers and to the decision makers to pinpoint where (locally and globally) high probabilities of urban growth are expected to happen (in other words: if a developer wants to know where are the best parcels of land to purchase in the metropolitan area he only needs to select the cells with high probability of urbanisation; similarly, if a local authority realises that some of these cells with high probability of urbanisation are close to relevant areas for some planning purpose they can purchase them in advance). It is also possible to compare different scenarios and evaluate if specific actions to countervail urban growth will result in the same land consumption, and in the same local pressures or in the same regional urban image. This will help reflecting upon questions such as: what is better, a high probability of having for example 44,544 urban cells of 100x100m urbanised or only 27,220 urban cells if another planning strategy is to be used? What is the resulting metropolitan image? Where are the urban pressures? (see Table 11.2).

This level of dynamic analysis and the complexity of including so many variations at the local level are impressive and are a good indication of the importance of Cellular Automaton and the inclusion of this complexity in an outcome that is quite simple to see, to quantify, to read and to understand.

Colours represent urban probabilities: light grey represents cells of existent urban areas; dark grey represents cells with high probability of urban growth. For the purpose of this paper cells with average probability of urban growth were not accounted for. The development of CVCA is also relevant as a good example of the

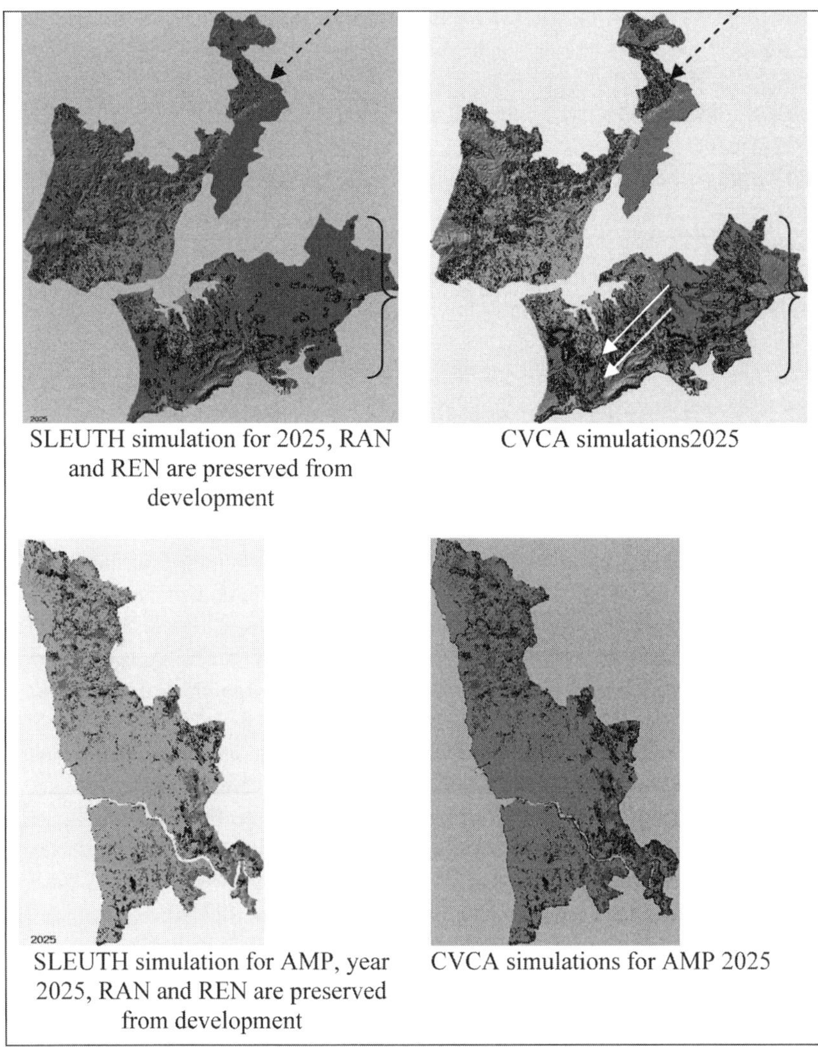

2025
SLEUTH simulation for 2025, RAN and REN are preserved from development
CVCA simulations2025
2025
SLEUTH simulation for AMP, year 2025, RAN and REN are preserved from development
CVCA simulations for AMP 2025

Figure 11.3 The Lisbon Metropolitan Area (AML) and the Porto Metropolitan Area (AMP): Two different scenarios of urbanisation (RAN: Agricultural Reserve, REN: Ecological Reserve)

need to include expert decision, actions by the imposition of central government directives and/or regional master plans, or local constrains that promote other kinds of local self-organisation. For instance, this will be important to see if an intended impact really happens and enables expected land dynamics.

Table 11.2 The cell values for each future simulation of the AML and AMP

AML		
	A1	**E1**
Light Grey	5,147	51,417
Dark Grey	44,544	27,220

AMP		
	A1	**E1**
Light Grey	56,249	56,249
Dark Grey	8,068	3,332

Note: A1 – SLEUTH simulation, year 2025. The Agricultural Reserve (RAN) and The Ecological Reserve (REN) are preserved from development E1 – Simulation of CVCA coupled with SLEUTH, year 2025.

The inclusion of different landscape strategies, in order to guide urban growth, has a relevant impact on the future image of the metropolitan area. Setting up landscape strategies around all the main important patches will prevent urban growth to occur in those areas. The impact of having a predominant strategy of defensive behaviour that imposes more compactness (as observed when implementation CVCA to AML and AMP), will tend to develop with time, a more concentrated urban development.

As a result of applying landscape strategies again, assuming any strategy, Figure 11.3 (simulations using CVCA) presents several patches of 'green areas' (represented in the images by open space of grey cells – between the dark cells of high probability of urban growth and the light grey existent urban cells) scattered throughout the Lisbon Metropolitan Area (AML) and several corridors connecting the patches. The two arrows define a region where a green corridor can be observed for an extensive area. Figure 11.3 presents several findings: one is the ability to have a very extensive corridor and a large patch in the municipality of Palmela (arrow in the image). It is also interesting because the establishment of several corridors works as a barrier to prevent urbanisation to happen in the heartland of the Peninsula de Setúbal.

The Porto Metropolitan Area (AMP) reveals the same importance if the landscape strategies are applied. A visual analysis of the importance of the landscape strategies is not as clear as in the case of the AML, nevertheless some 'open areas' (resulting from the application of the landscape strategies) are disclosed in the images.

The comparison of the number of urban cells resulting from applying the SLEUTH and the CVCA models, confirms the importance of the strategies. When comparing the number of high probability of urban cells, resulting from the simulations running one or both models, applying the landscape strategies as a means to control and direct urban growth presents fewer urban cells for the Lisbon and Porto Metropolitan Areas. The values for the year of 2025 in the case of applying the landscapes strategies are 27,220 for AML and 3,332 for AMP (Table 11.2).

Table 11.3 The Landscape Strategy cells and Urban cells for AML and AMP

Classes	AML, Year 2025	AMP, Year 2025
Light Grey	51,417	56,249
Dark Grey	27,220	3,332
Protective	115	50
Offensive	447	26
Defensive	40,636	8,052

From the previous analysis, several conclusions point to the fact that Cellular Automaton models are a good tool to simulate the behaviour of metropolitan systems, not only from the past, but also into the future. The images resulting from the scenarios (and associated probabilities of urban growth) are not only useful for planning practice. They are also important for planning theory, as new thinking is being developed in particular exploring the phenomena of complexities and cities.

In Table 11.3 it is possible to evaluate the classes that represent urban probabilities: light grey represents cells of existent urban areas; dark grey represents cells with high probability of urban growth. For the purpose of this chapter cells with average probability of urban growth were not accounted for. Also for the purpose of this chapter, 'opportunistic' cells were not included due to the reduced number of cells, proposed by the model. 'Opportunistic' cells are for instance cells resulting from an Ecological Reserve Patch that has a Nearest Neighbour that allows establishing a corridor between the two patches of Ecological Reserve. The Dark Grey Cells represent in CVCA the strategy of 'Let it grow'.

An analysis of Table 11.3 allows us to see that the Lisbon Metropolitan Area (AML) has more cells resulting from the application of the Landscape Strategies, while this metropolitan area is bigger when comparing with the Porto Metropolitan Area (AMP). It seems to be clear that urban dynamics are more intense, but there are still significant patches of RAN (Agricultural Reserve) or REN (Ecological Reserve) to allow landscape strategies to be implemented in a successful way.

In order to fully understand the importance of using SLEUTH or CVCA and to compare the resulting scenarios, besides comparing numbers of cells one should also compare the shape and size of the areas affected by the different scenarios. The next section will explore these issues, understanding the amount of urban cells is important, but comparing how these are organised in space is equally important.

11.5 The image of a metropolitan area: self-organisation, urban shape and size

This section highlights the ability of using computer simulations to consider the density, the spatial pattern and the total amount of urban growth when computer simulations are used to create scenarios for the future. Consequently, it is possible to influence the image of a metropolitan area. The elements that can promote that change are among those framed within our simulation model: *(i)* the elements related to the layers used as space variable (input layer); *(ii)* the elements that control the behaviour of the system; *(iii)* elements promoting future phase-transitions (i.e. identify the amplitude of the metrics/indicators necessary to promote a specific change in density, amount or shape of urban growth); *(iv)* elements establishing landscape strategies that promote connectivity; *(v)* elements regarding strategic decision input to develop scenarios the reflect expert's requirements.

Figure 11.4 and Figure 11.5 oppose several 'images' of what the metropolis might look like in the future. The trend scenario is opposed to an urban growth boundaries scenario; these two contrasted images promote two different metropolitan areas (dispersed metropolitan area, or a more concentrated metropolitan area). The image of what would be the future if Agricultural Reserve (RAN) and Ecological Reserve (REN) were to be preserved since the 1970s. These scenarios demonstrate that legally defining RAN and REN delimitations in the past had a clear objective of promoting a more concentrated kind of growth. Nevertheless, it seems also to reveal that the level of implementation did not manage to reach the goals to be established once the fact that today's urban shapes of Lisbon and Porto are very different from the one simulated if RAN and REN had been accounted for.

The scenario of preserving of RAN and REN, can also be contrasted to Landsat images for the same years (used as 'control' years), representing what is happening in the field, and therefore characterising the real image of the scattered urban character of the AMP and AML. In this case the decision maker can evaluate if the law is being followed and where/why some areas are being urbanised (Figure 11.4 and Figure 11.5).

The previous paragraphs introduced the importance of these dynamic models that address complexity as a means generating different scenarios. Besides this fact, it is important to study the resulting images of these models in terms of urban shape and size. Previous deterministic models tended to propose urban growth that was very dependent of existent growth poles, the rhythms of growth were the same throughout the metropolitan area, and the resulting urban forms tended to be of organic growth from the existent nuclei. CVCA and SLEUTH, as many CA models, overcome these problems by generating realistic simulations where this diversity of urban shapes is visible and different growth rates are allowed.

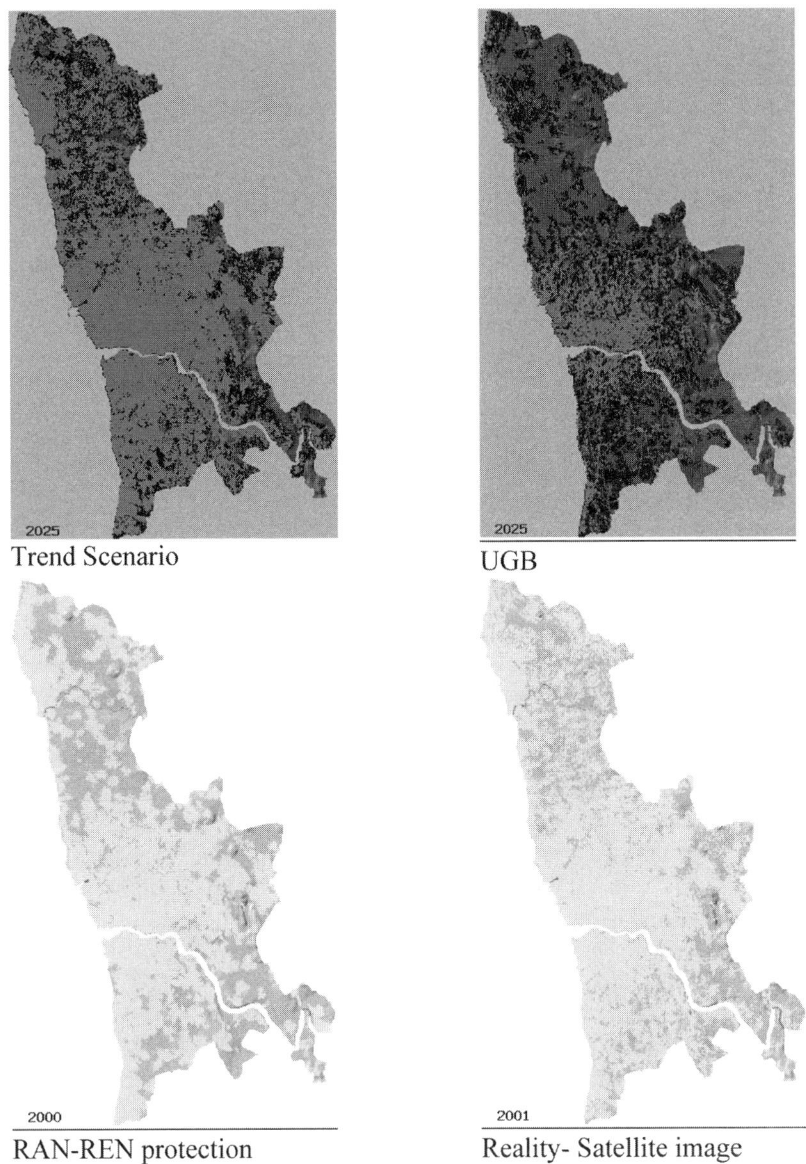

Figure 11.4 Discussions about the image of AML

Note: The 'Trend Scenario' identifies sustainable urban growth, including an Urban Growth Boundary (UGB) that seems already impossible at the moment of reflection. The two images of 'RAN-REN protection' and 'Reality' oppose what is today the AMP and what it could be in case the RAN (Agricultural Reserve) and REN (Ecological Reserve) law was strictly followed.

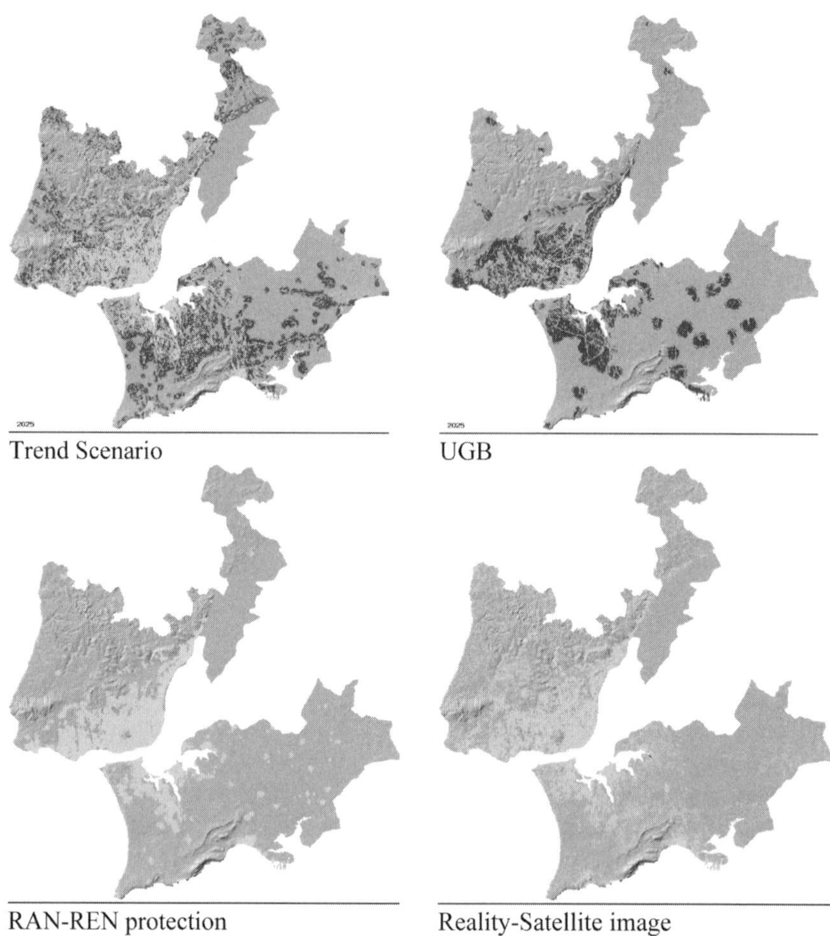

Figure 11.5 Discussions about the image of AML

Note: The 'Trend Scenario' identifies sustainable urban growth, including an Urban Growth Boundary (UGB) that seems already impossible at the moment of reflection. The two images of 'RAN-REN protection' and 'Reality' oppose what is today the AML and what it could be in case the RAN (Agricultural Reserve) and REN (Ecological Reserve) law was strictly followed.

Figure 11.6 identifies the different kinds of urban growth (organic, sprawl, road influenced and new nuclei). It identifies the major axis of urban growth, and where the main channels of urban growth flow to the countryside are. In the Porto Metropolitan Area the phenomena of infill predominates, but, as will be demonstrated in the next point of this chapter dedicated to the analysis

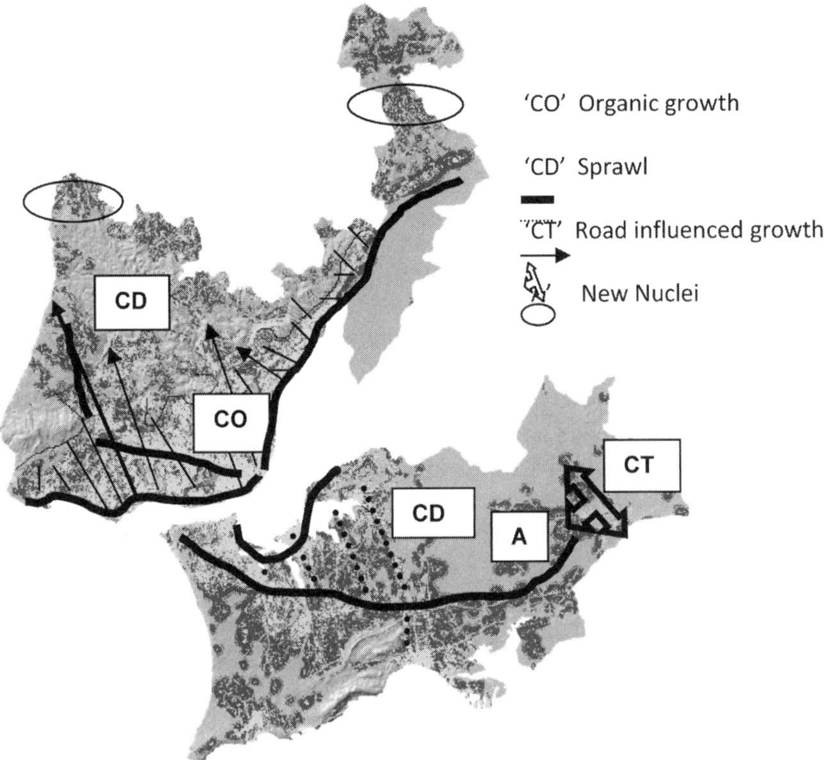

Figure 11.6 The urban elements of AML, year 2025 (simulation that allows some urbanisation in RAN areas)

of phase-transition, a change is happening in the AMP, not only at the level of spatial structure, but (we might induce) already at the level of socio-economic relationships (i.e. in terms of the importance of major developers in the area, and the impact of industrial areas).

The questions raised by these scenarios make it very clear that the future of the AML and AMP is a question of option, of showing to the decision makers the possible future and present the advantages and disadvantages. It is a question of keeping the traditional character of AMP of small farms, two-story homes, private wells, corn and grapevines as main economic activities. Or alternatively, to allow a more dense urban growth, with several-storey apartment buildings, very different from the traditional single family home. At this moment, the main conclusion points to the fact that the simulations of both models for the two metropolitan areas present an intense process of change; the objective was not to prevent growth to happen, but to accommodate growth in a way that was not overly detrimental to the environment and the human scale.

Table 11.4 The SLEUTH metrics before and after self-modification

	AML final calibration	AML after self-modification	AMP final calibration	AMP after self-modification
Diffusion	16	19	20	25
Breed	57	70	20	25
Spread	50	62	40	51
Slope	25	38	45	100
Roads	30	43	20	75

11.6 Spatial and temporal analysis through self-organisation

The advantages of using cellular automata (CA) are presented in Chapter 17 and in the first part of this chapter. The sensitivity to local conditions, the ability to detect regional patterns through local behaviour of cells, the scalability of the analysis from local to regional patterns, the dynamic analysis of time and space, are among some of the main advantages.

The Cellular Automaton (CA) sensitivity to local analysis was clear when studying the Lisbon and Porto Metropolitan Areas. Through calibration it was possible to narrow down the values that best described the elements that controlled the behaviour of the system. SLEUTH and CVCA allow to perform one more action that will be very helpful to explore another issue of complexity, the importance of recent events in the behaviour of systems. For the purpose of this chapter the existence of phase-transitions and the impacts of DNAs will be explored using the SLEUTH model.

When running SLEUTH, during the calibration phase boom and boost phases of urban growth are detected and recorded. This is important once systems do not progress with the same intensity and speed through time and space (i.e. in a metropolitan area there will be locations with intense development and other areas with less or no development), understanding and comparing these urban boom and boost phases. And re-calibrating the system accordingly to these variations is equally important. This requires the inclusion of another level of complexity in the model, that is to say a second level of self-organisation that is different from the self-organisation reported in the previous section (resulting from the interaction of the urban cells along the past 30 years). It focuses on the recent past and the observation throughout the metropolitan area of boom and boost phases that otherwise would be hidden by the overall dynamics along a 30-year period. This second level of self-organisation is called 'self-modification'.

As already introduced, it was possible to detect the relative weight of the indicators that control the behaviour of the system. Therefore, after this process of self-modification was introduced, the most important indicators in the behaviour of the Lisbon Metropolitan Area were detected (the breed factor, resulting in the creation of new nuclei, and the spread factor); in the case of the Porto Metropolitan

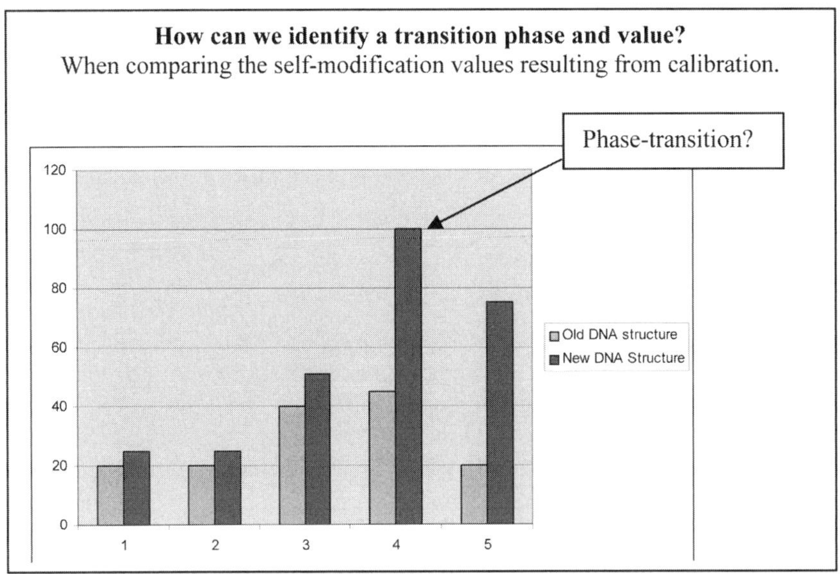
How can we identify a transition phase and value?
When comparing the self-modification values resulting from calibration.
Phase-transition?
120
100
80
60
40
20
0
1
2
3
4
5
Old DNA structure
New DNA Structure

Figure 11.7 Is a Metropolitan Area suffering due to a phase-transition? (The values of the calibration from the Porto Metropolitan Area were used in order to make it simpler to understand)

Area the most important indicator was the slope factor (Table 11.4). This DNA key of values for each metropolitan area testifies to the aptitude of CA to reflect local characteristics of each metropolitan area.

The analysis of the time evolution when boom and boost phases are included as a self-modification mechanism, discloses another element recently happening in the Porto Metropolitan Area. Changes in the transportation system of the AMP seem to be reorganising the behaviour of the metropolitan area and the degree of importance and value of the DNA metrics. The second most important element in the behaviour of the AMP was the 'spread factor'. Using self-modification, the second most important element becomes the 'road factor', instead of the previous second position of the 'spread factor' before self-modification.

The ability to assess phase-transitions presents other advantages. Running SLEUTH allowed the identification of an important phase-transition for AMP (Table 11.4, Figure 11.7, Figure 11.8, and Figure 11.9). Figure 11.7 presents a simplified graph of what the old and new values of DNA for the Porto Metropolitan Area (AMP) represent before and after self-modification, and questions to which extent we are in a phase-transition (once the variables that control the behaviour of the system have changed as well as the intensity of change is very significant). If in fact this points to a phase-transition, this changing reality might raise some questions, since this will have major implications for the landscape and socio-

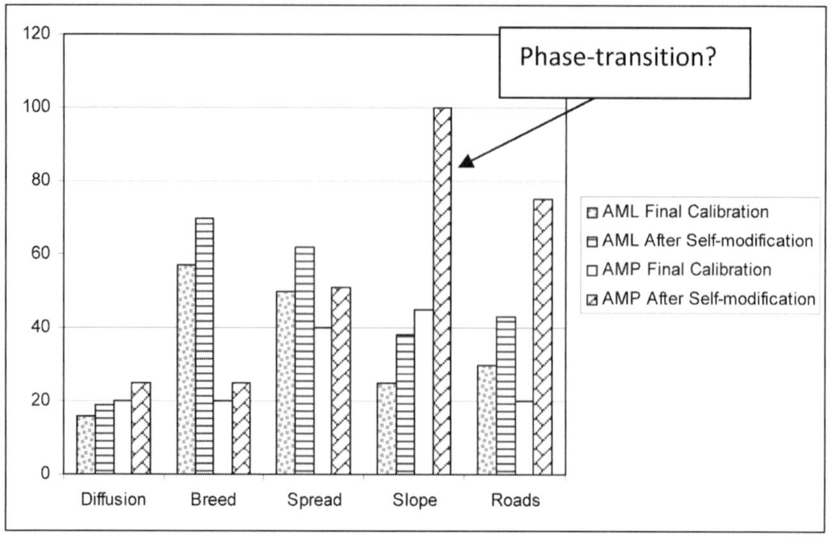

Figure 11.8 Evolution for AML and AMP, what to expect?

Note: The Lisbon Metropolitan area has an historic pattern of successive phases of intense growth, followed by phases of relative stability. The Porto Metropolitan Area had a more constant growth. The new phase-transition might be inducing a new kind of urban growth for the Porto Metropolitan Area.

economic life of the AMP. Are the municipal and regional planning departments ready for this change? If so, what is the impact of the new DNA structure and when in time it will be spatially explicit?

Figure 11.8 contrasts both DNAs for the Metropolitan Areas. The intensity of the self-modification values for the Porto Metropolitan Areas allows to raise the question: are we observing a phase-transition? If so, several assumptions can be asked (if indeed it is possible to define a moment in time when these phase-transitions are happening): if we can define clearly phase-transitions it is also possible to establish criteria that would reveal when the next phase-transition is going to happen, and if so, we also can assume that we can cause our own controlled phase-transitions.

11.7 Conclusions

Planning and complexity is certainly a subject that is generating much attention and research. It is now clear that pure deterministic models are not able to cope with the dynamics that city systems require. Analyses need to include variability across space, and they also need to allow for scalability accordingly to the phenomena under study.

In the same token, to account for complexity is to include spatial diversity but it is also to include the evolution of phenomena through time. Consequently, to understand such complex city systems one needs to understand how self-organisation happens in space and through time; also, understanding complexity is to accept that evolution exists, and that change might be so substantial that a phase-transition will be inevitable.

This chapter addresses complexity by implementing, in a computer environment, many of the theories developed in other chapters (such as Chapter 17), using Cellular Automata. As mentioned, CA are very well suited to simulate cities' complex systems due to the cellular matrix of space that allows to represent different land uses, and the possibility to simulate dynamically across space and in time (allowing for a high sensitivity to local conditions). The results of applying CA can be assessed in terms of the visual output, but also in terms of quantitative statistics they generate. This chapter explores the application of the CA models CVCA and SLEUTH to two Portuguese Metropolitan Areas and assesses the results of this implementation both in terms of its visual and quantitative outputs.

The first part of this chapter explores the importance of understanding urban growth as an evolution from the past into the future and the importance of past history and landscape characteristics to grant sensitivity to local conditions and as an enabler of self-organisation of urban and environmental cells. By exploring this point the reader can understand how important is the individual behaviour of cells to generate regional patterns, and how these cells in their individual behaviour might contribute to the local and regional diversity. This adaptability to local conditions is one of the keys for the success of CA, particularly in this case, the CA adapts itself to reality, generating its own identity (its own DNA).

The importance of these dynamic models goes beyond the simulation of past evolution. With this key knowledge from the past, it becomes possible to simulate future scenarios. The second and third parts of this chapter explore the different scenarios, not only in terms of its visual assessment and on how local dynamics of cells produce regional images that will vary accordingly to the developed scenario; but also in terms of comparing how many future urban cells each scenario will generate.

The possibility of 'playing' with different scenarios allows us to compare outcomes of (and select the best) planning strategies. This is important when comparing different scenarios, to select planning strategies that will produce different future urban images with different economic, social and environmental implications. Both SLEUTH and the CVCA models, attempt to provide several scenarios of what that image might be. The fourth part of the chapter discusses how the shape and size of urban growth will vary for both metropolitan areas. The objective is not to impose a specific view, but rather to integrate the visions that result from different needs (urban, environment, people). It is a tool to learn and to communicate to the decision maker what the implications are for opting for certain planning strategies.

CVCA and SLEUTH are also good tools to discuss the implications of spatial dynamics through time and the possibility of detecting phase-transitions and bifurcations. The fifth part allows us to raise the question of having the Porto Metropolitan Area register a phase-transition, and if so, what is the implication of having self-organisation of the spatial cells into a different regional image from the past? How are the activities being organised, how is urban growth happening, how are we accounting for environmental concerns? Questions of self-organisation, shape and size and phase-transitions disclose underlying processes that reflect the visual and quantitative analyses in the images.

As mentioned, besides the more quantitative research questions of spatial metrics, phase-transitions, and predominant strategies, it is possible to reflect on the different public response to each scenario. It is a tool to learn and to communicate with lay audiences that sometimes do not have the technical planning or modelling knowledge, but can distinguish the kind of image they want for their metropolitan regions.

In conclusion, the characteristics of the urban and environmental phenomena make it very hard to model with deterministic models, since most of the analysis and planning strategies deal with uncertainty and subjectivity, hence the need for dynamic models. Added to this is the increasing need to have models that are more inclusive regarding the decision maker's expectations. Therefore, the need for a new generation of models that deals with complexity is clear. Cellular Automaton models are an important modelling approach in order to deal with complexity and planning, as this chapter reports.

References

Ahern, J. (1998) 'Spatial concepts, planning strategies and future scenarios: A framework method for integrating landscape ecology and landscape planning', in J. Kopatek and R. Gardner (eds.), *Landscape Ecological Analysis: Issues and Applications*, Springer-Verlag Inc., New York, pp. 175-201.

Alan, W. (2008) 'Urban and regional dynamics, 3: "DNA" and "genes" as a basis for constructing a typology of areas', CASA Working Paper 130, UCL, London.

Barredo, J., Kasanko, M., McCormick, N. and Lavalle, C. (2003) 'Modelling dynamic spatial processes: Simulation of urban future scenarios through cellular automata', *Landscape and Urban Planning*, vol. 64, pp. 45-160.

Batty, M. (1998) 'Urban evolution on the desktop: Simulation with the use of extended CA', *Environment and Planning A*, vol. 30(11), pp. 1943-1967.

Batty, M. (2007) 'Cities and complexity: Understanding cities with cellular automata, agent-based models, and fractals', *Journal of Regional Science*, vol. 47(3), pp. 624-627.

Batty, M. and Longley, P. (1994) *Fractal Cities: A Geometry of Form and Function*, Academic Press, London.

Clarke, K.C. and Gaydos, L. (1998) 'Loose coupling a cellular automaton model and GIS: Long-term growth prediction for San Francisco and Washington/ Baltimore', *International Journal of Geographical Information Science*, vol. 12(7), pp. 699-714.

Clarke, K.C., Gazulis, N., Dietzel, C.K. and Goldstein, N.C. (2007) 'A decade of SLEUTHing: Lessons learned from applications of a Cellular Automaton land use change model', in P. Fisher (ed), *Classics from IJGIS: Twenty Years of the International Journal of Geographical Information Systems and Science*, Taylor and Francis, Boca Raton, Florida, pp. 413-425.

Gazules, N. and Clarke, K.C. (2006) 'Exploring the DNA of our regions: Classification of outputs from the SLEUTH model', in S. El Yacoubi, B. Chapard and S. Bandini (eds.), *Cellular Automata: Lecture Notes in Computer Science*, No. 4173. Springer, New York.

Piyathamrongchai, K. and Batty, M. (2007) 'Integrating Cellular Automata and regional dynamics using GIS', *Modelling Land-use Change*, vol. 90, pp. 259-277.

Kocabas, V. and Dragicevic, S. (2007) 'Enhancing a GIS Cellular Automata model of land use change: Bayesian networks, influence diagrams and causality', *Transactions in GIS*, vol. 11(5), pp. 681-702.

Liu XiaoPing, L., Gar-On Yeh, A., Jin Qiang, H. and Jia, T. (2007) 'Discovery of transition rules for geographical Cellular Automata by using ant colony optimization', *Science in China Series D: Earth Sciences*, vol. 50, pp. 1578-1588.

Openshaw, S. and Openshaw, C. (1997) *Artificial Intelligence in Geography*, John Wiley and Sons, Chichester.

Silva, E.A. (2002) 'Beyond modelling in environmental and urban planning: Planning support systems and the case study of Lisbon and Porto Metropolitan Areas, Portugal', PhD Dissertation, University of Massachusetts, Amherst.

Silva, E.A. (2004) 'The DNA of our regions: Artificial Intelligence in regional planning', *Futures*, vol. 36(10), pp. 1077-1094.

Silva, E.A. and Clarke, K. (2002) 'Calibration of the SLEUTH urban growth model for Lisbon and Porto, Portugal', *Computers, Environment and Urban Systems*, vol. 26(6), pp. 525-552.

Silva, E.A. and Clarke, K. (2005) 'Complexity, emergence and cellular urban models: Lessons learned from applying SLEUTH to two Portuguese Cities', *European Planning Studies*, vol. 13(1), pp. 93-115.

Sudhira, H.S. (2004) 'Integration of agent-based and Cellular Automata models for simulating urban sprawl', available via: http://www.itc.nl/library/ Academic_output/ 2004/MSc_theses_2004.asp.

Webster, C. (1996) 'Urban morphological fingerprints', *Environment and Planning B: Planning and Design*, vol. 23, pp. 279-297.

Wileden, J, Silva, E.A. and Ahern, J. (2003) 'The CVCA model: A cellular automaton model of landscape ecological strategies', *European Simulation and Modelling Society: ESM*, pp. 206-209.

Chapter 12

Complexity and Travel Behaviour: Modelling Influence of Social Interactions on Travellers' Behaviour Using a Multi-Agent Simulation

Yos Sunitiyoso, Erel Avineri and Kiron Chatterjee[1]

The planning and design of transport systems have an important part in leading travellers to more sustainable and efficient choices. Car dependence is a prominent problem to be solved in order to reduce traffic congestion. It also affects the general efficiency with which people can travel in urban areas, the environmental impacts of traffic, the structure of towns and settlements and consequently the liveability of the cities. Traditional models of travel behaviour, commonly looking at aggregated choices tend to ignore the complexity of the travel choice problem, where many decision makers influencing each other in a dynamic process of social interactions in various domains and through various types of social network. In this chapter we present a methodology to model social interactions and their influence on travel choices. The methodology, based on multi-agent simulation, is explained using an example demonstrating the influence of the social interactions on travellers' behaviour during the implementation of a demand management measure.

12.1 Background

The problem of car dependence is a key issue to be solved in order to reduce traffic congestion, which is responsible for a considerable part of environmental pressures. By reducing traffic congestion people can travel more efficiently (e.g. less travel time/cost, less environmental pollution) and with equal importance, to keep the existence of public transport services. Many practical transportation policy issues

1 Yos Sunitiyoso is a Research Fellow at the Transport Research Group, University of Southampton, United Kingdom. Erel Avineri is a Reader in Travel Behaviour, Centre for Transport and Society, Faculty of the Built Environment, University of the West of England, Bristol, United Kingdom. Kiron Chatterjee is Rees Jeffreys Senior Lecturer in Transport and Society, Centre for Transport and Society, Faculty of the Built Environment, University of the West of England, Bristol, United Kingdom.

are concerned with people's choice of transportation mode. It affects the general efficiency with which people can travel in urban areas, the environmental impacts of traffic, the structure of towns and settlements and consequently the liveability of our cities.

The private car is the dominant means of transportation in most areas and it contributes considerably to traffic congestion. Public transport has a key role in travel mode choice-related policies since it makes use of road space more efficiently than private cars. If some car users could be persuaded to use public transport instead of cars then the rest of the car users would benefit from improved levels of service as the traffic is less congested (unless further car traffic is generated). However, car use provides the individual driver with a number of immediate advantages which make the users unwilling to switch to public transport. A car appears to be a cheap form of transportation (Van Vugt et al., 1998), effective and efficient for multi-purpose trips (Mackett, 2003), and has a link to feelings of independence and convenience (Tertoolen et al., 1998).

A demand management measure (or often called Transportation Demand Management or TDM) is the application of a plan or policy aimed at changing or reducing demand for car use by encouraging the behavioural change of people's choices of travel. Demand management measures are utilised to address the problem of car dependence by incorporating structural interventions ('hard' measures) as well as psychological interventions ('soft' measures). Hard measures include policy interventions that alter the objective features of the decision situation by changing the incentive patterns associated with cooperation and non-cooperation. Examples of hard measures may include changing payoff structure (e.g. congestion charging), reward-punishment (e.g. incentives for public transport users, restriction on car parking), and situational change (e.g. residential or workplace relocation). Soft measures can be defined as policy interventions that are aimed at influencing attitudes and beliefs that may guide people's cooperative and non-cooperative behaviours. Soft measures are more persuasive than hard ones. They include increasing individuals' awareness of the environmental impacts of excessive car use (e.g. travel awareness campaign), providing advice and information to encourage the use of alternative modes of travel (e.g. travel plan, individualised marketing) and promoting alternative ways of using the car (e.g. car sharing).

Hard measures, which concentrate on changing personal material incentives associated with travel mode options (e.g. time, cost, and comfort), seem to be more effective than psychological interventions, since enforcements by the authority are also at force. Soft measures are voluntary by nature and have no economic consequences (e.g. penalty from the authority) if travellers do not participate in the measures, so that the measures may become attractive for travellers as they are not obliged to participate in. Some success stories have been reported in recent pilot projects on soft measures (Jones and Sloman, 2003; Cairns et al., 2004; Stopher, 2005). However, soft measures also have drawbacks as it is difficult to ensure the sustainability of travellers' participation in a long run.

It may be argued that the effectivenesses of a soft measure could be enhanced if more consideration and emphasis is given to the support of social aspects of human behaviour. Given the fact that behavioural change does not take place in a social vacuum, broader society and its social values have important roles to play. Social-psychological aspects of travel behaviour, including *social interaction*, *social learning/imitation*, and *social influence*, may influence travellers' behaviour. Better understanding of these aspects will provide us with some informed behavioural insights about the potential for utilising them to encourage travellers' change of behaviour. An agent-based simulation is used in this study to model the roles that social aspects may have in influencing travellers' behaviour during the implementation of a policy measure.

The diffusion process of compliance with a demand management measure has become our interest as it may have an important role in encouraging behavioural change. Jones and Sloman (2003) argued that the existence of the 'snowball effect', a phenomenon where long-term effects may be greater than short-term ones, would increase the effectiveness of soft measures over time. They stated that, there is some evidence that the change may be very slow at first, but then accelerate as people see their colleagues and neighbours changing their travel behaviour. In the implementation of voluntary household travel behaviour change programs, Ampt (2003) argued that strategies that require households to diffuse information both between households and ultimately across communities are likely to be effective. Stopher (2005) added the importance of diffusion effects in the implementation of voluntary programs by stating the need to measure the effects in schools, workplaces, and other locations. When a person tells someone about what he is doing, he is both reinforcing his own behaviour in the process and giving a level of commitment. This way of communicating is often called 'word-of-mouth' communication. Spreading information by 'word-of-mouth' is the most effective way for diffusion and reinforcement (Stern et al., 1987). A study by Shaheen (2004) also considered this word-of-mouth communication as a means to diffuse the change of behaviour in a car sharing program.

To gather understanding on the social aspects, it is important to explore their influence on travellers' behaviour using empirical and experimental studies based on observations of their choices during field and laboratory studies (see examples in Sunitiyoso et al., 2007/2008). However, a simulation-based study is also a valuable line of research. Jager et al. (2002) argued that a simulation research does not replace empirical research, but it has two main functions. First, it may function as a complementary research tool which enables researchers to explore complex (multi-factorial) research fields and to identify promising conditions for further (empirical) research. Second, a simulation model may be used to answer questions emerging from empirical research (laboratory or field), demonstrating that complex phenomena are sometimes resulted from simple dynamics.

12.2 The complexity of social interactions in travel behaviour

Travel behaviour is a result of a complex and dynamic process involving a sequence of adaptations overtime. The timing and frequency of many events may lead to different patterns of travel behaviour. As a complex system, the main element of travel behaviour is travellers themselves as the actors of travel decision making. Personal factors such as attitudes, preferences, and habits influence the behaviour of a traveller. Interactions between travellers in various interaction domains (neighbourhood, school, workplace, etc.) using various types of social network (lattice structured, random network, etc.) may also have important roles to play. Travellers are also heterogeneous; some travellers interact with other travellers and take other travellers' behaviour into consideration before making a travel choice decision. Other travellers may stick to the same travel choice by habit. They are not easily influenced to change their choice to another choice. The aggregate interactions of the interacting travellers would later contribute to the dynamic of aggregate behaviour of travellers in the transportation system. Other elements such as policy interventions by the transportation authority are external elements that may also influence travellers' behaviour. The large number of variables involved and the variety of their interactions contribute to the complexity of travel behaviour.

Social interaction

Social interaction is necessary for a successful social learning and influence from an individual to other individuals. The interaction exists whenever an individual is involved in an interdependence situation with other individuals. Interdependence can be explained by a collective action (e.g. social dilemma) where there exists impossibility of exclusion, which means that no member of the group engaged in collective action can be excluded from enjoying the benefits of the group's efforts (Huberman and Glance, 1993). Messick (1985) defines interdependence in relation to preferences by stating the fact that individuals are not indifferent to the outcomes received by others. Interdependence of choice may create a situation where travellers sometimes take into account and are concerned about choices by other travellers (Van Lange et al., 2000).

In this study, we consider that social interactions occur beyond residential neighbourhoods. There may be multi-dimensional relationships between individuals, which are built based on similarities of 'social club' domains, including workplace, non-work activity club and also within a household. However, we do not focus on intra-household interactions. The possibility of repeated interactions between individuals differs from one social club to another. For example, a workplace gives more opportunity for interaction than a sport/leisure club since colleagues of the same workplace work around five days a week at the same place, whereas members of a sport/leisure club may only meet once or twice a week.

A social network may affect the spread of influence (Kempe et al., 2003). The structure of a network has an important role to determine a successful diffusion process of information. There are many kinds of communication structures that may exist between individuals. Nakamaru and Levin (2004) investigated four structures: complete mixing (each individual interacts with the others at random), lattice (each individual interacts with his neighbours with some probability), power-law-network (a few influential people have more social contacts than the others) and random graph network (the number of contacts follows a Poisson distribution). The types of social network may differ between different 'social club' domains. For example, a lattice-structured network is more likely to exist in a neighbourhood domains while complete mixing in a non-work activity club domain.

Social learning

Change of behaviour is a dynamic process that occurs over time and may involve a learning process. The concept of *individual learning* suggests that individuals learn from their past experience and utilise an adaptive decision making process to cope with uncertainty. There is also another form of learning, *social learning*, where individuals learn from others' experiences or observed behaviours. In travel behaviour modelling, the individual learning concept has often been studied (for review, see Arentze and Timmermans, 2005), while social learning has not been investigated intensively. It is quite surprising since some evidence from other disciplines (e.g. economics and behavioural sciences) have shown that this kind of learning process is influential and important (e.g. Pingle, 1995; Offerman and Sonnemans, 1998).

In social learning, decision makers observe the behaviours or preferences of others prior to making a choice, therefore they can reduce their efforts in comparing and analysing all possible choices by themselves. Individuals can use several mechanisms in order to learn from others as suggested by Henrich (2004); these include conformist transmission (imitating high frequency behaviours), payoff-biased transmission (imitating other individuals who are more successful), self-similarity transmission (imitating other individuals with similarity in some traits) or normative transmission (following the common behaviour in the group according to social norm).

Social influence

There is a slight difference between social learning and social influence. In social learning, the change of judgments, opinions and attitudes of an individual is a result of active search for information by the individual, where as in social influence, the change is a result of being exposed to other individuals (Van Avermaet, 1996).

There are two types of social influence: majority influence (conformity) and minority influence (innovation). Majority influence can be shortly defined as the majority's efforts to produce conformity on the part of a minority, whereas minority influence can be defined as the minority's effort to convert the majority to its own way of thinking (Sampson, 1991). Majority influence has a strong relation with a form of social learning transmission, the conformist transmission, which is a psychological propensity to preferentially imitate high frequency behaviours or the most common (majority) behaviours.

In this research, minority influence becomes the point of interest as other studies indicated the importance of considering the influence of 'key people' in diffusion of participation in a demand management measure (e.g. Ampt, 2003). 'Key people' are not necessarily traditional leaders, but they can be 'trusted persons' with a respected reputation in community. The influence of these 'key people' is called minority influence. In the model, minority influence is investigated by introducing a situation where a few influential agents (independently or in group) have more power to influence others whom they communicate with. The strength of their influence is derived from the reputation built from their consistency of choice to comply with the measure (Van Avermaet, 1996; Sampson, 1991). Involving key people (not necessarily traditional leaders, but 'trusted others' in the community) will provide more advantages since people are more willing to hear from someone who is trusted, respected or perceived to have similar values. This is related to the idea of minority influence where a few influential agents are able to influence the opposing majority to the minority's way of thinking. Individuals are more willing to hear from someone who is trusted and respected as a consistent person. For example: a suggestion to car share by a consistent car sharer, who has been car sharing regularly in a considerable period of time, would have more influence than that of other individuals' who have not done so.

The potential effects of these three social aspects on travellers' decision making and behaviour – social interaction, social learning and social influence – are investigated using a multi-agent simulation model as discussed in the following section.

12.3 Agent-based approach for simulating travellers' behaviour

An agent-based model can be defined as a computational model, which represents individual agents and their collective behaviour (Parunak et al., 1998; Shalizi, 2003). An agent-based model represents individuals, their behaviours, and their interactions, rather than the aggregate of individuals and their dynamics. The application of this approach in transportation modelling is still in infancy, although it offers many benefits in the study of behaviour (in transportation context: e.g. Nakayama et al., 2001; Arentze and Timmermans, 2006; Avineri, 2006; in non-transportation context: Henrich and Boyd, 1998; Kameda and Nakanishi, 2002).

In travel behaviour modelling, the idea of utilising a multi-agent model to better understand the dynamic of travellers' change of behaviour has not been given much consideration until recently, despite its potential to provide a different 'flavour' on travel behaviour studies by deriving informed insights from the results of simulation experiments (e.g. Kitamura et al., 1999; Sunitiyoso and Matsumoto, 2007; Sunitiyoso et al., 2006). In a multi-agent model, decision making rules and parameters used by individuals can be based on decision making processes revealed from empirical studies (e.g. behavioural survey, laboratory experiment) as well as behavioural theories. A multi-agent simulation model is able to elucidate the dynamics of decision making processes, showing what course of 'evolution' a certain behaviour could have looked like over time. Travellers' behaviour can be represented by the behaviour of autonomous agents in a simulation model. The model is also used to represent social interactions between agents which occur through various interaction domains (e.g. neighbourhood, workplace/school, etc.).

In studying the effects of a treatment/intervention on individuals, a simulation experiment is able to handle the interactions of a large number of individuals with each other in a large and complex transportation system. It also makes possible for conducting a large number of repetitions (time periods), which enable the researcher to observe whether individuals' choices converge to an equilibrium point or not, how they converge and the dynamics before convergence. It may also provide predictive value in forecasting travellers' behaviour in different kind of situations, and to know how robust the results are in different parametric conditions.

The multi-agent simulation approach presented in this study focuses on (intangible) interactions between individuals, while physical interactions between the individuals and transport or urban environment are beyond the scope of the study. Other studies have indicated that agent-based models are also able to represent the interactions of physical entities such as pedestrians on streets or cars on roads (e.g. Batty, 2005, pp. 263-318).

In the next section, we present an example of the way a multi-agent simulation model can be used to simulate and understand the influence of these social-psychological aspects on traveller's behaviour and the performance of the overall system.

12.4 Simulating the influence of social interactions on travellers' behaviour

The research methodology consists of two stages, a behavioural survey and a simulation experiment. In the first stage, a *behavioural survey* is conducted to obtain information regarding mechanisms of social interaction and social learning in addition to those derived from literatures, as well as parameters required for the simulation model. The survey respondents (N=178) are students in the Faculty of the Built Environment, University of the West of England, Bristol. Car sharing, as a 'soft' demand management measure, was used as a case study in the survey (and is used in the second stage of study, the simulation experiment). The survey enables an estimation of some of the simulation model's parameters (e.g. weights of other agents' influence, the proportion of influential minority, reputation of agents) and initial values for the variables (e.g. agents' preferences, choices,

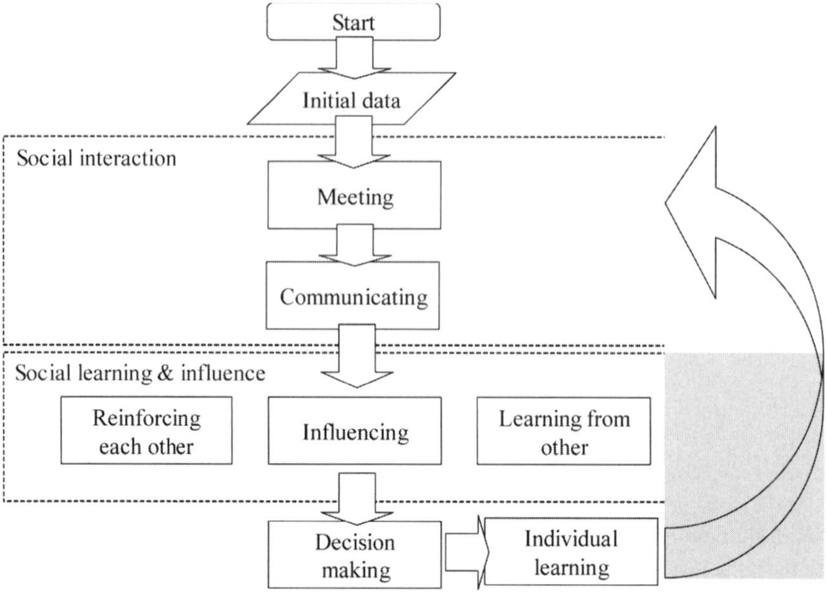

Figure 12.1 Algorithm of the multi-agent simulation model

level of compliance), while other parameters and variables are estimated based on theoretical assumptions as they are difficult to be measured empirically. In the second stage of the study, the *simulation experiment* utilises an agent-based simulation model to simulate and analyse behaviours of individuals. We focus our discussions in this chapter on the second stage of study, the simulation experiment.

The model consists of four main sections: social interaction, social learning and influence, decision making, and individual learning (from the outcome of previous decisions). The algorithm of the model is then developed as simply illustrated in Figure 12.1. The algorithm starts with an initialisation process of assigning a number of agents into so-called 'social' club domains (*neighbourhood*, *course of study*, and *non-study social club*). It is assumed that within each club each member can meet (not necessarily followed by communication) any other members in a lattice structured network for the *neighbourhood* domain and in random manner (complete mixing) for other type of 'social' clubs. The frequency of meeting depends on the type of interaction domain. For example, an agent (individual student) meets other agents (fellow student) more often in a course of study than in a non-study social club (see Table 12.1).

In the simulation model, social interaction is represented by two processes: *meeting* and *communicating*. These processes may occur in any social club domain depending on the day of the week whenever agents (who represent individuals) involve with activities in the domain. Meeting is defined as a process where two agents meet each other without engaging in an intensive communication involving an exchange of information. Communication may follow the meeting if there is a 'mutual agreement' between them, which depends on whether they are both closely connected or not (represented by the value of perceived degree of relationship) and on whether a threshold for communicating has been exceeded or not.

There are two types of agents: an influential agent (which is a member of the minority) and a common agent. An influential agent is given a higher *reputation score* than a common agent. The process of social learning and social influence may exist during a process of communication between two interacting agents. If both communicating agents have the same choice on a particular day then they are *reinforcing each other*. If they have different choices, there are two possibilities. First, if one of the communicating agents has a higher reputation than the other then the exchange of information will only be one way, from the agent with a higher reputation to the other with lower reputation. This is a process of *influencing the other*. Second, if they both have the same reputation, then only the agent who initiates the social interaction learns from his interaction partner's choice by updating its preference, since the initiator is considered as the one who is looking for information. This process is called a process of *learning from the other*.

The decision of whether to comply with a demand management measure is made based on the agent's preference value. Each agent learns individually from past decisions, learns/imitates other agents' decisions and is influenced by 'influential' individuals, and then updates his preference value in a reinforcement process. The higher the preference to comply, the more the probability that the agent will comply with the measure. The decision making of each agent is based on a social influence model with each agent taking into consideration previous choices and choices of other agents (see Sunitiyoso et al., 2006) for detailed formulation of the model.

Table 12.1 Scenarios of simulation run based on existence and location of influential minority and social interaction domains

Scenario	Existence and location of influential minority	Interaction domain (neighbourhood, course of study, non-study social club)	% of car sharers (average of the last 90 days)
1	No	No social interaction	49.0
2	No	All domains	55.9
3	Yes, spread in population	All domains	61.4
4	Yes, spread in population	Neighbourhood only	55.9
5	Yes, spread in population	Course of study only	58.5
6	Yes, spread in population	Social club only	55.8

The decision making process of each agent is repeated from time to time. The population of agents also displays inertia, which means that they all may not change decisions at the same time. Some of them change their decisions but the others continue with their previous choices. And also each agent does not have perfect information about the choice of all other agents in the population. He only knows the choice of other agents whom he communicates with.

In the simulation model, a number of agents are generated and given attributes (parameters and initial variables) according to the attributes of respondents in the survey (see for details Sunitiyoso et al., 2006). Since the number of respondents is limited (N=178), a technique so-called 'cloning' is used to produce a larger number of agents (N_s=4,096). This means that a number of agents are generated with similar attributes which come from the attributes of a respondent. So that approximately each respondent has 23 'clones' (N_s/N=4,096/178≈23) in the population of agents. Each simulation run has a period of T=1,460 days (four years). The domains of interaction are *neighbourhood*, *courses of study*, and *non-study activity clubs*. There are eight scenarios used in the simulation runs. Each scenario is repeated for ten runs.

Table 12.1 shows the results of six scenarios in the last 90 days of simulation runs. In Scenario 1, where social interaction between agents does not exist, the number of car sharers goes up gradually up to 2008 agents, which means the level of compliance (LC; the proportion of car sharers in population) is 49.0 per cent. When social interactions (in all domains of interactions: neighbourhood, course of study, and non-study activity club) exist between agents (Scenario 2), the number of car sharers increases with a slower trend than in Scenario 1. However, the level of compliance in this scenario is higher than in Scenario 1 with 2,290 car sharers (LC=55.9 per cent). The situation becomes better for car sharing when a number of influential minority agents (6.18 per cent of total number of agents) exist in the population as seen in Scenario 3. These influential minority agents are able to increase the level of compliance up to in average of 2,514 car sharers (LC= 61.4 per cent).

Figure 12.2 presents the results of Scenarios 1 to 3. These results represent the first 365 days (one year) of simulation run, since the system is in equilibrium after that until the end of the run (1,460 days=four years). Each point in the graph is an average of ten simulation runs. Average preferences of agents (Figure 12.3) in Scenarios 1 to 3 reach almost similar points to their levels of compliance (Figure 12.2), since they are highly correlated based on the fact that the decision of each agent is made with regard to his preference.

In Scenario 1, where social interaction does not exist, the average of preference is stable day to day with an average of 0.49 in the last 90 days of simulation runs. This result is close to the initial average preference based on survey results, which is 0.47. Scenarios 2 and 3 have similar patterns of changes. In early interactions, average preferences in these scenarios decrease since a majority of agents, who have low preferences to car share, decide not to car share causing the decrease of average preference. After the effects of initial, conditions can be minimised, as agents involve

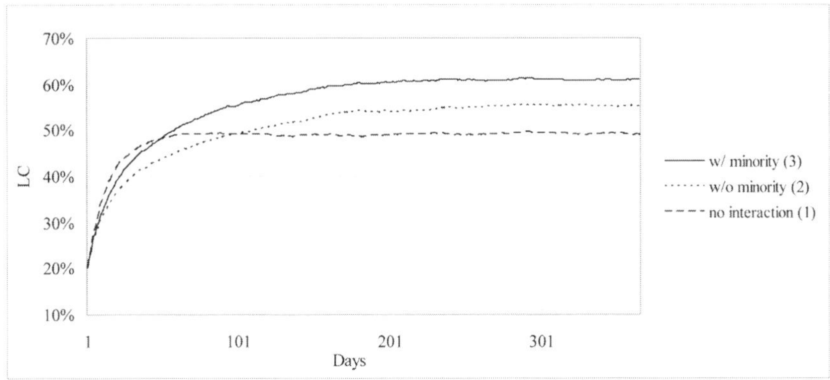

Figure 12.2 Level of compliance (LC) in Scenarios 1 to 3

Note: Scenario numbers in parentheses.

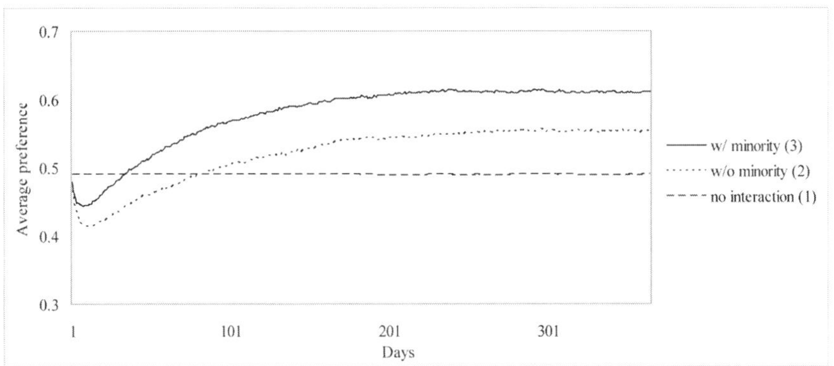

Figure 12.3 Average preferences to car sharing in Scenarios 1 to 3

Note: Scenario numbers in parentheses.

in interactions with each other, the average preferences in Scenarios 2 and 3 increase higher than that of Scenario 1.

These processes show an adaptation where travellers make decisions to initiate changes of preferences based on their own experiences and due to process of social interaction, social learning and social influence. Some travellers were influenced by other travellers but some were not. When influential minority agents are in charge, a higher level of compliance can be achieved in Scenario 3 (with minority) than that of Scenario 2 (without minority).

The effects of interaction domains are studied by comparing the system's behaviour whenever interactions happen in different sets of domains, as in Scenarios 3 to 6. Level of compliance has the highest level in Scenario 3 where all domains of

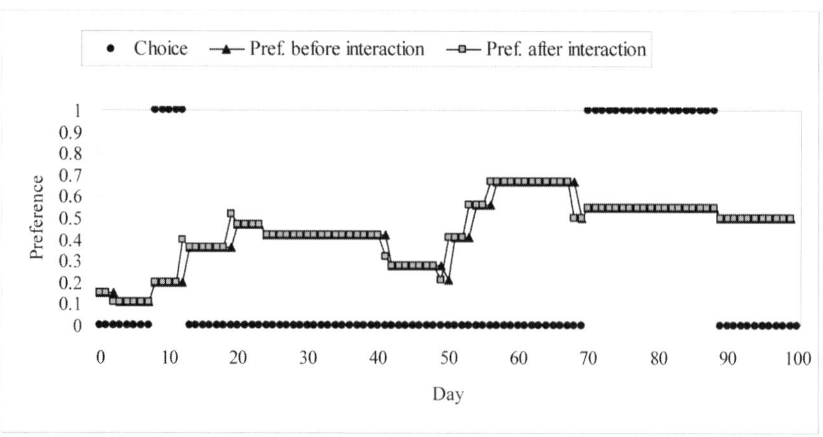

Figure 12.4 Changes of an individual preference

interaction (neighbourhood, course of study and non-study activity club) are in use. It is followed by Scenario 5 where the domain is course of study, and then Scenario 4 (neighbourhood only) and Scenario 6 (non-study activity club).

To give an example of the dynamics of an agent's behaviour in the simulation, Figures 12.4 and 12.5 show the behaviour of an individual agent. Figure 12.4 shows dynamic changes of an individual's preference during the first 100 rounds of a simulation run with Scenario 3. The changes are the results of the individual's experience as well as in the influence of other people's choice. The agent starts with an initial preference to car sharing of 0.15 and by day 100, the preference reaches 0.5.

Figure 12.5 presents the agent's frequencies of activities in social interaction, learning and influence. It is shown that among the whole social interaction processes (*meeting* and *communicating*), there are some *meeting* processes which were not followed by *communicating* (exchanging ideas). The process of *communicating* resulted in mostly in the processes called *reinforcing each other* and *learning from others*, and few occasions where the individual was being influenced by influential individuals (minority agents). This example is one of many patterns of behaviour that exist within agents in the simulation.

12.5 Behavioural insights

The simulation experiment described in the example provides some behavioural insights regarding the influence of social aspects on travellers' behaviour during the diffusion process of compliance with a demand measure. It is revealed that social interactions between individuals helps diffuse the information between them through

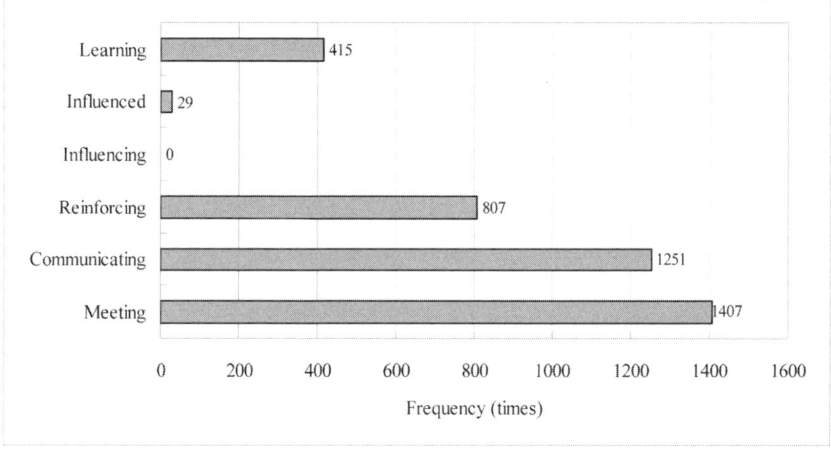

Figure 12.5 Frequency of activities in social interaction, learning and influence over a full simulation run (T=1460 days)

various interaction domains ('social club'), such as neighbourhood, workplace, school, community, and activity clubs, thus increasing the level of compliance to a demand management measure. Repeated interactions between individuals would generate high propensity for communicating which later give more opportunity for social learning and social influence to induce compliance in the population. Higher levels of compliance (participation) with the measure is then produced with the support of 'minority' agents who are able to strongly influence other travellers' behaviour through various social interaction domains. Neighbourhood is a domain which has often been used in existing simulation models, however it may have a smaller role than other 'social' clubs where interactions occur more often (e.g. school, workplace) since the interactions between neighbours, particularly in an urbanised city, are incidental and not as frequent as, for example, interactions within students in a school or university.

The insights support empirical findings of the role of *word-of-mouth* communication as a tool for diffusion. Ampt (2003) reported that involuntary behaviour change projects messages delivered by any other way are reinforcing, but much less efficient. When the behaviour change has had a positive benefit to the individual it is likely that they will tell others of the benefits. Since they are more likely to practise diffusion in the company of trusted others, the message is more likely to lead to further change. Taniguchi and Fujii (2007) in their study of promoting community bus service found that word-of-mouth advertising through recommendations to friends and family plays an important role in promoting bus use. Spreading information by 'word-of-mouth' may help solve a concern stated by Cairns et al. (2004) about the implementation of personalised travel planning. They stated that the effects may be short-lived, if people may quickly slide back into their old travel habits once the monitoring is over. A laboratory experiment conducted to study the effect of communication on travellers' behaviour (Sunitiyoso et al., 2007) found that communication does influence their behaviour, although the effects are not consistent for different groups of individuals.

The simulation model also shows how travellers' behaviour 'evolves' over a long period of time when travellers interact with other travellers. This shows the importance to study the dynamic not only in short-term but also in long term. Cairns et al. (2004) reveals the need to study the dynamic build-up of effects over time during the implementation of soft measures. Empirical research has shown that the long-term effect of policy interventions (e.g. Goodwin, 1992) can be much stronger than the short-term effect. The same holds true for possible negative side effects which often occur in the long term.

It can be inferred from the example that involving 'key people', which were represented as influential minority agents in the model, in diffusing compliance with the measure into population would increase the level of participation. Identifying the influential individuals (the minority) is as important as involving them in promoting changes of behaviour using their influence. An influential individual is not necessarily a traditional leader, but he can be a 'trusted person' with a respected reputation in the social club as individuals are more willing to hear from someone who is trusted and respected as a consistent person. For example: a suggestion to car share by a consistent car sharer, who has been car sharing regularly in a considerable period of time, would have more influence than that of other individuals' who have not done so. In practice, the minority could be some opinion leaders and credible sources who are drawn from the community and trained to do so. These influential people have a 'minority' influence which is strong in influencing change of behaviour of other people even though they are small in number. They can help people overcome barriers to action and give ongoing support beyond their households. Jones and Sloman (2003) added the importance of involving key employees in the relevant organisations, so that they are aware of and supportive of the campaign in their dealings with members of the public.

In general, the study provides useful information for investigating the role of minority influence in the diffusion process of compliance with a soft policy measure. Some informed insights regarding the spread of compliance with a soft measure from an individual to other individuals through various kinds of interaction domain are obtained. The results are produced by self-organisation and complex interaction processes between travellers in the system.

12.6 Conclusions

The study demonstrates the potential of utilising a multi-agent simulation model to simulate the effects of social aspects, particularly social interaction, social learning and social influence, on the diffusion process of travellers' compliance with a demand management measure, which in this study is a car sharing program.

The model is also able to show the 'evolution' of behaviour over time and to demonstrate how agents can be equipped with decision rules that are based on social-psychological theory of social interaction, learning and influence and experimented with different settings. It has been indicated that the diffusion process of compliance with a demand management measure may depend on the way a traveller interacts with others (social interaction), the way he learns socially (social learning), and the existence of influential people (social influence) who strongly influence other people.

We may consider that the findings produced by the study are more in 'qualitative' rather than 'quantitative' sense, since they are used to explore or to understand theoretically the causal relationships of interaction between people which underlie the real world society rather than to represent societal dynamics in a precise way. Much elaboration is needed to produce sufficient sensitivity and accuracy in order to ensure that the findings are substantially important. The insights obtained from the simulation model in the example may be useful for understanding and finding possibilities for influencing travellers' change of behaviour during the implementation of a demand management measure. For example, the simulation shows that involving 'key people', represented as influential minority agents in the model, in diffusing compliance with the measure into population would increase the level of participation.

Before making use of a simulation model in real-world application, it is important to have credible parameters for the model which can be obtained from an intensive behavioural survey or laboratory-based experiments with people. A synergetic combination between empirical research and simulation research would yield benefits in our research. In this study, empirical data collected from a longitudinal study, which is a research study that involves repeated observations of the same subjects over long periods of time (e.g. months, years or decades), with several waves before and after the implementation of a soft measure would serve best for supporting the findings of a multi-agent simulation model.

In studying the effects of a treatment/intervention on individuals, a simulation experiment is able to handle the interactions of a large number of individuals with each other and with the transport system. The multi-agent simulation model described in this work highlights the potential results of social interactions of a large number of individuals in making a choice whether to participate in a travel demand management measure and shows how the interactions affect the overall system behaviour as well as individual behaviour. Behavioural changes in a wider societal scope are expected to differ from those of a smaller group of individuals, since interdependence between individuals becomes complicated whenever the number of interacting individuals increases. Dealing with this situation, the ability of a multi-agent model to handle a complex form of interactions becomes a major advantage. With agent-based simulation, it is possible not only to model the dynamics of the system but also to represent behavioural change of every single individual; therefore, it may become a powerful approach in understanding and predicting travellers' change of behaviour.

It also makes it possible to conduct a large number of repetitions (time periods), which enable the researcher to observe whether individuals' choices converge to an equilibrium point or not, how they converge and the dynamics before convergence, and how many repetitions are required. Many patterns of change within travellers' behaviour during the implementation of a demand management measure can be observed in a multi-agent simulation. This may help transport planners in anticipating the potential effects of the measures at the individual level.

The capability of multi-agent simulation for predicting potential travellers' behaviour in different scenarios or parametric conditions which resemble scenarios of a potential travel demand management measure in order to gain informed insights of how travellers would respond to each scenario. The insights could later be useful in designing demand measures that are potentially effective in changing travellers' behaviour. For example by incorporating social interactions and taking into consideration their potential effects into the design of transport measures (e.g. behavioural change programmes, user communication feature of ATIS).

We believe that the agent-based approach presented in this work provides a first step towards the creation of a novel tool for use by transport researchers and practitioners that can be incorporated in travel plans and other demand management measures.

References

Ampt, E. (2003) 'Voluntary household travel behaviour change: theory and practice', paper presented at the 10th International Conference on Travel Behavior Research, Lucerne.

Arentze, T. and Timmermans, H. (2005) 'Modelling learning and adaptation in transportation context', *Transportmetrica*, vol. 1(1), pp. 13-22.

Arentze, T. and Timmermans, H. (2006) 'Social networks, social interactions and activity-travel behavior: A framework for micro-simulation', paper presented at the 85th TRB Annual Meeting, Washington.

Avermaet, E. van (1996) 'Social influence in small groups', in M. Hewstone, W. Stroebe and G. Stephenson (eds.), *Introduction to Social Psychology: A European Perspective*, Blackwell, Oxford.

Avineri, E. (2006) 'Measuring and simulating altruistic behaviour in group travel choice decisions', paper presented at the 11th International Conference on Travel Behaviour Research, Kyoto.

Batty, M. (2005) *Cities and Complexity: Understanding Cities with Cellular Automata, Agent-based Models and Fractals*, MIT Press, Massachusetts.

Cairns, S., Sloman, L., Newson, C., Anable, J., Kirkbride, A. and Goodwin, P. (2004) *Smarter Choices: Changing the Way We Travel*, DfT, London.

Goodwin, P. (1992) 'A review of new demand elasticities with special reference to short and long run effects of price changes', *Journal of Transport Economics and Policy*, vol. 25, pp. 155-169.

Henrich, J. and Boyd, R. (1998) 'The evolution of conformist transmission and the emergence of between-group differences', *Evolution and Human Behavior*, vol. 19, pp. 215-241.

Henrich, J. (2004) 'Cultural group selection, coevolutionary processes and large-scale cooperation', *Journal of Economic Behavior and Organization*, vol. 53, pp. 3-35.

Huberman, B.A. and Glance, N.S. (1993) 'Diversity and collective action', in H. Haken and A. Mikhailov (eds.), *Interdisciplinary Approaches to Nonlinear Systems*, Springer, Berlin.

Jager, W., Janssen, M.A. and Vlek, C.A.J. (2002) 'How uncertainty stimulates over-harvesting in a resource dilemma: Three process explanations', *Journal of Environmental Psychology*, vol. 22, pp. 247-263.

Jones, P. and Sloman, L. (2003) 'Encouraging behavioural change through marketing and management: What can be achieved?', paper presented at the 10th International Conference on Travel Behavior Research, Lucerne.

Kameda, T. and Nakanishi, D. (2002) 'Cost/benefit analysis of social/cultural learning in a nonstationary uncertain environment: An evolutionary simulation and an experiment with human subjects', *Evolution and Human* Behavior, vol. 23, pp. 373-393.

Kempe, D., Kleinberg, J. and Tardos, E. (2003) 'Maximizing the spread of influence through a social network', paper presented at the 9th ACM SIGKDD International Conference on Knowledge Discovery and Data Mining, Washington.

Kitamura, R., Nakayama, S. and Yamamoto, T. (1999) 'Self-reinforcing motorization: can travel demand management take us out of the social trap?', *Transport Policy*, vol. 6, pp. 135-145.

Mackett, R.L. (2003) 'Why do people use cars for short trips?', *Transportation*, vol. 30, pp. 329-349.

Messick, D.M. (1985) 'Social interdependence and decision making', in G. Wright (ed.), *Behavioral Decision making*, Plenum Press, New York, pp. 87-109.

Nakamaru, M. and Levin, S.A. (2004) 'Spread of two linked social norms on complex interaction networks', *Journal of Theoretical Biology*, vol. 230, pp. 57-64.

Nakayama, S., Kitamura, R. and Fujii, S. (2001) 'Drivers' route choice rules and network behavior: Do drivers become rational and homogeneous through learning?', *Transportation Research Record*, vol. 1752, pp. 62-68.

Offerman, T. and Sonnemans, J. (1998) 'Learning by experience and learning by imitating successful others', *Journal of Economic Behavior and Organization*, vol. 34, pp. 559-575.

Parunak, H.V.D., Savit, R. and Riolo, R.L. (1998) 'Agent-based modelling vs. equation-based modelling: A case study and users' guide', in J.S. Sichman, R. Conte and N. Gilbert (eds.), *Multi-agent Systems and Agent-based Simulation*, Springer, Berlin, pp. 10-25.

Pingle, M. (1995) 'Imitation versus rationality: An experimental perspective on decision making', *The Journal of Socio-Economics*, vol. 24(2), pp. 281-315.

Sampson, E. (1991) 'Innovation and the minority-influence model', in E. Sampson (ed.), *Social Worlds Personal Lives: An Introduction to Social Psychology*, Harcourt Brace Jovanovich Inc, Orlando.

Shaheen, S. (2004) 'Dynamics in behavioral adaptation to a transportation innovation: A case study of Carlink – a smart carsharing system', PhD Thesis Report, Institute of Transportation Studies, University of California, Davis.

Shalizi, C.R. (2003) 'Methods and technique of complex systems science: An overview', Research Report, Center for the Study of Complex Systems, University of Michigan, Detroit.

Stern, P.C., Aronson, E., Darley, J.M., Kempton, W., Hill, D.H., Hirst, E. and Wilbanks, T.J. (1987) 'Answering behavioral questions about energy efficiency in buildings', *Energy*, vol. 12(5), pp. 339-353.

Stopher, P. (2005) 'Voluntary travel behavior change', in K.J. Button and D.A. Hensher (eds.), *Handbook of Transport Strategy, Policy and Institutions*, Elsevier, Amsterdam, pp. 561-578.

Sunitiyoso, Y., Avineri, E. and Chatterjee, K. (2006) 'Role of minority influence on the diffusion of compliance with a demand management measure', paper presented at the 11th International Conference on Travel Behaviour Research, Kyoto.

Sunitiyoso, Y., Avineri, E. and Chatterjee, K. (2007) 'The role of social interactions in travel behaviour: Designing experimental tools to explore the behavioural assumptions', paper presented at the Workshop of Frontiers in Transportation: Social Interactions, Amsterdam.

Sunitiyoso, Y., Avineri, E. and Chatterjee, K. (2008) 'Influence of social interaction and social learning on travellers' behaviour', paper presented at the 40th Universities Transport Study Group Conference, Southampton.

Sunitiyoso, Y. and Matsumoto, S. (2007) 'Modelling a social dilemma of mode choice based on commuters' expectations and social learning', *European Journal of Operational Research*, vol. 193(3), pp. 904-914.

Taniguchi, A. and Fujii, S. (2007) 'Promoting public transport using marketing techniques in mobility management and verifying their quantitative effects', *Transportation*, vol. 34, pp. 37-49.

Tertoolen, G., Kreveld, D.V. and Verstraten, B. (1998) 'Psychological resistance against attempts to reduce private car use', *Transportation Research A*, vol. 32(3), pp. 171-181.

Van Lange, P., Vugt, M. van and Cremer, D. de (2000) 'Choosing between personal comfort and the environment: solutions to the transportation dilemma', in M.V. Vugt, M. Snyder, T. Tyler and A. Biel (eds.), *Cooperation in Modern Society*, Routledge, London.

Van Vugt, M., Lange, P.A.M. van, Meertens, R.M. and Joireman, J.A. (1998) 'How a structural solution to a real-world social dilemma failed: A field experiment on the first carpool lane in Europe', *Social Psychology Quarterly*, vol. 59, pp. 364-374.

Chapter 13
Complexity Theory and Transport Planning: Fractal Traffic Networks

Erel Avineri[1]

One of the important procedures in many applications of transport planning is the analysis of the performance of traffic networks that is related to the supply and demand of transport (commonly measured by the road capacity and the predicted traffic volume, accordingly). This chapter demonstrates the possibility of incorporating complexity analysis in the modelling of traffic networks. One may argue that many traffic networks are structured in a rather hierarchical form, featuring complex and fractal characteristics of the geometric structure of the networks, as well as the spatial distribution of flows on it. Illustrated by a numeric example we demonstrate the relevance of complexity theory to the analysis of the performance of traffic networks. Conceptual and methodological issues that could be addressed by further research in transport planning are suggested.

13.1 Introduction

Transport systems are comprised of many elements – services, prices, infrastructures, vehicles, control systems and users, which are been taken by transport planners as a whole. Characteristics and performances of transport systems and their components are usually defined on the basis of quantitative evaluation of their effects, considering the objectives and the constraints of the transport system. The planning, design and operation of transport systems may vary much by its focus and methodologies. For example, a detailed level of representation may be used in the functional design and control management of transport systems, while in the transport planning of a region only the major roads of the traffic network may be represented. One of the important aspects of the transport planning process is assigning the predicted traffic volumes on the road segments. This is followed by an analysis of the transport network and its performance, mainly by observing its ability to satisfy the travel demand of persons and goods in a given area. The scale

1 Erel Avineri is a Reader in Travel Behaviour at the Centre for Transport and Society, Faculty of Environment and Technology, University of the West of England, Bristol, United Kingdom.

Table 13.1 Public roads in Great Britain: Length by class of roads

Road Type	Length (km)
Motorways	3,466
Trunk	12,189
Principal	42,446
B roads	30,189
C roads	84,459
Unclassified roads	223,184
TOTAL	388,008

Source: Based on UK National Statistics, DfT, 2005.

of the network is generally depended on the stage of the planning and its detailed level.

Segments of the traffic network (such as road links) can be classified into hierarchies according to the size and type of traffic flow they are supposed to carry. Public roads may be classified by types, such as motorways, trunk roads, principle roads and local B and C type roads. The design of such roads is based on their purposes and their roles in accessibility and mobility. This leads to specific recommendations on the level of service provided by different types of road, and guidelines on the geometric design of such roads (such as the number of lanes and the lanes width, and the design of other elements such as intersections, parking, and traffic calming). Table 13.1 represents the length of public roads in Great Britain. While motorways and trunk roads carry large volumes of transport, they hardly represent the size of the transport system (motorways themselves carry about a quarter of the traffic volume although they account for only one per cent of the total length of the transport network). This illustrates a dilemma transport planners are faced with; in order to reduce the complexity of the planning process, would it be enough to analyse a network comprises only of main roads, but representing most of the traffic volumes?

It has been observed that transport networks may exhibit properties of regularity and self-similarity (Thomson, 1977; Benguigui and Daoud, 1991; Marshall, 2005). Complexity properties of the traffic network have been applied in different contexts. Marshall (2005) uses complexity properties in order to gather a better understanding of the relationships between streets and patterns, forming a basis for a broader framework that may be used to underpin streets-oriented urban design agendas.

The conventional process of transport modelling involves generating and analysing a traffic network, which is a sub-network of the physical road network. The represented network may include existing components, planned ones, or a mix. Physical dynamic changes in the road network often consist of adding new capacities or deleting existing capacities. While some of these changes may already been introduced to the transport system, others may be suggested and considered as part of an alternative plan to be appraised. Transport modellers do not have access to detailed information about the minor roads, and are not able to calibrate the travel time functions on these segments. Moreover, when modelling a planned transport system, some of its elements may not be fully planned or designed. For example, the planning of some minor roads in residential areas may be based on partial information on its geometric shape and capacity. Another unknown in some cases may be the expected traffic flow measures as a function of the traffic volumes. For example, the link volume-travel time functions may be described as following:

$$(13.1)\ t_{ij} = \alpha_{ij} + \beta_{ij} f_{ij}$$

where

t_{ij} is the travel time on link *ij*
α_{ij} is the free flow time on link *ij*
β_{ij} is the delay parameter for link *ij* (the increase in travel time per unit increase in the flow on link *ij*), and
f_{ij} is the flow on link *ij*.

(the above notation is based on the assumption of linear relationship between traffic volume on a link and the travel time on it).

The addition of a link to an existing transport system may lead to undesired situations. For example, in heavily congested areas, some of the medium and long-distance trips use minor roads as 'rat runs' (see p. 365 in Ortúzar and Willumsen, 2001). In a town planning context, some researchers argue that the complex characteristics of urban traffic networks can be explained by a fractal growth of cities (or vice versa) (Shen, 1997; Chen and Lou, 1998; Lu and Tang, 2004; Yerra and Levinson, 2005). Most of these studies explore the complexity of traffic network in the context of its spatial characteristics. In this chapter we are going to reflect on this.

13.2 Definitions

Marshall (2005) introduced several concepts to define the complex structure of traffic networks. *Depth* is a measure of network 'distance' – steps of adjacency – between network components. Calculating the depth of any axial line to any other, the average depth of a network can be measured. *Recursivity* is defined by the number of depths divided by the number of routes (where the number of depths is simply equivalent to the maximum depth). *Complexity* is defined as the number of distinct types of route present over and above the number of distinct types generated by difference in depth alone (which is the number of distinct types present less the value of the maximum depth) divided by the number of routes. (for illustrative examples see Marshall, 2005). Many traffic networks can be described as fractals. While some mathematicians avoid giving the strict definition, *fractal* is a geometric object that is generally 'a rough or fragmented geometric shape that can be subdivided in parts, each of which is (at least approximately) a reduced-size copy of the whole' (Mandelbrot, 1982).

Traffic flow parameters of link *ij* (α_{jj} , β_{ij}) may be typical to distinct route type or depth. Different types of road links, classified by hierarchical configuration of the traffic network, may be assigned with a limited range of parameter values to represent the typical traffic flow characteristics on such road types. A specific issue this chapter is dealing with is the effect of introducing a new link to a congested traffic network, and the likelihood of this additional capacity to improve the system's performance (traditionally measured by users' aggregated cost or travel time). The ratios between traffic flow parameters of two roads are assumed to be related to the difference in the hierarchical level of these roads, as follows:

$$(13.2)\ \alpha^n = k^{n-1}\alpha\ ;\ \beta^n = l^{\,n-1}\beta$$

where α and β are traffic flow parameters typical to roads classified by the highest hierarchical level of the traffic network; assuming recursivity and self-similarity of the traffic flow characteristics in different hierarchical levels, α^n and β^n are used to represent traffic flow parameters typical to roads classified by the *n*-hierarchical level of the traffic network. Assumptions about fixed linear ratios are made for demonstration purposes only, and may be over simplistic to represent the fractal nature of road hierarchy in real traffic networks.

Following this recursive definition of traffic flow parameters (Eq. 13.2), traffic networks (or sub-networks) that have a recursivity of about *1* and a complexity of about *0* (both properties as defined by Marshall, 2005) may be described as fractals. The recursivity of traffic flow measures can be represented by *k* and *l* (see Eq. 13.2). Complexity properties of roads' traffic flow parameters may help transport planning to determine under what circumstances the addition of a new link to an existing transport network improves or worsens the overall system performance, as demonstrated in the next section.

13.3 Numeric example

Let us consider a simple network problem, represented in Figure 13.1. The nodes of the traffic network are represented by a, b, c, and d. There are three possible paths to get from the origin to the destination, and the total traffic, *Q*, is equal to the sum of traffic volumes on these paths (F_1, F_2, F_3):

$$(13.3)\ Q = F_1 + F_2 + F_3$$

where:

$$(13.4)\ f_{ab} = F_1 + F_3\ ;\ f_{bd} = F_1\ ;\ f_{ac} = F_2\ ;\ f_{cd} = F_2 + F_3\ ;\ f_{bc} = F_3$$

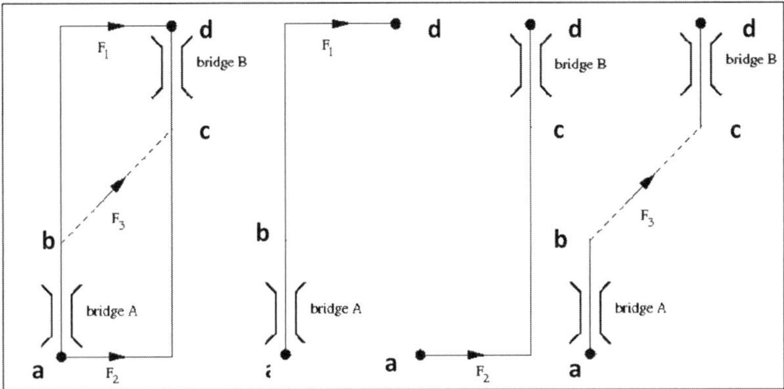

Figure 13.1 The traffic network and three possible paths

And the travel time experienced by travellers on each of the paths are:

$$(13.5)\ T_1 = T_{ab} + T_{bd};\ T_2 = T_{ac} + T_{cd};\ T_3 = T_{av} + T_{bc} + T_{cd}$$

As in the classical problem for Braess' paradox[2] we assume that the problem is symmetric, so that:

$$\alpha_{ab} = \alpha_{cd} = 0$$
$$\alpha_{bd} = \alpha_{bd} = \alpha^1$$
$$\beta_{ab} = \beta_{cd} = \beta^1$$
$$\beta_{bd} = \beta_{bd} = 0$$

The parameters were used in this numeric example are presented in Table 13.2.

These parameter values were used in Braess' (1968) classical example. Link *bc* has a lower hierarchical level in the traffic network. Following Eq. 13.2, its traffic flow parameters may be represented as follows:

$$(13.6)\ \alpha_{bc} = \alpha^2 = k\alpha;\ \beta_{bc} = \beta^2 = l\beta$$

Network equilibrium models are commonly used for the prediction of traffic flow on the network links. Wardrop (1952) provided a simple behavioural principle to describe the distribution of traffic volume on a traffic network, widely used in transport planning. Each user seeks to minimise travel cost or time. The traffic flows that satisfy this principle are usually referred to as 'user equilibrium', since

2 Breass' paradox, also known as the Road Network Paradox, is about the possible consequences for traffic flow when adding a road to a road network: it can actually slow traffic instead of enhancing its through-put. In such a situation the conclusion is controversial: the only way to speed up traffic is to close one of the roads.

Table 13.2 Parameter values of the road segments

link (ij)	α_{ij}	β_{ij}
Ab	0	10
Bd	50	0
Ac	50	0
Cd	0	10
Bc	10	1

each user chooses the route that is the best for him. In equilibrium, no user can decrease his/her route travel time by unilaterally switching routes. This condition may be represented by:

$$(13.7)\ T_1 = T_2 = T_3$$

The user equilibrium solution for this 3-path network with overall traffic volume of $Q=6$ is $T_1=T_2=T_3=88.3$ minutes, while the user equilibrium solution for a 2-path network (by omitting the link *bc*) is $T_1=T_2=80$ minutes. This illustrates the Braess' Paradox (Braess, 1968): 'adding new capacity (such as an extra link) in a congested network does not necessarily reduce congestion and can even increase it'. This situation happens because the users of the network do not face the 'true' social cost of an action.

Pas and Principuo (1997) do not find it appropriate to refer to this phenomenon as a paradox. Exploring the general expression of the network presented in Figure 13.1, they found that Brasess' paradox occurs when:

$$(13.8)\ \frac{2\,(\alpha^1-\alpha^2)}{3\beta^1+\beta^2} < Q < \frac{2\,(\alpha^1-\alpha^2)}{\beta^1+\beta^2}$$

For Q values outside of the above region, Braess' paradox does not occur, either because the demand is too low or because the demand is too high. Pas and Principuo (1997) show that for the values of Braess' original example, the paradox occurs for Q value between 2.58 and 8.89. Can the occurrence of Braess' paradox in a traffic network be predicted by the complexity properties introduced in the previous section? Using the recursive definitions of traffic glow parameters (Eq. 13.2), we find that Braess paradox occurs when:

$$(13.9)\ \frac{2\alpha(1-k)}{\beta(3+l)} < Q < \frac{2\alpha(1-k)}{\beta(1-l)}$$

The depth represented in this equation is 2, but the hierarchical difference between the added link and the existing routes may be more than that. Eq. 13.9 can be generalised for an added link of *n*-hierarchical level as follows:

$$(13.10) \quad \frac{2\alpha(1-k^{n-1})}{\beta(3+l^{n-1})} < Q < \frac{2\alpha(1-k^{n-1})}{\beta(1-l^{n-1})}$$

It is easy to see that Braess' paradox does not occur when $l^{n-1}>1$ and $k^{n-1}<1$, or when $l^{n-1}<1$ and $k^{n-1}>1$. The region of Q-values that satisfies Eq. 13.10 depends on the depth of the sub-network (n) and the recursivity of the hierarchical traffic flow properties. Thus, exploring the sensitivity of Eq. 13.10 to these values, the likelihood of Braess' paradox effects may be predicted for given estimation of traffic flow entering the sub-network (Q). The probability of overall performance of the network to be worse off than before a link is added $p(T_{new}>T_{old})$ (or in other words, the probability of Braess' paradox to occur) is:

$$(13.11)\ p(T_{new}>T_{old}) = \Sigma\, p(q)*l(q,k,l,n)*J(q,k,l,n)$$

Travel demand has a stochastic nature, thus the traffic volume that enter a traffic network is changing over time, reflecting changes in the demand for travel. In Eq. 13.11 $p(q)$ stands for the probability that the traffic volume enters the network is q.

$$l(q,k,l,n) = \begin{cases} 1 & q > \dfrac{2\alpha(1-k^{n-1})}{\beta(3+l^{n-1})} \\ 0 & otherwise \end{cases} ;$$

$$j(q,k,l,n) = \begin{cases} 1 & q > ; \dfrac{2\alpha(1-k^{n-1})}{\beta(1-l^{n-1})} \\ 0 & otherwise \end{cases}$$

The following example illustrates how the complex nature of the traffic network may be related to the probability of Braess' paradox to occur. The distribution of the traffic volume entering the network presented in Figure 13.1 is estimated as follows: Q (traffic flow) is *0* with a probability of *0.05*, *1* with a probability of *0.1*, *2* with a probability of *0.2*, *3* with a probability of *0.3*, *4* with a probability of *0.2*, *5* with a probability of *0.1*, *6* with a probability of *0.05*. The traffic flow parameters are presented in Table 13.2.

The probability $p(T_{new}>T_{old})$ for different levels of hierarchy ($0\leq k\leq 2$ and $0\leq l\leq 2$) and for a depth of *2* is represented in Figure 13.2. The probability $p(T_{new}>T_{old})$ for different measures of hierarchy ($0\leq k\leq 2$ and $0\leq l\leq 2$) and for a depth of *4* is represented in Figure 13.3. A general property of the traffic network's complexity may be observed here: the higher the depth of the network system is, the lower is the probability of Braess' paradox to occur, and the safer is the assumption that introducing a new link will improve the overall performance of the system. A transport modeller may find use in such analysis even if he is not provided with accurate and precise properties of the traffic complexity.

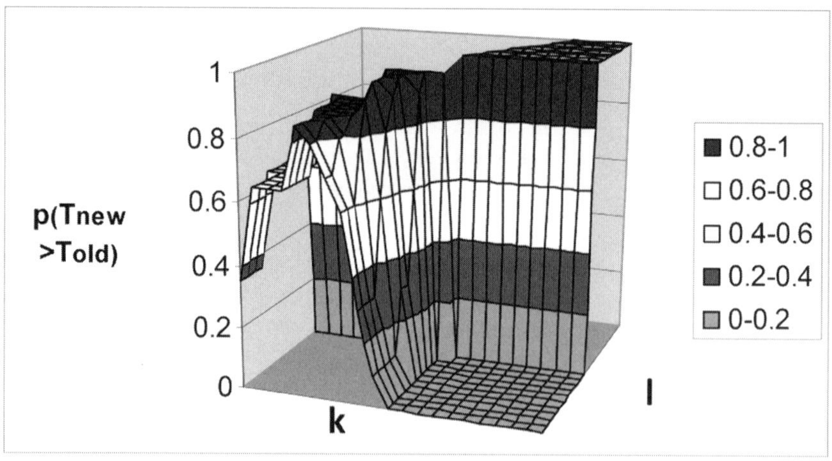

Figure 13.2 Probability of Braess' Paradox as a function of the Network Recursivity 0≤k≤2, 0≤l≤2, n=2

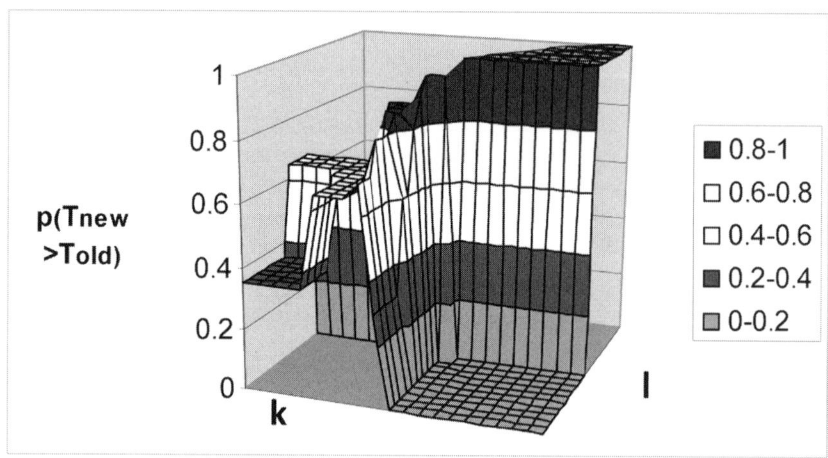

Figure 13.3 Probability of Braess' Paradox as a function of the Network Recursivity 0≤k≤2, 0≤l≤2, n=4

13.4 Conclusion

A traffic network can be described as a complex system; one may argue that it may be characterised by self-similarity and symmetry across scales. This chapter describes conceptual and methodological issues for presenting and exploring complex traffic systems and illustrates the application of complexity properties in the analysis of traffic networks.

Facing rather large and complex traffic networks, parts of those may not be completely planned or design, transport modellers may use complexity analysis of the traffic network in order to identify situations where added capacity might not be followed by improved performance of the traffic system. Using complexity terms presented in this work, as well as other complexity terms, in the description of traffic networks can form the structural basis for a broader modelling framework.

Complexity modelling of the traffic network may also help in the conceptual representation of the minor parts of the road network, which in many cases are not represented fully due to limited knowledge of the modeller or limited resources by him (see, for example, Bovy and Hansen, 1983). The level of spatial detail (i.e. zone side and network detail) used in transport analysis is an important factor affecting the correctness and the accuracy of the resulting estimates of the impact of changes in the transport system.

In order to incorporate complexity properties into traffic modelling, further empirical and theoretical investigation of the complexity of road networks in the context of traffic flow are required. The example presented in this chapter is rather simple and does not address other dimensions of real traffic networks, such as recursivity or connectivity. An obvious generalisation of the presented approach is to develop a systematic analysis of any complex traffic network.

References

Benguigui, L. and Daoud, M. (1991) 'Is the suburban railway system a fractal?', *Geographical Analysis*, vol. 23, pp. 362-368.

Bovy, P.H.L. and Jansen, G.R.M. (1983) 'Network aggregation effects upon equilibrium assignment outcomes: An empirical investigation', *Transportation Science*, vol. 17(3), pp. 240-262.

Braess, D. (1968) 'Über ein paradoxon aus der verkehrsplanung' ['About a paradox from infrastructure planning'], *Unternehmensforschung*, vol. 12, pp. 258-268.

Chen, Y. and Luo, J. (1998) 'The fractal features of the transport network of henan province', *Journal of Xinyang Teachers College*, vol. 11, pp. 172-177.

De Ortúzar, J.D. and Willumsen, L.G. (2001) *Modelling Transport*, John Wiley & Sons, Chichester (third edition).

Department for Transport (2005) 'Road lengths in Great Britain: 2005', available at http://www.dft.gov.uk/pgr/statistics/datatablespublications/roadstraffic/roadlengths/regionclass/.

Lu, Y. and Tang, J. (2004) 'Fractal dimension of a transportation network and its relationship with urban growth: A study of Dallas, Fort Worth area', *Environment and Planning B: Planning and Design*, vol. 31, pp. 895-911.

Mandelbrot, B.B. (1982) *The Fractal Geometry of Nature*, W.H. Freeman & Co., San Francisco.

Marshall, S. (2005) *Streets and Patterns*, Spon Press, London/New York.

Pas, E.I. and Principio, S.L. (1997) 'Braess' paradox: Some new insights', *Transportation Research B*, vol. 31, pp. 265-276.

Shen, G. (1997) 'A fractal dimension analysis of urban transportation networks', *Geographical and Environmental Modelling*, vol. 1, pp. 221-236.

Thomson, J. (1997) *Great Cities and Their Traffic*, Victor Gollancz, London.

Wardrop, J.G. (1952) 'Some theoretical aspects of road traffic research', *Proceedings, Institution of Civil Engineers*, part II, vol. 1, pp. 325-378.

Yerra, B.M. and Levinson, D.M. (2005) 'The emergence of hierarchy in transportation networks', *The Annals of Regional Science*, vol. 39, pp. 541-553.

Chapter 14
Going Beyond the Metaphor of the Machine: Complexity and Participatory Ecological Design

Joanne Tippett[1]

Many of the social and environmental problems faced by post-industrial societies will not be solved without a fundamental re-think of how citizens and organisations interact with the environment. Despite the fact that sustainability is often touted as a core goal of spatial planning, planning practice still struggles to achieve long-term sustainable solutions (Owens et al., 2006). This gap points to the need for new approaches, in order to develop resilient human settlements which allow people *and* ecosystems to thrive. We contend that achieving sustainability requires a shift from the mechanistic paradigm underlying current planning practice. This should enable effective integration of civic engagement and ecologically informed planning. Complexity and systems thinking could act as a source for such a new paradigm.

This chapter explores the nature of scientific paradigms and metaphorical understanding in the context of ecological design. It does this through the lens of action research, in which a new planning methodology, entitled DesignWays, was developed and tested. This represented a systems-based effort to develop more effective ways to incorporate participatory processes into ecological planning. Development of the methodology was based on a realisation that we need new ways of thinking about the relationship between humans and ecosystems.

14.1 Introduction

One of the greatest challenges facing humankind is learning how people worldwide can best realise their potential and improve their quality of life, whilst safeguarding the natural systems on which human well-being ultimately depends. Ecosystems worldwide are under threat. Decline in the state of the world's ecosystems was highlighted by the findings of the Millennium Ecosystem Assessment. This assessment was initiated under the auspices of the United Nations in 2001.

1 Joanne Tippett is Lecturer at the Centre for Urban and Regional Ecology, Planning and Landscape, School of Environment and Development, University of Manchester.

The initial report was published in 2005, following a major effort to assess the consequences of ecosystem change for human well-being, involving more than 1,360 experts from a wide range of fields worldwide. The summary of main findings starts with this statement:

> Over the past 50 years, humans have changed ecosystems more rapidly and extensively than in any comparable period of time in human history, largely to meet rapidly growing demands for food, fresh water, timber, fibre and fuel. This has resulted in a substantial and largely irreversible loss in the diversity of life on Earth (Millennium Ecosystem Assessment, 2005, p. 1).

This worsening has occurred despite the rise in environmental concern during the last several decades (Commoner, 1992), starting with the publication of Carson's (1962) *Silent Spring* and more recently with major global environmental summits, such as the World Commission on Environment and Development (1987) and the United Nations Conference on the Environment and Development in Rio (1992). Conversely, there have been improvements in environmental quality in some areas during the last several decades, such as improvements in water quality in many European rivers. These have stemmed from a combination of de-industrialisation (with much manufacturing moving out of Europe), cleaning up industrial processes and from improved sorting of waste streams (e.g. Wood and Handley, 1999). There are, however, limits to the improvements that can be made through such incremental approaches, especially when considering the system of production and consumption on a global scale. In the context of continued environmental degradation, Ison (1998) talks of the need for second order change, stepping out of the confines of the system and developing 'change which changes whole systems'.

We contend that what is needed is a focus on 'upstream solutions', such that the *causes* of pollution and waste are designed out of manufacturing, energy and infrastructure provision, land management and buildings. The challenge is how to develop such 'upstream solutions', and how to encourage their implementation.

Spatial arrangements and patterns play a key role in mediating flows of material and energy, and in determining the long-term environmental effects of development. Spatial planning, in its broadest sense, involves thinking about the interaction of society and place. It is a mechanism through which new visions for places are developed and implemented. New planning methodologies are needed in order to move towards a sustainable society, in which nature is seen as an integral part of the fabric of human settlements and urban regions, and 'waste' is designed out of the system.

Discussion about sustainability necessarily includes discussion of people's actions. In the book *Supply-Side Sustainability*, Allen (Allen et al., 2003, p. xiv) states: 'Social science is inextricable from ecological sustainability and central to the future'. In this chapter, ecology is seen in a broad sense, and defined as the organisation and interactions of complex communities, both natural and human, from the local to the global scale (Centre for Urban and Regional Ecology, 2007). Such a definition goes beyond a debate between an anthropocentric or biocentric view of nature, as it adopts a non-dualistic view in which humans are seen as part of nature. It is, however, still useful to discuss human and natural systems if we are to talk about sustainability. Whilst the two systems are interrelated, it is possible to achieve greater clarity by analysing them both as integrated wholes and separately (Allen et al., 2003, p. 55). The concept of sustainability is often related to the idea that human activity has a significant impact on the functioning of global ecosystems and geo-chemical cycles, which otherwise would be capable of being sustained over time. Thus, if we are to continue to benefit from the services ecosystems provide to human kind, new ways of interacting with these ecosystems will be needed (e.g. Holmberg, 1998; Robert et al., 2002). To discuss sustainability thus implies considering the way in which humans interact, both with and within ecosystems.

Recent policies, such as the European Union Water Directive (European Commission, 2000) and the Convention on Access to Information, Public Participation in Decision making and Access to Justice in Environmental Matters (UN ECE, 1998), have required an enhanced level of participation of community members and stakeholders in environmental and natural resource management. These are reflected in shifts in spatial planning policies, such as the recent changes to the planning system of England and Wales, which requires increased stakeholder involvement early in the planning process (Office of the Deputy Prime Minster, 2005). Increased participation is seen as leading to more effective planning. Local knowledge can be incorporated into plans, giving fuller information (Handley et al., 1998). And the inclusion of local people's interests and concerns in the plans helps to close the 'implementation gap' between plans and changes on the ground (Luz, 2000). A major benefit of increased participation in planning is seen as the increased likelihood of changes in behaviour, as participants gain a new understanding about environmental impacts of their actions increasing the potential to change behaviour of actors (e.g. Allen et al., 2002; Tyson, 1995). New planning methodologies aiming to create ecologically sound visions for the future thus need to involve stakeholders and community members in the planning process.

In a review of shifts towards sustainability in leading organisations, Doppelt (2003) argues that changes in mental models and assumptions are essential to achieve these shifts. They facilitate the organisational and cultural change he suggests is necessary to achieve changes in management and practice. This chapter explores participatory ecological planning in the light of this need to change mental models.

The discussion draws on action research, which tested a participatory ecological planning methodology developed by Tippett (author of this chapter) (1994/2004). This methodology, entitled DesignWays, combines attention to the process of participatory communication and the use of eco-systemic metaphors for perceiving and interacting with the environment. These metaphors are developed into practical tools for developing new possibilities through ecological design.

The DesignWays methodology is introduced below, followed by an exploration of metaphors in relationship to construction of thought and planning. Ecological design is introduced, with a more detailed section looking at how the metaphors of living systems are incorporated into the DesignWays methodology. The chapter concludes with a discussion of the nature of mental models associated with complexity and systems thinking.

14.2 A new methodology for participatory ecological planning

Tippett has been developing the DesignWays methodology since 1993, refining it through application in practice, including rural regeneration in Southern Africa, teaching environmental studies in the United States and urban regeneration in Northern England (Tippett, 2005a). The initial impetus for development stemmed from two realisations: firstly, 'business as usual' (even with a green tint) was not going to deliver a sustainable future; secondly, changing mental models of the nature of human relationships with the environment could play an important role in achieving change that had a possibility of going beyond 'business as usual' (as discussed in Capra, 1982; De Rosnay, 1975; Ornstein and Ehrlich, 1995).

There was an active attempt to learn from many different methodologies in the development of DesignWays, including ecological design (Holmgren, 2003; Mollison, 1990), sustainability frameworks (e.g. Holmberg, 1998; Robert et al., 2002) and participatory planning methodologies, such as Participatory Rural Appraisal (Chambers, 1994) and Planning for Real (Gibson, 1996). There are several participatory planning processes that include an element of sustainability thinking, but it is not a given in most of the methodologies. Several ecological planning methodologies include attention to participatory processes. Ecological design does not necessarily, however, involve a participatory process (methodologies reviewed in depth in Tippett et al., 2007). Indeed, Fletcher and Goggin (2001, p. 16) contend, 'the success of a range of approaches to ecodesign is at least partly contingent on people and this largely has been overlooked'.

The aim was to build on the strengths of earlier attempts to plan for sustainability, whilst developing an effective way to integrate participatory approaches and ecological planning. There are six interrelated attributes of DesignWays that enable it to meet the challenges of sustainable development: creative involvement of stakeholders; common design language (a platform to link across contexts and levels of scale); sustainability guidelines; practical ecological design process; experiential learning approach; and a systems thinking framework (Tippett, 2005b). As a methodology, DesignWays offers a vehicle for exploring the relationship between metaphors and participatory ecological planning. It is not seen as the only approach, or necessarily the best approach. Choice of appropriate methodologies, of which DesignWays is just one, requires careful attention to context and the goals of the project or programme.

The following section elaborates the theoretical background to this approach and its wider context, that of attempts to explore the nature between humans and natural systems.

14.3 Systems and complexity in planning

Capra (1982) discusses the deeply entwined link between scientific paradigms and the organisation of society. He suggests that recent shifts in scientific paradigm have profound implications for the organisation of society. Innes and Booher (1999) discuss the need for a new world view in this time of turbulence and constant change. They state: 'Under such conditions, the predominant Western world view since the Enlightenment is no longer as useful as it once was' (ibid., p. 145).

The last century has seen several significant shifts in scientific understanding, those of particular relevance to this discussion are summarised below:

i. a sense that uncertainty is irreducible, as we are not able to predict outcomes precisely in complex systems (e.g. Funtowicz and Ravetz, 1994; Ravetz, 1997);
ii. shifts in understanding of the nature of objectivity and scientists' ability to observe systems objectively (captured for the imagination in the phrase 'the uncertainty principle' Heisenberg, 1962);
iii. the nature of emergent properties from the interaction of different components of a system, which are not reducible to the parts of the system (e.g. Allen and Hoekstra, 1992; Koestler, 1969; Miller, 1995);
iv. an increased understanding of self-organisation and non-linearity in systems far from equilibrium (e.g. Portugali, 2000; Prigogine, 1997);
v. increased awareness of the impact of contextual factors and starting conditions on the development of complex systems (e.g. Capra, 1996; Kay et al., 1999);
vi. realisation of the irreversibility of time in terms of the trajectory of complex systems (as opposed to Newton's laws which imply 'equivalence between past and future' Prigogine, 1997, p. 746) (elucidated in Coveney and Highfield, 1991);
vii. understanding the interaction of geo-chemical flows and living organisms in terms of the planet as a self-organising system (e.g. Lovelock, 1991; Margulis and Sagan, 1987).

To help meet the challenge of sustainable development, practitioners and stakeholders need to learn to explore and experience connections between different areas of knowledge. Capra (1996, p. 297) suggests that 'the theory of living systems [...] provides a conceptual framework for the link between ecological communities and human communities'. The report, 'The Law of Sustainable

Development' produced by the European Commission, explores the 'legal theory of sustainable development' and states: 'today, no serious study and application of the principles of sustainable development is possible without the help of systems science' (Decleris, 2000, p. 8). The report goes on to state, 'The control system for sustainable development is based on a new philosophy and a different design' (ibid., p. 56).

Systems thinking is an emerging discipline, its origin often credited to Ludwig van Bertalanffy, who in the late 1940s argued that 'the ideas derived from the behaviour of organisms which organism biologists had developed, could actually be applied to "wholes" of any kind' (Checkland, 1992, p. 1024). It has developed over the last 40 years in many different fields and through a range of applications. A system is 'an integrated whole whose essential properties arise from the relationships between its parts' (Capra, 1996, p. 27). Systems thinking can be characterised as an attempt to find common principles that apply at different levels of scale and across different types of phenomena. It is 'a methodology that makes possible the collection and organisation of accumulated knowledge in order to increase the efficiency of our actions' (De Rosnay, 1975, p. 57).

There are methodologies within systems thinking that are closely associated with management and operations research (Mingers and Taylor, 1992). The discipline goes beyond particular methods for management, however, as it is a way of thinking about systems in terms of 'connectedness, relationships and context' (Capra, 1996, p. 36).

The publication of the book *Collapse: How Societies Choose to Fail or Survive* (Diamond, 2005) highlighted increased awareness of the inherent nature of change and uncertainty in socio-ecological systems. The systems approach has emerged in response to the shifts in scientific understanding outlined above, as a means to help understand and develop strategies within complex systems and their emerging properties.

In the last several decades, new mathematical tools and increased capacity to model complex interactions on high-speed computers have led to new insights, commonly termed complexity theory. Complexity theory and planning is a rapidly developing field, particularly in urban dynamics and spontaneous order (Webster and Lai, 2003), but the potential for complexity to inform the practice of planning for sustainability is not yet fully realised. Complexity theory can offer new ways to understand natural systems, in particular in looking at the nature of change and resilience (Berkes et al., 2003). This understanding can be developed into new approaches to planning, endeavouring to design and develop human systems that sit more comfortably within ecosystems (e.g. Pulliam, 2002). This work described in this chapter represents one such attempt, working at the intersection of systems thinking and complexity. The theoretical context of DesignWays, and that of the methodologies referenced in its development, is rooted in a paradigm shift from reductionist to more holistic ways of thinking, as exemplified in complexity and systems thinking paradigms.

Systems thinking can be seen as an approach to understanding complex systems at different levels of scale, offering some tools and insights to help initiate and manage change within them. Complexity theory adds a nuanced understanding of the nature of change and interactions between elements of a system. As systems thinking is multi-faceted and developing, complexity theories are still evolving (Zchichang, 2007, p. 458). The interface between these intellectual fields, and their development through application in different areas of operation, offers a rich seam of future theoretical and practical learning. This chapter makes a contribution to this learning, whilst recognising the need for further development.

Development of DesignWays, represented an endeavour to respond to Capra's (1996, pp. 4-5) insight into environmental problems:

> Ultimately these problems must be seen as just different facets of one single crisis, which is largely a crisis of perception. It derives from the fact that most of us, and especially our large social institutions, subscribe to the concepts of an outdated worldview, a perception of reality inadequate for dealing with our overpopulated, globally interconnected world.

Responding effectively to this problem, in terms of engendering a change in perception, requires attention to metaphors and metaphorical understanding. In a study of ways to use metaphorical understanding to improve management, Morgan (1997, p. 351) states 'Metaphor encourages us to think and act in new ways. It extends horizons of insight and creates new possibilities'. The important role of metaphor in the creation of meaning is discussed in the following section. Metaphors are not merely useful mental constructs, but can provide a powerful generative framework for rethinking the way in which humans interact with the environment. We contend that changing the metaphors of planning is central to a shift in both our *conceptions* of planning and the way in which we *can* plan.

14.4 Metaphors and changing views of planning

Lakoff and Johnson (1999) offer a new way of looking at the nature of knowledge and meaning. They illuminate the ways in which humans construct meaning through metaphor (Lakoff and Johnson, 1980), and suggest that the way in which we are able to reason is fundamentally linked with the way in which our bodies orientate spatially in the world and interact with the environment. These basic relationships between our bodies and the world help to build primary metaphors, which are used in abstract thought. How we can know is not just influenced by what we see, but also fundamentally by *how* we can see and feel. In *Philosophy in the Flesh* (1999, p. 3) they develop this concept of '*embodied realism*' and make three central assertions:

i. The mind is inherently embodied.
ii. Thought is mostly unconscious.
iii. Abstract concepts are largely metaphorical.

Embodied realism rejects a 'Cartesian separation' of mind and body. Instead it is 'a realism grounded in our capacity to function successfully in our physical environments' (Lakoff and Johnson, 1999, p. 95). The concept of embodied realism was developed in the field of cognitive science and linguistics. This exploration of the functioning and development of living systems can be traced back to Gregory Bateson's work on ecology and mind (Tognetti, 1999).

In their critique of analytical philosophy and the concept of disembodied realism, Lakoff and Johnson suggest that the concept of metaphorical structuring of thought does not imply an inability to discuss stable truths in the world and to engage in rational scientific reasoning, but rather that the commonalties of responding to the physical environment that we share, allows for the exploration of shared truths. They suggest that imaginative capacity enhances scientific ability and the possibility of discovering abstract concepts.

Lakoff and Johnson (1999) explore two major shifts in an understanding of truth. One is that any discussion of truth may need to be multi-levelled, and that concepts of truth when seen at different levels may be contradictory. This aspect of reality does not necessarily mean that there is no such thing as 'truth', but rather that human perception of reality is a complex and many-layered phenomenon. They suggest that abstract reasoning requires metaphorical thought, and that more than one metaphor can be used to describe abstract thoughts, which can lead to different interpretations of reality. They see metaphors as essential in constructing worldviews, and suggest that often this is an unconscious process.

Metaphors are 'live' when they are used to actively construct meaning in society, and many societies have different metaphors for the same concepts. They suggest that scientific paradigm shifts involve fundamental changes in the metaphors underlying scientific thought. This is illustrated through a discussion of the western cultural metaphor, Time is Money. They show how cultures that do not have this metaphor conceive of time in a different way. They suggest that it is important to examine our metaphorical constructs and see how they influence our thinking; both to illuminate the thought process and to see which metaphors may be limiting or misleading. Lakoff (pers. comm. 1998) suggested the utility (especially in academic discourse) of replacing the Argument is War metaphor with Argument is a Dance, as a thought experiment, if not as a practical means of changing the tenor of academic polemic.

14.5 The metaphor of the machine and the ecosystem

A 'mechanistic worldview' sees components of the world (e.g. living organisms) acting 'like machines', in which the whole can be understood through an analysis of the parts, within a closed system independent of its wider context. This can be contrasted with a holistic worldview, in which the world is seen 'as an integrated whole rather than a dissociated collection of parts' (Capra, 1996, p. 6). Discussing the western world view, Innes and Booher (1999, p. 145) say 'the dominant, though tacit, metaphor was that natural and social systems are like machines: composed of separable parts that can be analysed and understood individually'. In another paper, they discuss the way indicators are seen in the mechanistic worldview: 'the idea of indicators is to measure different parts of the machine and their purpose is to help us find out what part of the machine is not working, and to fine tune possibilities to make the machine produce the right outputs' (Innes and Booher, 2000, p. 178).

By contrast, in a holistic worldview, each part of reality is seen as embedded in a larger whole. An understanding based on relationships is seen as essential to comprehension of the system. The very building blocks of matter are not indivisible billiard balls responding to the rules of Newtonian physics, but rather waves of energy where the appearance of matter emerges from a dance of relationships. This is a fundamentally different view of reality than that espoused by much of modern science, but it is increasingly recognised as a more accurate description of the world than that of a mechanistic worldview (Coveney and Highfield, 1991). These shifts in understanding are echoed in the field of ecology amongst others, with an increased awareness of the importance of flows of energy and materials, and maintenance of process integrity at multiple scales (e.g. Allen and Hoekstra, 1992).

There have been major shifts during this period of changes in scientific thought in terms of our knowledge of how people understand the world and construct meaning from their experience. In contrast to the positivist understanding of meaning, where there are objective truths in the world that can be apprehended by the observer, a constructivist position views reality as mentally constructed, so that multiple realities exist in different contexts. The underlying metaphor for the process of learning about the world from a constructivist position is that of 'making meaning', not 'finding' it. Some ecological economists have criticised this paradigm, as it denies the biological arena that provides constraints on social life. Tacconi (1998, p. 99) suggests the following reformation of the constructivist position: 'There exists a physical reality subject to different interpretations by human beings. Thus, there exist multiple socially constructed realties'.

We posit that we are both meaning makers in a social context and biological entities. Such a realisation has parallels in several fields, such as in the work of the educationalist Dewey (1925/1937/1954), 'who focused on the whole complex circuit of organism and environment interactions that makes up our experience, and he showed how experience is at once bodily, social, intellectual, and emotional' (Lakoff and Johnson, 1999, p. 97).

If the aim is to design in a way more consistent with living systems, it is worth asking: 'What is life?'. It is a question which lead Maturana and Varela (1992) to develop the theory of autopoiesis. They found that the answer was inextricably interwoven with the question 'What is cognition?'. They found that the process of a living organism maintaining its identity in an environment of flux and change is inherent in the act of living (Maturana and Varela, 1987). Maturana and Varela coined the term autopoiesis to denote the organisation of living beings. It is derived from the root 'auto', or self, and the Greek word 'poiesis', which means making, and shares the same root as the word poetry. Thus autopoiesis can be seen as self-making. Living organisms are characterised by the process of self-reproduction. An organism's behaviour is affected by its environment, but at the same time its actions shape and change the ecosystems of which it is a part. The theory of 'autopoiesis' provides a view of life that is characterised by processes and patterns, in which emergent properties arise from dynamic interactions of the components of a system.

The concepts of embodied realism and autopoiesis suggest that a stark division between ontology, the nature of the world, and epistemology, the nature of how we can know about the world, is in itself problematic. We can only know the world through being in the world, thus any description of 'reality' is inherently filtered through, or created by, physical bodies and their interactions in the world.

Ideas about the relationship between humans and the environment play an essential role in how we are able to make changes in the environment. The former president of the Czech Republic, Vaclev Havel (1994) suggests that a '*meaningful world order*' needs different underlying metaphors to those that have underpinned modern, reductionist science. He suggests that the Gaia Hypothesis might provide an alternative source of metaphors. It allows us to see that 'we are parts of a greater whole. Our destiny is not dependent merely on what we do for ourselves but also on what we do for Gaia as a whole' (ibid.).

At the heart of the research discussed in this chapter lies the concept of ecological wisdom, which allows us to 'appreciate and better understand the intricate web of interactions between human and natural processes' (Ndubisi, 2002, p. 239) and to develop these lessons into new methodologies for planning human settlements. A conscious attempt to embed living systems metaphors into participatory ecological planning lies at the core of the development of DesignWays. The core metaphor underlying DesignWays is to 'think like an ecosystem'.[2] The challenge is to design human settlements and systems that run off the sun (and the wind), build soil, biodiversity and freshwater reserves. The outputs from these systems would be clean water, biodiversity and useful products that can be composted or completely recycled at the end of their use.

The use of the word 'like' is deliberate. In this research, we make the assumption that it is desirable to design human physical and social infrastructure that behave

2 The term 'think like an ecosystem' was derived from Aldo Leopold's phrase 'think like a mountain' (Leopold, 1968). Rowe (2000) suggests that shifting the concept of a mountain to an ecosystem represents a further step on a 'road to wisdom'. As Wheeler (1990), California's Secretary for Resources 1991-1999, said 'To halt the decline of an ecosystem, it is necessary to think like an ecosystem'.

more like ecosystems, with their cycles, than linear flows of resources that create pollution and ecological degradation. Discussing value judgements and science, O'Riordan (1998) says the process of considering values should be seen as *part of* the scientific process and notes that what is deemed as fact is often decided by consensus. This research took an inherently normative approach, as it was seen that new approaches to planning were needed in which values were considered as part of the planning process. The ethical imperative is 'to preserve the integrity, stability and beauty of the biotic community' (Leopold, 1968), seen as essential in preserving a viable human community.

The principles of ecological design provide the practical way in which the DesignWays methodology endeavours to plan for sustainability. The way in which this new metaphorical approach was embedded in DesignWays is discussed in the next two sections. First, ecological design is introduced, then the way in which ecosystem metaphors are used to animate and structure participatory ecological design in DesignWays is discussed.

14.6 Introduction to ecological design

> To alter a disappointing present course and assure a more promising and gratifying future, we must allow ourselves the luxury of dreaming. In this context, visioning is considered the most powerful tool for escaping from the confines of ideas and paradigms that lock us into many undesirable patterns of behaviour and practice (Mebratu, 1998, pp. 516-517).

Design can be seen as a hinge between a desired future and the present. It involves conceiving new patterns, forms and relationships between elements at different levels of scale. In ecological design, forms of production, housing and infrastructure are integrated into the landscape, with the aim of enhancing natural systems where possible, and of causing minimal environmental impacts. The aim is to design and develop human settlements so that they sit as comfortably as possible within ecological systems without degrading them. This is a process of actively designing alternative possibilities for the future, in which sustainability is seen as 'an active condition, not a passive consequence of doing less' (Allen et al., 2003, p. 12). Ecological design can be applied to production and manufacturing processes, building design and spatial planning, in short to all aspects of designing human settlements and infrastructure. Ecological design is most effective when these are seen as whole systems in and of themselves (e.g. Delin, 1979), as well as interacting components within larger wholes.

Ecological design has a long history of precedents. In the UK in the late 19th century, John Ruskin and William Morris questioned the emerging industrial model of production and explored instead how to learn from 'nature' in design. Ebenezer Howard developed this work into the idea of the Garden City (1850-1928), exemplified by Letchworth and Welwyn Gardens (Farmer, 1996). Fuller (1969) was an early advocate of applying ecological principles to human settlements, and the influential design thinker Papanek (1995) has extended his work on design for human needs to include what he calls the *'Green Imperative'*. The philosophical roots of much of the recent work on appropriate technology and green design stems from two influential thinkers, Schumacher (1973), with his focus on 'Small is Beautiful'; and Illich (1987), with his focus on the role that technology plays in structuring social interaction, power relations and learning.

McHarg (1992) promoted the idea of designing with nature, within the context of landform, watersheds and vegetation of an area. He set out a comprehensive approach to analysing ecological and cultural characteristics of landscapes, in order to determine the best areas for development for particular purposes. In a similar development, Lewis (1996) has devised an integrated methodology for sustainable design, which offers a framework for interdisciplinary planning on a regional scale. Mollison and Holmgren developed permaculture, an early form of ecological design, in the 1970s in Australia. Permaculture is now promoted and taught by an internationally recognised institution (Mollison, 1990). It was originally conceived as an approach for applying ecological principles to productive land management, and has been developed into a holistic system for designing human landscapes and settlements (Holmgren, 2003). Permaculture was seen as a way of learning from ecosystems, to create more productive and ecologically sustainable human landscapes which mimic the structure and processes of mature ecosystems, such as in agro-forestry, which mimics the structure of the forest edge. The development of permaculture was inspired by insights from the emerging living systems approach, in particular systems ecology (Mollison, 1990).

Criticisms of the concept of ecological design fall into two categories, the practical and the theoretical. On the practical level, ecological design is difficult to implement, requiring different skills and competencies, both in design and construction, than those for common practices. There are high up front costs from the time spent in design. This is the case especially in strategic and large-scale plans, and where there is a high degree of stakeholder involvement. These costs may be mitigated by efficiency gains through streamlining of later projects (e.g. Bass and Herson, 2000; Brooke, 2000; Verheem, 2000).

Within the theoretical realm, there are thinkers who suggest that design aimed at reducing damage to ecosystems is not necessary. The approach of 'technological optimism' suggests that human ingenuity will always be able to solve problems created by technology, so there is no need to limit the application of technology in consideration of ecosystems (e.g. the debate between Norman Myers, a well known environmentalist, and Julian Simon, an economist and outspoken critic of environmentalism, in Myers et al., 1994).

Botkin (1990) discusses the recent revision of the theory of climax ecosystems to a more dynamic view of change in ecosystems. He contends that the historical role of humans in maintaining ecosystems implies that ecosystems are inherently capable of adapting to human changes. He suggests this means that ecosystems will be able to adapt from human induced changes, without the need for us to be overly concerned about our effects on those systems.

In any endeavour to create more sustainable systems, it is important to ask the question, 'Do we really know that ecological design will produce results that are more sustainable than any other process of design?'. Several researchers caution about the difficulty of 'measuring' or assessing relative ecological sustainability of options, emphasising uncertainty in any scientific endeavour to understand ecosystems (e.g. Carpenter, 1995; George, 1999). Bateson (1972, p. 481) reminds us:

> There are, in a sense, no facts in nature; or if you like, there are an infinite number of potential facts in nature, out of which the judgement selects a few which become truly facts by that act of selection.

Professor Rayner from Oxford University's Saïd Business School suggests, with regards to using scientific knowledge to attempt to move towards sustainability, 'We know enough'. He calls on scientists to cease calling for more research into precise effects of actions, but rather to advance sustainability politics based on our current understanding, ethics and aesthetics. He says:

> While better knowledge is generally a good thing, what we already know ought to be sufficient to start taking decisive steps to protect the planet and address the needs of its poorest citizens. Knowledge deficit does not seem to be the key obstacle (Rayner, 2002, para. 8).

In the spirit of endeavouring to develop new ideas to move towards sustainability, given the best state of knowledge that we have at the moment, the following section describes the way in which a metaphorical understanding of ecosystems has been developed into a hands-on, participatory process for applying ecological design principles in DesignWays.

14.7 Learning to 'think like an ecosystem'

DesignWays was initially developed in Southern Africa as a means of applying permaculture design within rural regeneration. This involved working with local communities who had very little direct experience of climax ecosystems, due to extreme soil erosion and ecological degradation in the lowland areas. This meant that many of the ways commonly used to talk about ecological design, such as asking participants to think of a forest, were difficult for participants to engage with. This difficulty sparked the development of new ways to explain these principles and making them meaningful for participants.

Living systems metaphors are expressed in DesignWays in the communication tools (the graphics and the way of presenting information) as well as in the process of design. The metaphor of a river flowing through its catchment is used to introduce the process of design. One participant commented on the metaphor of the river, 'the whole thing is about cycles, sustainability is about cycles. So to start off with this metaphor as a cycle [...] was a good way to do it [...] one of the benefits was the fact that it made us think in systems and cycles' (Creative Director of Countryscape, 2003). A few participants found this metaphor difficult to start with, but said that as they went through the process, it began to make sense. One participant said she found it confusing at first, but at the end of the process that she felt it was important, giving a sense of a goal and a journey to the process.

Each part of the water cycle metaphor used to structure the overall design process embodies a further metaphor related to a stage of the design process. For instance, the assets and context of the area are seen to channel design decisions, echoed in the metaphor of water formed into channels by the underlying geology of the mountain slope. The process of testing ideas developed in brainstorming sessions against principles of sustainability acts as a filter for the flow of ideas emerging from the workshops, as wetlands act as filters in the water cycle.

There are several stages of thinking about the elements of the design and their associated resource flows. Participants are encouraged to learn to 'think like an ecosystem' through the application of ecological design principles. There are several different formulations of these principles (Holmgren, 2003), but at heart they offer a heuristic for turning basic ideas derived from observations of ecosystems, such as 'all waste equals food', into a way of approaching design. As they are used in DesignWays, they can be summarised as:

i. multiple uses for each element;
ii. multiple sources for each need;
iii. use of local and biological resources;
iv. cycling of energy and materials;
v. beneficial location and connective strategies;
vi. use of appropriate technology;
vii. stacking in space and time;
viii. designing for resilience within surges and pulses.

These ecological design principles are tied together through a metaphor of organisms embedded in ecosystems, turned into mnemonic in DesignWays as the DNA Framework. This provides a graphic representation of ways of thinking of design as an analogy of an ecosystem, under the headings: **D**esigning edge, **N**odes and Networks and **A**nalysis of Flow (see Figure 14.1).

Each part of the DNA Framework has a set of principles and processes associated with it. Interactive, hands-on toolkits, with moveable pieces, help participants to understand and apply these principles. These are described below.

In '**A**nalysis of Flow', flows of energy, water, biological nutrients, technical nutrients, money and information are considered as inputs and outputs to a design element (e.g. building, factory, farm, community forest). These are analysed in terms of their impact on the wider regional and global systems, and in terms of

Figure 14.1 DNA – Designing Edge, Nodes and Networks and Analysis of Flow

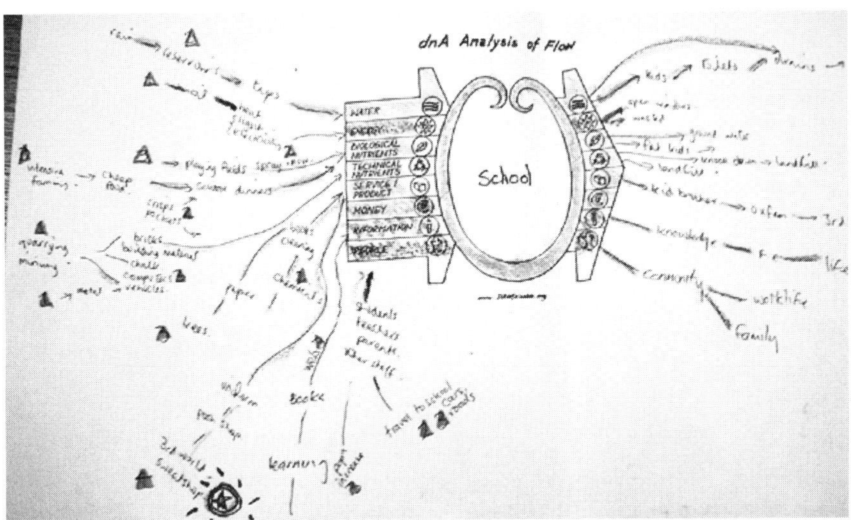

Figure 14.2 'Analysis of Flow' template

alternative ways of supplying the inputs to the system, applying the ecological design principle of 'multiple sources for each need'. There is careful consideration of the sources, uses and sinks of water and energy, aiming to maximise the 'use of local and biological resources'.

The information from the 'Analysis of Flow' charts is used to brainstorm about more ecologically sound ways of supplying the inputs to elements (such as schools, households, or businesses), and new ways of using the outputs, thus applying the principle 'multiple uses for each element' (see Figure 14.2). The 'Nodes and Networks' charts animate the process of finding ways to maximise the productive use of material flows through developing connections between elements in the landscape (see Figure 14.3). Along with careful attention to how clusters of elements are designed, this process helps participants apply the principle 'stacking in space and time'. The consideration of different types of flows of materials allows participants to develop designs in which technical nutrients (any non-biodegradable materials, such as metals, persistent plastics) can be re-used and are not wasted and biological nutrients (materials that can be composted) are kept free of contaminants to that they can be returned safely to the soil at the end of their use (e.g. McDonough and Braungart, 2002). Thinking of resource flows in this way helps participants apply the principle: 'cycling of energy and materials'.

Using maps and surveys, there is a parallel consideration of the spatial configuration of resources, including the networks of hydrological systems and existing ecosystems in the area under consideration. The metaphor of 'Nodes and Networks' is used to help participants to analyse the key spatial connections in the landscapes and the areas (nodes) where there are high concentrations of cultural and ecological value. These are seen as dynamic, emergent properties of change over time. As Forman (1998, p. 445) suggests 'Natural patterns and forms result from a geomorphic template on which natural flows and natural disturbances take place'. These templates of natural form offer a valuable basis for thinking of the location of elements within the design, in order to enable natural ecosystems to continue to function effectively in the landscape.

Figure 14.3 Participants using a 'Nodes and Networks' template

This can be illustrated with the example of ecological approaches to flood risk management, as opposed to 'hard engineering' solutions. There is an increased awareness of the value of attempting to restore rivers to as natural a state as possible, for reduced flood damage, habitat and wildlife gains and as well as for aesthetic value (e.g. Riley, 1998). A realisation of the unintended consequences of engineered approaches to river management has led to a more humble, precautionary approach in many professional quarters, in which '*the dangers of intervening unnecessarily to manipulate the water environment*' are acknowledged (Newson, 1997, p. 14). In particular, this approach requires a longer time scale for planning, and an awareness of geological change and ecological resilience, as opposed to simply human induced change, in the landscape (Forman, 1998). DesignWays encourages participants to design new elements in the landscape in such a way as to allow natural systems and human systems to adapt and change over time as much as possible.

The concept of '**D**esigning Edge' in the DNA Framework helps to clarify the relationships between design options and the 'whole system'. Every element is embedded in a whole; it cannot exist without the whole. Each element, however, has an edge, an area which can be seen as the transition from the organism itself as an entity and its context. It is defined as an entity through the interaction of this edge with the larger whole of which it is a part, whilst still maintaining its own identity, despite possible exchanges of matter and information between the organism and the wider environment (Capra, 2002, p. 7).

In DesignWays, participants are encouraged to think about the identity of the various systems they are designing, to ask, 'what are the essential features and attributes they wish to conserve in any future design'. This involves thinking of the historical development of the system and in relationship to future goals for sustainability. This understanding is seen as essential for allowing the character and context of a particular place to be allowed to develop, instead of imposing a blueprint idea of a sustainable future onto places. In this way, the context of the place and its history can be taken into account in any plan. The importance of managing for the 'context for whole ecosystem functions' is emphasised in Allen, Tainter and Hoekstra's (2003, p. 14) book, *Supply-side Sustainability*.

An essential process in systems thinking is ascribing boundaries around the systems to be discussed. This has been criticised as an artificial imposition, as the boundaries are inherently human constructs and do not actually exist in the phenomenon themselves. Zchichang (2007, p. 461) addresses this criticism, stating 'If there is any hint for the future, that is the past and present conversations of the community. Sometimes, it even does not matter much whether the boundaries we draw are wrong, so long as they give us the confidence and the sense of purpose to act'. Thus a cognitive tool, that of drawing boundaries around systems for the purpose of learning and planning, is useful in creating plans for action, as long as there is a realisation that these boundaries are only heuristic concepts, and should be subject to critical discussion.

In a similar vein, no matter how well thought through a design process is, we need to take a humble approach to the realisation of ideas that are developed in any design process. The concept of emergence in complexity theory refers to 'the appearance of patterns, structures, or properties that cannot be adequately explained by referring only to the system's pre-existing components and their interactions' (Huaxia, 2007, p. 431). Not only can we not know exactly what the impacts of design ideas will be on the system, we do not know how the different parts of a system will interact to produce new, emergent properties. This can include changes in people's perceptions and goals as a plan is implemented, and people have new experiences with the changed environment.

Accepting that unpredictability and change are the norm does not have to stop us from trying to develop and implement new concepts for the future, rather it is an appropriate response to do this in a way that recognises emergence and allows for the unexpected. Discussing new approaches to management in the light of complexity theory, Axelrood and Cohen (1999, p. xvi) suggest 'in return for accepting complexity, we have a more systematic approach to harnessing it'.

A design process needs to be seen as a learning system, with an inbuilt process to allow for changes in response to reflections upon action. In DesignWays, the process is seen as a cycle. This idea of a cycle of learning was inspired by Holling's (1978/1986) concept of adaptive management, recognising that surprise and complexity require a constant process of learning in attempt to 'manage' natural systems. There should be regular periods of reflection, when the effects of the changes that have been made are assessed, and questions about the direction of the plan and the overall goals are asked. It is this linking together of the design and adaptive management of implementation that makes DesignWays a planning process. A cycle of reflection is built into the metaphor of the water cycle, through the image of transpiration, which rejuvenates the water cycle and keeps it flowing.

The DNA Framework provides a practical way to apply ecological design principles to spatial planning. The process through which it is applied encourages participants to explore their own understandings and to stretch these to new ways of thinking about whole systems. The metaphors help participants to understand their locales and the relationship between human and natural systems in new ways, as illustrated in the following quote:

> I think it was very effective in [helping people link between different areas], because you often don't think about something being linked to something else, like when we were doing the flow exercise, and the DNA ones at the end, where you had things coming in and all the arrows going across linking to each other (Community Liaison Officer at City Council, 2003).

14.8 Discussion

The metaphors and principles used in DesignWays are not claimed to be absolute truths, or a description of how nature *is*, but rather to represent a shift in understanding of how we interact with the environment. The underlying principles of this process represent a useful framework for action. It strives to incorporate what Lakoff and Johnson (1999) term 'stable truths' in a context of social construction of meaning.

The value of learning through 'holistic gestalts', and the way that experts are able to access such 'whole' impressions through intuition and bodily experience, was recognised by Dreyfus and Dreyfus (2000) in their analysis of the nature of learning. In their critique of analytical philosophy and the concept of 'disembodied realism', Lakoff and Johnson suggest that our responses to the physical environment allows for exploration of shared truths. They suggest that because 'our conceptual system is grounded in, neurally makes use of, and is crucially shaped by, our perceptual and motor systems', we are able to construct metaphors from basic physical experience of the world. These metaphors enable us to communicate about this world (Lakoff and Johnson, 1999, p. 55). They suggest that metaphorical thought allows a rich and evocative means of constructing higher-level thought and abstraction. This epistemology suggests that ways of thinking are to an extent structured by the evolutionary adaptation of organisms living in the physical environment.

We posit that it is possible to communicate about sustainability because of some very basic similarities we share as biological organisms. No matter how advanced human technologies become, we still need to eat and to drink clean water. To date, no substitutes have been found for the action of ecosystems in creating fresh water reserves on land and the recharging of aquifers, nor for the capacity of plants to turn sunlight into carbohydrates on a scale large enough to provide food for the human population. The value of these essential ecosystem services has been valued at a minimum of US$33 trillion per year, in a year when the global gross national product was US$18 trillion (Constanza et al., 1997). Humans are reliant on the workings of ecosystems for our well-being. The challenge is how to think of our settlements as ecosystems, so that they are integrated with, rather than disrupting, these ecosystem services. This chapter has discussed the relationship between such a change and the metaphorical structuring of thought.

The process of industrialisation and urbanisation has cut across the connection between people and nature. If we are to develop new possibilities for ecologically sustainable human settlements, we will need new metaphors for design. The metaphor of the machine has underpinned much of our thinking about design and planning. The underlying metaphor of the ecological design approach outlined in this chapter is that of an ecosystem. Advances in the science of dynamic systems, including complexity theory, provide an opportunity to '*learn from the principles involved as they apply to various circumstances*' (O'Riordan 2000, p. 16). There needs to be a continuous process of questioning the underlying conceptual models, which can be stimulated by such application in different contexts. Thus we can improve both the usefulness of the constructs in achieving more sustainable development, at the same time as contributing to our understanding of the principles and constructs of dynamic systems themselves.

14.9 Conclusion

> The environment is not an 'other' to us. It is not a collection of things that we encounter, rather, it is part of our being. It is the locus of our existence and identity. We cannot and do not exist apart from it (Lakoff and Johnson, 1999).

Systems which are open to a flow of energy, information and materials self- organise in unpredictable ways, dependent on the interaction of the parts, and on the context in which this interaction takes place (Kay et al., 1999). Human settlements and the systems that are the subject of planning display complex behaviour, where the interactions of the parts produce emergent properties and display unpredictable behaviours.

Ecological design can be seen as a normative process, in which attributes commonly ascribed to natural systems, such as resilience, diversity, and adaptive capacity, are seen as desirable attributes for human designed systems to emulate. A lack of absolute certainty in science, especially when dealing with complex systems, has been highlighted recently by discussions about the possible effects of the rise in greenhouse gases. This impossibility of predicting outcomes with absolute certainty is recognised in the term 'irreducible uncertainty' (Funtowicz and Ravetz, 1994). An increased understanding of the unpredictable nature of change, emerging from the interaction of many agents and elements, shows that it is not possible to 'regenerate' an area through applying a formula or imposing a development plan. A process of participatory ecological planning cannot guarantee any particular outcome. It is only possible to create the conditions in which regeneration and sustainable development might flourish.

Each ecosystem develops in relationship to the context of the place, and is both affected by, and affects, its surroundings. Life is not simply an accident on inert rock. Living organisms are engaged in a dynamic interplay of matter and energy, a sun-driven dance that connects rock, water and atmosphere. There is a tendency towards a self-organising state, embodying resilience. This research represented an attempt to test the metaphor of ecosystems in participatory planning as a tool for social learning. The research on which this chapter draws suggests that a participatory process animated through a living systems paradigm can contribute to development of more integrated, ecologically sound plans. It does this through increasing participants' capacity to 'think like an ecosystem' and to see connections between their actions and the wider context. A participatory planning process that has ecological metaphors embedded in its language and tools can help create the conditions for people to consider new alternatives. If this planning is seen as a cycle of learning, such that changes in the system give rise to reflection on the change and the trajectory of the development, it can help create the conditions for sustainable regeneration.

Acknowledgements

The research that informed this writing was supported by The Economic and Social Research Council (awards PTA-026-27-0068 and S42200124048), Mersey Basin Campaign and Newlands (Forestry Commission and North West Development Agency). Many people contributed their time and insights, and we would like to thank in particular Professor John Handley and Joe Ravetz at the University of Manchester and Walter Menzies at the Mersey Basin Campaign.

References

Allen, T.F.H. and Hoekstra, T.W. (1992) *Toward a Unified Ecology*, Columbia University Press, New York.

Allen, T.F.H., Tainter, J.A. and Hoekstra, T.W. (2003) *Supply-Side Sustainability*, Columbia University Press, New York.

Allen, W., Kilvington, M. and Horn, C. (2002) 'Using participatory and learning-based approaches for environmental management to help achieve constructive behaviour change', Contract Report LC0102/057, Landcare Research, Ministry for the Environment, Lincoln, New Zealand, http://www.landcareresearch.co.nz/research/ social/par_rep.asp.

Axelrood, R. and Cohen, M.D. (1999) *Harnessing Complexity: Organizational Implications for a Scientific Frontier*, Free Press, New York.

Bass, R. and Herson, A. (2000) 'SEA of water management plans and programs: Lessons from California', in M. Partidario and R. Clark (eds.), *Perspectives on Strategic Environmental Assessment*, Lewis Publishers, Boca Raton, Florida.

Bateson, G. (1972) *Steps to an Ecology of Mind*, Ballantine Books, New York.

Berkes, F., Colding, J. and Folke, C. (2003) *Navigating Social-Ecological Systems, Building Resilience for Complexity and Change*, Cambridge University Press, Cambridge.

Botkin, D. (1990) *Discordant Harmonies: A New Ecology for the 21st Century*, Oxford University Press, Oxford.

Brooke, C. (2000) 'Strategic EA and water resource planning in Europe', in M. Partidario and R. Clark (eds.), *Perspectives on Strategic Environmental Assessment*, Lewis Publishers, Boca Raton, Florida.

Capra, F. (1982) *The Turning Point: Science, Society, and the Rising Culture*, Simon and Schuster, New York.

Capra, F. (1996) *The Web of Life*, Anchor Books, New York.

Capra, F. (2002) *The Hidden Connections: Integrating the Biological, Cognitive and Social Dimensions of Life into a Science of Sustainability*, Doubleday, New York.

Carpenter, R.A. (1995) 'Limitations in measuring ecosystem sustainability', in T.C. Trzyna (ed.), *A Sustainable World: Defining and Measuring Sustainable Development*, Published for IUCN – The World Conservation Union by the International Center for the Environment and Public Policy, Sacramento and Claremont, pp. 175-197.

Carson, R. (1962) *Silent Spring*, Fawcett Crest, New York.

Centre for Urban and Regional Ecology (2007) *Constitution and Modus Operandi*, available at http://www.sed.manchester.ac.uk/research/cure/.

Chambers, R. (1994) 'The origins and practice of participatory rural appraisal', *World Development*, vol. 22(7), pp. 953-969.

Checkland, P. (1992) 'Systems and scholarship: The need to do better', *Journal of the Operational Research Society*, vol. 43(11), pp. 1023-1030.

Commoner, B. (1992) *Making Peace With the Planet*, New Press, New York.

Community Liaison Officer at City Council (2003) Interview by Author, Manchester.

Constanza, R., Arge, R. d', Groot, R. de, Farber, S., Grasso, M., Hannon, B., Limburg, K., Naeem, R., O'Neill, J., Paruelo, J., Raskin, R., Sutton, P. and Belt, M. van den (1997) 'The value of the world's ecosystem services and natural capital', *Nature*, vol. 387(6230), pp. 253-260.

Coveney, P. and Highfield, R. (1991) *The Arrow of Time*, Flamingo, London.

Creative Director of Countryscape (2003) Interview by Author, Manchester.

Decleris, M. (2000) 'The law of sustainable development: General principles, A report produced for the European Commission', European Commission, Environment Directorate-General, Luxembourg, Belgium, p. 147, http://europa.eu.int/comm/environment/pubs/home.html.

Delin, S. (1979) *What is the Energy Crisis? A Systems Analysis*, National Swedish Board for Energy Source Development, Stockholm.

De Rosnay, J. (1975) *Macroscope: A New World Scientific System*, Harper & Row, New York.

Dewey, J. (1925) *Experience and Nature*, Open Court Publishing Company, Chicago.

Dewey, J. (1937) 'The democratic form, an address before the National Educational Association', *School and Society*, February 22, 1937.

Dewey, J. (1954) *The Public and its Problems*, Ohio University Press, Athens.

Diamond, J. (2005) *Collapse: How Societies Choose to Fail or Survive*, Penguin, London.

Doppelt, B. (2003) *Leading Change Toward Sustainability: A Change-Management Guide for Business, Government and Civil Society*, Greenleaf, Sheffield.

Dreyfus, H.L. and Dreyfus, S.E. (2000) *Mind Over Machine: The Power of Human Intuition and Expertise in the Era of the Computer*, Free Press, New York.

European Commission (2000) 'Directive 2000/60/EC of the European Parliament and of the Council of 23 October 2000 establishing a framework for Community action in the field of water policy', *Official Journal* L 327, December 22 2000, pp. 1-73, http://europa.eu.int/ comm/environment/water/water-framework/index_en.html.

Farmer, J. (1996) *Green Shift, Towards a Green Sensibility in Architecture*, Butterworth Heinemann, Oxford.

Fletcher, K.T. and Goggin, P.A. (2001) 'The dominant stances on ecodesign: A critique', *Design Issues*, vol. 17(3), pp. 15-25.

Forman, R.T.T. (1998) *Land Mosaics, The Ecology of Landscapes and Regions*, Cambridge University Press, Cambridge.

Fuller, R.B. (1969) *Operating Manual for Spaceship Earth*, Pocket Books, New York.

Funtowicz, S. and Ravetz, J.R. (1994) 'The worth of a songbird: Ecological economics as a post-normal science', *Ecological Economics*, vol. 10(9), pp. 197-207.

George, C. (1999) 'Testing for sustainable development through environmental assessment', *Environmental Impact Assessment Review*, vol. 19, pp. 175-200.

Gibson, T. (1996) *The Power in Our Hands: Neighbourhood-based World Shaking*, John Carpenter, Oxford.

Handley, J.F., Griffiths, E.J., Hill, S.L. and Howe, J.M. (1998) 'Land restoration using an ecologically informed and participative approach', in Fox, Moore and McIntosh (eds.), *Land Reclamation: Achieving Sustainable Benefits*, Balkema, Rotterdam.

Havel, V. (1994) *Acceptance Speech: The Philadelphia Liberty Medal, Philadelphia, July 4, 1994*, viewed September 12, 2002, available at http://www.hrad.cz/president/ Havel/speeches/1994/0407_uk.html.

Heisenberg, W. (1962) *Physics and Philosophy*, Harper and Row, New York.

Holling, C.S. (1978) *Adaptive Environmental Assessment and Management*, John Wiley and Sons, Chichester.

Holling, C.S. (1986) 'The resilience of terrestrial ecosystems: Local surprise and global change', in W.C. Clark and R.E. Munn (eds.), *Sustainable Development of the Biosphere*, Cambridge University Press, Cambridge.

Holmberg, J. (1998) 'Backcasting: A natural step in operationalising sustainable development', *Green Management International: The Journal of Corporate Environmental Strategy and Practice*, vol. 23, pp. 30-51.

Holmgren, D. (2003) *Permaculture: Principles and Pathways Beyond Sustainability*, Holmgren Design Services, Hepburn Springs.

Huaxia, Z. (2007) 'Exploring dynamics of emergence', *Systems Research and Behavioral Science*, vol. 24(4), pp. 431-443.

Illich, I. (1987) *Tools for Conviviality*, Heyday Books, Berkeley.

Innes, J.E. and Booher, D.E. (1999) 'Metropolitan development as a complex system: A new approach to sustainability', *Economic Development Quarterly*, vol. 13(2), pp. 141-156.

Innes, J.E. and Booher, D.E. (2000) 'Indicators for sustainable communities: A strategy building on Complexity Theory and Distributed Intelligence', *Planning Theory and Practice*, vol. 1(2), pp. 173-186.

Ison, R.L. (1998) 'The future challenge: The search for system', 9th Australian Agronomy Conference, The Regional Institute Ltd., Wagga Wagga, viewed August 12 2003, available at http://www.regional.org.au/au/asa/1998/plenary/ison.html.

Kay, J., Regier, H.A., Boyle, M. and Francis, G. (1999) 'An ecosystem approach for sustainability: Addressing the challenge of complexity', *Futures*, vol. 31(7), pp. 721-742.

Koestler, A. (1969) 'Beyond atomism and holism: The concept of the Holon', in A. Koestler and J.R. Smithies (eds.), *Beyond Reductionism: New Perspectives in the Life Sciences*, Hutchinson, London, pp. 192-216.

Lakoff, G. and Johnson, M. (1980) *Metaphors We Live By*, University of Chicago Press, Chicago.

Lakoff, G. and Johnson, M. (1999) *Philosophy in the Flesh, The Embodied Mind and its Challenge to Western Thought*, Basic Books, New York.

Leopold, A. (1968) *A Sand County Almanac and Sketches Here and There*, Oxford University Press, London.

Lewis, P.H. (1996) *Tomorrow by Design, Regional Design Process for Sustainability*, John Wiley and Sons, New York.

Lovelock, J. (1991) *Gaia, The Practical Science of Planetary Medicine*, Gaia Books Ltd., London.

Luz, F. (2000) 'Participatory landscape ecology: A basis for acceptance and implementation', *Landscape and Urban Planning*, vol. 50(1-3), pp. 157-166.

Margulis, L. and Sagan, D. (1987) *Microcosmos*, Allen and Unwin, London.

Maturana, H. (1992) *Autopoiesis, Structural Coupling and Cognition: A History of These and Other Notions in the Biology of Cognition*, viewed January 18, 2004, available at http://web.matriztica.org/555/article-28335.html.

Maturana, H. and Varela, F. (1987) *The Tree of Knowledge*, Shambhala Publications, Boston.

McDonough, B. and Braungart, M. (2002) *Cradle to Cradle: Remaking the Way We Make Things*, North Point Press, New York.

McHarg, I. (1992) *Design with Nature*, John Wiley and Sons, New York.

Mebratu, D. (1998) 'Sustainability and sustainable development: Historical and conceptual review', *Environmental Impact Assessment Review*, vol. 18, pp. 493-520.

Millennium Ecosystem Assessment (2005) *Ecosystems and Human Well-being: Synthesis*, Island Press, Washington.

Miller, J.G. (1995) *Living Systems*, University of Colorado Press, Niwot.

Mingers, J. and Taylor, S. (1992) 'The use of soft systems methodology in practice', *Journal of Operational Research*, vol. 43(4), pp. 321-332.

Mollison, B. (1990) *Permaculture, A Practical Guide for a Sustainable Future*, Island Press, Washington.

Morgan, G. (1997) *Images of Organization*, Sage Publications, Thousand Oaks.

Myers, N., Myers, N.J. and Simon, J.L. (1994) *Scarcity or Abundance? A Debate on the Environment*, W.W. Norton and Co., New York/London.

Ndubisi, F. (2002) *Ecological Planning: A Historical and Comparative Synthesis*, Johns Hopkins University Press, Baltimore.

Newson, M. (1997) 'Time, scale and change in river landscapes: The jerky conveyor belt', *Landscape Research*, vol. 22(1), pp. 13-23.

O'Riordan, T. (1998) 'Civic science and the sustainability transition', in D. Warburton (ed.), *Community and Sustainable Development*, Earthscan, London, pp. 96-115.

O'Riordan, T. (2000) 'Environmental science on the move', in T. O'Riordan (ed.), *Environmental Science for Environmental Management*, Prentice Hall, London, pp. 1-28.

Office of the Deputy Prime Minster (2005) Planning Policy Statement Number 1 - Delivering Sustainable Development. London, http://www.odpm.gov.uk/stellent/groups/odpm_planning/documents/downloadable/odpm_plan_034815.pdf.

Ornstein, R. and Ehrlich, R. (1995) *New World New Mind*, Doubleday, New York.

Owens, S., Petts, J. and Bulkeley, H. (2006) 'Boundary work: Knowledge, policy, and the urban environment', *Environment and Planning C: Government and Policy*, vol. 24(5), pp. 633-643.

Papanek, V. (1995) *The Green Imperative: Ecology and Ethics in Design and Architecture*, Thames and Hudson, London.

Portugali, J. (2000) *Self-Organization and the City*, Springer Verlag, Berlin.

Prigogine, I. (1997) 'Non-linear science and the laws of nature', *Journal of the Franklin Institute*, vol. 334(5-6), pp. 745-758.

Pulliam, H.R. (2002) 'Ecology's new paradigm: What does it offer designers and planners?', in B.R. Johnson and K. Hill (eds.), *Ecology and Design, Frameworks for Learning*, Island Press, Washington, pp. 51-84.

Ravetz, J.R. (1997) 'The science of "what-if"?', *Futures*, vol. 29(6), pp. 533-539.

Rayner, S. (2002) 'We know enough', viewed September 2, 2002, available at http://education.guardian.co.uk/higher/sciences/story/0,12243,784962,00.html.

Riley, A. (1998) *Restoring Streams in Cities: A Guide for Planners, Policymakers, and Citizens*, Island Press, Washington.

Robert, K.H., Schmidt-Bleek, B., Aloisi de Larderel, J., Basile, G., Jansen, J.L., Kuehr, R., Price Thomas, P., Suzuki, M., Hawken, P. and Wackernagel, M. (2002) 'Strategic sustainable development: Selection, design and synergies of applied tools', *Journal of Cleaner Production*, vol. 10(3), pp. 197-214.

Rowe, S.J. (2000) 'An earth-based ethic for humanity', *Natur und Kultur: Transdisciplinare Zeitschrift fur Okologische Nachhaltigkeit*, vol. 1(2), pp. 106-120.

Schumacher, E.F. (1973) *Small is Beautiful: Economics as if People Mattered*, Blond and Briggs, London.

Tacconi, L. (1998) 'Scientific methodology for ecological economics', *Ecological Economics*, vol. 27, pp. 91-105.

Tippett, J. (1994) 'A pattern language of sustainability', B.A. thesis, submitted to the Bachelor of Arts Dissertation submitted to the Department of Independent Studies, Lancaster University, available at http://www.holocene.net/dissertation.html.

Tippett, J. (2004) 'A participatory protocol for ecologically informed design within river catchments', thesis submitted to PhD Dissertation, submitted to the School of Planning and Landscape, University of Manchester, Manchester, 537, available at http://www.holocene.net/research/phd.html.

Tippett, J. (2005a) 'Participatory planning in river catchments, an innovative toolkit tested in Southern Africa and North West England', *Water Science and Technology*, vol. 52(9), pp. 95-105.

Tippett, J. (2005b) '"Think like an ecosystem": Embedding a living system paradigm into participatory planning', *Systemic Practice and Action Research*, vol. 17(6), pp. 603-622.

Tippett, J., Handley, J.F. and Ravetz, J. (2007) 'Meeting the challenges Of sustainable development: A conceptual appraisal of a new methodology for participatory ecological planning', *Progress in Planning*, vol. 67(1).

Tognetti, S.S. (1999) 'Science in a double bind: Gregory Bateson and the origins of post normal science', *Futures*, vol. 31, pp. 689-703.

Tyson, J.M. (1995) '*Quo Vadis*: Sustainability?', *Water Science and Technology*, vol. 32(5-6), pp. 1-5.

UN ECE (1998) 'Convention on access to Information, public participation in decision making and access to justice in environmental matters', ECE/CEP/43, entry into force 30 October 2001, United Nations Economic Commission for Europe, Aarhus, http://www.unece.org/env/pp/.

United Nations (1992) 'Report of the United Nations Conference on the Environment and Development', UNCED Report A/Conf.151/15/Rev.1, United Nations, New York.

Verheem, R. (2000) 'The use of SEA and EIA in decision making on drinking water management and production in the Netherlands', in M. Partidario and R. Clark (eds.), *Perspectives on Strategic Environmental Assessment*, Lewis Publishers, Florida.

Webster, C.J. and Lai., L.W.C. (2003) *Property Rights, Planning, and Markets: Managing Spontaneous Cities,* Edward Elgar Publishing, Cheltenham.

Wheeler, D.P. (1990) *EPA Journal*, http://www.epa.gov/Region2/library/quotes.htm.

Wood, R. and Handley, J.F. (1999) 'Urban waterfront regeneration in the Mersey basin, North West England', *Journal of Environmental Planning and Management: Policy and Practice*, vol. 42(4), pp. 565-580.

World Commission on Environment and Development (1987) *Brundtland Commission Report, Our Common Future*, Oxford University Press, Oxford.

Zchichang, Z. (2007) 'Complexity science, systems thinking and pragamatic sensibility', *Systems Research and Behavioral Science*, vol. 24(4), pp. 445-464.

Chapter 15
Rethinking Brownfields: Discourses, Networks and Space-Time

Nikos Karadimitriou, Joe Doak and Elisabete Cidre[1]

This chapter argues that the current UK policy fixation on brownfield redevelopment is built on a particular conceptualisation of the land redevelopment process which intertwines the economic logic of neo-liberalism with the emphasis placed on environmental efficiency by proponents of sustainable development. By focusing on the heritage dimension of brownfield redevelopment, the chapter notes the apparent conceptual contradictions of policy discourses. In the same way that certain sites are deemed ripe for redevelopment as 'Previously Developed Land', certain other sites are deemed as worth preserving as 'Heritage'.

The chapter explores the economic logic underlying this apparent contradiction and conceptualises policy discourse formulation as an outcome of the interactions of socio-spatial webs of interacting actors whose communicative interaction gives rise to meanings, attached to spaces. Therefore, land development and redevelopment can be seen as a complex dynamic social and temporal network process that creates and uses places and physical structures 'inscribed' into time and space. By exploring the evolving socio-spatial relations attaching meaning to space the chapter highlights the contingencies of spatial planning and the fragile role of planners in their efforts to mediate spatial change.

15.1 Introduction

It has been more than a decade since the redevelopment of previously developed land assumed a central role in Britain's urban policy. This shift was based on the argument that by re-using brownfield land government policy is simultaneously achieving multiple environmental, social and economic goals with the minimum cost. Although this argument has not been without criticism the view that the redevelopment of previously developed land is a sustainable approach to urban development is now dominant. The question then is how can the political, social

---

1 Dr. Nikos Karadimitrou is Lecturer at the Bartlett School of Planning, University College London, UK. Joe Doak is Senior Lecturer at the Department of Real Estate and Planning, University of Reading. Elisabete Cidre is Postgraduate Teaching Assistant at the Barlett School of Planning, University College London, UK.

and spatial dynamics of sustainable brownfield redevelopment be understood within the context of the complex set of interactions generated between actors with sometimes conflicting interests?

This chapter will go about answering this question by examining the relationships between space, time, networks, brownfields and heritage. Based on Luhman's ideas (1990) it will conceptualise the discursive construction of brownfields and heritage as an emergent quality of actor interactions that generate meanings and will explore the subsequent discursive legitimation of brownfield redevelopment and heritage preservation. The 'brownfields vs. greenfields' debate and the sustainability discourse that is underpinning it resonates of '[...] the deliberations, strategies, tactics and devices employed by authorities for making up and acting upon a population and its constituents' (Rose, 1996). In their attempt to make this possible, authorities often construct concepts and discursively position them in dialectic relationship to each other, this construction helps to highlight the appropriateness of the proposed action or to frame the debate in a way that will facilitate further action.

We will treat brownfield redevelopment and heritage preservation in terms of Massey's (2005, p. 122) spatial-temporal stabilisation. Brownfields, lately more revealingly referred to in literature as Previously Developed Land (PDL), are discursively constructed as 'surfaces' with a dirty past and devoid of a present (to use Massey's terminology). They are spaces 'emptied' of their history so that they can legitimately be re-discovered and 'conquered'. The historical aspects of heritage sites on the other hand, become pronounced during a similar process of re-discovery. Eventually then we will argue that what drives this process is not so much some intrinsic quality of space itself but the meaning attached to this space by constellations of interacting actors for purposes aligned with their goals and interests. Interestingly, these processes resonate of the approaches pursued in Brenner and Theodore (2002) ultimately relating to Lefebvre's theorisation of capitalism as a spatially embedded process.

Finally we will attempt a redefinition of brownfields in terms of space-time, to recognise that a brownfield site is not an empty vessel but a place where the complex dynamics of varying socio-spatial networks are reflected and reciprocally affected. As such, brownfield sites do possess a past and their present and future is under constant negotiation by human and non-human elements (plants, animals, etc.) alike. The example of heritage highlights not only the contradictions inherent in the conceptualisation of brownfields as dead and empty spaces but also the social re-construction and the re-negotiation of these places. Heritage sites resonate within long and well established discourses emphasising their preservation or evolutive conservation (i.e. mostly in historic urban centres) regardless of their present or future use.

In this chapter we will frame PDL reuse within the context of policy discourses. We will argue then that whereas conceptually brownfields are seen as redevelopable spaces redundant to their original production purpose, heritage sites are associated with culture and consumption aspects which require the preservation of their character in order to generate value. Previous contributions recognise these value generative aspects of the conflict between 'old' and 'new' spaces (see Peck and Tickell, 2002; Weber, 2002) as well as the importance of meaning attached to spaces (Beauregard, 1993). These, in our view, are important aspects underpinning the debates about brownfields and the associated governing processes. Our contribution theorises the processes that generate these meanings as processes of communicative interactions of social systems and focuses on policy discourse formulation as indicative of how this meaning is generated.

Interestingly for planning and planners these processes can also be seen under the lens of 'governing' as defined by Kooiman (2003). Many of the current debates underpinning government policies can be seen as 'establishing a normative foundation' (ibid., p. 4) in order to bridge spatially embedded processes of production and consumption. These processes are generated by public and private actors who sometimes fail to interact or whose interaction is underlined by objectives that may not always be in alignment.

Therefore, the balance between the brownfield and heritage aspects of a site and the subsequent degree of redevelopment and preservation can also be seen as an indication of the particular spatial arrangement that various interacting actors (involved in policy, development, community, etc.) have reached. Examples range from the gasometers in Vienna or Kings Cross; to waterfront urban regeneration in Expo'98 Lisbon and Newcastle; to landmarks like the Tate Modern and Guggenheim Bilbao. What is conceptually interesting in such processes from a planning point of view is the spatially embedded nature of the meaning generating processes previously described. Spatial planning and planners are not isolated from this intersubjective process and its spatial expressions. Indeed in our view planners are immersed into it, actively communicating and thus generating and replicating meanings. As the social systems in which planners participate by definition reduce the complexity of their environment in an attempt to describe it during the process of meaning generation (see Luhman, 1990) so does the planners' responsibility increase in view of the choices at hand.

What is then the scope for planning within this 'brave new conceptual world' where definitions are elusive and where the mere adoption of a term may tilt the balance towards a certain spatial outcome? Here is where our chapter will argue that planning and planners are inevitably embedded in the process of meaning generation, since the mediation of spatial change is also a mediation of the meanings that are attached to those spaces.

Following the introduction the chapter will try to place previously used land within a network-based approach of the production and consumption of space. Consequently, in Section 15.3, the chapter will focus on analysing brownfield policy discourses. Section 15.4 will analyse how the creation and consumption of heritage came about and will attempt a comparison with the PDL discourses. Finally, Section 15.5 will propose to re-conceptualise brownfields as places, as the outcomes of complex sets of network relations, simultaneously belonging to a variety of different socio-spatial 'trajectories', actively created by the planners' efforts to intervene, amongst other things.

15.2 The making and remaking of brownfields: A network perspective

In his examination of social phenomena and material reality Capra (2002) tries to integrate four 'perspectives'. Form (networks), matter (material objects), process (communication) and meaning are all interconnected and 'each contributes significantly to the understanding of a social phenomenon' (ibid., p. 64). Capra agrees with Luhmann (1990/1995) that communicative interactions between the components of social networks are necessary in order to maintain 'coordination of behaviour' and 'create thoughts and meaning, which give rise to further communications' (Capra, 2002, p. 72). Furthermore, communicative systems are 'self-referential' and 'totalising', each 'operating within a world of its own' by '[…] communicating about themselves […] using distinctions that differentiate the observing system from something else' (Luhman, 1990, p. 7). Events disappear but memory, writing, objects 'have their function in preserving – not the events, but their structure-generating power' Luhman continues (ibid., p. 9) and we would add that this capacity is also shared by physical spaces.

These networks also have a material aspect. They 'generate material structures' and 'material goods' which are 'created for a purpose, according to some design, and they embody some meaning' (ibid., p. 73). The interpretation of this meaning relies upon contextualisation, relating it to 'other things in its environment, in its past, or in its future', things like 'concepts, values, beliefs or circumstances' (ibid., p. 73). The importance of meaning is paramount in the function of social networks because human beings act in accordance to the way they understand their environments. Therefore action and meaning in social networks are intertwined, 'the network continually generates mental images, thoughts and meaning on the other hand, it continually co-ordinates the behaviour of its members' (ibid., p. 74) but this behaviour in turn generates new meaning, affecting action, requiring further coordination in a self-generating loop.

The production and consumption of the built environment then, are two aspects of the function of social networks that are engaged in wider processes of resource transformation. This process of transformation of resources for the production of material structures and objects that constitute the built environment is inextricably attached to the creation of images, thoughts and meaning, embodied in buildings, spaces and places.

The key point behind the post-structuralist argument about the relational nature of space is that space does not exist independently, it is constantly re-created and re-negotiated by actors who attach meaning to a material reality (the earth's surface) by their action. At the same time their actions are shaped by the meanings that actors attach to their environments. Time is not 'out there' either. Similarly to space, the physical dimension of time is re-shaped and re-negotiated through human action. Attaching meaning to spaces, turning them into 'places' is in essence a social process, that of the manipulation of space and time. Relevant here are Murdoch's comments (1998, p. 359) on Actor Network Theory as a theory that:

> ... sees spaces and times as emerging from processes and relations, and concerns itself with the topographical textures which arise as relations configure spaces and times.

That eloquent conceptualisation of relational space is enriched with 'a concern with networks' (ibid., p. 359). Murdoch's view of these 'translated spaces', emphasises that *(i)* networks are 'the sets of associations which define and constitute spatial qualities'; *(ii)* spaces are arranged so that certain types of action can be conducted, and thus 'the action in actor-networks configure space'; and *(iii)* these actions, and the relations through which they are conducted, are 'grounded' within these networks which transcend spatial scales (ibid., p. 361).

What one could further argue here is that space and time and social actors are facets of the same thing, a network of relations between human and non-human actors. Social interaction takes place in space and time and therefore inevitably space and time become attributes of the network. Although this relationship might not always be entirely obvious it is particularly apparent in cases where the reasons why the networks were formed are directly related to the transformation of space. These are not only the webs of actors involved in construction but all these networks whose function depends on the physical transformation of space. Most production processes would fall within that category.

We have argued elsewhere (Doak and Karadimitriou, 2007a) on the need to build a 'holistic' or 'integrated' understanding of brownfield redevelopment and how it

> ... could start by recognising that existing 'brownfield' sites are embedded within, and are therefore part and product of, an existing network of actors that draws value and meaning from the land that we call 'brown', 'derelict' or 'unused' (ibid., p. 221).

The concept of 'brownfield development' has arisen within a set of socio-political relationships which have shaped its construction. Recognition that urban policy formulation and implementation is a discursive process involving a range of interest positions has been emphasised by other authors. Atkinson (1999, p. 59) builds his analysis of regeneration partnerships on the contention that,

> ... there is no single authentic mode of assigning meaning to terms such as partnership and empowerment, that their meaning is constructed (i.e. produced and reproduced) in a context of power and domination which privileges official discourse(s) over others.

Tait and Franklin (2002) and Biddulph, Tait and Franklin (2003) approached their analysis of the urban village model through similar processes of discourse construction and reconstruction. Along the same lines Doak and Karadimitriou (2007b, p. 69) also highlighted that:

> The important aspect about this emphasis on discourse construction within a web of social (and other) relations is that these constructs provide the framework within which action takes place and these relations are structured and restructured.

Murdoch (1998) explored how this framing is applied in the material world through the use of technologies and resources.

15.3 The brownfield policy discourse

So, in order to explore the networking processes that construct, reconstruct and materialise the concept of brownfields we need to un-pick the concept somewhat and find out what (and who) constructs the term as it has been developed in government policy and practice. In doing that, we also need to understand how the concept of heritage has taken shape in the construction of official policy discourses. But we begin with deconstructing the term 'brownfield'.

There is a long lineage and an evolving history of the brownfield concept in policy documents. Within these documents and the debates surrounding them, we have identified a number of linked or competing discourses (see also Doak and Karadimitriou, 2007b, p. 69): The Sustainable Brownfield Development/Sustainability Discourse, the Market Generated Brownfield Development/Neo-liberal Discourse, the Negotiated (or Equitable) Brownfield Development/Participatory Discourse, the Organisationally Efficient Brownfield Development/Managerial Discourse and the Technically Efficient Brownfield Development/Scientific Discourse.

We focus our attention on the two dominant discourses (sustainability and neo-liberalism) and concentrate on two of the key UK policy documents: PPG 3[2] (DETR, 2000) and The Sustainable Communities Plan (ODPM, 2003).

Sustainable brownfield development: The sustainability discourse

The discourse (or 'discourses') of sustainable development had already entered, and structured planning policy when the new era of brownfield development took off in the mid-1990s (Doak, 2004). It is significant that the priority placed on brownfield redevelopment by the previous Conservative administration, quickly became a surrogate concept for sustainable forms of urban development. What

2 Planning Policy Guidance (PPG), a policy instrument particular to the UK, providing central government guidance on planning matters.

is also significant is that this discourse was influenced by the well-organised and proactive countryside conservation lobby (fronted by the CPRE)[3] which could be viewed as a relatively coherent and self-differentiated network of agents promoting a specific agenda. The Labour Government that followed the Conservatives helped construct a policy framework that was summarised by Nick Raynsford as 'brownfield first, greenfield second' (2000, p. 262). As Murdoch suggests (2004, p. 53):

> The new political rationality that came to dominate the planning for housing arena in the late 1990s effectively involved the rather selective appropriation of elements within the sustainability discourse by CPRE and central government. Sustainability was now interpreted not in its usual sense as a balancing of economic, social and environmental criteria with the development process but rather as the re-development of already-developed land.

This narrowing-down of sustainability is clearly evident in the 2000 version of PPG 3 when it offers guidance, 'to promote more sustainable patterns of development and make better use of previously-developed land', in which 'the focus for additional housing should be existing towns and cities'. The emphasis on re-using brownfield sites is consistently used as the touchstone of sustainability. The main policy statement about housing land-release is clear that:

> The Government is committed to promoting more sustainable patterns of development, by:
>
> *(i)* concentrating most additional housing development within urban areas;
> *(ii)* making more efficient use of land by maximising the re-use of previously-developed land and the conversion and re-use of existing buildings;
> *(iii)* assessing the capacity of urban areas to accommodate more housing;
> *(iv)* adopting a sequential approach to the allocation of land for housing development;
> *(v)* managing the release of housing land and;
> *(vi)* reviewing existing allocations of housing land in plans, and planning permissions when they come up for renewal (DETR, 2000, para. 21).

Although the efficient use of land dominates the guidance note, other sustainability concerns such as the greening of the development process, public transport provision and the conservation of heritage and ecological resources are included in PPG 3. However, they do not receive the same kind of emphasis and are treated as subsidiary additions to the main policy criteria of reusing previously developed land. This is also reflected in the way in which the policy for housing development

3 Campaign to Protect Rural England (CPRE), formerly known as Council for the Protection of Rural England.

was to be taken forward into implementation or, as Murdoch suggests, materialised through 'governmental technologies'.

Urban capacity study were the main planning technique (or 'technology') advocated in the guidance note to secure the aims of sustainable development. Arising from earlier work on environmental capacity studies developed by an emerging network of environmental consultants, environmental pressure groups (including the CPRE and FoE[4]) and some proactive local planning authorities (see Jacobs, 1993 and West Sussex CC, 1992), this required local authorities to identify and quantify previously developed sites in their (urban) areas that could accommodate new housing development. As Murdoch shows in his study of the use of this technology, local authorities have been able to bend the technique in various ways to bring the findings more in line with local political priorities. In terms of theory, it illustrates that:

> The operation of the capacity study is part of a network-building process, one that ties the deliberations of central policymakers to the many urban sites that are to be enrolled into the planning-for-housing process. In effect, the capacity study allows the government network to place a (particular kind of) 'sustainability frame' around local development decisions.

But also:

> By selectively appropriating elements of the guide, local planning decision makers can steer their conduct in line with local, rather than national, sensibilities (Murdoch, 2004, p. 55).

Of course, urban capacity studies are not the only technology of governance constructed to take forward the discourses of sustainability. Other examples, with their own actor-networks of construction and implementation, include: environmental impact assessment; sustainability appraisal; the listing of historic buildings; the designation of ecological or heritage areas or sites; environmental audits; the application of sustainability indicators; the BRE's Environmental Appraisal Method; and life cycle analysis. Indeed there is some indication that some of these technologies are 'competing' with urban capacity studies in more recent government legislation and guidance (for example, the 2004 Planning and Compensation Act's requirement that local planning authorities undertake sustainability appraisals of the new Regional Spatial Strategies and Local Development Frameworks). So the discourse of sustainability is in a constant process of construction, stabilisation and (re)construction, aided and abetted by various technologies of governance. However, in the same way that sustainability is a product of many sub-discourses, so too that of 'brownfield development'. The

4 Friends of the Earth.

greenness of sustainability is not the only colour that contributes to the brownness of previously developed land.

Market generated brownfield development: The neo-liberal discourse(s)

The importance of the development industry and market processes to the delivery brownfield development shapes the policy discourse in many, often imperceptible, ways. When emphasis is placed on ideas of economic utility, market demand, private sector involvement, the polluter pays principle, promotion of owner-occupied housing or cost minimisation, it indicates the pervasiveness of the market in structuring the processes of brownfield redevelopment.

The neo-liberal project of (re)introducing the market into public policy making and implementation is well-acknowledged (see Brenner and Theodore, 2002). Numerous contributions describe neo-liberal strategies seeking to: promote competition; reduce the role of law and the state; privatise public services; introduce quasi market criteria into the remaining areas of the public sector; free international patterns of trade; and increase consumer choice (and reduce or keep down taxation). The 'rolling-back' of the state under Margaret Thatcher has been restructured into a softer, but equally pervasive, 'rolling-out' of neo-liberal ideas and technologies by the Blair governments during the last decade. The construction of the policies and tools for brownfield development has indeed been part of this process.

In its various guises since the mid-1980s (and in other Government Circulars before that date) PPG 3 has consistently been about making sure that the planning system provides land for housing 'in the right place and at the right time' (DETR, 2000, para. 3). As the private house-building industry is (or has become) the dominant producer of that housing, so market-based principles and interests have been incorporated into the guidance. However, the sustainability discourse outlined above provides a major challenge to the house-building industry as it seeks to cut-off or severely reduce the supply of greenfield land, which has been the mainstay of the industry since the planning system was established. What we finally get therefore is a hybrid; a combination of neo-liberalism and other discourses, the most significant of these being 'sustainability'.

Given the apparent 'policy switch' implied by the pro-brownfield strategy, it is interesting to find regular references to the role of brownfield regeneration in supporting continued economic growth (a suitably neo-liberal principle[5] now enshrined in the UK Sustainable Development Strategy). In a statement that perfectly illustrates the coming together of the two discourses, PPG 3 says:

> The aim is to provide a choice of sites which are both suitable and available for house building. This is important not only to ensure that everyone has the

5 As opposed to the concept of 'sustainable economic development', which is advocated by members of the environmental movement.

> opportunity of a decent home but also to maintain the momentum of economic growth. Economic growth should not be frustrated by a lack of homes for those wishing to take up new employment opportunities: but to promote sustainable development, the need for economic growth has to be reconciled with social and environmental considerations, particularly those of conserving and enhancing the quality of our environment in both town and country (DETR, 2000, para. 3).

Interestingly, one of the 'old' technologies used to maintain housing land supply for house building has been retained in the new version of the PPG; that of 'housing land availability studies', which were introduced in the late 1970s to secure an immediate supply of identified (and market tested) housing sites. This is back-up by the policy that:

> Sufficient sites should be shown on the (local) plan's proposals map to accommodate at least the first five years (or the first two phases) of housing development proposed in the plan. Site allocations should be reviewed and updated as the plan is reviewed and rolled forward at least every five years. Local planning authorities should monitor closely the uptake of both previously-developed and greenfield sites and should be prepared to alter or revise their plan policies in the light of that monitoring. However, it is essential that the operation of the development process is not prejudiced by unreal expectations of the developability of particular sites nor by planning authorities seeking to prioritise development sites in an arbitrary manner (DETR, 2000, para. 34).

This emphasis on market-led development processes appears to have grown more prevalent in recent government policy statements. The Sustainable Communities Plan (ODPM, 2003) reacts to the 'market failure' of low house-building rates in the South of England and market collapse in certain economically depressed areas, by stressing the need to a stepped-change in housing supply for owner-occupation.[6] Thus, the government aims to tackle the housing shortage by, 'creating the conditions in which private house builders will build more homes of the right type in the right places' (ibid., p. 30). This is to be supported by the reform of the planning system (carried out through the 2004 Planning and Compensation Act) into a more efficient and streamlined facilitator of housing land provision.

A number of additional resources and technologies have been used to consolidate the neo-liberalist ethos emphasised within the Communities Plan. Reform of the planning system has been complemented by new resources channelled into increasing the number of planning officers and 'changing the culture' of planning. The Best Value regime of government targets, incentives and penalties is being revised to reflect these priorities and numerous guidance and best practice documents are being produced.

6 Reported to be the 'preferred-choice' in housing tenure for most people.

In this way, we can see the meshing of two dominant discourses as they evolve over time through the policy wording and implementation techniques deployed to secure 'network enrolment' in line with the ideas and principles that are negotiated through a shifting pattern of 'policy coalitions'. The dominant discourses outlined here are also subject to challenge and modification through the construction and deployment of other framing discourses.

As we mentioned at the beginning of this chapter, within both PPG 3 and the Communities Plan (and other policy and supporting documents) other discursive regimes are evident. These put emphasis on community participation, managerial efficiency and the use of 'good science'. These both reflect and open up opportunities for different interests to structure the brownfield development process and influence the types of outcome produced.

Having analysed the dominant discourses surrounding brownfield redevelopment, or the redevelopment of Previously Developed Land as we should refer to it, we can now proceed to examine, in some less detail, how the concept of heritage has emerged and evolved as an outcome of similar processes associated to a completely different set of discourses.

15.4 The making and remaking of brownfield histories: 'Heritage' and the folding of time-space

The first arguments in favour of heritage protection stressed the moral and ethical reasons to preserve and enhance the built heritage of the past for the use and delight of future generations. Lord Clark (1969) had defined civilisation as a 'sense of permanence' and stated that a civilised man 'must feel that he belongs somewhere in space and time that he consciously looks forward and looks back' (in Larkham, 1996, p. 6). We have moved a long way from that conceptualisation, so reminiscent of the ethical and moral obligation to promote sustainable development.

Past, history and heritage are three related words with a different scope in their meanings the past being 'what has happened' while history is the selective attempts to describe this. Heritage today encompasses a contemporary product shaped from history, a resource that responds to the specific needs of the present generations making use of selective criteria that is influenced by all agents involved in the development process.

Although both history and heritage conceive of and use the past in similar ways there are differences in the detailed practice (Ashworth and Tunbridge, 1996, p. 5). Both make a selective use of the past for current purposes and transform it through interpretation while having regard to what has already happened, but history can be said to be what a historian considers as worth recording and heritage as what contemporary social networks choose to inherit and to pass on. 'The distinction is only that in heritage current and future uses are paramount, the resources more varied, including much that historians would regard as ahistorical, and the interpretation is more obviously and centrally the product that is consumed' (ibid., p. 6).

'By definition, heritage exists only in terms of the legatee and thus the heritage product is a response to the specific needs of actual or potential users' (Ashworth and Tunbridge, 1996, p. 8) multiplying as a resource for cultural, social, economic and political uses. Since the concept of heritage is culturally constructed, there is a variety of possible heritages, each shaped for the requirements of specific consumer groups and reflecting different understandings of culture. It is not the physical components of heritage that are actually traded, such as historic monuments or sites, but intangible ideas and feelings, such as fantasy, nostalgia, pleasure, pride and the like, which are communicated through the interpretation of the physical elements (ibid., p. 8).

Heritage is a potential political instrument when involved in the creation or support of states at various spatial jurisdictional scales and the legitimating of their governments and governing ideologies. The practice of government involves the development of the discourses through which the exercise of power is conceptualised and the use of mechanisms (programmes, techniques, documents and procedures) through which discourse is implemented at different scales (Murdoch, 2004, p. 52). Mechanisms (such as allocation of resources, funding, etc.) are dependent on discursive practices that can either lead to stigmatisation or promotion of sites targeting them for demolition or redevelopment (Weber, 2002, p. 520).

Heritage also acts as the supporter of economic activities, either directly as an industry itself (heritage tourism) or indirectly as a contributor to the location preferences of other economic activities. It can certainly be said that the rehabilitation of historic structures and nuclei are highly beneficial local economic activities. And it can be argued here that the special features of brownfield sites are reference elements that strengthen the character of the site. Rypkema (2001) stresses the economic value of conservation and argues that historic preservation is an economic generator of jobs, household income, heritage tourism, small business incubation, downtown revitalisation, small town revitalisation, neighbourhood stability, and neighbourhood diversity.

States discursively constitute, code and order the meaning of place through policies and practices that are often advantageous to capital (Beauregard, 1993), legitimating real estate as a spatially embedded commodity and taming value of the physical structure as context-dependent. As Weber so clearly puts it (2002, p. 524):

> […] because the presence or absence of value is far from straightforward states attempt to create a convergence of thinking around such critical issues as the economic life of buildings, the priority given to different components of value, the sources of devaluation and interrelationships between buildings and neighbourhoods [… hence] the discursive mutates in tandem with the changing market logics of real estate (dis)investment, as words take on new meanings and new themes shape spatial tactics.

The nature of the heritage product is determined, as in all such market-driven models, by the requirements of the consumer not the existence of the resources. The production of heritage becomes a matter for deliberate goal-directed choice about what uses are made of the past for what contemporary purposes. The goals of the commodification of the past have been explored in Newcomb (1979) nevertheless, heritage has a much broader if indirect commercial use in its contribution to place amenity, its exploitation in the projection of place images and thus its influence upon the location choices of economic actors. Paramount to this commodification is the re-use/reinstatement into activity of Previously Developed Land that has to comply with heritage objectives. Ultimately we could say that all heritage is brownfield. But focusing merely on individual sites, we argue its importance for the deliberate promotion for 'place images designed to shape the perception of a place as a suitable location for investment, enterprise, residence or recreation' (Ashworth and Tunbridge, 1996, p. 59).

Heritage is inherently linked to sustainability. The word sustainability first appeared in 1980 in 'The World Conservation Strategy' report prepared by the International Union for the Conservation of Nature and Natural Resources (IUCN).[7] Several follow-up meetings followed, culminating in 1987 with the Brundtland report 'Our Common Future', by the World Commission on Environment and Development (WCED). The initial ecological concerns are seen in a much wider scope, where 'heritages can reinforce our economic interests and survival imperatives' (WCED, 1987, p. 1). Heritage is linked to the concept of sustainability and seen as a new indicator outside the economic scope where the argument is not about growth and profit but about the right direction for growth (WCED, 1987, p. 44 and 364). In these discourses heritage is linked to the concept of sustainability and seen as a new indicator outside the economic scope where the argument is not about growth and profit but about the right direction for growth.

In the late 1980s the concept was redefined to include economic development and growth in the well-known 'development that meets the needs of the present without compromising the ability of future generations to meet their needs' (WCED, ibid.). In the World Heritage Convention held in Kyoto in 1998, Article 5 urged for the 'necessity of integrating conservation in the sustainable development process' (UNESCO, 1998). Likewise, it was also emphasised the importance of community and stakeholder involvement and a participatory approach in all efforts to integrate conservation and development.

Following from the sustainable development approach, 'the city is understood to be a unique ensemble that needs to be conserved in its historical integrity' (Zancheti and Jokilehto, 1997, p. 46). This means understanding the city as a dynamic process and as a structure in continuous change. This structure concentrates 'important cultural values of society (identity, memory, self-consciousness and artistry) and is a resource capable of attributing values to new things through the creation of new processes based on established values' (ibid., p. 47).

With these assumptions, a new discourse can be constructed associating the sustainable heritage dimension to Previous Developed Land redevelopment. This

7 One of the advisory bodies of the UNESCO World Heritage Convention.

would shift the existing conceptualisation of brownfield as an undesirable commodity and would reason on the networks of actors and material artefacts that make-up the brownfield places and structures and on the evolving relations that give meaning to them. By appropriating elements from the sustainable heritage discourse a new rationality is established, ready to be appropriated by the government's agenda.

Discourses shape the environments, contexts and frameworks within which political-economic and socio-institutional restructuring takes place (Peck and Tickell, 2002, p. 400). Reconceptualisation would allow the established decision making coalitions and the existing mechanisms to redefine their principles. When thinking about concrete cases where this reconceptualisation has occurred, two relevant examples spring to mind:

1. The first by Murdoch (2004, pp. 53-56), who explored the coalition between the DETR[8] and CPRE which resulted in PPG 3 (2000) asserting the re-use of previously developed land in accordance with 'sustainable patterns of development' while making use of the Urban Capacity Study mechanism.
2. The second by Weber (2002, pp. 527-533), who looked into the 'blight' designation in the USA during the 1970s and at the standards used to devalue and dispose of properties and prepare space for new rounds of investment. During that process narratives would re-construct themselves to take on more comprehensive approaches (i.e. the change from urban renewal for urban redevelopment spelled out in the 1954 Act).

15.5 Conclusions: Reconceptualising brownfields and the role of planners

We have argued in this chapter that production and consumption of the built environment are organised in networks of humans and non-human elements. These networks produce their own meanings and attach them on space, creating a socio-spatially embedded system. In order to apply those meanings, and in order to 'govern' in the broad sense, these webs create their own discourses and subsequent action. These complex networks need to adapt to their external environment in order to survive. This adaptation is expressed through actions emanating out of discourses in a process well described by Murdoch amongst many other authors.

A dominant and underlying 'global' discourse of neo-liberalism serves as the normative background for the webs of production and consumption that are based on free market competition for their survival. Therefore, although the basic tenets of the neo-liberal discourse do not change, elements of it 'adapt' as the networks generating it adapt to the changing circumstances of the environment. The discourse of neo-liberalism has a global claim but it is not total as it cannot encompass all the complexity of the environment within which it is situated. It

8 Department for the Environment Transport and the Regions, a UK government ministry.

therefore suffers from the same 'partiality' that every other discourse suffers in the sense that it cannot transcend the limits of the networks that produce it.

Another global discourse is 'sustainability'. It has arisen through a slow process of realisation that capitalism as it was practised by the West in the late 1960s was leading to environmental degradation and was endangering social cohesion and eventually capitalism itself. Two of the many streams or concepts arising in the sustainability discourse are those around heritage and brownfield sites.

Although superficially unrelated, the two concepts are profoundly related in more than one way. Both refer to spaces that were previously developed 'embedded' in networks of production and consumption that have been destroyed or replaced by others which no longer make the 'highest and best' use of the spaces they occupy. However, the heritage discourse was constructed in a positive way. It is presenting the preservation of previously used land as a means to increase value added and unlock opportunity through the use of culture and its consumption as a tool of economic development. In contrast, the brownfield/PDL discourse was constructed in a negative way, brownfields are messy, contaminated and in need of radical measures if they are to be returned to 'proper' use. The change in UK government policy in favour of the diversion of urban growth back into urban areas was accompanied by strong images of the idyllic pastures that would be saved and of the vibrant cities of Tuscany that the average Briton should strive to emulate. These strong metaphors were invoked not necessarily in order to 'justify' but more so in order to provide the backdrop, to 'set the scene'.

In that sense heritage and brownfields are logically incompatible with one another, previously used land cannot simultaneously be a good thing and a bad thing. Our emphasis on the intersubjective nature of meaning generation goes a long way in explaining why that is the case. Each concept was generated through the interactions of a different set of actors pursuing their own rather unrelated agendas and referring to their own, internal, sets of meanings. However, under the guise of community building and regeneration a compromise is reached with the aid of the state whereby the regeneration discourse bridges the gap and allows for heritage to be accommodated within brownfield redevelopment schemes which have now become 'sustainable community-building projects'.

Understandings of urban change and policy intervention may be moving from urban renewal, to redevelopment, to regeneration, to sustainable communities, but essentially they are describing the same thing: the re-incorporation of spaces into new networks of production and consumption which rarely operate at a local spatial scale. As far as these networks are concerned it is important to keep unchanged the principles around which economic production is structured while at the same time be flexible enough to incorporate new elements, to constantly adapt but to never completely dissolve or shift the main ideological 'attractors' around which these networks are shaped. In that sense the constant change in our conceptualisation of brownfields and heritage and the discourses surrounding their reuse is a reflection of this adaptation.

Within this context it would be interesting to reflect on the role of planning and planners. The relatively recent focus towards spatial planning and its emphasis on the mediation of spatial change is posing interesting questions about how this mediation takes place. In the previous chapters we described exactly such a process of spatial change through the lens of meaning creation and its attachment on space. We argued that spatial change is a socio-temporal process deeply embedded in networks of actors and spaces whose communicative interaction gives rise to meanings, attached to spaces and reciprocally affected by those spaces. Yet these networks by their nature cannot embrace the complexity of their environment in its totality. Their internal complexity, as Luhmann first argued, is lower than that of their environment. And therefore the meanings that the communicative interaction between the elements of those networks is generating never are a total description of the world but a selective interpretation of the world. By the same token there are always alternative meanings generated by networks with different scope and composition, i.e. with a different selectivity.

Sections 15.3 and 15.4 indicated how the concepts of brownfields and heritage emerged and evolved and how policies related to brownfield regeneration and heritage conservation were formulated under the influences of a variety of actors with a wide array of interests. Thus the basic underlying phenomenon of value generation through spatial transformation has been translated into quite distinct and seemingly contradicting sets of policies and their implementation tools. In our view this is not an unexpected consequence but rather an inherent capacity of policy making, emerging out of the interaction of different socio-spatial webs of actors. According to this logic therefore planners are left with little scope for any attempt to 'neutrality'. Instead their involvement with mediating these processes will inevitably affect the meaning generation processes of all the networks involved and therefore any choice of language and terminology will eventually have an impact on the physical outcomes of these processes, even by implication. This is not necessarily a view shared by all the conceptualisations of planning, we would claim however that such a conceptualisation would deeply enhance the capacity of planners to improve their understanding of the environment in which they find themselves. As such it would allow them to embrace more aspects of the complexities facing them and therefore it would provide them with a capacity to act more effectively in their effort to steer the constellations of socio-spatial interactions they are meshed into.

References

Akrich, M. (1992) 'The de-scription of technical objects', in W.E. Bijker and J. Law (eds.), *Shaping Technology, Building Society: Studies in Socio-technical Change*, MIT Press, Cambridge.

Ashworth, G.J. and Tunbridge J.E. (1996) *Dissonant Heritage: The Management of the Past as a Resource in Conflict*, Wiley & Sons, Chichester.

Atkinson, R. (1999) 'Discourses of partnership and empowerment in contemporary British urban regeneration', *Urban Studies*, vol. 36(1), pp. 59-72.

Beauregard, R. (1993) *Voices of Decline*, Blackwell, Cambridge.

Biddulph, M., Franklin, B. and Tait, M. (2003) 'From concept to completion. A critical analysis of the urban village', *Town Planning Review*, vol. 74(3), pp. 165-192.

Brenner, N. and Theodore, N. (2002) *Spaces of Neoliberalism. Urban Restructuring in North America and Western Europe*, Blackwell Publishing, Oxford.

Bridge, G. (1997) 'Mapping the terrain of time-space compression: Power networks in everyday life', *Environment and Planning D*, vol. 15, pp. 611-626.

Brueckner, J. (1980) 'A vintage model of urban growth', *Journal of Urban Economics*, vol. 8, pp. 389-402.

Byrne, D. (1998) *Complexity Theory and the Social Sciences*, Routledge, London.

Capra, F. (1996) *The Web of Life: A New Scientific Understanding of Living Systems*, Anchor Books, New York.

Capra, F. (2002) *The Hidden Connections: A Science for Sustainable Living*, HarperCollins, London.

DETR (1998) *Planning for the Communities of the Future*, The Stationary Office, London.

Doak, J. (1999) 'Planning for the reuse of redundant defence estate: Disposal processes, policy frameworks and development impacts', *Planning Practice and Research*, vol. 14(2), pp. 211-224.

Doak, J. and Karadimitriou, N. (2007a) '(Re)development, complexity and networks: A framework for research', *Urban Studies*, vol. 44(2), pp. 209-229.

Doak, J. and Karadimitriou, N. (2007b) 'Actor networks: The brownfield merry-go-round', in T. Dixon, M. Raco, P. Catney and D. Lerner, *Sustainable Brownfield Regeneration*, Blackwell, Oxford.

Gore, T. and Nicholson, D. (1991) 'Models of the land development process: A critical review', *Environment and Planning A*, vol. 23, pp. 705-730.

Guy, S. (1998) 'Developing alternatives: Energy, offices and the environment', *International Journal of Urban and Regional Research*, vol. 22(2), pp. 264-282.

Guy, S. and Henneberry, J. (2000) 'Understanding urban development processes: Integrating the economic and the social in property research', *Urban Studies*, vol. 37(13), pp. 2399-2416.

Guy, S., Henneberry, J. and Rowley, S. (2002) 'Development cultures and urban regeneration', *Urban Studies*, vol. 39(7), pp. 1181-1196.

Harvey, D. and Reed, M. (1997) 'Social science as the study of complex systems', in D. Kiel and E. Elliott (eds.), *Chaos Theory in the Social Sciences: Foundations and Applications*, University of Michigan Press, Ann Arbor.

Healey, P. and Barrett, S.M. (1990) 'Structure and agency in land and property development processes: Some ideas for research', *Urban Studies*, vol. 27(1), pp. 89-104.

Holland, J. (1998) *Emergence: From Chaos to Order*, Oxford University Press, Oxford.

Jacobs, M. (1993) *Sense and Sustainability: Land Use Planning and Environmentally Sustainable Development*, CPRE, London.

Jessop, B. (2002) 'Liberalism, neoliberalism and urban governance: A state-theoretical perspective', *Antipode*, vol. 24(3), pp. 452-472.

Kauffman, S. (1995) *At Home in the Universe: The Search for the Laws of Self-Organisation and Complexity*, Oxford University Press, New York.

Kooiman, J. (2003) *Governing as Governance*, Sage, London.

Lane, S.N. (2001) 'Constructive comments on D. Massey: "Space-time, 'science' and the relationship between physical geography and human geography"', *Transactions of the Institute of British Geographers*, vol. 26, pp. 243-256.

Larkham, P.J. (1996) *Conservation and the City*, Routledge, London.

Latour, B. (1993) *We Have Never Been Modern*, Harvester Wheatsheaf, Hemel Hempstead.

Law, J. (1999) 'After ANT: Complexity, naming and topology', in J. Law and J. Hassard (eds.), *Actor-Network Theory and After*, Blackwell, Oxford, pp. 1-14.

Local Government Association (2002) 'Something old, something new: A report of the LGA inquiry into the development of brownfield land', LGA, London.

Luhmann, N. (1990) *Essays on Self-Reference*, Columbia University Press, New York.

Luhmann, N. (1995) *Social Systems*, Stanford University Press, Stanford.

Manson, S.M. (2001) 'Simplifying complexity: A review of complexity theory', *Geoforum*, vol. 32, pp. 404-414.

Massey, D. (1999) 'Space-time, "science" and the relationship between physical and social geography', *Transactions of the Institute of British Geographers*, vol. 24, pp. 261-276.

Massey, D. (2001) 'Talking space-time', *Transactions of the Institute of British Geographers*, vol. 26(2), pp. 257-261.

Massey, D. (2005) *For Space*, Sage, London.

Murdoch, J. (1998) 'The spaces of actor-network theory', *Geoforum*, vol. 29(4), pp. 357-374.

Murdoch, J. (2004) 'Putting discourse in its place: Planning, sustainability and the urban capacity study', *Area*, vol. 36(1), pp. 50-58.

Newcomb, R. (1979) *Planning the Past: Historical Landscape Resources and Recreation*, Dawson, Folkestone.

ODPM (2000) Planning Policy Guidance Note 3: Housing, ODPM, London.

O' Sullivan, D. (2004) 'Complexity science and human geography', *Transactions of the Institute of British Geographers*, vol. 29(3), pp. 282-295.

Parker, D. and Stacey, R. (1994) *Chaos, Management and Economics: The Implications of Non-Linear Thinking*, Institute of Economic Affairs, London.

Peck, J. and Tickell, A. (2002) 'Neoliberalising space', in N. Brenner and N. Theodore, *Spaces of Neoliberalism: Urban Restructuring in North America and Western Europe*, Blackwell Publishing, Oxford.

Raper, J.F. and Livingstone, D. (2001) 'Let's get real: Spatiotemporal identity and geographic entities', *Transactions of the Institute of British Geographers NS*, vol. 26, pp. 237-242.

Raynesford, N. (2000) 'PPG 3: Making it work', *Town and Country Planning*, September 2000, pp. 262-263.

Rose, N. (1996) 'The death of the social? Re-figuring the territory of government', *Economy and Society*, vol. 25(3), pp. 327-356.

Rypkema, D. (2001) 'The (economic) value of national register listing', *CRM*, vol. 1, 2002.

Selman, P. (2000) 'Networks of knowledge and influence: Connecting "The Planners" and "The Planned"', *Town Planning Review*, vol. 71(1), pp. 109-121.

Tait, M. and Franklin, B. (2002) 'Constructing an image: The urban village concept in the UK', *Planning Theory*, vol. 3(1), pp. 250-272.

Taylor, M. (2001) *The Moment of Complexity: Emerging Network Culture*, University of Chicago Press, Chicago.

Thrift, N. (1996) *Spatial Formations*, Sage, London.

UNESCO (1998) World Heritage Committee, SESSION XXII Report. Kyoto, Japan, UNESCO, Paris.

WCED (1987) *Our Common Future*, Oxford University Press, Oxford.

Weber, R. (2002) 'Extracting value from the city: Neoliberalism and urban redevelopment', in N. Brenner and N. Theodore, *Spaces of Neoliberalism. Urban Restructuring in North America and Western Europe*, Blackwell Publishing, Oxford.

West Sussex County Council (1992) 'Environmental capacity study', WSCC, Brighton.

Zancheti, S.M. and Jokilehto, J. (1997) 'Values and urban conservation planning: some reflections on principles and definitions', *Journal of Architectural Conservation*, vol. 3(1), pp. 37-51.

Chapter 16
Urban Governance and Social Complexity

Joris Van Wezemael[1]

In this chapter we try to explore how the invention of complexity as an event in the academic understanding of dynamics, flows, emergence, and adaptivity may impact on the field of urban governance. We will introduce DeLanda's *assemblage theory of social complexity* to be followed by our arguments how planners could use this conception for a better understanding of their 'reality'. We will therefore discuss various fields such as social movements, hybrid government/non-government assemblages, political feed-forward loops, socio-technical collectives, firms and networks, spatial individuals and assemblages of location-networks. We will develop the argument that there is no bird's eye perspective and no master process in urban governance; the only position to view, affect, or even think an assemblage is another assemblage. At the end of the chapter we introduce concepts of conversion and temporality, which yet have to be explored empirically.

16.1 Introducing complexity and the aims of urban planning

We see the invention of complexity with Isabelle Stengers as an event. Through a transformation in scientific practices in several dimensions this event puts into variation what appears as 'given', and puts at risk what counts as the object of knowledge (Stengers, 2000).[2]

---

1 Dr Joris E. Van Wezemael is Professor of Human Geography, Department of Geosciences, University of Fribourg, Switzerland.

2 Let us illustrate this 'event' with this anecdote quoted from Manuel DeLanda: 'If you read the essays by the first guy who saw spontaneously oscillating chemical reactions, you find out he was unable to publish his essays. This was in the 1950s, not long ago. The idea that orderly behaviour could arise spontaneously from matter was so counter-intuitive. At that time, the only two ways they could see stable things arising in nature was through rational perfection – the best possible outcome – or heat-death. What nonlinear science brings about is a complete new range of structurally stable forms of behaviour, which has absolutely nothing to do with rationality or the heat-death of entropy. Now attractors are appearing all over the place. We've discovered a whole new reservoir of forms of stabilization. It's a paradigm warp' (Davies, 2007).

This chapter asks how complexity may impact on the field of urban governance. Today, complexity is used in a metaphorical (Thrift, 1999) as well as in a conceptual sense throughout many disciplines; in planning and in urban governance the metaphorical use is predominant.[3] Metaphorical use, however, does not take complexity as an event and therefore does not push the limits of how we think our topics and problems. However, in recent years, authors such as Brian Massumi (Massumi, 2002), Manuel DeLanda (DeLanda, 1997/2002/2006), or Adrian Mackenzie (Mackenzie, 2002) introduce non-metaphorical accounts into social sciences.[4]

A number of authors, which engage with complexity and/in social sciences, draw on Gilles Deleuze's work on the virtual. It provides a non-metaphorical understanding of creation on the basis of productive difference. The use of Deleuze's oeuvre as a shared background eases the combination of the work of different authors since it provides a largely shared ontological (or maybe more appropriate: ontogenetic) basis. Manuel DeLanda is working towards a philosophy of generation and elaborates on the key concept of assemblage. In his latest book DeLanda further develops his philosophy of generation and explicates a theory of social complexity on the basis of Deleuzes' (partly with Guattari) fragments of an assemblage theory (DeLanda, 2006a/b).

We suggest that assemblage theory can be very helpful since it establishes a great number of *connections* between more traditional approaches in social sciences (e.g. the work of Giddens, Bourdieu, Tilly, Weber) on the one hand and intensive sciences and complexity theories on the other. The starting point for the assemblage approach is DeLanda's critique that many social phenomena or entities beyond the micro or the macro[5] such as interpersonal networks, organisations, cities and regions, etc. lack a proper ontological basis and are wrongfully either reduced to a micro-, macro-, or a meso-position. In most cases their ontogenetic status is simply ignored, which means that an implicit ontology is uncritically accepted as in Network Governance (Sørensen and Torfing, 2004). In his attempt to solve this shortcoming DeLanda gets rid of totalities and essences and also of some unnecessary mystifications in social sciences.

As a brief outline of the assemblage approach we would like to highlight three aspects:

1. Assemblage theory criticises oversimplifications that attribute causes to posited systems,

3 With some noteworthy exceptions like Hillier (2005) or De Roo (2003).

4 They do so largely on the basis of mechanism-independencies. The most popular example may be the Lorenz attractor.

5 One family of solutions to the linkage of the micro (level of the individual subject) and the macro (level of society as a whole) has been a strategy to reduce one to the other. It views society as an aggregate of social action in the sense described above.

2. it calls for an adequate ontological conceptualisation of entities which draws on the processes that produce them,
3. and it highlights those theories, which begin with 'actual', physically perceived systems, do not adequately explain the origins of those systems.

As a first aspect DeLanda's major concern refers to oversimplifications that attribute causes to posited systems such as 'modernist planning' or 'urban governance' without describing the causal interaction of their parts, which would change in different contexts. DeLanda's theory owes a lot to population thinking rather than to the worldview of typologists. Population thinking argues that variation is the fuel of any kind of evolution (see also Bertolini, Chapter 5). For population thinkers *heterogeneity* is the state we would expect to exist spontaneously under most circumstances, while homogeneity is a highly unlikely state which may be brought about only under very specific selection pressures, abnormally in space and time. Moreover, while the typologist thinks of the genesis of form in terms of the expressions of single types (*the European City*, *the American Suburb*, *the Garden City*, *the Medieval City*, etc.), for the populationalist the forms always *evolve within collectives* (DeLanda, 2002, p. 48) and they display variation. Therefore the populationalist stresses the uniqueness of everything: whereas for the typologist, the type is real and variation is an illusion, for the populationist the type is an abstraction and only the variation is real (Mayr, 1978). Population thinkers use probabilistic terms (rather than linear causality) in order to overcome homogenising typology. We suggest assemblage theory as a way of theorising populations (of human subjects, social groups, organisations, cities, etc.) by means of *conceptualising the generative processes from which they emerge*.

The focus on generative processes and emergence introduces an important second aspect of assemblage theory. It challenges the ontological solution of hitherto social theory, which did not properly conceptualise the ontological status of 'intermediate' levels such as social movements, institutional organisations, social networks or city regions, and instead reduces them to a micro, macro, or lately also to a meso-level:

1. One family of solutions to the linkage of the micro and the macro has been a strategy to reduce one to the other.
2. Classical sociology in a Durkheimian or Parsonian tradition as well as many forms of Marxist social theory do not pretend that individuals would not exist, but they assert that *society makes the individual*. On the basis of socialisation and thus the internalisation of the societal rules – traditional regulations and cultural values – individual persons are an epiphenomenon to social structures (DeLanda, 2006a). This macro-sociological reductionism was heavily criticised since the 1960s by what we can call a micro-sociological reductionism, which views society as a mere aggregate of social action. Similar arguments apply to neo-classical economics. Society as a resulting macro entity thus does not have emergent properties of its

own; it is an epiphenomenon from the point of view of phenomenological experiences or choices of (bounded) rationality, respectively.

3. A third reductionist position has gained popularity more recently in governance related topics such as planning (Healey, 2006b; Healey, 2004). Authors such as Giddens (1984) or Bourdieu (1979) point out that both agency and structure are mutually constructed by practice – they are both sides of a single coin. The constitution of society thus can be reduced to social practice as ultimate reality, or to the habitus as a master process.

In either of the reductionist strategies the generative processes that govern systems and also the complex interactions among their parts (which give rise to the system – 'emergence') remain hidden below the shadow of final products.

Assemblage theory is based on the understanding that theories, which begin with 'actual', physically perceived systems, do not adequately explain the origins of those systems. This refers to the third key aspect of assemblage theory: the subordination of the term 'real' to the terms 'virtual-actual'. What we usually understand as the 'real world' in an assemblage perspective is merely the experience of the 'actual' state of final products; they are devoid of their virtual becoming. In order to remedy the situation DeLanda (2002) introduces the Deleuzian virtual *as a deeply materialist concept*. For this he borrows concepts from complexity and chaos theory, as well as from differential geometry and other fields. He points a way out of the dichotomy between either taking the actual for the real (and the virtual for the non-real), or following the linguistic turn and view the world as a mere social construction. Assemblage theory, we could say, takes the virtual as the *more-real* and thus focuses on the (virtual) generative processes which produce systems and the actual world which we can (more or less) perceive.

Let us be very clear about this: in our perspective the 'real' includes, in addition to the physically perceived, sensuous world of the actual, the virtual properties inherent in assemblages and the intensive processes that select and animate them. This composes a sort of *passage* from the virtual to the actual. The virtue of a Deleuzian ontology of processes is that, in considering 'the virtual' alongside 'the actual', it is able to explain generation (morphogenesis as the birth of metric space, but also the production of places), and bridge virtual and actual viewpoints (Pease, 2005).

Complex systems as well as assemblages display behaviour that results from the interaction between components and not from characteristics that are inherent to components themselves. The according concept of emergence is at centre stage in assemblage theory, but this theory rejects the idea that systems be perceived as a 'whole', which then would explain the behaviour of component parts. DeLanda's (DeLanda, 2002) reference to non-linear models and their multiple attractors in assemblage theory define a world capable of surprising us through the emergence of unexpected novelty, a world where there will always be something else to explain.

Assemblage theory implies self-organisation as a direct consequence of the lack of a top-level of organisation. Since there is no pre-supposed global level or god's eye perspective from the 'top-level' of a system, the only position to think, view or affect an assemblage is another assemblage. However, its conceptual development stems from differential geometry (manifold), vector field theory, and the theory of groups, rather than from systems theory.

In this chapter we firstly conceptualise the entities that regional sciences deal with (interpersonal networks, organisations, cities and regions, etc.) by means of assemblage theory. We will illustrate the concepts by referring to examples from the Swiss context of urban governance and planning. Thus the first aim is an inquiry into the (ontological) status of the 'ingredients' of urban governance and spatial planning by means of assemblage theory. Then we moot a concept to re-formulate the problem of governance and strategic spatial planning in a non-metaphoric complexity approach in order to re-think attempts of steering from the field of decision making in planning and urban governance as *ontogenetic modulation*.

16.2 Urban regions, governance and complexity

Apart from the perspective on complexity as an event there is a growing belief that the world we deal with *really* has become more complex itself, rendering linear/Eucledian modes of social sciences increasingly inadequate for the task. As Law and Urry rightly state, social and physical changes in the world need to be paralleled by changes in the methods of social enquiry (Law and Urry, 2004). On the planning agenda there are e.g. various aspects of increased global-local interplay, which affect the management of metropolitan areas; another example refers to Edge-Cities with their tangential connections, which interfere with the traditionally radial built transportation networks and pose serious challenges for the governance of urban areas. This is especially the case in areas with small political entities as in Switzerland. The intensification of societal complexity in recent decades deepens systemic interdependencies across various social, spatial, and temporal horizons of action (Jessop, 1999, p. 1) and calls for new modes of governance.[6] Governance networks are believed to provide advantages if compared to hierarchical government organisations. Sørensen and Torfing (2004) define them as relatively stable horizontal articulation of interdependent, but operationally autonomous actors, who interact through negotiations, which take place within a regulative, normative, cognitive and imaginary framework, that to a

6 In respect of metropolitan governance Kübler (2003, pp. 535-537) identifies the disintegration of urban areas in socio-economic, political and cultural aspects as a driver in the quest for new organisational forms in metropolitan regions.

certain extent is self-regulating, and which contributes to the production of public purpose within and across particular policy areas.[7]

The present phase of re-orientation in planning and related disciplines such as economic, regional and urban geography may reflect these attempts as paralleled changes in the ways of doing research. A relational perspective (see Amin, 2002/2004; Healey, 2006a; Massey, 2005; Thrift, 1996/2000) views cities and regions as agglomerations of heterogeneity which are 'locked into a multitude of relational networks of varying geographical reach' (Amin, 2004). Furthermore, in urban governance literature there is a lot of vocabulary used, which more or less directly points towards complexity (e.g. relational complexity, unpredictability, self-regulation of regions, heterogeneity, creativity, experimental practice, etc.). However, as mentioned before, the use of 'complexity-terms' within planning and the regional sciences is largely metaphorical. Furthermore, many concepts which are used do link back to reductionist positions (DeLanda, 2006a).

16.3 Links in regional sciences

Assemblage theory puts the topics of regional sciences at the very heart of social complexity. There are innumerable links, which connect regional studies, urban governance, etc. to complexity. We will illustrate this and refer to relevant issues in our outline of assemblage theory below. In several academic discourses there is a growing awareness of dissatisfactory theoretical frameworks. As Sorensen and Torfing (2004) state, in the case of network governance:

> ... most scholars in the first generation [of network governance research] tended to borrow concepts and arguments from other scholars in the field, thus producing a somewhat eclectic and confusing theoretical landscape. [...] when people refer to concepts and arguments developed in a different and even contradicting theoretical context, it is problematic.

Indeed, the theoretical frameworks juxtapose concepts, which are based on different ontological strategies. The assumed ontological status of 'intermediate' levels between a micro and a macro such as social movements, institutional organisations, social networks or cities and regions is a key problem of urban governance[8] research (Van Wezemael, 2006). The linkage of '*individual and society*', '*agency and structure*', '*choice and order*' is one key question for *any* social ontology and thus for the respective social theory (DeLanda, 2006a/2006b). However, it is *a paramount question* for regional sciences because their *key concern* is the *linkage*

7 For a conceptualisation of democratic network governance on the basis of assemblage theory and minor politics see Van Wezemael (2006).

8 In this chapter we will treat the terms of urban, regional and metropolitan governance as synonyms and use the term 'urban governance'.

of manifold heterogeneous agents (e.g. social groups, private organisations, firms, public institutions, quangos, etc.) in spacing and their interplay in a context of various kinds of 'negotiation' (see next sections).

Even regional sciences, which predominantly deal with the hybrid forms of socio-technical entities, modes of regulation and the question of building regions do fall into the trap of uncritically accepting implicit ontologies (this is particularly true for some literature on regional innovation models such as in Cooke (1996)). For an excellent survey of the field of 'regionalism' see Moulaert and Mehmood (2007). The tools of analysis often are mixed with normative concepts. Although to a varying degree, various schools conceptualise regional development and the attempts of steering it. For example regulation theory[9] has identified the importance of the hybrid intermediate-scale entities in socio-technical, politico-institutional, and economic respects. Evolutionary economics thinking and more elaborated approaches to path-dependency were introduced through the literature on innovation systems (Dosi, 1988/1994; Lundvall, 1992).

We argue that taking on ontological questions as outlined above is the very basis for an adequate academic engagement with urban governance. The invention of complexity can boost this debate.

16.4 Assemblage theory and the 'ingredients' of urban governance

The theory of social assemblages and the processes that create and stabilise their historical identity opens up towards a great number of Deleuzian concepts.[10] Its core ideas, however, are rather straightforward. The predominant conceptualisation of the relations between parts and wholes in social sciences can be addressed as 'relations of interiority'. Here, the parts are constituted by the very relations they have in the whole.[11] In contrast, assemblages, are made up of parts which are self-subsistent and articulated by *relations of exteriority* (here DeLanda draws on Deleuze's (1991) reading of David Hume). In this perspective organised beings are the result of large numbers of relations between parts, which have no significance on their own: 'A flash of red, a movement, a gust of wind, these elements must be

9 As Bathelt (1994) argues regulation theory was an important step since it aimed at *drawing together the interplay* of economic-technical and socio-institutional structures in a national economy and to put them into a development context with an attempt of learning how they steer themselves (learning regions, etc.) as well as how to intervene into their dynamics (mostly in order to increase regional competitiveness). For a careful discussion of regulation approaches see Jessop, 1997a/1997b; Moulaert and Swyngedouw, 1989.

10 The most important ones are: abstract machines, quasi-causal operator, (de/re)territorialisation, diagrams, individuation/morphogenesis.

11 This is clearly the case in functionalism, however it is also true in less obvious cases such as in Structuration Theory (Giddens, 1984): agency and structure mutually constitute each others and produce a seamless whole (DeLanda, 2006, p. 10).

externally related to each other to create the sensation of a tree in autumn' (NN, 2006).

Every relation thus has a localised motive, not a transcendent one: there is no Aristotelian ideal type or essence of a tree in autumn (or a governance network or the European City) – only an immanent world of relations, from which such entities may emerge by means of exterior relations of their component parts. Exterior relations therefore may change without their terms changing (Deleuze and Parnet, 2002). The relations in assemblages are not logically necessary but contingently obligatory; an entity therefore is never fully defined by its relations. Whereas necessary relations could be investigated by thought alone, contingently obligatory ones involve a consideration of empirical questions (DeLanda, 2006b, p. 11). Exteriorly joined components remain certain autonomy from the whole they compose, and they are neither mutually constituted nor fused into a seamless whole. As opposed to relations of interiority, the parts which make up an assemblage are self-subsistent. It 'is always possible to detach an entity from one particular set of relations, and insert it instead in a different set of relations, with different other entities' (Shaviro, 2007). Assemblages are secondary to the relations of their constituent components. Larger assemblages emerge from the interactions of their component parts.

DeLanda's ontology really rather is an ontogenesis. Since there is no pre-given identity which could be drawn form an Aristotelian essence a thing is determined by what it can do (rather by what it 'is'). Assemblage theory is a thoroughly relational, non-metaphorical (meta-) theory of creation. As soon as assemblages emerge on the basis of their component's connections they start providing resources for their components as well as constraining them. This introduces a top-down aspect into the so far bottom-up approach.

On the basis of the argument so far it becomes clear that in an assemblage approach there are *many levels of emergence*, which cannot be reduced to naturally 'given' entities (such as 'society' or the 'individual'). Assemblage theory moves us below and above the subject.[12] The move below the subject stems directly from Hume, but it also connects to the 'society of mind' thesis in cognitive sciences.[13] The subject becomes an intermediate level of organisation. In DeLanda (2006b) an individual person, a population of individual persons, friendship networks, interpersonal networks, organisations, interorganisational networks (clusters, etc.), cities, and territorial states are all conceptualised as assemblages on different

12 Since both individualism and collectivism are reductionist and essentialist concepts, the antipole to both is relationalism.

13 In his thesis that 'minds are what brains do', Minsky (1986) views the human mind and any other naturally evolved cognitive system as a vast society of individually simple processes known as agents.

'scales',[14] which do not differ in ontogenetic status: they are all historically produced, unique individuals.

The world of assemblages is populated by hybrids: human and non-human, technological and social components give rise to entities by means of their connections. The social practices are inseparable from the material roles of their component parts. A social movement usually consists (besides its counter-movement) of both populations of interpersonal networks and of organisations (both government and non-government organisations). For example, the social movements in Switzerland, which urge for an alternative traffic policy and which are component parts in governance networks regarding metropolitan transport systems, produced an association in 1979.[15] Today we can find a hybrid of a number of local (more or less organised) movements which are based on interpersonal networks and *at the same time* an institutionalised lobby organisation on various institutional levels of the federal state in Switzerland. Similarly, government hierarchies at all jurisdictional scales form networks with non-governmental organisations in order to be able to implement centrally decided politics. E.g. the Swiss Federal Office for Spatial Development (ARE) needs non-governmental or para-governmental association like 'glow. Das Glattal' (Oehler, 2005) or 'Idee Seetal'[16] in order to develop an intercommunal governance project in the metropolitan area of Zürich and Lucerne, respectively. Further the Federal Office needs them in order to implement and to re-formulate its metropolitan politics (see Agglomerationspolitik des Bundes, 'Modellvorhaben').[17]

The 'dimensions' of assemblages

An assemblage can be defined along two analytical dimensions: *(i)* the roles which assemblages play and *(ii)* the processes which stabilise or destabilise their identity.

1. Dimension 1: The role assemblages may play can be *material* (infrastructure needed for communication, labour put into the moderation of conflict in an organisation, etc.; see below) or *expressive* (DeLanda, 2006a) and usually they are a combination of both. Expressive components may

    a. rely on specialised vehicles for expression (e.g. coded systems such as language, genetic code), or;

14 'Scale' is not used in a strictly geographical sense. It rather follows a topological sequence of emergence.

15 See http://www.vcs-ate.ch.

16 See http://www.idee-seetal.ch.

17 For further information visit http://www.are.admin.ch/themen/raumplanung/02114/index.html?lang=de.

b. be directly expressive (e.g. architecture of a building, gesture of a subject, skyline of a city; traditionally but wrongly lumped together under the label 'symbolic' (DeLanda, 2006a)).

The focus on the roles, which assemblages *really play* transgresses the distinction of traditional concepts like 'facts' versus 'values' and points out that both do not exist as such beyond the concrete relations in assemblages.

Along this first dimension are specified the roles which component parts may play (from a purely expressive role to a purely material role, and predominantly mixtures of the two). The material parts of a social movement consist of the energy and labour involved in maintaining its relations, patching together provisional coalitions, negotiating which of the numerous agendas brought forward by the participants will be mounted as collective action, and hiding internal struggles from public view. The communication hardware used in stabilising the relations play a material role, too (the deprivation from computers or telecommunication hard- and software in totalitarian regimes or the censorship of the world wide web e.g. in the People's Republic of China illustrate the importance of such material roles for politically relevant networks). Furthermore the production of outputs such as brochures, etc. and running an office makes part of the material components. In order to affect its audience and be a legitimate claim-maker both in the eyes of its rivals and the government a movement has to be respectable, unified, numerous and committed. Although these possessions can be expressed linguistically (e.g. by publishing a webpage with the number of associated individuals and institutions) it will be displayed more convincingly if a large crowd congregates peacefully in a place in town (DeLanda, 2006b, p. 60).

DeLanda argues that the processes in which specialised expressive media (e.g. language) can be seen as an additional dimension or a differentiation of the expressive roles in social assemblages (third dimension, or dimension 2.1).[18] Specialised expressive media consolidate and rigidify the identity of the assemblage (e.g. by shared stories or myths of origin) or allow the assemblage certain latitude for more flexible operation while benefiting from e.g. linguistic resources in processes of coding and decoding (DeLanda, 2006b, pp. 18-19). Thus an expressive role should not be confused with a linguistic one.[19] In an assemblage perspective e.g. populist movements cannot be analysed merely, not even

18 Specialised expressive media can be seen as a form of interiorisation of intensive individuating factors.

19 For instance, many organisations are closely associated with e.g. a building (Petronas Tower, Chrysler Building), cities with a skyline (skyline of Manhattan, Paris with the Eiffel tower), firms with colours (Ferrari with Maranello-red).

mainly, by means of their political (linguistic) argument. They are too ludicrous to imagine without their colours, the lights, the music,[20] etc. as elements which form assemblages with sub-personal 'agents' (in the sense of the 'society-of-mind' thesis, see above) as well as many assemblages 'above' the individual level. However, these non-linguistic expressive components must not be lumped together under the label symbolic – the roles they play in order to affect and be affected and to stabilise and maintain the identity of the individual assemblage have to be examined empirically and experimentally.

2. Dimension 2: Stabilising and destabilising the identity of an assemblage

    a. Stabilising = (re-)territorialisation (sharpening its borders, homogenising its components, etc.).
    b. Destabilising = deterritorialisation (free up fixed relations).

The second dimension characterises processes in which these components are involved: processes which stabilise or destabilise the identity of assemblages. Interpersonal networks, social movements or associational organisations can be stabilised by conflict with their opponents. For instance, advocates of an expansion of public transport can be more or can be less radical in their claims, which is likely to generate internal struggles in the respective movement. However, when confronted with an initiative of the road traffic lobby they will unmistakably be 'one voice' in favour of their core requests.[21] Stories and categories play important boundary-defining roles, as DeLanda shows with regard to the work of Charles Tilly (1999), but these are *real* group boundaries not just phenomenologically experienced or linguistically constructed borders. Therefore it is not the linguistic label of a category which deserves our main focus of interest but the outcome of sorting processes of inclusion and exclusion that produce concretely bounded groups. Let us explain this point.

Take 'foreigners' which cannot participate in the direct democratic processes in Switzerland (even if they constitute the majority of the population of a borough). It is not the category 'foreigners' that produces this exclusion, but a *real process of differential inclusion and exclusion works as a sorting process* regarding the access to formal democratic political power. The category 'foreigner' merely catalyses the process and sharpens the border of the real boundary. The linguistic category territorialises the exclusion of a group of people. Or take the segregation

---

20 This argument refers to the before mentioned 'society of mind' approach.

21 This may be illustrated in the struggles about the distribution of resources for metropolitan regions versus transit roads in Switzerland. For further information see http://www.parlament.ch/do-avanti.

of foreigners into an area (which will be denominated as a 'migrant area'). However, this refers not to linguistic categories but to the enforcement of *real categorical boundaries*. Thus, for example, the housing market should be viewed as a *real sorting process* of people and life-chances. The change in relations of the components of that sorting machine can deterritorialise an existing order and thus modify the outcomes of the sorting process (see Van Wezemael, 2000). Naming or coding of neighbourhoods can sharpen the neighbourhood's borders and the over coding of the residents in the neighbourhood with categories such as e.g. foreigners can catalyse the enforcement of uneven life chances. Specialised expressive media thus rigidify the identity of the assemblage, however they do not produce it.

Assemblages avoid reifications

Assemblage theory makes clear that government organisations in terms of internal heterogeneity and complexity do not differ from economic organisations. Joint action by many (heterogeneous) governmental organisations is *objectively complex and problematic* and not something that can be taken for granted. Concepts such as 'the state' not only tend to reify generalities but they veil the relations of exteriority which exist among the heterogeneous organisations that form a government hierarchy (DeLanda, 2006b, p. 85).

Political feed forward[22] loops can be dealt with as 'autocatalytic dynamics'[23] (DeLanda, 1997, pp. 49-52), which foster new developments on the basis of their self-stimulating dynamics. The process of formulation-implementation-reformulation is reflected in the Swiss-German term *rollende Planung* (a basic concept in Swiss spatial planning). However, such feed-forward loops do not occur on an idealised plane of policy formulation and implementation, rather they move in relational settings with non-governmental organisations and they always work on the basis of the various material and expressive roles their components may play. Thus *concrete government organisations are precarious entities, which always intertwine with a number of non-governmental entities in order to be effective.*

In an assemblage view the difference between 'government' and 'governance' (Healey, 2006b) clearly is not a fundamental one. However, the component parts of the relational entities may play different roles and thus actualise a set of specific temporary solutions to the 'problem of governance'. Whereas the hitherto governance debate generally locates governance as an alternative 'to market

22 Political feed-forward processes can be dealt with as 'autocatalytic dynamics' (DeLanda, 1997, pp. 49-52), which foster new development on the basis of their self-stimulating dynamics.

23 Autocatalytic systems refer to coupled, looped reactions that lead to conditions in which the component parts of the system depend on one another in more than proportional ways (forward loop).

anarchy and organisational hierarchy' (Jessop, 1999), an assemblage approach stresses the necessary intertwining of manifold organisations and networks, which all are socio-technical collectives rather than pure 'political' or 'economic' entities. Thus they do not merely 'use' material resources and technology in order to follow their goals. Furthermore, assemblage theory makes clear that hierarchies and networks display similar relations of exteriority on different levels of their relational constitution.

Another crucial aspect of an assemblage perspective is the distinction of the assemblage(s) that produce the hierarchy of a federal government (as in the Swiss case) on the one hand, and the territorial entity which it controls, on the other hand. The territorial entity includes populations of organisations of various kinds, populations of persons and interpersonal networks, cities, regions, provinces, etc. The governmental hierarchies are intertwined with those populations and do not refer to a separated or 'upper' level.

16.5 Non-metaphorical creation

DeLanda criticises the linguistic turn in social sciences as 'the worst possible turn' (DeLanda, Protevi and Thanaem, 2006, p. 8) and he disapproves of the predominant social constructivist perspectives, which use the term 'construction' in the sense of how our minds 'construct' the world of appearances via linguistic categories. The processes that literally – not phenomenologically – create a region (processes of morphogenesis or individuation), exceed the constructions of linguistic categories. Similarly, politics is not about the construction of categories, as the example of segregation above may illustrate. New technologies 'space' areas long before they are coded by means of categories (see below). The linguistic coding of clusters, etc. may stabilise a setting and increase the homogeneity of a location ('Motor City', 'Silicon Valley'). However it cannot *create* it as many attempts to 'create' economic clusters on the basis of a decision of a city marketing or planning agency shows (for a Swiss example see e.g. 'winlink').[24] Social-constructivists falls short because they use a merely metaphorical concept of the term 'creation' and ignore the non-linguistic roles that component parts in assemblages do play (DeLanda, Protevi and Thanem, 2006). They furthermore neglect the respective de/re-territorialising tendencies.

Almost unperceived by many, a sort of linguistic idealism has become a predominant paradigm for most social scientists. The inherent anthropocentrism creates fundamental difficulties when dealing, as regional scientists do, with socio-technical and environmental issues. In their conceptualisations of urban regions and their (political) steering most contemporary authors follow a social-constructivist strategy (although hardly ever in an explicit way). Amin's (2004)

---

24 http://www.winlink.ch/home.html.

summoning up of regions[25] and Healey's (2006a/2006b) relational complexity are only two recent and influential examples. In the sense of Gidden's (1984) double hermeneutics this also establishes a broadly shared attitude in many practioner's communities.

As explained above, the roles components can play in an assemblage are combinations of material and expressive ones. Whereas the material ones refer to the whole repertoire of causal interaction (and should be treated as such), the expressive ones typically involve catalysis.[26] The mechanisms to synthesise assemblages therefore include (mostly non-linear)[27] *causality* as well as, in the case of social assemblages, *reasons* and *motives*. For the latter DeLanda draws on Max Weber's concept of *Verstehen* in order to stress that ignoring the hybrid nature of social mechanisms (we mean the combination of causes, reasons, and motives which must not be reduced to only on of them) can be a source of misunderstanding and mystification in social sciences.

What can we learn from this for decision making? DeLanda explains that social activities in which means are successfully matched to ends are traditionally labelled as 'rational'. However, this label obscures the fact that the activities involve *problem-solving skills of different kinds* and not a single mental faculty like 'rationality'. Thus the explaining of successful solutions of practical problems will involve consideration of relevant causal events in socio-technical collectives, and not just calculations in the actor's head (DeLanda, 2006a, p. 24). The capacity of human beings to be affected by linguistic triggers consequently demands (besides a number of physiological preconditions such as e.g. a nervous system) explanations, which include *reasons* for acting (e.g. referring to traditional values or personal emotions) and *motives* (choices and goals, matching means to ends). Whereas matching means to ends will be at the forefront in situations when *intensity is high* (e.g. in a crisis situation when one must solve a new planning problem), traditional routines tend to dominate in situations with a *lower intensity* (reproduction of the existing social order)[28]

25 Amin argues that material formations such as a region must be summoned up as temporary placements of ever moving material and immanent geographies, as 'hauntings' of things that have moved on but left their mark as situated moments in distanciated networks, as contoured products of the networks that cross a given place.

26 This means that they mainly trigger or ease processes like a catalyst.

27 The two basic assumptions of linearity are: large causes will produce large scale effects (and vice versa), and the same cause always produces the same effect. Non-linear science systems display multiple determinations, which is why the two basic assumptions of linearity do no longer apply. Complexity thus implies a move in social sciences away from the linear analysis of structure or agency. The assumptions of complexity are that *(i)* there is no necessary proportion between 'causes' and 'effects', that *(ii)* the individual and statistical level are not equivalent, and that *(iii)* systems do not result from simple addition of individual components (Law and Urry, 2004).

28 The argument of high and low intensity can be related to questions of temporality. Problems are posed differently in the course of a planning procedure, and the procedure

(DeLanda, Protevi and Thanaem, 2006, p. 8). In such a schema of high-versus-low-intensity-situations we can talk about *degrees of freedom of human action.*[29] Assemblage theory means a relevant approach to issues of strategic spatial planning and urban governance because it takes 'creation' at face value and qualifies the role of language in respect of other expressive as well as to material roles that components play. Let us illustrate our line of argument with a Swiss case as discussed by our colleague Alain Thierstein.

Spatial development 'in secrecy': Creation beyond categories

As part of the Interreg III B project 'Polynet' Thierstein et al. (2006) investigate what they call 'spatial development in secrecy' ('Raumentwicklung im Verborgenen'). In the process of coping with distinct knowledge/skill-resource dependencies[30] enterprises in the so-called knowledge-economy (which mainly includes finance and consulting industries, high-tech branches, life-sciences) tend to display specific material and expressive roles (see above), which their component parts play. Expressivity of an organisation's intentions can be explicitly phrased and thus linguistically coded. However, usually they will be a manner of assessments of *strategic significance* (and not: signification) (DeLanda, 2006a, p. 81).[31]

Requested premium services are a limiting resource to organisations in the knowledge-economy. Since they are scarce and unevenly distributed, specific economies of agglomeration emerge. The production of knowledge-intensive goods (which are 'assembled' from a variety of highly specialised material and non-material elements) critically depends on specific material and expressive roles of their component part. This includes personal interaction, face-to-face communication ('trust') and interpersonal networks ('strength of weak ties', see Granovetter, 1973). The specific roles modulate relations between locations and thus relational spaces, which deviate from the outcome of the firm's hitherto location-strategies. Firms choose (and eventually create) a set of specific locations in order to solve the problem of sets of resource-dependencies in highly specialised domains.[32] Components of the organisation are at the same time part

---

is more or less sensitive to changing demands, to new demands or to alterations of the (supposed) conditions. We will return to this line of reasoning towards the end of the chapter (see Section 16.6).

29 This could be linked to Christensen's concept of 'degrees of complexity' (see also (Zuidema and De Roo, 2004).

30 This means that firms need (knowledge and other) resources which they either cannot produce in one place or which they have to buy from or exchange with other forms.

31 In general terms a main expressive component in organisations is legitimacy, the material one refers to the enforcement of authority structures.

32 Since resource dependency is a general problem to which all firms will develop a 'solution' we can refer to these topological invariants as *universal singularities*. The specific

of socio-technical networks in the region (relations of highly specialised staff, laboratories, sets of legal rules, natural resources used, public infrastructure such as fire-optic cables and airports, etc.) and of rather dispersed 'in-house' networks, which connect the various component parts of the organisation as an assemblage.

The *populations* of socio-technical collectives (parts of firms, transportation infrastructure, shared resources, government organisations, etc.) give rise to another scale of assemblages: relational spatial individuals. They provide resources (beneficiary effects) and constraints (agglomeration costs) for their component parts. Since component parts of an assemblage usually are also simultaneously parts of a number of other assemblages and therefore connect (to) them, modulations in one population of assemblages introduces further modulations to sets of relations between elements in other populations of assemblages. This of course launches ongoing ontogenetic transformations throughout populations of assemblages, which each emerge *differently*[33] from the modulated relations. At this point it becomes obvious that assemblages are only *meta-stable*.

Spatial individuals specifically relate to other localised individuals and relationally produce assemblages of the knowledge-economy on various spatial scales. The relations of the firms are mediated across a large variety of distances by using different kinds of transportation and communication technologies. Eventually this produces simultaneous changes to assemblages on various scales.[34] The change in the kind of resource dependencies in the knowledge-economy produces specific relations between metropolitan areas on a European level (pentagon London – Paris – Milano – München – Hamburg), but it also de/re-territorialises the relations of Swiss locations and clearly conflict with key strategic goals of Swiss spatial development.

The modulation of relations (on the basis of inventions and innovations in local and remote socio-technical collectives) re-territorialises Swiss location networks. Value added chains in knowledge economy seriously produce sorting processes, which de/re-territorialise *spatial individuals*. The analysis of Thierstein (2006, pp. 14-15) detects a 'gap' in the perception of the relevant political institutions regarding spatial development in Switzerland. This means that the (invisible)

---

solutions of an assemblage (a firm or a network of firms) can be referred to as *individual singularities*. See DeLanda (2006b, pp. 28-29).

33 Mind that the equation 'same reason = same effect' is only true in linear relations (Law and Urry, 2004).

34 For instance the above mentioned association 'glow. Das Glattal' deals with the recent breathtaking dynamics of economic, traffic, building, etc. in the area between the city of Zürich and the Airport in Kloten/Rümlang. Its effort to create shared projects e.g. in traffic infrastructure and the like may provide provisory solutions. However, if we put the tracing of the relations in connection with knowledge-economy back on the map, it becomes clear that processes with vectors working on other scales pose more singular problems.

processes which produce places have changed while planners only focus on 'actual', physically perceived changes. They thus do not grasp the origins of the dynamics, tend to miss the changes altogether and increasingly render themselves unfit for their very task.

Thierstein et al. (2006) believe that the way ahead is to perceive the 'problem' of the so-called *spatial development in secrecy* differently, and to make planners more aware of changing chains of value creation in the knowledge-economy. However, we must keep in mind that we must not reduce the whole set of material and expressive relations to mere 'perception'. On the basis of our argument so far, we would rather say that the material and expressive roles of the counterparts in governmental/non-governmental hybrids do *really* have to change. While government organisations need other organisations in order to implement their policies, the same relational settings may prevent alternative relations from emerging. Therefore spatial policies as real relational networks have yet to be modulated.

This can be illustrated with the federal metropolitan politics ('Agglomerationspolitik'), which puts a lot of energy and labour into the formation of assemblages with networks such as the mentioned 'glow. Das Glattal'. It awaits its implementation because of feed forward relations between sets of nested assemblages in the relational networks of policy-formation and implementation in Switzerland.[35]

Conclusion of the case

As a conclusion of this digression into knowledge-economy and spacing[36] in Switzerland we can state that *(i)* new modes of dealing with resource dependencies in the driving knowledge-economy is modulating sets of relations, which again drive spatial development in Switzerland. And that *(ii)* there is a lacking 'conversion' between the domain of knowledge-economy (populations of firm networks and their connections in agglomeration economies) and the domain of urban governance (concrete government/non-government assemblages with regard to strategic spatial development).

35 Switzerland is often called a *Verbandsdemokratie* ('association-democracy') because powerful stakeholders form very dense connections (assemblages) on interpersonal and organisational scales with government organisations and build a hybrid para-state domain, which has more effective power than parliament (see Hotz-Hart, 1995). The federal parliament, however, plays an important expressive role. It has a strong ceremonial role in Swiss democracy.

36 Assemblage theory can also be embedded in an evolutionary trajectory of space-related research. It moves from an ontological perspective to ontogenesis, from space to spacing. Space (as in relativity theory) can be seen as the emergent product of populations of relational networks. Space therefore is a becoming, and the processes, which produce space are those very processes that create all the individual assemblages.

However, on the basis of the arguments so far the problem cannot be reduced to perception and negotiation. Rather in the outlined perspective 'governance' would relate to a plane of *potential conversions* between the populations of firm networks and their connections in agglomeration economies, and the concrete government/non-government assemblages with regard to strategic spatial development. We could say: *'governance' builds an interface*. In the course of actualisation (from virtual to actual, see above) a set of potential connections is actualised while other connections remain potentials. Actualised 'governance-structures' thus refer to *realised (or actualised) conversions* between the above domains. On the other hand, 'governance' also refers to an event of de/re-territorialisations, which modulates the actualisation of both domains in respect of each other.[37] How can we address those conversions, which modulate the relations on an interface between the domains?[38] In the next part we will introduce the concept of transduction in order to engage with conversions on the basis of non-metaphorical complexity and we address temporality as a crucial problem when dealing with eventful de/re-territorialisations or conversion respectively. This brings us one step closer to posing the question of urban governance and strategic planning *differently* in the aftermath of the invention of complexity.

16.6 Governance, transduction and heterochrony

How can we conceptualise 'governance' within a non-metaphorical complexity approach? On the basis of the above ontogenetic conceptualisation of the relevant scales of urban governance it is not adequate to limit the analysis to (linguistic) negotiations. Besides the linguistic roles (referred to in network governance as negotiation) other expressive as well as material roles have to be considered. Furthermore, assemblage theory makes it clear that there cannot be any entity, which is 'above' or 'beyond' assemblages. *There is no bird's eye perspective and no master process; the only position to view, affect, or even think an assemblage is another assemblage.* Therefore planning organisations, social movements, specialised associations, etc. are component parts of the processes of self-organisation. 'Governance' becomes a problem of affecting and being affected. This perspective of being one element in a relational socio-technical collective of spacing actors legitimises a pro-active role of *planners as catalysts* (as in Albrechts, 1999) and the use of all available means in order to affect. In order to

37 We must distinguish actualised governance structures (which are effects of actualised relations), governance as an event (which de/re-territorialises both domains) and governance as the potential of all conversions between domains in the process of their reproduction.

38 The domain refers to the assemblage, which emerges from the relation of sets of lower-scale assemblages.

grasp governance in a non-metaphorical approach to social complexity we moot the concept of transduction (see below).

The relational fundament of assemblage theory makes clear that assemblages are *secondary* to the relations from which they emerge. Therefore by *beginning from the relation*, individual things (people, interpersonal networks, cities) can be understood as effects of relationality. Now an operation, in general terms, modulates the relations between elements of a set. If a process specifically occurs at some kind of limit or interface between different orders, the operation is called a transduction. E.g. a microphone converts sound into electrical energy; a computer screen converts electrical energy into rays of light; an eye converts rays of light into neuro-electrical signals. Transductions thus convert between different domains; a particular domain undergoes a kind of ontogenetic modulation, which means that the way it is actualised changes. A transduction is an event, which cuts through existing lines of actualisation and folds together previously unconnected elements across domains.

Something new actualises, something that was pre-individual or virtual.[39] Doing research on urban governance means in a first step tracing the topologies of transductions within spacing.

If we view the population of socio-technical collectives in knowledge-economy and government/non-government hybrids in the field of strategic spatial development as two relatively separate domains, urban governance (as a real event) means a transduction between them. As we stick to our ontogenetic design transduction is no metaphor. Since in assemblage theory a thing *is* what it *does*, *urban governance is what transduces between domains in spacing*.

What does this mean in terms of actualisation and thus the ontogenetic perspective as outlined in this chapter? In the case of regional studies the interface is topologically, but also temporally, complicated. Ongoing actualisation occurs since transductive operations are nested with each other (on the basis of *exterior relations* assemblages relate outward to other assemblages). Petersson (2005) discusses time in non-linear processes.[40] With Deleuze (in DeLanda, 2002, p. 84) he views actual time as the coexisting plurality of time-formations which – as assemblages do – relate outwards (to other time-formations). A time-formations refers to the intrinsic time of a system. A straightforward example may be the individuation cycle of an organism (duration necessary for replacing the cells of an individual without affecting the organism's identity).[41] But business cycles,

39 Transduction refers to the Deleuzian abstract machines of a 'probe head' that searches among neighbouring systems for relations of loose singularities or 'singularities of resistance, ready to modify these relations, overthrow them and change the unstable diagrams' (Deleuze, 1990, p. 130).

40 He refers to a set of concepts which are all implicitly or explicitly founded on the work of Deleuze. We keep ontogenetically sound by introducing his elaboration on temporality into the assemblage approach.

41 For a detailed discussion see DeLanda, 2002, Chapter 3.

project cycles, electoral cycles, planning cycles, innovation cycles, etc. can also be understood as the heterochronous time-formations of the respective assemblages. This means that their positions in their intrinsic time-cycles usually will be different. They are not governed by a shared interval of time in the sense of a synchronisation of cycles, of phases of higher and lower (in)stability or if you like changing degrees of freedom. If we recall that the degree of freedom alters with the connections in heterogeneous entities (assemblages) and if we also mind our non-linearity foundation it becomes evident that the same disturbance produces a *different* effect in relation to varying positions of assemblages in a time cycle. Thus a governance network displays nested cycles of time-formations (plurality of intrinsic times in the assemblages which give rise to a governance network).

Assemblages therefore display a high sensitivity to the positions, which they occupy in their time-cycles. This means that the same modulation will have different effects according to the relative temporal positions in the cycles of the two domains; the same event thus can produce a set of various consequences. This corresponds to the notion that explanations in an assemblage approach must include non-linear causality. Think, for example, of representations in a planning process. They do produce different consequences according to their relation to the time cycle of the planning procedure. Or as DeLanda (2002) puts it: 'A process may change too slowly or too fast in relation to another process, the relationship between their temporal scales determining in part their respective capacities to affect one another. Even when two processes operate at similar scales, the result of their interaction may depend on their coupled rates of change'.

Petersson argues that if an evolutionary process (as in spacing) occurs in parallel development of relatively independent processes, then an altering of the duration of one process relative to another creates new problems and triggers the actualisation of new designs. The actual 'heterochrony of becoming' thus fuels processes of creation. Since the intrinsic time of a system always relates outwards, alterations in one system may produce radical change (a bifurcation) in a different system (Petersson, 2005). This may cause a phase-transition among a set of nested cycles of time-formations. This means that cycles alter their intrinsic rhythm in relation to each other (since they relate outwards). Transductions thus are likely to alter the individuation of time-formations in affected domains. For example, one outcome of urban governance processes involving organisations and associations from the building industry and governmental and non-governmental organisations is the adjustment of planning cycles with the time-formations in real estate industry, which, again, tends to synchronise with market cycles. A conversion between domains thus also means a re-actualisation of the time-formations. In a topologically and temporally complex field such as urban governance the modulation of one time-formation will almost certainly trigger another problem in respect to different time-formations. In complicated topologies and temporalities a synchronisation in one domain may trigger the potential of heterochrony in related assemblages and further introduces change.

16.7 Conclusion

Why bother with social complexity? In this chapter we have tried to explore how the invention of complexity as an event may impact on the field of urban governance. In order to clear the field we followed Manuel DeLanda in his assemblage approach. With this planners can clarify the ontogenetic status of the things they deal with and also with their own role in the actualisation of places. We introduced the theoretical framework into the field of urban governance by referring to social movements, hybrid government/non-government assemblages, political feed forward-processes, socio-technical collectives, firms and networks, spatial individuals and assemblages of location-networks. This may prove that there are many connections between complexity sciences and more mainstream research in terms of relevant issues and as addressed by various theories.

The relationality foundation of the assemblage approach on the basis of exterior relations shows that collectives emerge from elementary relations. Therefore understanding of how relationality can trigger *different actual solutions* to one virtual problem is crucial for urban governance. The inclusion of forms of causality in combination with linguistic and non-linguistic expressivity transforms the view on 'governance' – interaction cannot be limited to negotiation but must include direct expressive and material roles which component parts of assemblages play. In general terms assemblage theory urges us to put our focus on *real processes of inclusion and exclusion* rather than reify terms and typologies (this leads to homogenisation which is no longer adequate on the basis of non-linearity). It puts the term creation into a very prominent though non-metaphorical position (move beyond social constructivism).

The ontogenetic design of assemblage theory helps to clarify the role of planning. There is no god's eye perspective. Each (planning) intervention is a potential effect between externally related elements – self-regulation and autopoiesis are a direct consequence of the 'flat ontology' of radical relationality of this view on social complexity. Furthermore the ontogenetic perspective on socio-technical assemblages and the material roles that components play move the focus of research and theorising away from an anthropocentric view and manoeuvres analysis around the cliffs of social and technological determinism. The origin of events is as relational as individual things.[42]

Furthermore the outlined approach opens up into a number of potentially useful domains of contemporary theory-building. Concepts such as transduction or heterochrony seem potentially relevant to spatial planning and governance

42 Individual things are effects of relationality.

research. We believe that urban governance as a field of research provides a useful empirical fund for empirical research in social complexity – the illustrations in this chapter may underline this. However, the next step in this line of research comprises of careful empirical tracings of the roles component parts play and of the consequences, which (modulations of) relations produce. However, it is not adequate to merely trace actual things and thus fall back on describing things instead of engaging with their dynamics and their potentials for difference. Since in our ontogenetic perspective the actualisation of things is problematic, 'history' has to be doubled with a becoming. Thus the tracing has to be put back on the map (Deleuze and Guattari, 1987, pp. 99-100).

References

Albrechts, L. (1999) 'Planners as catalysts and initiators of change: The new structure plan for Flanders', *European Planning Studies*, vol. 7(5), pp. 587-604.

Amin, A. (2002) 'Spatialities of globalisation', *Environment and Planning A*, vol. 34, pp. 385-399.

Amin, A. (2004) 'Region unbound: Towards a new politics of place', *Geografisker Annaler*, vol. 86(B), pp. 33-44.

Bathelt, H. (1994) 'Die bedeutung der regulationstheorie in der wirtschaftsgeographischen forschung' ['The relevance of regulation theory for research in economic geography'], *Geographische Zeitschrift*, vol. 2, pp. 63-90.

Bourdieu, P. (1979) 'La distinction: Critique sociale du jugement' ['The distinction: Social review of judgement'], *International Social Science Journal/UNESCO*, Paris, p. 155.

Cooke, P. (1996) 'Reinventing the region: Firms, clusters and networks in economic development', in P. Daniels and W. Lever (eds.), *The Global Economy in Transition*, Longman, Harlow.

Davies, E. (2007) 'DeLanda destratified', available at http://www.techgnosis.com/delandad.html, viewed December 20, 2007.

DeLanda, M. (1997) *A Thousand Years of Nonlinear History*, Zone Books, New York.

DeLanda, M. (2002) *Intensive Science and Virtual Philosophy*, Continuum, London.

DeLanda, M. (2006a) *A New Philosophy of Society: Assemblage Theory and Social Complexity*, Continuum, London/New York.

DeLanda, M. (2006b) 'Deleuzian social ontology and assemblage theory', in M. Fugslang and B. Meier Sorensen (eds.), *Deleuze Connections*, Edinburgh University Press, Edinburgh, pp. 250-266.

DeLanda, M., Protevi, J. and Thanaem, T. (2006) 'Deleuzian interrogations: A conversation with Manuel DeLanda, John Protevi and Torkild Thanem' (electronic version), *Journal of Critical Postmodern Organisation Science*, available at www.tamarajournal.com, viewed January 15, 2007.

Deleuze, G. (1990) *The Logic of Sense* (trans. Mark Lester and Charles Stivale, orig. 1969), Columbia University Press, New York.

Deleuze, G. (1991) *Empiricism and Subjectivity*, Columbia Press, New York.

Deleuze, G. and Parnet, C. (2002) *Dialogues II*, Columbia Press, New York.

De Roo, G. (2003) *Environmental Planning in the Netherlands: Too Good to be True*, Ashgate, Aldershot.

Dosi, G. (ed.) (1988) *Technical Change and Economic Theory*, Pinter, London.

Dosi, G. and Nelson, R.R. (1994) 'An introduction to evolutionary theories in economics', *Journal of Evolutionary Economics*, vol. 4, pp. 153-172.

Giddens, A. (1984) *The Constitution of Society: Outline of the Theory of Structuration*, University of California Press, Berkeley.

Granovetter, M. (1973) 'The strength of weak ties', *American Journal of Sociology*, vol. 78(6), pp. 1360-1380.

Healey, P. (2004a) 'Creativity and urban governance', *Policy Studies*, vol. 25(2), pp. 87-102.

Healey, P. (2004b) 'Relational complexity and the imaginative power of strategic spatial planning', *European Planning Studies*, vol. 14(4), pp. 525-546.

Healey, P. (2006a) 'Network complexity and the imaginative power of strategic spatial planning', in L. Albrechts and S. Mandelbaum (eds.), *The Network Society: The New Context for Planning*, Routledge, London.

Healey, P. (2006b) *Urban Complexity and Spatial Strategies: Towards a Relational Planning for our Times*, Routledge, London.

Hillier, J. (2005) 'Straddling the post-structuralist abyss: Between transcendence and immanence?', *Planning Theory*, vol. 4(3), pp. 271-299.

Jessop, B. (1997a) 'Survey article: The regulation approach', *The Journal of Political Philosophy*, vol. 5, pp. 287-326.

Jessop, B. (1997b) 'Twenty years of the (Parisian) regulation approach: The paradox of success and failure at home and abroad', *New Political Economy*, vol. 2, pp. 503-526.

Jessop, B. (1998) 'The rise of governance and the risks of failure: The case of economic development', *International Social Science Journal*, issue 155, pp. 29-46.

Jessop, B. (1999) 'The governance of complexity and the complexity of governance: Preliminary remarks on some problems and limits of economic guidance', http://www.lancs.ac.uk/fass/sociology/papers/jessop-governance-of-complexity.pdf, accessed May 20, 2006.

Law, J. and Urry, J. (2004) 'Enacting the social', *Economy and Society*, vol. 33(3), pp. 390-410.

Lundvall, B.A. (ed.) (1992) *National Systems of Innovation. Towards a Theory of Innovation and Interactive Learning*, Pinter, London.

Mackenzie, A. (2002) *Transductions: Bodies and Machines at Speed*, Continuum, London.

Massey, D. (2005) *For Space*, Sage, London.

Massumi, B. (2002) *Parables of the Virtual: Movement, Affect, Sensation*, Duke University Press, Durham.

Mayr, E. (1978) *Evolution und Vielfalt des Lebens* [*Evolution and Life in Manifold*], Springer, Berlin.

Moulaert, F. and Mehmood, A. (2007) 'Analysing regional development: From territorial innovation to path-dependent geography', in W. Dolfsma and J. Davies (eds.), *The Elgar Handbook of Socio-Economics*, Edward Elgar, Camberley.

Moulaert, F. and Swyngedouw, E. (1989) 'A regulation approach to the geography of flexible production systems', *Environment and Planning D: Society and Space*, vol. 7, pp. 327-334.

Roffe, J. (2006) 'Gilles Deleuze', in, *The Internet Encyclopaedia of Philosophy*, available at www.iep.utm.edu/d/deleuze.htm, Last updated on July 12, 2005, accessed August 12, 2009.

Oehler, S. (2005) *Entwicklungsstrategien und Kooperationsformen im mittleren Glattal* [*Development Strategies and Cooperation in the mid Glattal*], University of Zürich, Zürich.

Pease, A. (2005) 'Manuel DeLanda's *Art of Assemblage*', *Electronic Book Review*, available at http://www.electronicbookreview.com/thread/criticalecologies/morphogenetic, viewed October 17, 2007.

Petersson, D. (2005) 'Time and technology', *Environment and Planning D*, vol. 23, pp. 207-234.

Sonntag, R.E. and Wylen, G.J. van (1991) *Introduction to Thermodynamics*, John Wiley & Sons, London.

Sorensen, E. and Torfing, J. (2004) 'Making governance networks democratic', Centre for Democratic Network Governance, Working Paper Series 2004(1), Roskilde University, Roskilde.

Stengers, I. (2000) *The Invention of Modern Science*, University of Minnesota Press, Minneapolis.

Thierstein, A. (2006) *Raumentwicklung im Verborgenen* [*Spatial Development in Secrecy*], NZZ Verlag, Zürich.

Thrift, N. (1999) 'The place of complexity', *Theory, Culture and Society*, vol. 16(3), pp. 31-69.

Thrift, N. (2000) 'Afterwords', *Environment and Planning D: Society and Space*, vol. 18, pp. 213-255.

Thrift, N. (1996) *Spatial Formations*, Sage, London.

Tilly, C. (1999) *Durable Inequality*, University of California Press, Berkeley.

Van Wezemael, J.E. (2000) 'Verändert die Marktmiete die residenzielle Segregation? Die Marktmiete aus sozial- und wirtschaftsgeographischer Sicht' ['Does Uncontrolled Rent Change Residential Segregation? Uncontrolled Rent from a Social and Economic Geography Perspective'], *Geographica Helvetica*, vol. 4, pp. 251-261.

Van Wezemael, J.E. (2006) 'The contribution of assemblage theory and minor politics for democratic network governance', Conference on Democratic Network Governance in Europe, Centre for Democratic Network Governance, Roskilde.

Zuidema, C. and Roo, G. de (2004) 'Integrating complexity theory into planning: truth or dare?', paper presented at the 18th Annual Aesop Conference at Grenoble, available http://www.ruimte-rijk.nl/index/ publicaties/publicaties/ DeRoo%20Zuidema%20 2004%20Aesop, accessed October 24, 2007.

Chapter 17
Waves of Complexity: Theory, Models and Practice

Elisabete A. Silva[1]

This chapter explores the importance of phase-transitions and bifurcations in order to understand complexity. The first part of the chapter starts by briefly addressing the evolution of complexity in the natural and physical sciences and the transposition of knowledge from these scientific fields into mainstream research and to the land use related subjects (i.e. Geography, Planning, Architecture, Spatial Econometrics and Urban Sociology). Two relevant approaches are going to be explored: Cellular Automata and Genetic Algorithms. The second part of the chapter addresses the importance of clearly defining what is complexity and what are complexity's main characteristics, concluding that a graphical representation of 'waves' is good to explain and classify what complex and non-complex phenomena are. Once this is done it is possible to explain what bifurcations and phase-transitions are and their importance in complexity studies. The third part of this chapter addresses how to represent in a quantitative way these graphical waves of complex and non-complex phenomena, detailing some of today's relevant data models available to represent the complexity of the different phenomena.

17.1 Introduction: The awakening to the complex systems approach

Until recently, complexity was generally associated with randomness. An objective of science was to reduce this randomness and reveal underlying order, either by inferential statistics or through the construction of analytical models. A consequence of the resulting studies of the previously used analytical/deterministic models was the loss of relevant information that could help to explain processes and patterns in the study of urban systems. Complexity Thinking might offer us alternative solutions.

The understanding of the importance of complexity came from two main scientific areas: *(i)* the dynamics of the micro behaviour and the formation of patterns, particularly in the chemical and biological fields, *(ii)* and the production of patterns of behaviour, through the behavioural social sciences.

---

1 Dr. Elisabete A. Silva is University Lecturer at the Department of Land Economy, University of Cambridge, United Kingdom.

The study of complexity has become important to understand self-organisation and chaotic systems (Wilson, 2000; Phillips, 1999; Kay, 1999; Toffoli, 1998; Holland, 1995; Kauffman, 1993; Prigogine, 1984). One of its assumptions is that simple processes can lead to intricate spatial patterns. Therefore, complexity that was long dismissed as randomness, in fact represents an alternative order inherent in a system (White, 1994). One of the disciplines that first simulated complex, dynamic and self-organising processes was Biology; using the field of Artificial Life, natural 'organic' processes were simulated in an artificial computational environment (Delorme, 1999; Goles, 1996; Resnick, 1995; Langton, 1991).

At the basis for this change towards an understanding of complexity is the work of Von Neumann and Morgenstern's theory of games and economic behaviour (1944); these researchers initiated a very important pan-disciplinary paradigm change. The theory of games was particularly important, it demonstrated that far from determinism, continuity, calculus, it is indeterminism, probability, and discontinuous changes of state that control the behaviour of most systems. The emphasis in modelling shifted therefore from the determinant to structure, in particular to the behaviour of the elements of systems and their contribution to the overall patterns and processes in a system.

Von Neumann's work with Standislav Ulam, during the 1950s, linked game theory and micro behaviour, through the development of simple Cellular Automaton (CA). CA provides local rules which could generate mathematical patterns in two-dimensional and three dimensional space. Therefore global order could be produced from local action.

Von Neumann called his proposed systematic theory the 'theory of automata'. This theory of automata was to be a coherent body of concepts and principles concerning the structure and organisation of both natural and artificial systems, the role of language and information in such systems, and the programming and control of such systems (Von Neumann, 1966, p. 18).

Conways's game of life, popularised by Gardner in 1970, widened these ideas through other fields of science. Simulations of death and life in a game showed the striking similarities between real life and simulated life in a computer. Cells would survive or die in function of competition for space, crowdness, minimum number of neighbours required in order to live in society and reproduce.

More recently, Wolfram's book *A New Kind of Science* (2002) explores the importance of having a new science that does not dismiss complexity, instead that tries to understand it. Batty's *Cities and Complexity* (2005) assembles one of the first books with a clear and consistent body of theory in the subject of complexity and planning.

17.2 Cellular Automata and Genetic Algorithm models in spatial analysis

Cellular Automata

Complexity analysis came into the field of spatial analysis later in time, during the 1970s particularly through Waldo Tobler's work. Tobler had contact with Arthur Burks who exposed him to Von Neumann's works, which became a source of inspiration to write 'Cellular geography' (1979). Helen Couclelis, influenced by Tobler, and by Prigogine's work on molecular interactions and the resulting large-scale spatial structure, published 'Cellular worlds' (Couclelis, 1985). Finally, decades of research on dynamic systems and computer applications by Michael Batty culminated in the publication of the seminal book *Fractal Cities* (1994).

Tobler and Burks work are particularly important in the field of Cellular Automaton (CA). They were the first to explain the spatial components that a CA should be comprised and what kind of structure spatial systems should have in order to represent its dynamic behaviour. Nowadays, Cellular Automaton theory has evolved greatly from the initial concepts of: *(i)* A grid or raster space – organised by cells which are the smallest units in that grid/space; *(ii)* Cell States – cells must manifest adjacency or proximity. The state of a cell can change according to transition rules, which are defined in terms of neighbourhood functions; *(iii)* The neighbourhood and dependency of the state of any cell on the state and configuration of other cells in the neighbourhood of that cell; *(iv)* Transition rules that are decision rules or transition functions of the cellular model and can be deterministic or stochastic; *(v)* Sequences of time steps. When activated, the Cellular Automaton proceeds through a series of iterations. For each iteration (time step), the cells in the grid are examined. Based on the composition of cells in the neighbourhood of that central cell, transition rules are applied to determine the central state of the cell in the next iteration.

Wolfram (1994, pp. 3-7) outlined a number of characteristics that CA possesses:

i. The correspondence between physical and computational processes is clear;
ii. CA models are much simpler than complex mathematical equations, but produce results that are more complex;
iii. CA models can be modelled using computers with no loss of precision (degree of closeness with real world systems);
iv. CA can mimic the actions of any possible physical system;
v. CA models are irreducible.

These characteristics are of outmost importance for Complexity Theory once they proove that CAs have properties that imply that there is no pre-knowledge of a global structure and that any global pattern created by CA is not prescribed or predetermined but rather emerges from purely local interactions. Therefore, the complex systems can be understood at its most pure state, including, and not dismissing, some of the most important elements that are non-linear, and consequently less obvious.

At the present day CA models have evolved and are able to include other processes that might impact local behaviour (such as government policies). Nevertheless those initial characteristics were fundamental to understand that local action had an important impact in the generation of global patterns and that, for instance, individuals and their daily options could justify for instance the formation of the regional patterns of movement. Therefore if researchers want to understand these complex system dynamics they need to start by simulating their behavioural interactions.

Cellular Automata models are based on the premise that it is possible to describe the complex patterns of natural phenomena (and human resulting phenomena) by modelling the simple rules that govern the actions of the component parts, and consequently, emergent patterns, and properties can be identified.

Cellular Automata can be seen, in their more primary state, as discrete models of spatio-temporal dynamics obeying local laws. The work of Prigogine pioneered the relationships between molecular interactions in chemical reactions, and demonstrated the importance of this micro-macro interaction in pattern identification. In the same way the works of Holland (1999), Crutchfield (1995), and Kauffman (1984) have been important in pointing out the emergent properties of random complex automata.

While the patterns obtained with different rules differ in detail, they appear to fall into four qualitative classes, in what concerns one-dimension (1-D) Cellular Automata:

i. Evolution leads to a homogenous state;
ii. Evolution leads to a set of separated simple stable or periodic structures;
iii. Evolution leads to a chaotic pattern;
iv. Evolution leads to complex localised structures, sometimes long-lived (Wolfram, 1984:5).

The observation that micro-simulations led to macro-patterns, and that main patterns were imprinted at several scales, raises the question of the existence of a fractal character in their CA simulations, pointing to other similarities between CA and the bifurcation paradigm (Silva and Clarke, 2001; Batty, 1996). If results reveal to be correct, this implies that there are patterns that have a repetitive behaviour at multiple scales (Batty, 1996) and therefore the repetition of the same urban structures at multiple scales is possible. If this is a case, this would be the first demonstration that at a certain moment of urban evolution a leap/bifurcation of scale would allow the same repetitive process and the generation of a similar pattern at a different scale.

The bifurcation paradigm assumes that the transition between states is not constant and continuous. Instead it is composed by a set of variations, phase-transitions that can explain sudden increase or decrease of intensity, or totally different directions of evolution. If this is the case, not only bifurcation phases are an expression in the explanation of fractal dimensions, but also that the quantification and qualification of these fractal dimensions will be at the basis of unveiling the understanding of urban form in a more quantitative way.

Genetic Algorithms

While CA development seemed to be decisive to the understanding of complexity at the spatial scale, a second stream of research was also being developed. In the case of Genetic Algorithms (GA), the goal is to focus in behavioural and social systems. This second stream of research focuses on the different behavioural options that human beings are faced with, using for instance decision trees and neuronal nets, and extrapolating such concepts to a new modelling environment called Genetic Algorithms (GA). While today research starts to integrate both approaches of CA and GA, during several decades these were studied apart.

While Genetic Algorithms (GA) usually do not have a direct representation in space as is the case with CA, they are very important as representations of phenomena in terms of explaining what is at the basis of decisions and options (i.e. why do we choose to perform a specific option). Therefore GAs play a major role in explaining decisions making processes that leads to specific spatial actions. The core theory of GA is in the work developed by John Nash exploring research results by Merrill Flood and Melvin Dresher at RAND corporation[2] (1950s); in doing so he open up a new field of computational exploration of human behaviour (Nash, 1950a; Nash, 1950b; Nash, 1953).

The research developed by Flood and Dresher at RAND Corporation are at the basis of the understanding of human behaviour and how to extrapolate that behaviour to understandable rules. Their most known finding is 'the prisoner's dilemma' (the formalisation and name came from Albert W. Tucker – PhD adviser of John Nash). The prisoner's dilemma states that if two prisoners (players) have a choice each on whether to betray the other, and thus to decrease one's own jail time, while increasing the jail time for the other, common sense tell us that in this competitive environment a cooperative strategy should be the best option, nevertheless, because of the uncertainly both will tend to choose to 'betray'. This leads to what is commonly known as a 'non-zero-sum game'. They have the option to cooperate or 'betray' each other. Nash was able to prove that if each person/player has chosen a strategy and no person/player can benefit by changing his or her strategy while the other players keep theirs unchanged, then the current

2 Besides RAND Corporation, a second group contributed fundamentally to research in GAs at the Santa Fe Institute. While RAND Corporation (**R**esearch **AN**d **D**evelopment, Corporation) is a post war non profit company dedicated to research, the Santa Fe Institute is a 1980s development, as a result of research practiced at the Los Alamos National Laboratory. Both of these research centres have strong links with universities and university research laboratories.

set of strategy choices and the corresponding payoffs constitute an equilibrium (what is now called a Nash equilibrium).

If human behaviour could be classified accordingly to patterns in a more quantifiable way and Nash's equilibrium represents the first clear demonstration of the outcome of players in a game, this implied that more research could be performed. Some of Nash's conclusions opened the doors to more developments in the social and economical sciences (i.e. in Psychology the demonstrations of the Pavlovian behaviour, in the Economic field the exploration of the formation of Cartels). Therefore, the post Second World War explanations of behaviour in a more mathematical way, by attempting to incorporate the complexity associated to individual behaviour, using game theory and strategising techniques, has brought us another important element of the theory by focusing on public-individual choice and option.

Genetic Algorithms (GA) are constituted of: *(i)* agents that do not have the constraints of neighbourhood effects, *(ii)* behavioural roles among agents and the environment itself, *(iii)* independence from central command/control, but able to act if action at a distance is required, *(iv)* states of agents tend to represent behavioural forms. These models tend to behave as populations of simple agents that interact locally with each other and their environment and produce swarm intelligence (machine resulting intelligence, or emergent behaviour in machines not directly resulting from code development, in CA and GA has the attribute of generating similar local behaviour for several agents or cells with no prior knowledge – its outcome is self organising group behaviour with no prior knowledge. In real life this would be similar to a flock of birds – while they behave individually, overall there is a pattern in the skies).

While Cellular Automata (CA) has a spatial explicit representation that makes it very apt to model urban and environmental systems (i.e. land parcels, transportation infrastructures), Genetic Algorithms (GA) are important for their behavioural roles that are very apt to model individual agents and their behaviour (i.e. households, vehicles and pedestrians).

During the 1960s, 1970s and 1980s the basic elements of complexity analysis both in the natural and social sciences were draft. Some of them were at that time still conjectures that are now being explored with more detail. During the 1990s it started to become clear that these two approaches of modelling with Cellular Automaton or with Genetic Algorithms had become the two most used approaches to work with complexity in a quantitative formulation.

Nevertheless, researchers would tend to separate both approaches. These tended to be in opposing fields, defending one or another approach. These were almost hermetic areas of research where little information would cross-fertilise the development of new methodologies. For those not familiar with the subject it would be very hard to argue for one or another method. And the result tended to be a blind option disregarding the questions being answered and the selection of the best methodology for that purpose. At that time, the meaning of complexity in itself was still unknown to the majority, and therefore it was very difficult to describe what complexity was, what were its elements and mechanics. For some of us it becomes clear that without this explanation it would be difficult to select the best methodological option (CA or GA) or to develop hybrid methodologies that included CA and GA.

It is important to understand when and how we should use CA and GA in order to optimise their application, and when we should use other methodologies that might be more deterministic in approach and still give the best result. Consequently, first we need to clarify what is complexity, and how to model it.

17.3 What is complexity and what are its elements and mechanics?

As described in the previous chapters, the subject of complexity and complex systems is a growing subject of research both in the development of application and theory. Nevertheless, while complexity studies are now considered very important in order to understand reality, much confusion exists on what is complexity and how it can be described. Complexity can be described accordingly to several key elements/variables and a specific set of mechanics that dynamically contribute to complex system behaviour. This chapter will focus on two of the elements that best describes complexity. These elements are bifurcations and phase-transitions.

When answering to the question 'What is complexity and what are its elements and mechanics' the use of the concepts of bifurcations or phase-transitions is of paramount importance to the definition and understanding of complexity and some of its elements that compose complexity. In other words it is important to answer the following questions:

1. What are the mechanics of complexity?
2. What make the mechanics of complexity different from other non-complex phenomena?
3. Are there complex and non-complex phenomena?
4. If so, when can we state that we are in one or another state (a complex and a non complex state)?
5. Is complexity an attribute of a particular time and space (i.e. there are specific time frames and specific scales where complexity is more evident)?
6. If so how can we measure its transient identity?
7. Can we state that time plays a very important function in complexity?
8. If so, how can we asses complexity time-frames?

The next paragraphs will try to answer these questions in separate parts, starting by the attempts to explain what complexity is.

When representing various phenomena, it is possible to represent, for instance, their intensity or frequency through time. Figure 17.1 presents a graphic representation of the behaviour of specific phenomena through time. Usually, physics literature tends to use the evolution of temperature and the formation of patters of convection cells in water progressing to a boiling phase. For planning purposes we can transpose this to a transportation system and the evolution to a congested state or the competition for land among different land use types.

This figure assumes that the behaviour of a variable or a set of variables is not constant through time (i.e. there will be moments in time it will present different intensities). Therefore there will be certain moments in time that the amplitude of occurrence of a specific variable will manifest itself with different intensities. For instance, in the case of a transportation system, we will have more traffic in streets during the morning and late in the afternoon as a result of commuting to work. Therefore the graphical representation of this transportation system will be a curve representing the number of cars in a street having at least two peaks.

As it is possible to observe, at the graphic image of Figure 17.1 there is a moment in time where the intensity of a specific variable or phenomena reaches a maximum. As well there is a moment in time when it reaches its lowest intensity. Between the two there is a curve that describes that variation of intensity.

The slope of this curve describes an important attribute in the understanding of what is complexity and what is not complexity; that is to say when should we use complexity (in particular GA and CA approaches) to model a specific phenomena or a part of its behaviour.

In this context, Figure 17.1 is important because it can represent the variation in a phenomenon like water boiling, or when analysing a complex transportation problem. Understanding the dynamics of that system (and its different amplitudes and intensities) will help us in clarifying when to use models that need to incorporate complexity and/or when to use more deterministic models.

Trying to understand the dynamics of a system, water boiling might be a good example, as this tends to be the simplest explanation for those not directly involved in modelling of complex systems. Between the steady states of having water at air temperature and boiling water, if heat is provided water molecules will need to self organise (water molecules tend to organise accordingly to convection cells, but until they reach this, there is a 'chaotic' process of water molecules adjusting to the heat being inputted into the system). In order to represent this self-organisation of water molecules we need a different model that reflects this complexity.

Only through complex systems can we describe with a certain degree of validity and reliability such kind of transient phases (it is becoming very difficult to report reality only as a snapshot of time, we need to have dynamic models that report these self-organising systems and these far from equilibrium systems). In other words, complex systems specifically address the moments in time when a system is changing to something that does not belong to one or another state of equilibrium (i.e. a 0° temperature or a 100° temperature). In Figure 17.1 that state can be represented by the letter B, the specific moment in time when a system starts to present a kind of chaotic behaviour that makes it impossible to classify as steady-state water or as boiling water.

Therefore at Figure 17.1 one might conclude that, letters A and C can be described by complex systems, but there are other models (usually deterministic)

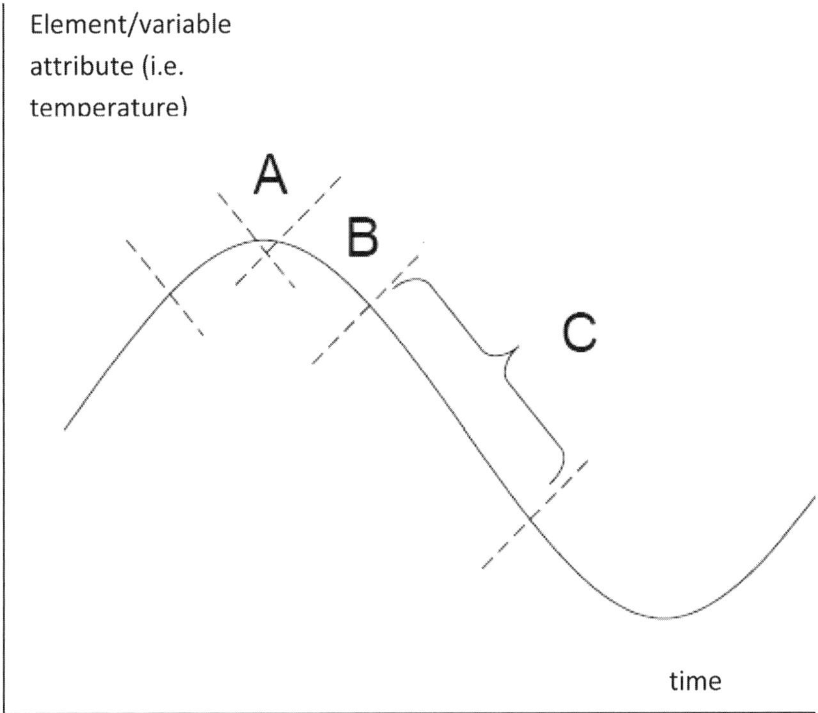

Figure 17.1 How to identify a complex element or phenomena in time

that also describe it. Particularly with regard to case 'C' it is possible to state that this is not a complex system.

The moment in time represented by the letter B can only be explained by complexity (i.e. water convection cells – at the edge of 'chaos'). B can only be understood by using complexity models (more stochastic in approach). Why is this the case? Because B represents a 'transient reality', something that will become something different (the trajectory is not 'linear').

If the understanding of phenomena such as the variation of the number of cars in a transportation system can be represented for a particular moment in time in Figure 17.1, it is also possible to describe it through time (i.e. day-by-day variation of flow of traffic in a roadway system), as presented in Figure 17.2. Therefore, for a specific variable C1 (i.e. cars flowing in the transportation system) it is possible to evaluate the moments in time where this transient reality emerges, that is to say the transition from a 'non saturate' to a 'saturated' state (at times t01, t02, t03, t04, t05, t06, t06, t07).

Using the example of a transportation system, it is possible to understand the moment when a system evolves from a non-congested to a congested situation.

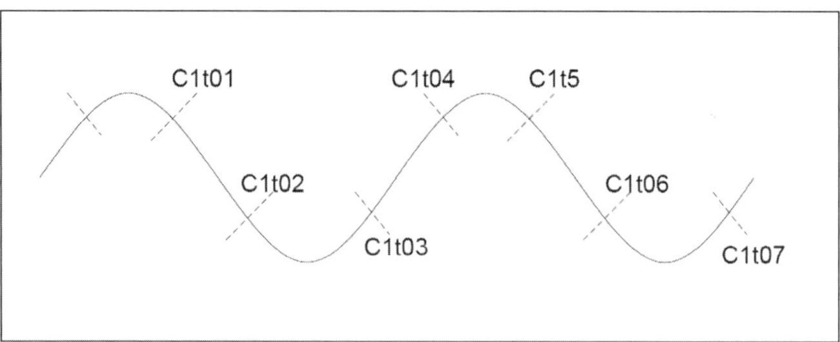

Figure 17.2 Identification of complex behaviour for an element or phenomena through time

Traditional transportation systems evolve from a set of radial roads to/from the CBD (Central Business District), to a net of radials, circulars, with different flow capacities, and high interoperability with other transportation systems (i.e. subway, trains). As such addressing solely origin/destination dynamics can not incorporate these dynamics and therefore are facing some planning problems. Understanding this transition phase when transportation systems start to be 'saturated' is of extreme importance, and for that, we firstly need to identify in Figure 17.2 when these transition phases are happening.

Following the same reasoning, if we can represent a variable through time and pinpoint where transition is happening, we also can represent the same process/ mechanics not only for one variable but for as many variables as one needs (Figure 17.3a).

Expanding from the previous reasoning, it is possible to state that as one is focusing on the representation of complexity for a specific variable along time, we can also analyse the evolution of specific phenomena (i.e. the moment in time and space when the 'saturation' of a transportation system is happening and what other variables, besides the number of cars that might be contributing to that specific phenomena of traffic congestion), and therefore trying to understand where are its most representative transition phases (i.e. the timing of traffic lights throughout the day, or the offer of parking places during a day/weeks).

Therefore, it is important to have a multidimensional representing of variables or/and phenomena (conjugation of different variables) and its associated transition phases (Figure 17.3b). That is to say that complexity analysis plays an important role in the analysis of these moments in time, and is particularly useful to define where these transition-phases are for each variable, for each phenomenon, for the different scales and for the different moments of time (these phases are portrayed in a simplified way as dashed lines in the figures).

Analysing Figure 17.3b it is possible to see the final image of the previous reasoning. This is a complex image of waves and its associated transient moments

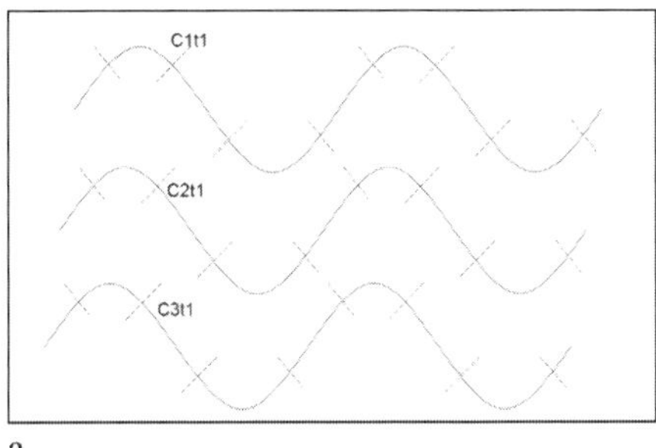

a

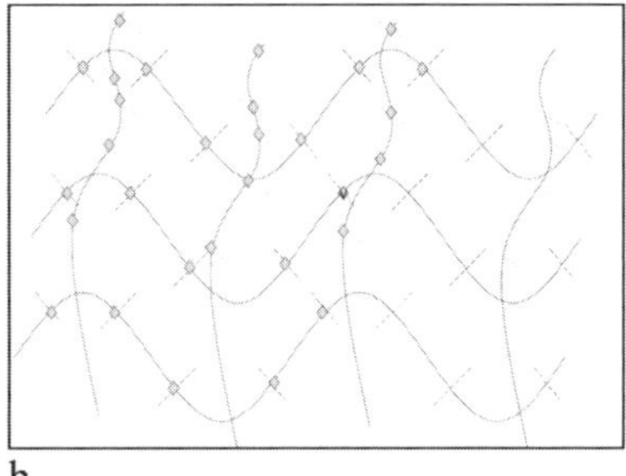

b

Figure 17.3 Identification of complex behaviour for multiple elements or variables through time and space

(dashed lines - for simplification purposes instead of having two dashed lines as in Figure 17.1, the option was to use a dashed line at Figure 17.2 and Figure 17.3a).

In other words, representing the moment in time and space when an event registers its phase-transition will allow to understand when an event is triggered (trigger points). The use of the term of trigger point is not new in system theory literature, and the reference here helps to clarify the importance of these processes as enablers of transitions of phases. Trigger points were conceptualised by Eccles and Jordan in 1919 and by Schmitt (1938) in electronics fields. This is now a term used in many subject areas, such as computer programming in particular in the group of event-driven programming; in the financial sector they are considered as trigger-lists. In its most general meaning it refers to actions or events that are used to initiate ('trigger') other actions/events. Therefore these phase-transition of Figure 17.3b can also have a representation as trigger points, particularly if we are considering a specific moment in space and time (these trigger points are onwards described in the figures by a shape like diamond) in the graphic. While a phase-transition reports self-organisation of a system accordingly to the variation of a specific attribute of a variable or accordingly to the variations registered in several variables though time, trigger points focus on one precise moment in time and space of that transition-phase that triggers the change process.

These trigger points can be described as enablers for boom or boost phases (Silva and Clarke, 2001). It is possible to observe in the curve these 'trigger points'. In the example of the water boiling, these represent the moments when the values tend to increase temperature – boom phase; or the moment in the curve when the values tend to reduce intensity – boost phase; and trigger the entire self-organisation of water molecules. These trigger points can have a more local representation resulting from local self-organisation dynamics (i.e. neighbourhood effect of different land uses in a CA model). They can also be the result of some kind of action at a distance that causes an immediate change of state (i.e. in the transportation system the existence of transportation policies that impact local

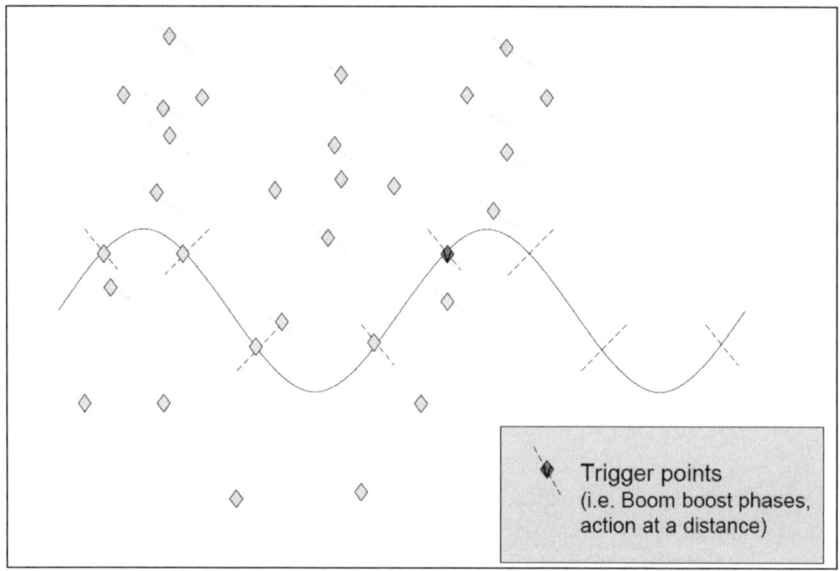

Figure 17.4 The identification of trigger points in space and time

dynamics such as imposition of higher parking fees by the city or government authorities).

Therefore, and for the purpose of complexity analysis, it is as important to make the graphical representation (and analysis) of these waves as it is the making of the graphical representation of the diamonds representing trigger points, once these pinpoint the trigger points of each transition (Figure 17.4).

If the identification of these transition phases is important for one variable, or phenomena, it is fundamental in the understanding of systems behaviour and the classification of a moment in time where multiple variables interact to produce a substantial change in a system. Therefore the 'triggers' that fundamentally constrain (or push) the behaviour of a system can be activated at different moments in time, scales and for different variables (Figure 17.5).

One of the conclusions that can be pointed out by the previous analysis is the fact that in some cases with phenomena aggregating multiple variables, it is reasonable to state that it is impossible to point out only one variable as its major cause of change; even if that change might manifest itself firstly in one particular variable, it is the result of multiple variables acting simultaneously. Therefore, in this case we should speak about a trigger point in time that enables an entire event.

The previous logical reasoning leads to the second fundamental question that also needs to be addressed: the mechanics of complexity (the first question was: what is complexity?). In other words, answering the question of what are 'the

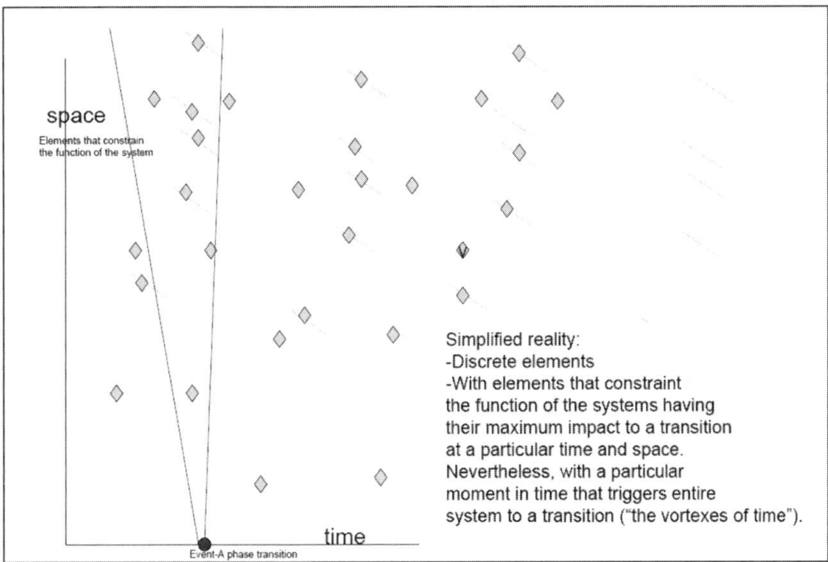

Figure 17.5 How a particular phase-transition is deployed: The vortex of time

mechanics of complexity' that allows us to understand and explain the behaviour of a variable/variables/system elementary for its change?

In this multi-dimensional environment (different variables evolving through time with different waves of intensity) it is possible to identify and search for different trigger points: *(i)* through time and for the same variable; *(ii)* through space, for the same moment in time, but at multiples scales; *(iii)* through time and for multiple variables and different scales; *(iv)* for a specific event at a particular time and its 'catchment area' (vortex of time) that enables changes in multiple variables through time (Figure 17.5). The term 'vortex of time' is relating to Einstein's relativity theory that states that time and space are woven together, forming a four-dimensional fabric called 'space-time' evolving 'objects' (i.e. earth) being the final visual form of that vortex.

This vortex concept adjusts to this image of multiple events in space and time generating a trigger point that will enable other events to succeed. In this context, a kind of 'catchment area' of multiple trigger points would enable a system to change its characteristics. For instance in order for a system to reach its maximum carrying capacity, multiple variables will contribute to that, but at a certain moment in time the entire system will be disrupted. In many cases we can see the moment in time that triggered that maximum carrying capacity and even assume that only one variable was responsible for that, when in fact it might happen that many other variables intervened in the process.

Figure 17.5 is particularly important, once it represents the main trigger points that contribute to a specific phase-transition or a bifurcation (the example of a systems' carrying capacity can be used here, once we can have many variables contributing to trigger a subsequent major event). This is important because this chapter argues that for land related subjects highly dependent on human actions, in the case of phase-transitions or bifurcations it is unreasonable to point out a specific change in a variable or a set of variables as the main driver for change (usually human related systems have a multitude of elements contributing to its actions and land impacts). Therefore it is important to understand the dynamics of the entire system in order to understand change. And this needs to be done through a complex systems approach (as traditional cause-effect determinist models produce far from satisfactory explanations).

Therefore it might be unacceptable to state for a great number of human induced dynamics that only one specific element can cause its own change. In terms of a classification of phase-transitions or bifurcations it is important to look at the behaviour of the entire system. And therefore, in some cases there might be a probability that the moment in time when a phase-transition happens that a specific individual event justifies the change. In other cases it might be the result of cumulative effects of different variables. Or, it might be the case that a phase-transition has a particular relevance in a variable but in order to address that change, other variables (probably more important) should also be considered.

17.4 Phase-transitions or bifurcations

The next question to be answered in the scope of complexity analysis is the importance of making a distinction between phase-transitions and bifurcations. There is a lot of confusion in the different research areas (including physics) regarding these two notions. There are several possible explanations for that confusion. Having in account research we have done with cellular automata, we will point out two of the factors that seem to have relevance when comparing the differences between bifurcations and phase-transitions:

a. If we are speaking about changing the fundamental 'being' of a variable or of a phenomena we have a bifurcation (i.e. mass extinctions, changes from migrant to sedentary societies, change in DNA).
b. If we are speaking about a change in 'state' we are speaking about phase/transition (i.e. water and its states).

Cellular Automata are particularly important in unveiling these two different characteristics (Silva and Clarke, 2002; Silva, 2004). Cities and regions also have 'unique' representations of main elements that constrain their behaviour making them different from each other. Because Cellular Automata are sensitive to local conditions (due to the cell-by-cell representation and its scale and time calibration) the values resulting from calibration are representative of the uniqueness of a region-city. These values tend to represent the 'intensity' of the variables that control the behaviour of a system, through time and space and by doing so they represent the uniqueness of that same region-city (Silva, 2004).

Artificial Intelligence models, such as Cellular Automaton and Genetic Algorithms, are the best modelling approaches to represent complexity in terms of phase-transitions or in terms of bifurcations. The main reason for that being the fact is that complexity, as presented in Figure 17.5, cannot be studied as a one-dimension representation. It requires a dynamic representation of time and space that even goes beyond simplistic planar (2D) representations. We need both time and space interactions working simultaneously. As a change in an element or in a phenomenon tends to be the result of multiple causes, objectively addressing it as a cause-effect kind of relation with one unique explanation would miss the multiple relations required to trigger a process. Therefore the mathematical representation of cause and effect would poorly represent the causes for change.

17.5 The representation of these waves of complexity and its best data models

Defining complexity would not be totally understood unless we select data models that best represent the behaviour of these systems (that is to say, the reality can be studied from multiple perspectives, in some instances it still makes sense to use more deterministic models, while in other cases this would be totally inadequate). Therefore, the next question to explore is: how to represent these waves of complexity? There are four ways of representing waves of complexity and they can be classified as follows:

Class membership (C1T1,C2T1)	CA and Fuzzy Sets
By the curve (stats. mean) (C1T03 – C1T06)	any statistic package
Moment of transition (C1T1)	GA and Neuronal Nets
Intersection of trajectories (<C1T1,<C1T2)	Fuzzy Sets

In order to explore these four groups it is important to bring back to memory Figure 17.1, 17.2 and 17.3 as the starting point to understand complexity and non-complex phenomena and to select the best model to study it.

In order to understand representations of waves in the group class membership represented in Figure 17.3a by 'C1T1, C2T1' the models that best describe this behaviour of the curve are Cellular Automaton and Fuzzy Sets. These models have the capacity of detecting particular phase-transitions or bifurcations (i.e. through the development of calibration methods that allow detecting trigger points. For instance in the work developed by Silva and Clarke, 2002, 2004) and Clarke, Hoppen and Gaydos (1998) trigger points can be represented for instance by 'boom' and 'boost' phases and self-modification phases). These models can be described as representing the complexity in a kind of 'Class Membership'. For instance when using CA, vast amounts of numbers are outputted each time we run the model. In order to cope with the vast amounts of information, the first thing researchers tend to do is to apply cluster analysis, aggregating outputs that are more representative of the behaviour of the different metrics. This basic data aggregation methodology (as more advanced data mining techniques are lacking) is of outmost importance, not only because it allows to calibrate the model to the known reality, but also because we can use the resulting values to compare different case studies (i.e. though the use of what we have been calling DNAs).

Perhaps the goal is to report processes represented in the figures as a continuous evolution of a variable that has a graphic representation of a curve. Take for instance an example of the analysis of temperature: for instance the decrease of air temperature at the letter C in Figure 17.1. Or take the average variation in one attribute along 30 years (Figure 17.2.). In both cases today's statistical packages can describe this progression.

In order to pinpoint the exact moment of the transition (at a specific time of the process described by C1T1 (in Figure 17.3A), CA could explore these kind of phenomena. However Genetic Algorithms and Neuronal Nets seem to be the best to describe the precise moment, once they are concerned with behavioural characteristics (and decision mechanisms are involved). These are more sensitive to the exact moment a decision process is triggered (the work of Openshaw (1997 and 1998) is relevant for this stream of research).

Finally in terms of intersection of different trajectories, Fuzzy Sets and the study of fractal dimensions seem to be the best methodologies. Some examples of the most illustrative work can be found in the publications of Batty (1997 and 2004), Clarke (1998, and 2006), Openshaw (1997), Portugali and Benenson (1997), and Silva and Clarke (2001, 2002, 2005), Martinez, Veigas and Silva (2007) and Silva (2002, 2004). In this research, the goal is to detect variations that justify important transitions without compromising the inherent variability of a system. For instance (in the case of Fuzzy Sets), in the past land use classes would be classified exactly by a line that would split for instance agriculture and forest. Nevertheless between these two land uses there tends to be a transition space that has plant species from both land uses. In this transition space it is difficult to speak about a pure land use. Fuzzy Set theory is particularly important in the acknowledgment that there are certain 'objects' in a geographic space with indetermine borders that need to be classified as such. In the case of the fractal dimension the best example has been presented by Batty showing edge city formation is a result of a fractal dimension than tends to repeat itself at multiple scales (therefore edge city formation is not nothing new, it is just a result of a city evolution). It is important to understand when these different trajectories intersect creating these different structures that repeat themselves at multiple scales. Accepting this line of reasoning, we will be able to predict, for instance, future shape and size of a metropolitan area.

The understanding of complexity and the understanding of the best methodologies to measure and understand complex and non-complex systems is addressed in the previous paragraphs. Nevertheless, this reasoning would be incomplete if we did not address the spatial representation of complexity through the use of spatial data models. Because we have been exploring land related systems it is important to consider the two models that are mostly used: the raster and the vector models. While the previous explanations of complex and non-complex models and the explanation of its associated models can be applied to non-spatial explicit data (a-spatial data is data that can have a spatial representation but, that usually does not appear with x, y, z, geographic coordinates or other spatial attributes, usually census data, can be a set of tables with no spatial attributes, for instance demographic statistics such as age – in this example there is no explicit reference to space), adding the dimension of explicit spatial data (spatial data requires more complex handling of data, such as relational data base that relates 'data tables' and vector or raster data models) builds in a new level of 'complicatedness' and therefore should be analysed as well.

One of the most distinctive features of the vector and raster models is the fact that the first one is an object oriented model and the second one is not (it is a 'matrix' base model). In other words the vector data model, represents the different objects of the world in its most faithful way in two or three dimensions and usually with an associated table of attributes that clearly and uniquely identifies each object in space (through its x, y, and sometimes z coordinates). The raster model is not dependent on the attributes of an object, and usually is represented by a matrix of rows and columns whose smallest unity is called a pixel.

While these data models do not answer to all needs of today's modellers, they tend to be used accordingly to the need at hand and through data manipulation (when required); we can transfer information from one data model to another. Nevertheless, both of these models are artefacts, they have been in use for decades, they are very well know by the modelling community and the degree of certainty and the knowledge we generated from them, makes them still the best data models.

While it seems clear that we need models that include in a more efficient way complex processes, these models are still needed for operational reasons. These are the models we use in the day-to-day work. Commercial software is prepared for receiving data organised accordingly to vectors or raster, and most data analysis is performed accordingly to the data model in use. The level of integration from data collection, to data manipulation and data analysis and representation makes it very hard to replace these data models.

In our opinion, and according to the previous analysis, the future will be in a first instance of CA and GA adopting both data model approaches, with an emphasis on the raster model in the case of the CA and an emphasis on the vector model by the GA users. In the future the use of these data models needs to be improved in order to fully explore the capabilities of CA and GA.

17.6 From complexity as a theoretical concept to its implementation and the development of new theories

Finally in order to address practical day-to-day demands of planning complex issues, the question how can we benefit from complexity studies should be addressed (now that we know what models to apply and what data models to use). At this moment it is possible to do this in two different ways, using statistical and dynamic analysis. Using statistical analysis implies the use of 'snapshots of time' applied to a particular system (as represented in the examples provided during the previous point for the evolution of temperature – letter C in Figure 17.1 and the average temperature in a 30 year record as in Figure 17.2).

Using dynamic analysis, implies the use of time as a discrete and synchronous update of characteristics on sequences of time. This dynamics can be analysed in time (as exemplified in Figure 17.2) and in space (as seen in Figure 17.3b) or from space-time interaction (as exemplified in Figures 17.3, and 17.4). At this moment this is the usual methodology in CA models. Each year and for each iteration the system updates synchronously for all cells in that specific moment in time, afterwards it does the same for each year.

In the future, dynamic analysis will need to include issues such as asynchronous time update and continuous evolution and adaptation. It is in this scope that vortexes of time are applied to a particular system (as presented in Figure 17.4). It is of extreme relevance to point out these multi-scale and time dimension approaches and the importance of dynamic analysis (for instance in the case of CA models, we cannot assume that each policy will be implemented at the same moment in time, or that throughout a metropolitan area all me municipalities will implement a policy at the same time, therefore we should have CA models that would allow us to implement different policies throughout a year and that the update of cells could be delayed or progressed in municipalities that are more efficient in implementing policies – we cannot assume that all cells in a system are updated exact at the same time). The elements that constraint the function of a system are multi-scale and their behaviour is enabled/disabled accordingly to trigger points, its complete understanding is improbable, but probability analysis can give a high degree of certainty when developing this models. Vortexes of time will be able to capture the moment of time that a set of trigger points enable another bifurcation or phase-transition.

The term 'arrow of time' was coined in 1927 by the astronomer Arthur Eddington used to distinguish a direction of time (i.e. from past to the future – there is a direction of time). For the social sciences and the natural sciences time will have a different concept and this need to be accounted for. While in the natural sciences the 'arrow of time' will usually refer to the second law of thermodynamics (entropy and 'chaos' increase with time) and the irreversible physic (arrow of time) of trajectories (particularly at the macro scale), or to Prigogine's work that states that order can be extracted out of chaos and therefore irreversibility is somehow relative (particularly at the macro scale). In the case of social sciences time will still be viewed as a concept of 'arrow of time' in its strict sense of irreversibility. Information theory for example states that no retrofit is possible, because human societies will increase knowledge with time and with that a different state of awareness.

In conclusion, in the future new theory will be developed in the fields of complexity (as already is perceived by the number of publications in the field). It will be possible to validate and confirm past theory with 'quantitative values', and new data-led theory will certainly increase in scope and application (i.e. from the discovery of phase-transitions in cities, to the proposal of DNAs to cities, and cities most important fractal dimensions are only some of the examples).

Finally, we can conclude the analysis with a question: is all of this possible? A straight forward answer would be: Yes – it already exists: *(i)* We have the computational capabilities *(ii)* We have the modelling technology studied and understood (for instance we are now coupling modelling approaches to common platforms of GA and CA), *(iii)* We are now exploring massive amounts of data and unveiling new relations and new models, *(iv)* We have personnel from different fields working together (increasing multi-disciplinarity).

One of the most interesting final conclusions for this chapter is that complexity is no longer only relevant for the natural and physical sciences, but also for the subject areas researching land dynamics, and for other areas, for instance process-oriented fields and decision making fields, making it one of the most interesting pan disciplinary developments at the beginning of this century.

17.7 Conclusion

This chapter clarifies the importance of clearly understanding what complex and non-complex phenomena are. Through the understanding of a graphical representation of a wave, it is possible to understand in time and space when complex and non-complex phenomena are happening and therefore point out the best models to use in order to describe variables and the phenomena itself (as well as the best data models that will support such analysis).

The description of phenomena as a wave kind of image also opens the door to the understanding of what phase-transitions and bifurcations are. And by doing so, it emphasises the importance of complexity in the understanding of dynamics processes that were not represented in the past because such dynamics were associated with randomness and therefore discarded.

Finally, this chapter points out the importance of Cellular Automaton and Genetic Algorithms as the best approaches to model complexity in the quantitative realm. Both approaches clearly reflect human related dynamics (CAs for physical land related processes of land change or transportation infrastructures; GAs for socio-economic related processes such as pedestrian movement, or shopping habits). While in the past both approaches were separate, nowadays they are becoming more integrated. An important conclusion is that much more can be done in terms of implementation of CAs and GAs. Nevertheless it is unquestionable that these are useful approaches to model complexity in a more quantitative way.

References

Batty, M. and Longley, P. (1994) *Fractal Cities: Geometry of Form and Function*, Academic Press, New York.

Batty, M. (2005) *Cities and Complexity*, The MIT Press, Cambridge.

Birkin, M., Clarke, G., Clarke, M. and Wilson, A. (1996) *Intelligent GIS. Locations Decisions and Strategic Planning*, Geoinformation International, Cambridge.

Clarke, K., Hoppen, S. and Gaydos, L. (1996) 'Methods and techniques for rigorous calibration of cellular automaton model of urban growth', Third International Conference/Workshop on Integrating GIS and Environmental Modelling, Santa Fe, New Mexico.

Gazulis, N and Clarke, K.C. (2006) 'Exploring the DNA of Our Regions: Classification of Outputs From the SLEUTH Model', in S. El Yacoubi, B. Chapard and S. Bandini (eds.), *Cellular Automata: Lecture Notes in Computer Science. No. 4173*, Springer, New York.

Couclelis, H. (1985) 'Cellular worlds: A framework for modelling micro-macro dynamics', *Environment and Planning A*, vol. 17, pp. 585-596.

Delorme, M. and Mazoyer, J. (1999) *Cellular Automata: A Parallel Model*, Kluwer Academic Publishers, Dordrecht.

Gardner, R. (1970) 'The fantastic combinations of John Conway's new solitaire game "Life"', *Scientific American*, vol. 223(4), pp. 120-123.

Goles, E. and Martinez, S. (1996) *Cellular Automata and Complex Systems*, Kluwer Academic Publishers, Dordrecht.

Holland, J. (1995) *Hidden Order: How Adaptation Builds Complexity*, Helix Books, Reading.

Holland, J. (1999) *Emergence: From Chaos to Order*, Helix Books, Reading.

Hubernman, B. and Glance, N. (1993) 'Evolutionary games and computer simulation', *Proc. National Academy of Sciences – USA*, vol. 90, pp. 7716-7718.

Itami, R. (1988) 'Cellular worlds: Models for dynamic conceptions of landscape', *Landscape Architecture*, vol. 78(4), pp. 52-57.

Kauffman, S. (1984) 'Emergent properties in random complex automata', *Physica, D*, vol. 10, pp. 145-156.

Kauffman, S. (1993) *Origins of Order: Self-Organization and Selection in Evolution*, Oxford University Press, Oxford.

Kay, J., Regier, H., Boyle, M. and Francis, G. (1999) 'An ecosystem approach for sustainability: Addressing the challenge of complexity', *Futures*, vol. 31, pp. 721-742.

Kok, J., Engelen, G., White, R. and Wind, H. (2001) 'Modelling land-use change in decision-support system for coastal-zone management', *Environmental Modelling and Assessment*, vol. 6, pp. 123-132.

Langton, C. (1986) 'Studying artificial life with cellular automata', *Physica D*, vol. 22, pp. 120-149.

Langton, C. (1995) *Artificial Life: An Overview*, Bradford and The MIT Press, Cambridge.

Leonard, R. (1995) 'From parlor games to social science: Von Neumann, Morgenstern and the creation of game theory 1928-1944', *Journal of Economic Literature*, vol. 33, pp. 730-761.

Martinez, L.M., Viegas, J.M. and Silva, E.A. (forthcoming) 'Modifiable areal unit problem effects on traffic analysis zones delineation', *Environment and Planning B*.

Nash, J. (1953) 'Two-person cooperative games', *Econometrica*, vol. 21, pp. 128-140.

Nash, J. (1950a) 'Equilibrium points in N-person games', *Proceedings of the National Academy of Sciences*, vol. 36, pp. 48-49.

Nash, J. (1950b) 'The bargaining problem', *Econometrica*, vol. 18, pp. 155-162.

Openshaw, S. and Openshaw, C. (1997) *Artificial Intelligence in Geography*, John Wiley and Sons, Ltd., Chichester.

Openshaw, S. (1998) 'Neural networks, genetic and Fuzzy Logic models of spatial interaction', *Environment and Planning A*, vol. 30, pp. 1857-1872.

Philips, J. (1999) 'Divergence, convergence, and self-organization in landscapes', *Annals of the Association of American Geographers*, vol. 89(3), pp. 466-488.

Phipps, M. (1992) 'From local to global: The lesson of cellular automata', in D. DeAngelis and L. Gross, *Individual-Based Models and Approaches in Ecology: Populations, Communities, and Ecosystems*, Chapman and Hall, New York, pp. 165-187.

Portugali, J., Benenson, I. and Omer, I. (1997) 'Spatial cognitive dissonance and sociospatial emergence in a self-organizing city', *Environment and Planning B: Planning and Design*, vol. 24, pp. 263-282.

Prigogine, I. (1999) 'Laws of nature, probability and time symmetry breaking', *Physica D*, vol. 263, pp. 528-539.

Prigogine, I. and Stengers, I. (1984) *Order out of Chaos: Man's New Dialogue With Nature*, Bantam Books, Toronto.

Remark, R. (1929) 'Kann die Volkswirtschaftslehre eine exakte Wissenschaft werden?' ['Is it possible for every-day-knowledge to become an exact science?'], *Jahrbucher fur Nationalokonomie und Statistik*, vol. 131, pp. 703-735.

Resnick, M. (1995) 'Learning about life', in C. Langton, *Artificial Life: An Overview*, Bradford and MIT Press, Cambridge, pp. 230-241.

Schmitt, O.H. (1938) 'A thermionic trigger', *Journal of Scientific Instruments*, (January) vol. 15, pp. 24-26.

Silva, E.A. (2002) 'Beyond modelling in environmental and urban planning. planning support systems and the case study of Lisbon and Porto Metropolitan

Areas, Portugal', PhD Dissertation. University of Massachusetts, Amherst, Massachusetts.

Silva, E.A. (2004) 'The DNA of our regions: Artificial intelligence in regional planning', *Futures*, vol. 36(10), pp. 1077-1094.

Silva, E.A. (2006) 'Waves of complexity: Bifurcations or phase-transitions', Complexity Group Meeting (AESOP Thematic group), Cardiff University, City and Regional Planning Department, Cardiff, June 5 and 6, UK.

Silva, E.A. and Clarke, K. (2001) 'Calibration of the SLEUTH urban growth model for two metropolitan areas of Portugal', Association of the American Geographers – 97th Annual Meeting, 2001, Abstracts: page 19. Conference program, p. 146.

Silva, E.A. and Clarke, K. (2002) 'Calibration of the SLEUTH urban growth model for Lisbon and Porto, Portugal', *Computers, Environment and Urban Systems*, vol. 26(6), pp. 525-552.

Silva, E.A. and Clarke, K. (2005) 'Complexity, emergence and cellular urban models: Lessons learned from applying SLEUTH to two Portuguese cities', *European Planning Studies*, vol. 13(1), pp. 93-115.

Tobler, W. (1979) 'Cellular geography', in S. Gale and G. Olosson, *Philosophy and Geography*, D. Reidel, Dordrecht, pp. 279-386.

Toffoli, T. and Margolus, N. (1987) *Cellular Automata Machines*, MIT Press, Cambridge.

Toffoli, T. (1998) 'Cellular automata as an alternative to (rather than an approximation of) differential equations', *Physica D*, vol. 10, pp. 117-127.

Von Neumann, J. (1966) *Theory of Self-reproducing Automata*, University of Illinois Press, Urbana.

Wagner, D. (1997) 'Cellular automata and geographic information systems', *Environment and Planning B: Planning and Design*, vol. 24, pp. 219-234.

White, R. and Engelen, G. (1994) 'Cellular dynamics and GIS: Modelling spatial complexity', *Geographical Systems*, vol. 1, pp. 237-253.

White, R. and Engelen, G. (1997a) 'Cellular automata as the basis of integrated dynamic regional modelling', *Environment and Planning B: Planning and Design*, vol. 24, pp. 253-246.

White, R. and Engelen, G. (2000) 'High-resolution integrated modelling of the spatial dynamics of urban and regional systems', *Computers, Environment and Urban Systems*, vol. 24, pp. 383-400.

White, R., Engelen, G. and Uljee, I. (1997) 'The use of constrained cellular automata for high-resolution modelling of urban land use dynamics', *Environment and Planning B: Planning and Design*, vol. 24, pp. 323-343.

Wilson, A. (2000) *Complex Spatial Systems: The Modelling Foundations of Urban and Regional Analysis*, Prentice Hall, Harlow.

Wolfram, S. (1984) 'Universality and complexity in cellular automata', *Physica* D, vol. 10, pp. 1-35.

Wolfram, S. (1994) *Cellular Automata and Complexity: Collected Papers*, Addison-Wesley Publishing Company, Reading.

Wolfram, S. (2002) *A New Kind of Science*, Wolfram Media, Champaign, IL.
Wu, F. and Webster, C. (2000) 'Simulating artificial cities in a GIS environment: urban growth under alternative regulation regimes', *International Journal of Geographical Science*, vol. 14(7), pp. 625-648.
Zermelo, E. (1912) *Uber eine Anwendung der Mengenlehre auf die Theorie des Schachspiels* [*On the application of Set Theory to the theory of Chessgames*], Proceedings of the Fifth International Congress of Mathematicians, Cambridge, 22-28 Aug. 1912, 1913, II, pp. 501-504.

Index